Agents of Apocalypse

Agents of Apocalypse

EPIDEMIC DISEASE IN THE COLONIAL PHILIPPINES

KEN DE BEVOISE

PRINCETON UNIVERSITY PRESS

PRINCETON, NEW JERSEY

Library of Congress Cataloging-in-Publication Data

De Bevoise, Ken, 1943–
Agents of apocalypse : epidemic disease in the
colonial Philippines / Ken De Bevoise
p. cm.
Includes bibliographical references and index.
ISBN 0-691-03486-9
1. Epidemiology—Philippines. I. Title.
RA650.7.P6D4 1995 614.4'2599—dc20 94-19328 CIP

This book has been composed in Bitstream Caledonia

Princeton University Press books are printed on acid-free paper and meet the guidelines for
permanence and durability of the Committee on Production Guidelines for Book
Longevity of the Council on Library Resources

Printed in the United States of America

1 2 3 4 5 6 7 8 9 10

CONTENTS

PREFACE   ix

ACKNOWLEDGMENTS   xiii

Map of Asia and the East Indies, 1875   2

Map of Philippine Provinces and Principal Islands, 1890   4

INTRODUCTION
Dimensions of the Crisis   6

PART ONE

CHAPTER 1
Probability of Contact   17

CHAPTER 2
Susceptibility   45

PART TWO

CHAPTER 3
Venereal Disease: Evolution of a Social Problem   69

CHAPTER 4
Smallpox: Failure of the Health Care System   94

CHAPTER 5
Beriberi: Fallout from Cash Cropping   118

CHAPTER 6
Malaria: Disequilibrium in the Total Environment   142

CHAPTER 7
Cholera: The Island World as an Epidemiological Unit   164

CONCLUSION
Intervention and Disease   185

ABBREVIATIONS USED IN THE NOTES   191

NOTES   193

BIBLIOGRAPHY   247

INDEX   267

THIS RESEARCH project began as an attempt to resolve a turn-of-the-century controversy as to whether United States soldiers had committed atrocities during the "Philippine Insurrection" of 1899–1902. A year of work in the American sources satisfied me that they had. The war records hinted at something more significant, however—an astonishingly high level of illness and death from disease among Filipino civilians. I went to Manila the following summer half intent on changing my focus. There the archival record fed my growing intuition that the historian would do better to explain the prevalence of epidemic malaria or smallpox than to reaffirm that armies engaged in wars of pacification are brutal and that some individuals commit war crimes. The Historical Data Papers, an extensive oral-history survey undertaken in the 1950s, revealed that what had remained most prominently in the Filipino historical memory of the American war was disease, not atrocities. Indeed, the Spanish colonial medical reports and demographic data made it clear that when the United States intervened in the Philippines in 1898, its soldiers had stumbled into the midst of a health crisis that had been ongoing for at least a couple of decades.[1]

A side trip to Cebu gave me a chance to put the documents aside for a few days so I could sort through their implications before deciding how to proceed. At the time, I had picked up a copy of biologist René Dubos's *Mirage of Health* and was considering his cautionary note to those of us in the developed world who may be overoptimistic about the promise of "modern" medicine. He insisted that some level of disease is inseparable from being human and thus utopias of perfect health, past or future, are purely imaginary. With those thoughts in mind and book in hand, I wandered into a barrio in the hills behind the city one afternoon and began talking with a group of six or seven persons. One of them was an elderly man who asked to see the book, less perhaps for any particular interest in its content than to establish his English-language credentials with me and the others. Several hours later, those of us who had remained broke off our talk so I could catch the last jeep back to the city. As I climbed in, the old man tapped me on the shoulder and said, "Don't forget your book—*The Miracle of Health*."[2]

That interchange defined this study. It was plain that the man's cultural frame of reference and life experience had taught him to think of health as something so unexpected, or perhaps inexplicable, as to be miraculous. His misreading of the book's title was evidently related to an assumption that its author shared his outlook. In fact, Dubos came from an intellectual and cultural tradition that entirely discounts religious or supernatural phenomena as determinants of health and has increasingly assumed that diseases can be controlled, if not eradicated completely. It suddenly seemed clear to me that to those who had lived in the islands a century ago, the soldiers I was studying had been less important as liberators or oppressors than as agents of disease. I sensed too that illness and dying was located at a historical and anthropological crossroads somewhere deep in the colonial heartland of the Filipino experience. Mapping the terrain would put the war and much else in a new perspective.

The context in which the late-nineteenth-century health crisis occurred subsequently became the focus of my research. In that light, the war assumes a new and relatively smaller dimension. Though it remains a crucial event in Philippine history as well as a proximate cause of disease, it appears here as just one strand in a much larger web of causation that stretches back at least to the mid-sixteenth century. On one level this book tries to explain why Filipino morbidity and mortality were so high during the last third of the nineteenth century, which I stretch into the first decade of the present one. On another, it has the broad objective of enriching our understanding of historical processes by emphasizing the complexity of cause and consequence. Embedding particular human interactions in a web of ecological interdependence provides an angle of vision that allows us to see them in a new light. I argue that the Philippine health crisis was a result of the conjunction of various long-term processes. Rapid population growth, initiated by more stable conditions of life after the mid-seventeenth century, was joined by far-reaching demographic, economic, technological, and political transformations during the following two and a half centuries. The changes were cumulative and gathered tremendous velocity by the middle third of the nineteenth century, upsetting ecological equilibrium. As a result, local epidemics grew in frequency, intensity, and scope amidst an increasingly mobile and debilitated population. Archipelago-wide contagion became a serious risk for the first time in the 1860s, and Filipinos were periodically overwhelmed by disease thereafter until settled conditions again prevailed during the first decade of the twentieth century.

Any historian working with issues raised by the presence of infection in past populations owes an enormous debt to Hans Zinssner, Charles E. Rosenberg, Alfred W. Crosby, William H. McNeill, and others for demonstrating the importance of disease as a critical force in human history. To answer the Philippine question, however, I thought it necessary to look outside of the discipline for my principal analytical tools. I found most of them in the health sciences. The *total environment* concept informs my interpretation of the archival record. As early as 1940, Sir Macfarland Burnet argued that interaction between human beings and infectious agents is so complex that it can only be understood in the context of their mutual relationship to the global ecosystem. Dubos conceived of the entire process as taking place within a total environment. He explained that "the process of living involves the interplay and integration of two ecological systems"—the community of interdependent cells, body fluids, and tissue structures that make up an organism's internal environment and all the living and inanimate things with which it comes into contact, its external environment. (Although he did not define it explicitly, the total environment evidently encompasses one's physical, biological, psychological, cultural, political, socioeconomic, and historical universe.) Living things ordinarily achieve an unsteady and temporary *ecological* equilibrium sufficient for survival, but any change in the "constellation of circumstances" under which the equilibrium evolved can upset the balance. Disease will swamp host defenses if the change is too sudden for adaptive mechanisms. George Macdonald has since underscored the delicacy of the balance by demonstrating that mathematically small variations in any one of those circumstances can trigger epidemic disease.[3]

To understand how disease worked in the Philippines, I have tried to think ecologically, seeing human health as an outcome of multiple, reciprocal, and continuing interactions among pathogens, hosts (both animal and human) and enveloping environment. Mervyn Susser explains that ecological thinking comprehends the broadest possible formulation of causality, one that "encompasses the whole system of relationships, and allows one to begin with either causes or effects." He conceptualizes a system as "a set or assembly of factors connected with each other in some form of coherent relationship." Building on Macdonald's empirical evidence, he emphasizes the tension between stability and change. Since all the persisting factors in a system are related, a change in any of them will affect the others. He envisions the universe as a complex of linked systems that "contain each other like the boxes of a Chinese conjuring trick." Such multidirectional reasoning highlights what we often overlook in our search for underlying historical causes—that each of those causes has numerous effects. That fact accounts for the unintended consequences that mark this history and for much of their irony.[4]

Metaphors also become conceptual tools when we try to comprehend something as complex as the nature of causation. Webs, networks, and intersections are some of the most common images. They suggest a system of highways, among other things, and indeed virologist Stephen S. Morse utilizes that analogy. He is concerned with the role of human agency in disease causation and takes the position that human activities, whether through changes in behavior or alteration of the environment, bear substantial responsibility for the emergence of "new" viruses. The social developments that create conditions favoring rapid viral dissemination he likens to highways, complete with "stop" and "go" indicators, and he explains that new viruses emerge as a result of changes in the patterns of "viral traffic." He calls for biomedical and social scientists to work closely toward a "science of traffic patterns." This book seeks to participate in that endeavor by trying to understand what cleared the way for epidemic disease among a people in Southeast Asia a century ago. Since political control was just one of many factors that shaped the flow of disease and because the political history of the Philippines has been written about extensively, I have chosen to underplay that aspect in this book. Thus, staples of traditional late-nineteenth-century histories like the Cavite mutiny, the Katipunan, José Risal, and William McKinley hardly appear. Indeed, I have given the years 1863–1903 their own ecological space rather than try to fit them unnaturally into the usual (and implicitly political) organizational scheme that divides Philippine colonial history in a "Spanish period" and an "American period." Because I have attempted a history of a past population group that looks at familiar events afresh, this study consciously and necessarily depends on previous scholarship, building on it as part of a cooperative effort to find new ways of understanding historical processes.[5]

After the introduction, which describes the late-nineteenth-century crisis, I attempt in the first two chapters to account for its occurrence. To do so, I use the classic epidemiological model, which was originally developed to explain the spread of infectious disease but is now informed by ecological thinking. This model holds that the patterns of disease in any population group depend on factors that determine the probability of contact between an agent of disease and a susceptible host. Whatever its shortcomings as an interpretive approach to illness in the developed world today, where noninfectious disease predominates, the model is a useful tool for the historian of past peoples in which contagious disease prevailed. Applying the formulation to the historical record helps us see the Philippine crisis approaching, and by mapping its journey we can understand why it arrived when it did.[7]

In the second part of the book, I select five disease subsystems for examination—five outcomes of the play of variables that had brought the population to epidemiological flashpoint. Each subsystem has been extracted from the mosaic of Philippine disease and treated separately to highlight a different aspect of the larger system and to show its interplay with other factors. That organizational strategy brings us to the same destination by five different routes, although we go through some of the same interchanges more than once, usually from a different direction. The multidimensional analysis tries to achieve a kind of "thick description" that will help us draw meaning from the complex of relationships. I conclude the book with a brief consideration of what the evidence has revealed about how human actions and interventions open the way for epidemic disease. We are after all the primary agents of apocalypse.[7]

ACKNOWLEDGMENTS

I WANT to thank the following persons for improving the substance of this book in various ways: Benjy Abellera, Richard Maxwell Brown, Lina Concepcion, Mike Cullinane, Ana De Bevoise, Petra Goedde, Amy Golden, Paul Greenough, Mila Guerrero, Laura Hein, Paul Holbo, Michael Hunt, Rey Ileto, David Joravsky, Sarah Maza, Resil Mojares, Bill Monter, Perlina Montilla, Bill Muraskin, Harold Perkin, Frank Safford, Michael Sherry, F. B. Smith, Allan Winkler, and Peter Wood.

I also want to acknowledge the help I received from the staffs of the various archives in which I worked and especially to the staffs of the University of the Philippines Cordillera Studies Center in Baguio City, the Philippine National Archives in Manila, and the Interlibrary Loan departments at the University of Oregon, New Mexico State University, and Northwestern University. Kathryn Deiss, Ed Fishwick, Carole Johnson, and Michael Nealon at the last-named library have been unfailingly helpful as well as persistent in tracking down printed material for me.

I am grateful for the financial support I received at various stages in my research from a Charlotte W. Newcombe dissertation fellowship, a Fulbright-Hays research grant, and a National Endowment for the Humanities summer stipend.

I would also like to thank the *Pacific Historical Review* for permission to use material from a previously published article.

I was particularly fortunate to have had Gail Schmitt as my copy editor. She improved the writing, clarified many ideas, and showed me others that needed more careful thought. She also prepared the index. My principal editor at Princeton University Press, Jenn Mathews, has been extraordinarily capable and professional, as have Margaret Case, Molan Chun Goldstein, and Lauren Osborne.

Special appreciation is reserved for Dan Doeppers, Al McCoy, Glenn May, Norman Owen, and Bob Wiebe. Each has gone out of his way on numerous occasions to provide documents, advice, or close critical readings of the manuscript as it was in progress. No scholar could hope for better assistance. The book's shortcomings are my own doing.

I depended on the personal support and encouragement of many persons, especially Barbara Drexler, Bob Drexler, Wynn Egginton, Michelle Johnson, Bob Johnson, and Li Hui.

Thanks also to the Archers of Loaf.

I dedicate the book to the memory of William Henry Scott, who passed away just as the manuscript was nearing completion. He was the inspiration for this project from the moment he took me in hand over a decade ago in the reading room at the U.S. National Archives. Subsequently, he guided me through the records in Manila and his own research source material in Sagada. He knew more Philippine history than anyone, and he spent many hours teaching me some of it. Scotty was a remarkable mentor, scholar, and person. I'll remember him most for his passionate commitment to the Filipino people and for his wonderful humor. All of us who are connected with Philippine studies in any way already miss him tremendously.

Agents of Apocalypse

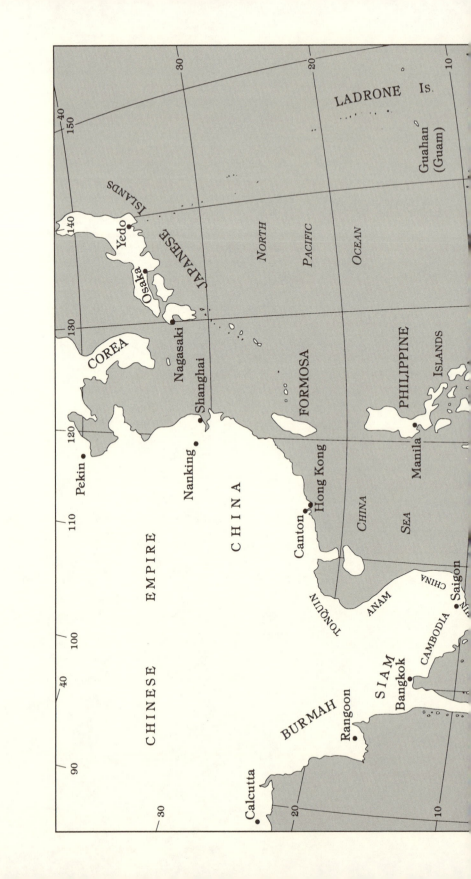

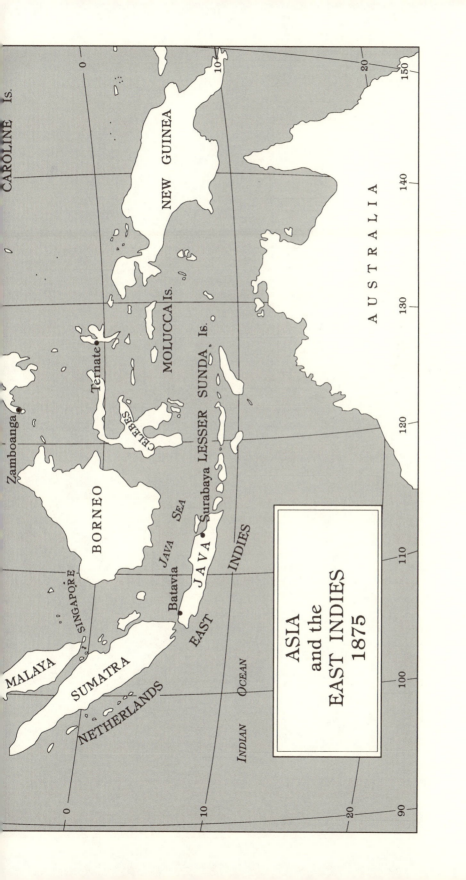

ASIA
and the
EAST INDIES
1875

PHILIPPINE
PROVINCES
and
PRINCIPAL ISLANDS
1890

CHINA

SEA

PACIFIC

OCEAN

BATAN IS.

BABUYAN IS.

LUZON

CAGAYAN

ISABELA

ABRA

LEPANTO

NUEVA
VIZCAYA

ILOCOS
NORTE
Laoag

ILOCOS
SUR

BENGUET

UNION

LINGAYEN GULF

PANGASINAN

TARLAC

ZAMBALES

PAMPANGA

NUEVA
ECIJA

BATAAN

BULACAN

Manila

MANILA BAY

CAVITE

MANILA
MORONG

LA LAGUNA

BATANGAS

PRINCIPE

INFANTA

MARIN-
DUQUE I.

MINDORO

CAMARINES
NORTE

TAYABAS

CAMARINES
SUR

Nueva
Caceres

ALBAY

CATANDUANES I.

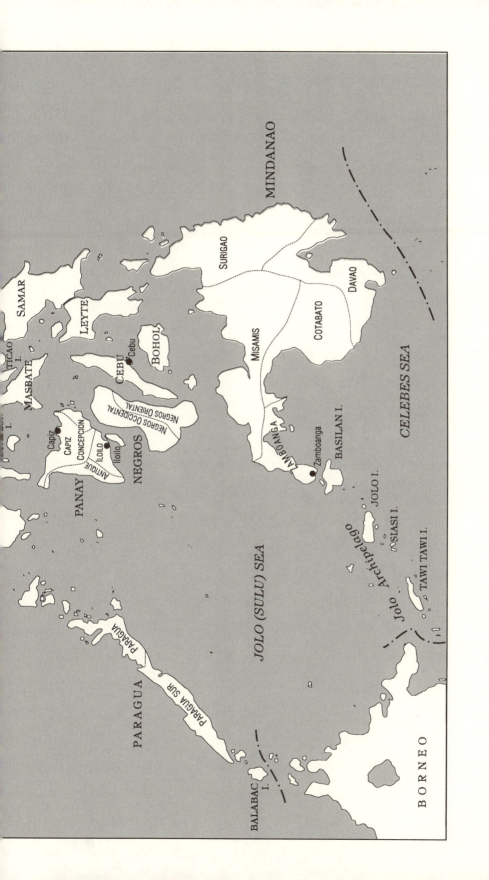

Dimensions of the Crisis

FEW PEOPLE had more opportunity to observe the course of public health in the late-nineteenth-century Philippines than the Spanish *médico titular* (licensed physician) José Gomez y Arce. He had already been in the islands for a decade when, in 1872, the colonial government appointed him chief physician of Iloilo province, where he then served for more than twenty years. Still passionate and outspoken but worn down by what seemed to him a losing battle against disease and ignorance, he capped a series of progressively gloomier annual reports by issuing an apocalyptic warning in 1892: Filipino defenselessness against disease was "annihilating the race, threatening their extinction not far off." No family survived beyond the third generation, he said, and as a consequence, the outcome of man's unending struggle against the land was in the balance. Only the extraordinarily high birth rate kept the ravages of disease from returning the land to nature. The physician had watched helplessly as major epidemics brought "sadness and desolation to a whole province" on six occasions during his tenure in Iloilo killing 100,000 persons altogether. And "to judge by the public knell," the situation was the same throughout the archipelago, where "today smallpox takes a million souls, tomorrow cholera."[1]

Dr. Gomez's overheated rhetoric was designed in part to goad the underfunded colonial administration into assigning public health as much importance as public order or tax collection, but his concern was genuine. Other doctors shared it. Two of his colleagues on Luzon had previously made similar predictions of doom despite five or six consecutive years of settled conditions following the dislocation wrought by the 1882 cholera epidemic. In 1888, Dr. Rafael Monserrat characterized life in Pangasinan as "a desperate battle between the inhabitants of this province and nature to determine whether catastrophe will occur or be prevented." Most people were so vulnerable to disease that "it is not strange that these catastrophes come periodically, causing mourning and wailing when an epidemic spreads its wings over our heads, punishing in this way the infringements of good hygiene." At about the same time, Dr. Julian de Arce reported from Ilocos Sur that many were prostrate from various diseases, going on to warn that "the indigenous people of the plain face imminent ruin." Writing in the middle of a period described by more than one contemporary in the Philippines as a time of "true mourning," neither physician would have been surprised to learn that a major disaster in the form of rinderpest, malaria, and cholera would strike in a matter of months killing hundreds of thousands of Filipinos and almost all of the draft animals, thus paralyzing agriculture and commerce in their region for several years. But even the direst forecasts failed to anticipate the six years of war after 1896 and the "conflagration of disease" that would result.[2]

Epidemic disease is by definition excessive, a sudden enlargement or growth of what exists normally *in* the people so as to become something visited *upon* them. For disease to affect many persons in the community at the same time, there must be an imbalance in factors of the total environment that would otherwise tend to ecological equilibrium. Filipinos saw the late-century epidemics as one manifestation of a society out of harmony with its universe, an outlook overlaid with Christian interpretation suggesting to many that the general chaos of the time was a sign of the approaching Apocalypse. Their worst fears were unrealized, of course, but the crisis was real. Scholars have since tended to overlook it for a couple of reasons, however. First, the commonly accepted statistics show that the population actually grew during the period, if at a negligible rate. But an overall population increase can hide suffering and death on a monumental scale, as the case of South Vietnam from 1965 to 1973 demonstrates. Second, attention has long been preempted by the development of the Filipino independence struggle after 1870 and its abortion by American intervention around the turn of the century. The fact that the public health crisis coincided almost precisely with such pivotal events is all the more reason to examine it closely.[3]

Plenty of evidence exists, but it must be used judiciously. The annual reports of the médicos titulares (the *Memorias médicas*) are the best source for prevailing diseases and causes of death, but because most people relied on local healers, the provincial physicians had only a hearsay knowledge of diseases outside their limited purview. To compile lists for the yearly reports, the doctors supplemented what they had observed firsthand and heard about by word of mouth with information that the parish priests sent them. From the sixteenth century, the five religious orders in the colony were responsible for recording vital statistics. Each padre enumerated his flock and kept a record of all baptisms, marriages, and burials in the parish register. No autopsies were conducted outside of Manila, so cause of death (when it was entered) was usually determined by what manifestations the deceased's relatives could recall. Fever (a symptom rather than a disease) was cited more often than not, duly inscribed as such, totaled with the other entries, and forwarded to the médico titular, who was left to make educated guesses. In 1894 health regulations were issued that required an examination and certification of death before burial could take place. Not surprisingly, the directives proved utterly impractical outside of Manila, given the shortage of qualified personnel and the problems of time and distance. The difficulties become clear in the light of a 1909 study of 176 cases in the capital in which the corpses had been examined and the cause of death certified. Autopsies suggested that up to 70 percent of the cases had been misdiagnosed before burial. Under those circumstances, Dr. Gomez's insight on causation is worth considering. He pointed out in 1893 that the cause of death was bound to be inexact because so much depended upon the deceased's preexisting state of health. Many Filipinos in the late nineteenth century were undernourished, debilitated, and riddled with multiple infection, as we shall see. He realized that it was often impossible to ascertain the actual cause and that simply knowing what provided the final blow was unimportant.[4]

Still, the evidence allows the general roster of diseases to be identified with some confidence, if not with anything like statistical precision. There can be little doubt that malaria, cholera, beriberi, dysentery and other diseases of the gastrointestinal tract, tuberculosis, and smallpox were implicated in more deaths than were any other diseases. Each increased in frequency and intensity during the last third of the century, and one of them, beriberi, was essentially new altogether. In a year when one or more were epidemic, as in 1902, the six diseases could account for as much as three-quarters of Filipino mortality. Next in importance were puerperal fever and other causes incident to childbearing, diseases of the respiratory tract, typhoid fever, measles, rheumatic fevers, influenza, whooping cough, meningitis, diphtheria, and tetanus. Helminthic infections predisposed individuals to one or more of the preceding diseases and were serious in themselves. Rinderpest, or cattle plague, had an indirect effect on Filipinos that was more serious perhaps than any human disease because of its role in the spread of malaria and the collapse of agriculture. Little death resulted from venereal disease, leprosy, or scabies, but each was a serious health problem, and the first was symptomatic of the increasing impoverishment that fueled the late-century conflagration.[5]

Population and birth-death totals that survive allow us to discern the demographics of the crisis, but it is well to recognize the limits of this data too. Filipinos were generally eager for church blessings, so most babies were baptized, most unions were sanctified in the church, and most corpses were brought in for burial. But not all. Those who could not afford the ceremonial fees or who were on the move or who were isolated by distance or the weather might escape the priest's notice. As late as 1889 Father Patricio Adell found that most of the people scattered about the sugar and rice fields in the hinterland of his parish in Silay, Negros Occidental, remained beyond his ministry. He reported that "of every hundred adults who live there hardly four receive the sacraments because it is impossible for me to attend to them, and at least once a month they bring over a corpse to be buried and they do not even know his name." Rainy season conditions made matters even worse. South of Silay, the Binalbagan River became impassable, and most people died without receiving the sacraments according to Father Francisco Ayarra, parish priest of Hinigaran: "Oftentimes the corpses are already rotting and the children are not baptized for weeks at a time."[6]

Everywhere during chaotic years, substantial portions of the local population seem to disappear so far as the parish registers are concerned. At all times and places a small segment of the Christian population purposely dodged administrative control and took to the hills for a variety of reasons—to avoid paying the annual tribute, to practice shifting agriculture, or to evade the law. Most of them probably left fleeting traces in the registers from time to time. Contemporaries alleged that fraud (by local officials who concealed immigrants and in effect used them as undocumented workers on their lands), negligence, and simple error contributed to the undercount of the Christian population. A larger proportion of Filipinos were never "reduced" (converted or subjugated) by either church or state and thus remained wholly outside the recording system. Muslims in the southern islands were the largest single such segment, but various ethnolinguistic groups faithful to neither of the two major religions lived in inaccessible hill regions throughout the archipelago. *Infieles* (non-Christians) probably comprised about 10 percent of the Filipino population late in the nineteenth century (and more earlier), but they do not appear in this book as statistics.[7]

If exactitude is impossible, the general trends the numbers describe are reliable. It is beyond question that the late-nineteenth-century health crisis brought two centuries of vigorous population growth to an abrupt halt. Population counts derived from church records of numbers of tributes indicate that after a probable demographic crisis during the first half of the seventeenth century, the Christian population of the islands increased about thirteenfold (from 433,108 to 5,567,685) between 1655 and 1877. Benchmark enumerations after 1735 indicate an average annual growth rate of 0.96 percent during the last two-thirds of the eighteenth century that then accelerated to 1.66 percent during the first three-quarters of the next before dropping precipitously to 0.85 percent (and probably lower) as disease and war swept the islands. The growth rate probably peaked during the first four decades of the century, topping out around an astonishing 2.5 percent a year.[8]

Other areas of Southeast Asia experienced accelerated population growth in the eighteenth century and eventually achieved average annual rates of increase well above 1 percent, which was extraordinarily high for the time. The available evidence is as yet restricted to Java and Siam, and in neither case is it conclusive. On Java the population grew somewhat more slowly than that in the Philippines, having an overall rate not exceeding 0.5 percent until about 1800. A declining death rate throughout the century after about 1820 was the principal determinant of estimated growth of 1.25 percent during the first half of the century and 1.6 percent in the second. The situation for Siam is not as well documented, but most estimates put growth at 1.3 percent in the 1860s and perhaps substantially higher in the 1890s. What is intriguing for comparative purposes and what emphasizes the exceptional nature of the Philippine experience is that in neither Java nor Siam did the growth not level off during the last quarter of the century as a result of abnormally high death rates.[9]

During the nineteenth century, birth and death rates started their long-term decline in the industrialized world and by 1900 were under 30 per 1,000 and 20 per 1,000, respectively, in some countries. The preindustrial model of high but stable birth rates combined with high and unstable death rates persisted elsewhere. The Philippine variation coupled a birth rate at the high end of that model with a moderately low but increasingly volatile mortality rate. It is difficult to generalize because the normal level of both rose steadily over time, at least during the nineteenth century, but under the best of conditions, deaths could dip below 25 per 1,000, while more than 50 births per 1,000 were attainable, a rate as high as any in the world. The less isolated an island or area, the smaller that differential tended to be. Disregarding the yearly and regional variations, we can see that the population took off from a reported base of 837,132 in 1735, and the rate accelerated until about 1840. Growth continued, but at a sharply reduced rate until about 1863, when it slowed even further during the four decades prior to the 1903 census, which found about 6.9 million "civilized" (that is, Christian) Filipinos.[10]

Since the birth rate fluctuated relatively little from year to year, the rate of population increase in the nineteenth century was controlled by what Peter C. Smith has termed *crisis mortality episodes*. Those were occasions on which deaths in any of the parishes reached abnormal levels, almost always from epidemic disease. Such episodes occurred throughout the century with increasing frequency and intensity. The sample of forty parishes gathered by Smith and Michael Cullinane is small, but it provides a statistical outline of the process this book will try to explain and elaborate. Their data show that regional mortality patterns became more similar as the islands figuratively grew closer together through shorter travel time and increased frequency of contact. Rates in the Bikol region first paralleled those on the rest of Luzon during the 1840s, and those in the Visayas began to follow suit as mortality there took its biggest jump in the 1860s. As the Philippine Islands approached an eventual epidemiological unity, larger population clusters were at greater risk from contagion imported from more places.[11]

Crisis mortality episodes became general for the first time in the 1860s. Prior to that time no epidemic had affected all regions of the archipelago. In 1863, however, imported cholera struck Manila, from where the disease was transported by steamship south to Zamboanga. Subsequently it was carried north on Mindanao to Misamis and eventually across the Bohol Sea to Cebu, where it raced around the island's southern tip, jumped the Tañon Strait and struck hard on the southeastern coast of Negros. The Smith-Cullinane sample of twenty-six parishes shows that sixteen of them, distributed throughout Luzon and Cebu, experienced abnormal mortality between 1863 and 1865. Cholera returned in 1882–1883, causing crises of far greater intensity in twenty-nine of thirty-eight sample parishes. Whereas the mortality in the earlier episode fell entirely within the lower and middle levels of Smith's intensity scale, twenty-one parishes now had mortality at the middle and highest levels. In 1888 the rinderpest virus reached the islands, killing most of the bovine population and thus triggering epidemic malaria. Cholera reappeared and mortality soared yet again, reaching crisis levels in twenty-six of thirty-nine sample parishes. The death toll was somewhat less than it had been earlier in the decade, but the recovery period was longer. Smith's analysis stops at the end of the century, but his sample was already detecting abnormal death rates in areas of U.S. Army activity on Luzon in 1899. Had the survey continued, it would have registered similar patterns wherever the Americans entered in force through 1901, followed by a general crisis of the greatest intensity brought on by cholera and malaria in 1902–1903.[12]

The average annual death rate of about 36 per 1,000 for the period 1863–1903 was, so far as I can tell, unprecedented in the history of the Filipino people. A serious crisis certainly occurred during the first half of the seventeenth century, but since the factors allowing wide diffusion of disease were lacking, it is probable that archipelago-wide death rates were lower. Although the late-nineteenth-century mortality fluctuated, moderating in the 1870s and 1890s, it seems not to have fallen below 30 per 1,000 for any ten-year segment. Increased dislocation, poverty, malnutrition, and infection provided a constant backdrop for the occasional but more dramatic Philippine pandemics. Unfortunately, the surviving documentation is mostly from the last half of this period. The *Memorias médicas* were not mandated by law until 1876, and although documents from a wide variety of archival sources supplement the medical reports, we still know almost nothing about the 1860s. Indeed, the demographic picture only begins to clear in the early 1880s, and even then variable data coverage makes it come in and out of focus thereafter.[13]

The 1903 census officials had access to birth and death totals from most of the parish registers for the years 1876 and 1885–1898. They had also found a record of birth and death rates for a year they misidentified as 1879. (The statistics almost surely pertain to 1882, and I tentatively advance them as such.) They published mortality (but not birth) statistics for 1902 and 1903 as well. The entire sample of about 6 million births and deaths, representing about 75 percent of all such events during those years, is more than adequately reliable, except for 1898, when Spain's defeat disrupted colonial record gathering. Birth-death ratios by province and by year can be calculated from that data and graphed along with the rates. The regional patterns are distinctive since they reflect episodes of purely local disease as well as variations in the timing, extent, and intensity of the spread of cholera in 1888–1889 and 1902–1903 from its original focus near Manila. For the most part, however, they are easily recognizable variations on the shape of the composite curve for the entire population. The degree of conformity shows the degree to which any given locality had been integrated into the late-century Philippine disease system, which appears statistically in table 1 and graphically in figure 1. In the table I have also included mortality data for 1904–1908 from the 1918 census to show the completion of the last major disease cycle.[14]

What emerges is a picture of three major crisis mortality episodes separated by recovery periods of varying completeness and duration. If adequate data allowed us to graph the entire century instead of the final quarter of the period only, the death rate would almost certainly appear as a series of foothills until about 1863, when the first and smallest of the four late-century peaks would rise over a line describing the slowly rising birth rate. The valleys in between those peaks in figure 1 illustrate the tendency toward a favorable equilibrium that could not be sustained for long. The peaks represent death on an enormous scale, accounting together for ten or eleven years in which at least 1 in every 25

TABLE 1
Birth and Death Statistics for the Philippines, 1876–1908

Year	Births	Deaths	Ratio	Birth Rate	Death Rate
1876	253,812	144,692	1.75:1	46.2	26.7
1882	—	—	—	43.4	106.3
1885	294,574	167,353	1.76:1	50.5	28.9
1886	157,817	81,078	1.95:1	51.5	26.5
1887	199,192	97,265	2.04:1	53.7	26.2
1888	210,228	142,821	1.47:1	50.2	34.0
1889	223,886	284,221	0.79:1	45.3	58.2
1890	118,897	123,555	0.96:1	43.2	48.1
1891	156,921	124,042	1.27:1	46.1	36.7
1892	246,516	182,162	1.35:1	48.1	36.7
1893	194,627	135,795	1.43:1	47.8	33.4
1894	258,078	180,206	1.43:1	48.5	33.9
1895	251,813	191,414	1.32:1	47.5	34.7
1896	262,257	176,180	1.49:1	48.6	32.5
1897	211,705	139,226	1.52:1	49.0	31.8
1898	61,467	39,324	1.56:1	47.6	30.5
1902	—	442,058	—	—	63.3
1903	—	329,671	—	—	47.2
1904	—	146,921	—	—	27.1
1905	—	166,555	—	—	27.8
1906	—	143,284	—	—	28.3
1907	—	138,464	—	—	21.6
1908	—	190,495	—	—	29.6

Note: The birth-death statistics for some years are fragmentary, nonexistent, or unavailable. The birth and death rates are per 1,000 persons.

Filipinos died, as opposed to the 1 in 40 during a "normal" year. Complete data would show their distinctive shapes, but it is at least evident that the 1882–1883 peak is not only the tallest but the narrowest of the three that we can see with reasonable clarity. The putative death rate of 106.3 per 1,000 may be too high, but it was probably at least 80 per 1,000. Contemporaries all agreed that the 1882 cholera epidemic was the worst; they failed, however, to appreciate that the final three episodes were progressively more complex, with crisis mortality spread over longer periods. Thus the 1888–1891 peak comprises not only cholera, but rinderpest and malaria as well, and the one for 1898–1903 includes those three plus smallpox, tuberculosis, and everything else that rode in war's train of evils.[15]

The wars of resistance against Spain and the United States (1896–1902) provided a terrible climax to a four-decade period in which the total number of deaths exceeded normal mortality by about 2.5 million persons and morbidity reached excessively high, though unquantifiable, levels. We will never be certain about the actual dimensions of wartime mortality since recordkeeping was

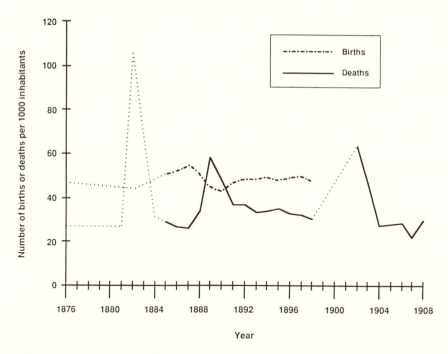

Figure 1. Comparative Birth and Death Rates for the Philippines from 1876 to 1908.

in disarray, but we do know that the population was literally decimated in one-eighth (129) of all Philippine municipalities during 1902 and that in a number of areas more than one out of every five inhabitants died. One reasonable estimate puts the death rate for the years 1899–1903 at 50 per 1,000, which indicates a total mortality of about 1.7 million, or an excess of about 775,000 over the number who would have died had no war taken place. The overall death rate dropped quickly when peace returned despite the exceedingly high levels of infant mortality that persisted for most of the decade in Manila, but the birth rate did not completely rebound. No direct statistics exist, but a statistical profile of the population in 1918 reveals a deficit of at least 400,000 persons who should have been in the cohort of those born between 1904–1908. When those missing people are combined with the excess deaths during the years of fighting, it appears that the American war contributed directly and indirectly to the loss of more than a million persons from a base population of about 7 million. If the Apocalypse never arrived, its agents had stalked the Philippine island world for forty years.[16]

PART ONE

Probability of Contact

CLASSIC epidemiological theory holds that the patterns of disease in any population group depend on factors that determine the probability of contact between an infectious agent and a susceptible host. That formulation still helps us understand the occurrence of the infectious diseases that weighed so heavily on late-nineteenth-century Filipinos, but it needs updating to account for patterns of others, the most important of which was beriberi, a noninfectious deficiency disease. Accordingly, an *agent* is understood in its current sense as "an organism, substance, or force whose relative presence or relative absence is necessary for a particular disease process to occur." In addition, the theory must be buttressed by a broadened awareness of critical host factors, especially immunologic states, as well as by an appreciation of the totality of the environment in which contact took place. Setting aside the susceptibility component of the model for now, this chapter considers the historical process that so dramatically increased the probability of contact between Filipinos and infection.[1]

The Filipino population as a whole was not at serious demographic risk from widespread epidemic disease before the mid-nineteenth century. Basic epidemiological principles explain why. Frank Fenner says that "the most important single parameter, from the point of infectious diseases, is the alteration in the size of the aggregates of men and the communications within and between these aggregates." No infection requiring transfers between human hosts for survival can maintain itself above the fade-out threshold for long in a static and dispersed population group where the probability of personal interaction is low. Diseases can neither be endemic (constantly present) nor epidemic (excessively prevalent) in a community whose members come in contact too infrequently to keep the chain of transmission alive. Mortality rates from infectious disease among such groups will be relatively low as a consequence.[2]

Relative size and isolation can also determine the extent of infectious disease within a community, as Fenner's statement of the principle suggests. Even where population density and interpersonal contact are sufficient to allow rapid diffusion, endemicity of many diseases is impossible in population groups below a critical size. As infection spreads, the remaining pool of susceptibles is quickly reduced below the level at which transmission can be sustained. Contact with an external population center where the infection is endemic or has been recently introduced is necessary for reintroduction of the disease, and a new epidemic must await the replenishment of the pool of susceptible hosts. Death rates will be high in small, isolated communities under epidemic conditions, but whether or not mortality is excessive over the longer term depends on the frequency with which the infection is imported. That frequency depends in turn on the size of the small community, its distance from the external reservoir, and the efficiency of the transportation network binding them. As a general rule, the smaller and more remote a community, the more irregular and discontinuous epidemic waves will be. Overall mortality is likely to be lower as well.[3]

The physical and cultural environments of the Philippine Islands set a relatively low limit on the probability of contact with infection from outside reservoirs. The archipelago seems to have been designed to encourage regional separateness and to inhibit extralocal human interaction. It comprises about seven thousand mostly tiny and uninhabitable islands, which are the unsubmerged portions of four major Southeast Asian tectonic provinces running roughly parallel to each other in a north-south configuration. The islands dot a half-million square miles of ocean, their total land area taking up somewhat more than one-fifth of that expanse. Four distinct climatological zones cut more or less longitudinally through the archipelago, bringing widely varying amounts of rainfall to different areas in distinct seasonal patterns. The various climates and geological histories have produced a corresponding diversity of soils, vegetation, and topography, though most of the larger islands are banded by a narrow and usually discontinuous coastal plain that rises abruptly to interior upland regions that are often mountainous and almost impenetrable. Physical barriers, poor roads, and rainy-season conditions have always made overland movement difficult and sometimes virtually impossible.[4]

At the time of Spanish intervention in 1565, which marks the start of recorded history in the Philippines, the archipelago was lightly populated. Probably no more than 1.2 million Filipinos inhabited up to a thousand islands for an average density of about ten persons per square mile. It would be seriously misleading to picture Filipinos living in "aseptic isolation" at any time, but from the epidemiological perspective, traditional settlement patterns were relatively small, dispersed, static, and isolated. Those qualifications are important because from another viewpoint, preconquest Filipinos were, in William Henry Scott's words, "a vigorous and mobile population adjusting to every environment in the archipelago, creatively producing variations in response to resources, opportunities and culture contacts, able to trade and raid, feed and defend themselves." Despite the sense of motion and interaction Scott conveys so well, the Philippine island world comprised archipelagos within an archipelago, islands within islands. That world was hardly impermeable to infection, and it became markedly less so over time, but imported disease from within and without tended to be localized and self-limiting until about a century and a half ago.[5]

Lowland settlement was generally based on the *barangay*, a kinship grouping of perhaps 20 to 100 families, most of whom lived in a primary village comprising an elongated cluster of houses several deep and ten to sixty long that hugged the shoreline or a river bank. (Cebu, Manila, Vigan, and a few others were exceptional, comprising as many as 2,000 families.) Shifting and seasonal cultivation produced a pattern of dispersed houses and hamlets scattered at some distance from the base village throughout its territory. The people harvested the fishing grounds in the shallow waters surrounding most of the islands and engaged in subsistence agricultural and handicraft activities ashore. Relations with other independent communities "whether of the same language or different, varied from isolation to cooperation or conflict according to circumstances," according to Scott. Miguel de Loarca noted the complexity of relationships between lowland and highland groups in 1582, remarking that although they "are almost always enemies," some peace was necessary because "those of the mountains cannot live without the fish and salt and other things and jars and plates which come from other parts, nor can those on the coast live without the rice and cotton which the mountaineers have."[6]

Since physical and cultural barriers to extensive overland contacts were so formidable, the sea presented the easiest route for diffusion of disease among the island populations. Scott explains that interisland waters were not a barrier but "the means of connecting Filipinos and culture exchange." The volume of interisland trade, and hence infectious agents as well, was sensitive to the difficulties presented by distance, contrary monsoon winds, and pirates, but evidence abounds of a vigorous commerce, especially in rice. Cebu, for instance, was the redistribution center for the Visayas at the time of conquest, receiving shipments from Panay and the east coast of Mindanao. Catanduanes shipbuilders went hundreds of miles to sell various types of sailcraft to barangay on Mindoro and southern Luzon, and the trade in porcelains extended to virtually every part of the archipelago and beyond. Slave raiding was even more important epidemiologically because of its capacity to terrorize the population and to disrupt normal living patterns. Power and prestige was based on control of slave labor, so attacks were continual and could come from any point on the compass. Scott points out that in Jesuit Father Francisco Alcina's day (mid-seventeenth century) "Bohol raids as far afield as Ternate [in the Moluccas] were still living memories, and he knew Samar parishioners who were the descendants of captives taken on the coasts of Luzon."[7]

Longer-range trade linked the various disease environments of insular Southeast Asia and the mainland to some extent. The Borneo-Luzon-Fujian (Fukien) route was perhaps the most active, but traces of Filipinos and their ships survive in virtually every part of the region. However, the relatively slow, small sailcraft held down the potential for the introduction of infectious disease into the Philippine Islands—the longer the travel time (the 640 miles between the Chinese mainland and Manila was an eight-day voyage in the sixteenth century) and the smaller the crew size, the greater the likelihood that the chain of transmission would be broken en route. The most accessible outside reservoirs of infection lay to the south. As trading sailcraft coming from Borneo, the Celebes, or the Moluccas hopped from island to island, the various populations served as "boosters" for new cases to be carried on to the southern reaches of the archipelago. Such disease as did arrive undoubtedly resulted in high levels of local mortality, but the potential for widespread dispersion was circumscribed.[8]

Although initial Spanish contacts did not wreak wholesale epidemiological havoc throughout the archipelago as in the Americas, the "pacification" (to use Philip II's euphemism) caused substantial death and suffering in many barangay. In 1571 Miguel López de Legazpi began the distribution of land and Filipinos among his soldiers by introducing the *encomienda* system, which Angel Martínez Cuesta has described as "a contract between the King, the *encomendero* and the natives to which only the King and the encomendero freely consented." Each encomienda holder received the right to collect the annual tribute from a specified group of Filipinos. In return he was to pacify them and procure their submission to the Crown, resettle them into townships, protect them from danger, and provide religious instruction. Detachments of soldiers went from community to community "tell[ing] the townspeople that if they want to be friends of the Spaniards they must pay the tribute at once." Those who refused or prepared to defend themselves were "killed or made prisoners, and their houses plundered and burned," according to the Augustinian friar Diego de Herrera. Even in "friendly towns" many of the common people were so poor that they destroyed their houses and hid in the hills for a few months rather than pay. Everything we know about the interaction of war and disease indicates that the "pain, tears, and blood" of the military conquest must have been accompanied by abnormal mortality.[9]

Administrative convenience, the imperatives of Christianization, and Spanish notions of civilization required a concentration of the population in the base villages so as to bring everyone "under the bells" of the church. That process of consolidation continued without abatement or complete success for more than three centuries. Ongoing resistance by Filipinos to leaving their fields and accepting "a way of life that was either unknown to them or which in the past had not pleased them" forced church and state to compromise. In the settlement pattern that evolved, the *población* (the administrative center of a pueblo containing the market, church, town hall, and major houses) acted as a magnet to the people in progressively smaller and distant satellite settlements known as barrios, *sitios*, and *rancherías*. The Spanish administration always despaired of its inability to induce more Filipinos to live in poblaciones, but substantial local population shifts took place wherever colonial rule took hold. Since disease inevitably accompanies dislocation and crowding, it is no surprise to find late-sixteenth-century missionaries in Cagayan reporting that greater exposure to pestilence was among the factors causing people to avoid resettlement. A century and a half later, Anton Malinski said that even "the rumor of a disease" caused the newly resettled hill people on Negros to "flee back into their forests." Others stayed and died, like those who had been forcibly resettled in the organized towns of Father Francisco Antolín's mission in north-central Luzon. About 1789 he wrote that many of them quickly became ill and expired. They "wasted away, weakened . . . and few could be kept alive."[10]

Sketchy evidence is accumulating of a demographic crisis that began near the end of the sixteenth century and extended through the first half of the next. A number of determining factors can be identified. The pacification and consolidation of Spanish control over Luzon and the Visayas coincided with the wars against the Dutch (1609–1648) for commercial supremacy in the region centering on the spice-rich Moluccas. It has long been recognized that the war years were extraordinarily hard. The colonial administration could not pay for the fighting, so it was prosecuted on the backs of the people. The *polo* (compulsory labor) and the *vandala* (compulsory sale of products to the government) were the most onerous means, as Horacio de la Costa has explained: "It was the forced-labor contingents drafted year after year from the provinces near Manila that felled the timber, built the ships, sailed them and manned their guns. It was the supplies requisitioned by the government from the same provinces that fed, clothed and armed their crews."[11]

At the same time, changed patterns of interisland raiding destabilized life in the Visayas. Forays by Christian Filipinos had ended, but Moro (Muslim Filipino) raids from Mindanao and the Sulu Archipelago in the south persisted and increased, eventually reaching their greatest extent in the third quarter of the eighteenth century. Father Rodrigo de Aganduru Moriz reported in 1632 on the sudden reversal of roles. Visayans told him that formerly "they would go to Mindanao where they took many captives, and terrified them; and now it is the opposite, because they are Christians and it is not licit for them to make those raids, and they are disarmed, they are paying for what they did then." The negative effects of the raids on public health and population growth should not be minimized. Moro incursions could destabilize a community as completely as American army depredations would centuries later. Raiders beseiged Ilog, Negros, for a month in 1722, finally destroying everything. Pedro Fariz reported that they burned all the houses in the town and fields as well as the growing rice. "As for plants, fruit trees and coconuts, they cut them down. They set fire to all the fields and killed all the pigs, cattle, fowl, dogs, and carabaos so that Ilog was completely razed." Raids took the form of frontal attacks against poblaciones on Samar, with seiges lasting as long as five weeks. One priest described the consequences: "When the Moros besiege the town, as they usually do, the people are subject to epidemics . . . despairing unto [the point of] surrender in order to eat since their fields and hills where there is plenty of food are far away."[12]

The colonial economy suffered during the years of the Dutch wars as well. It depended heavily on the transshipment of Chinese goods to New Spain (Mexico) in the Manila Galleon, especially since the Spaniards had closed all ports to direct outside commerce except Manila, where European vessels (other than Spanish and Portuguese) were banned. According to John L. Phelan the "string of calamities" that periodically interrupted the galleon trade during the war years "only aggravated an already desperate situation." Norman G. Owen has looked at the scant population data that exist and has derived figures for seven different years between 1586 and 1742 of persons from whom the colonial administration claimed tribute (tax and labor services). (The number of tributes can be multiplied by a number corresponding to presumed average family size, usually between four and five, to get a rough count of the population under Spanish control.) The numbers suggest the following rates of average annual population growth or loss during the period: +2.75 percent (1586–1591), −1.47 percent (1591–1608), +0.34 percent (1608–1621), −0.51 percent (1621–1655), +0.38 percent (1655–1686), and +0.94 percent (1686–1742). Anthony Reid has argued that the 35.1 percent decline in tributes between 1591 (166,903) and 1655 (108,277) is far too large to be explained solely by people fleeing to the hills to avoid colonial exactions. He links the apparent demographic loss not only to warfare but to the general seventeenth-century crisis, whose repercussions were felt in Southeast Asia as well. In addition, he cites climatological evidence (tree rings from Java and reports of drought elsewhere) indicating that the entire region experienced abnormally low levels of rainfall from 1600 to 1660, which he says would have induced famines and increased mortality from disease throughout Southeast Asia.[13]

Contemporary observers described the hardships of pacification, external war, polos and vandalas, and Moro raids but left no measurements of changes in precipitation, diet, or morbidity and mortality from disease. It will never be possible to reconstruct what happened with any certainty, but it is at least clear that the overall Philippine demographic downturn ended about the time the war did. What we do not know is how much of the rapid population growth thereafter was attributable to lower mortality (and from what causes) and how much to a higher birth rate. It may be that the latter factor was significant. The government had met its wartime need for labor and supplies by letting *cabezas de barangay* (local chieftains) force the people who could not meet polo or vandala obligations into debt peonage. We can safely presume elevated levels of morbidity and mortality under such conditions. With the return of peace in 1648, the cabezas lost that source of enrichment. New forms of onerous private labor arrangements founded on dependency relationships, like sharecropping evolved, but the worst of the misery must have eased. Levels of undernourishment and disease undoubtedly diminished, and as life became less precarious, the birth rate would have recovered quickly, especially in the provinces on Luzon that had supplied timber and foodstuffs during the wars. Earlier marriage may have become more common as well. When towns were organized in the Batanes Islands at a later date, the friars made sure that "the custom of not marrying before the age of thirty was eliminated [because] it held back the increase of population," according to Ana Maria Madrigal Llorente. If that experience is at all representative of church policy in other areas, consolidation of spiritual control would have initially increased the average number of births per mother. Since the demographic conditions did not exist for widespread epidemics (and indeed reports of devastating disease are not common in the early sources), the birth rate probably regulated population growth to a greater extent than it did in the nineteenth century.[14]

The population upsurge that began on Luzon as the Dutch wars ended was the first of the crucial changes in the Philippine total environment that would shape the health crisis two centuries later. The internal peace that generally prevailed after the consolidation of Spanish control was primarily responsible for the increase, just as the American conquest would create conditions favoring better health and population growth early in the twentieth century. That the effect of colonial rule was to nurture life as well as to destroy it is particularly difficult to accept in the face of the fact that the two periods of imperial peace were built on the suffering and death of so many. It is nevertheless the case that Spanish rule after 1650 ended interbarangay warfare and began the long process of freeing first Luzon and then the Visayas from the southern raiders. Commercial restrictions indirectly limited the volume of pathogenic microorganisms that could be imported into the islands and channeled most of what did arrive into Manila. Despite continuing resistance to Spanish rule, sporadic revolts, and the short-lived British conquest of 1762–1764, Philippine life became less subject to those kinds of upheavals that in the past had caused entire town populations to abandon their homes and flee to the forest. The main threat to dietary self-sufficiency, and thus better nourishment and health, was natural rather than man-made disaster. As a result, Father Joaquín Martínez de Zúñiga could affirm at the turn of the nineteenth century that Filipinos "multiply more than any other nation on earth."[15]

Mere growth in numbers did not by itself produce a critical level of contact probability; the islands had more than ample room even for the 7.6 million Filipinos who lived on some of them a century later. More important was the increasingly clustered pattern of settlement that developed and the volume and velocity of movement within and between those clusters. None of that was random, of course, so it is crucial to focus on the various factors—administrative, geographic, cultural, and economic—that caused the people to congregate and then to intermingle. The bonding process in nineteenth-century Philippine settlement patterns is central to an understanding of the increasing vulnerability of larger groups to epidemic disease.

Pueblo (town) formation was a centerpiece of Spanish civil and religious policy from the start. The friars quickly accommodated themselves to the Philippine reality of dispersed settlement by building rudimentary chapels in the larger outlying settlements of their missions. Those outstations were called *visitas* after the visits of the missionaries (and at a later time, the parish priests) to say Mass and administer the sacraments. Cullinane explains that pueblos were historically formed "by associating the *visitas* served by a particular mission station or established . . . *población*, which became the seat of the municipality." As settlement progressed, the municipality was eventually elevated to the status of parish and given a priest charged with spiritual responsibility for the inhabitants. By the eighteenth century, pueblos were territorial jurisdictions, more akin to an American county than city or town, comprising residential components that included a población, together with its numerous and widely dispersed barrios, sitios, rancherias, and scattered households. The people were organized into barangay (which had become tax collection units and had lost their original kinship bases) and governed by a civil administration of local Filipino functionaries known as the *principalía*.[16]

When Father Martínez de Zúñiga wrote his account of life in the nine provinces of the Manila archbishopric, the population there was said to have grown from 187,040 in 1735 to 493,770 in 1800, an average annual rate of 1.49 percent. The towns were still scattered and separated by large expanses of "desert," however, and he looked forward to the day, fast approaching, when new settlements would be founded to fill in those empty spaces. The process accelerated everywhere thereafter as the población-barrio-sitio system replicated itself. But even in Pangasinan, which had long been thoroughly missionized, most people lived far enough from the town centers to make it difficult for them to take part in the various religious and secular rituals. As late as midcentury, only about 18 percent of the residents of four major municipalities (Malasiqui, Calasiao, Dagupan, San Carlos) lived in the poblaciones. However, the fast-growing population, fueled by both natural increase and immigration from the Ilocos provinces to the north, soon made it possible to create more towns so that a greater proportion of the residents had easier access to municipal and parochial services.[17]

The normal procedure was straightforward enough, though in practice it varied according to region and circumstance. When enough families had settled together, they asked permission to erect a visita. As the settlement grew, a sense of community developed, "usually with the emergence of competing local . . . municipal elites" according to Cullinane, and when it could produce about five hundred tributes (which allowed it to pay a priestly stipend and meet the other municipal expenses), petition could be made for separation from its mother municipality and for recognition as an independent pueblo. The petitioners customarily affirmed that their distance from the municipality was so great that they could not fulfill their spiritual obligations (to the detriment of their souls), that many died without receiving the necessary sacraments, and that many crimes went unpunished for lack of law enforcement officials. They further affirmed that the settlement had sufficient land and water for agriculture and that a church, rectory, and municipal building had already been constructed. If all went smoothly, the petition was endorsed by the officials of the mother town, approved by the provincial governor, and granted by the superior government in Manila, which issued a royal decree creating a new municipality. Its establishment as a parish was not automatically concurrent, though it usually followed directly. Religious officials might set further conditions, such as the construction of more substantial church buildings, but in any case a new curacy depended on the availability of a priest.[18]

The burgeoning population made the creation of new towns possible, but pueblo formation in the nineteenth century was driven by a combination of factors. Church officials, government authorities, and private entrepreneurs all had complementary agendas. The civil administration, as we shall see, was increasingly concerned with facilitating agricultural and commercial development. Although regularly entangled in its own red tape, it was well aware of the need to rationalize tax collection, labor mobilization, and law enforcement in order to create favorable capital investment conditions as well as to consolidate its own tenuous hold over the colony. The church, as always, was intent on the spiritual care of its flock and the conversion of non-Christians, which required the "civilizing" environment of the población-barrio-sitio complex, or so it was believed.

Town creation on the fast-developing sugar frontier of western Negros after midcentury was such a joint endeavor. The process moved quickly in areas being developed for cash-crop exports. Upon return from an inspection trip in 1847, the Visayan governor notified the new bishop of Cebu, Romualdo Jimeno, of the need for additional parishes and better administration. The bishop immediately departed on a pastoral visit during which he was appalled to find seven goats lying on the benches in the sacristy of one church and a bull entering another. He resolved to remedy the "sorry neglect in which parish priests and their parishes could be found" by replacing the secular clergy with the Recollect order. About a year later, Governor Manuel Valdivieso Morquecho arrived in the province to find only Negrito bands peopling the "fruitful desert" on the future site of Valladolid, directly across the Guimares Strait from Iloilo City. A year later, six hundred taxpayers had settled there, impelling the governor to ask the Recollect provincial for a priest because "otherwise this development could fade or even die away." The provincial agreed and the government in Manila quickly authorized the foundation of a new pueblo and parish, joining to it the barrios of Pulupandan and Tinibagan. By 1866, Valladolid and neighboring San Enrique comprised a total of 7,448 inhabitants, most of whom were engaged in the production or export of sugar from the new haciendas. Missionaries took the lead on the less developed east coast, where they slogged about the extensive territory between Tanjay and Silay, converting infieles and then trying to keep them in the newly organized towns and parishes. That half of the island, Negros Oriental, was given its own politico-military government in 1882.[19]

We can recognize other determinants in Bruce Cruikshank's account of pueblo formation on the more slowly developing island of Samar. There private capital and production for the world market were not important factors, and new towns were established at the behest of the settlers as often as they were created on the motion of civil or religious authorities. New lands were settled by adventurous fishermen or hunters, farmers looking for new land for shifting-field agriculture, factions unhappy with their place in the power structure in a previous settlement, would-be patrons seeking clients, and even eloping couples. Most groups tried to retain ties with other settlements, if only to trade for iron and salt. Their leaders typically petitioned both church and civil government for recognition, usually by notifying the nearest parish priest. As Christians, the settlers wanted his visits, and as defenseless pioneers, they needed his leadership and his access to weapons when Moro raiders approached. Since a resident priest conferred substantial prestige, the principalía of growing splinter settlements continually pressured the authorities for recognition as the población of a new municipality. Hatred and jealousy between the principalía of rival settlements complicated the entire process.[20]

Seven towns were created in Pangasinan during the first half of the nineteenth century, bringing the total to thirty-four before the population explosion in the region compelled the drawing of new boundaries and the loss of about a third of the municipalities to other provinces. Still, more than three times as many people lived in Pangasinan at the end of the century as had lived there at the beginning despite the province's steady territorial shrinkage. The number of pueblos on Negros increased from seventeen in 1850 to forty-two in 1893 as the sugar-driven economy attracted massive immigration that multiplied the island's population more than ten times. Samar's municipalities increased at about the same rate, from nineteen in 1854 to forty in 1898. More important epidemiologically were the increasing population density and personal contact in each. Average town size on Samar grew from 2,800 in 1800 to 5,600 in 1854 to 6,100 in 1898, while the settlement pattern within pueblos contracted. Cruikshank estimates that between one-sixth and one-quarter of Samareños lived in poblaciones during the late eighteenth century. By 1898 about half (49.3 percent) did, and almost two-thirds (62.5 percent) lived in the población or within three miles of it.[21]

The bureaucratization of daily life and the economy's growing market orientation exerted a centripetal force on poblaciones, ensuring personal contact amongst a greater proportion of pueblo inhabitants. Religious and secular authorities used cultural imperatives to the same effect. In fact, Fedor Jagor claimed that it was only the priests (and the village prisons) who overcame the Filipino's "innate inclination to abandon the hamlets and retire into the solitude of the woods, or live isolated in the midst of his own fields . . . gradually turning the pueblos into visitas, and the latter into *ranchos*." But as Cullinane points out, most Filipinos accepted their religious duty to take part in parish celebrations and rituals and to receive the essential sacraments at the church in the población. Further, he says that "elaborate socio-religious activities (such as fiestas honoring the parish's patron saint and Easter and Corpus Christi celebrations) were sponsored by the población to form ritual links with the inhabitants of the barrios within its jurisdiction."[22]

As the uninhabited area was diminishing in accordance with Father Martínez de Zúñiga's vision, contact between the various municipal clusters became more frequent and regular. In Pangasinan "as each new town was erected, a road was built from it to the next or nearest town," according to R. Mendoza Cortes. Such a road was all the more necessary when the new pueblo did not immediately become an independent parish and remained tied to the mother parish for a time. Those connecting roads, however poorly maintained, together with rivers and short feeder paths and streams provided a transportation network more than adequate to tie a number of pueblos into significant population clusters in terms of the potential for epidemic transmission of disease. Once enough of those clusters were knit together by a critical volume and velocity of human movement, Filipinos suddenly found themselves at vastly increased risk from communicable disease.[23]

External population growth was another factor in the shifting ecological balance and was thus closely related to the Philippine system of disease. As the colony's commercial relations expanded in the nineteenth century, fast-growing port areas throughout Southeast Asia and beyond took on special importance as reservoirs of infection from which disease could be imported into the archipelago. Measles provides the clearest example of the process. In 1800 the Philippine population was too small and widely separated to support the virus on a permanent basis anywhere in the islands. The 100,000 residents in Manila and its environs were easily the largest grouping in the islands but fell far short of the 250,000 or so that is the threshold for endemicity. For the better part of the nineteenth century, the measles virus was unable to sustain itself in the Philippines without periodic replenishment from abroad. By the time the disease started arriving from California with the American army and its dependents in 1898, the bonded population clusters of Manila and surrounding provinces were capable of sustaining the infection endemically and exporting it directly throughout the archipelago.[24]

Much of what eventually made the population's increase so epidemiologically significant resulted directly from new economic policies that reflected a changed conception of the colony's role in the faltering Spanish empire during the eighteenth century. The agricultural and commercial transformations that followed are arguably the fundamental determinants in modern Philippine history. The internal economy, based on semisubsistence agriculture and local exchange of handicrafts, had traditionally been of little concern to the Crown since it held out no obvious promise of imperial gain. Despite some interchange with all surrounding countries, Philippine commerce centered on the galleon. The annual voyage yielded substantial profits to the colonial elite in Manila when all went well. Primarily, though, as Governor-General José Basco y Vargas put it in 1781, galleon profits "poured into the empires of China and Japan and the coasts of India, leaving nothing here but the rumor of their passage." The mother country gained little. Its Asian possession was a losing proposition financially, kept afloat by an annual subsidy from Mexico. As Spain lost ground to the "more advanced nations," the unproductive Philippines increasingly seemed an unaffordable luxury.[25]

The "precarious situation of the islands, so onerous for the Crown, made necessary a complete reconsideration of the sources of its wealth," according to Javier Ortíz de la Tabla Ducasse. Several decades before the 1762–1764 British occupation of Manila underscored the colony's vulnerability, liberal thinkers had begun to argue that Spain could only assure its own security and prosperity by stanching the outflow of silver. Each part of the empire should become a producer, contributing according to comparative advantage in order to reduce dangerous economic dependence on imperial competitors. The Philippine Islands were rich and fertile, a potential fount of agricultural produce for export situated as they were astride Asian trade routes. The "preoccupation with developing the archipelago's resources," as Antonio F. García Gonzales describes it, seems to have begun formally with a proposal in 1730 by the Marqués de Villadarias, though others applied for commercial licenses during that decade without effect. In the mid-1740s, Pedro Calderón Enríquez toured Pampanga and reported that "sugar alone would generate much money if producers were encouraged to build sugar mills and given complete freedom to extract." He argued that it was essential to organize a commercial entity charged with "encouraging and benefiting from the fabrics and fruits of the land." Pedro Murillo Velarde predicted a year or two later that strong governmental support in the form of a chartered company would initiate a cycle of prosperity. Once regional shipping capability was established, agricultural estates, textile factories, and extraction of raw materials would follow as a matter of course. Other *proyectistas* (people advancing projects) pointed out that export-generated wealth would encourage further cultivation of Philippine land and thus employ more people and increase tax revenues.[26]

Resistance to the proposed reforms from the Manila elite prevented their implementation until Governor Basco officially embraced the new approach. He argued that "the Philippines abounds in the treasures of the vegetable, animal and mineral kingdoms. Prudent management is all that is required to make it yield these hidden treasures." His administration (1778–1787) is associated with a number of innovations that laid the groundwork for the colony's entry into the world economy at a time when the other imperial powers in Southeast Asia were engaged in what J. Kathirithamby-Wells has characterized as *commercial adventurism*. Starting in 1785, a series of royal decrees had the de facto effect of removing restrictions on foreign shipping in the port of Manila. In order to take advantage of that move toward freer trade, the Real Compañía de Filipinas was created on the model of the successful Dutch and British East India Companies. The opening of the port legitimized much of the commerce that had long taken place under various covers, but the Crown still failed to benefit. The volume of shipping remained stagnant because the agricultural sector was unable to provide a regular supply of export goods, and the company lacked the resources to stimulate production in the provinces. Foreign firms did, however, and it was they that eventually profited. By 1815, the year of the last galleon crossing, foreign traders were taking steps to assure themselves of cargoes by leaving agents ashore to collect products and to advance money to cultivators against future crops. Thus were the foundations of the economic upsurge laid.[27]

Then in late 1820, a seemingly unrelated event gave the issue of economic development new urgency—cholera struck Manila for the first time. Terrified mobs, suspecting a plot to poison the waters, rioted for two days and massacred about thirty Europeans (but no Spaniards) and several times as many resident Chinese. Governor-General Mariano Fernandez de Folgueras called out the troops, but neither they nor he acted effectively to calm the enraged rioters. The main targets of the fury were precisely the kind of persons the administration wanted to attract to the Philippine storehouse of riches. Some of the victims were French naturalists, who had come to islands to make zoological observations, and others were potential investors or producers. The Russian consul, Peter Dobell, had already suspected that trade with the colony might not thrive because the Spaniards "held their productions two [*sic*] high & paid too low for European commodities." After the riots, he was certain that "its commerce is ruined forever." The "[F]rench and other foreigners, who were anxious to have established themselves in commerce or on estates in the country, are now frightened off and certainly no one will find himself confident enough to trust to a Government, which could permit such a massacre."[28]

The official response was a new commitment to facilitate agricultural and commercial development, a move designed not only to prevent the loss of foreign interest in trade but also to preempt the loss of the colony itself. The cholera riots must be seen in the context of the revolutions that broke up most of Spain's American empire during those years, thereby spurring official pessimism in Manila about the chances of retaining the Philippines. Governor-General Pascual Enrile y Alcedo later articulated that fear, which was in all Spanish minds, conceding that it was "illusory to expect that so small a force can hold down a determined revolutionary movement." Many, including Enrile, believed that the best chance of keeping the colony in the long run lay in bringing prosperity to the islands through a determined program to develop the public riches. Thus an unusually detailed royal decree was issued in early 1822 that recommended the establishment of agricultural experimental stations, the cultivation of enumerated commercial crops, the construction of roads and canals (for navigation and irrigation), the establishment of fairs and markets, and the formation of commissions to report regularly on the state of agriculture and methods to remove obstacles to its development. Supporting legislation was designed to stimulate agriculture by publicizing the existing privileges that the law gave to farmers and by announcing a wide range of new exemptions, incentives, and prizes.[29]

By the beginning of Governor Enrile's term (1830–1835), little or no official opposition remained to the idea, so controversial a half-century earlier, that the Philippines should function not simply as an entrepôt but as a producer and exporter of agricultural commodities. All agreed that the riches of the land should be exploited and that Spain should be the primary beneficiary. Everyone concurred on the need to eliminate the Moro threat once and for all, to foster coastwise trade, to provide credit to the agricultural sector, to welcome foreign merchant houses, and to develop cash-crop exports, but they disagreed passionately over the degree to which Philippine commerce should be free to the world. Protectionists no longer insisted on a closed system, but they believed that Spanish shippers should be awarded substantial preferences in the form of differential tariffs. Free traders, whether from a theoretical standpoint or from a more realistic appreciation of the Spanish merchant marine's limited capabilities, favored moderate customs duties and elimination of discriminatory rates on foreign bottoms and produce. The Junta de Aranceles (tariff board) had been established a couple of years earlier and charged with drawing a tariff that would increase the revenue of the treasury, nourish and protect the agricultural and manufacturing arts of the islands, and encourage the growth of national and foreign commerce. The board labored throughout the century under extreme pressure from adherents of both economic schools, attempting to steer a prudent and nonpartisan course between the twin evils of "forced isolation" and "an impudent and rash liberty." It nevertheless preferred freer trade. The port of Manila was officially opened in 1834, as were Sual, Iloilo, Cebu, and Zamboanga two decades later. Tariff differentials were narrowed, and the number of categories of dutiable goods was reduced by over 90 percent between 1831 and 1870 as the board attempted to attract capital and industry.[30]

It is difficult to argue that the junta failed to carry out its mandate. Customs receipts increased approximately nine times between 1831 and 1876, the value of agricultural exports multiplied almost fivefold, the volume of internal coasting trade to and from Manila registered even higher growth rates, and public revenues more than doubled. Yet, even though the Philippines had been forced to yield its "hidden treasures," as Basco had urged almost a century earlier, the empire never reaped the benefits the early reformers had envisioned. No sooner had the economy been opened than the mother country lost real control over it. It could not have been otherwise. As Jagor pointed out in 1873, Spain was almost entirely "without the power of turning [the Philippines] to any useful account." The initial strategy of welcoming foreign commercial houses but relegating them to a limited role backfired because foreign firms, especially British ones, had far more capital to invest in export stimulation and benefited accordingly. The secretary-general of Barcelona's society of credit and docks noted in 1883 that Spain's international commerce was insignificant in comparison with that of the other European nations, ranking twelfth among them. It was sad and disgraceful, he said, "to observe the silence that reigns in almost all of our ports." Few Philippine commodities arrived, either for domestic consumption or for processing and reexport, and more than 95 percent of the colony's overseas trade was in the hands of foreigners. In the meantime, too, Singapore and Hong Kong, and not Manila, had become the great commercial depositories in the Southeast Asian region.[31]

Spanish participation in the colony's internal development was almost as negligible. The removal in 1854 of judicial powers from the provincial governors so that they could concentrate their energies on government and development had made little difference. Chinese-Filipino mestizos increasingly owned the productive land, and resident Chinese functioned as middlemen between producers and foreign companies. Then, to compound the problem, the half-century of spectacular export-driven economic growth began fluctuating wildly in the 1870s as the dislocation in the world economic system rocked the colonial economy. Proyectistas sensed that time was running short for Spain to benefit from turning the Philippines into an "emporium of production" and proposed last-ditch development schemes without number. Antonio de Keyser y Muñoz called for the registration of land titles, establishment of experimental agricultural stations, and easily enforceable contracts between proprietors and farm laborers. José Jimeno Agius proposed the replacement of the "odious" personal tribute with a schedule of levies on local production. Toribio Ruíz de la Escalera y Oraá claimed that success rested upon fundamental administrative reform. Gabino Perez Valdez advocated a massive long-term loan from England or Holland on the guarantee of tobacco or customs revenues. And Manuel Azcarraga y Palmero argued for an all-out effort to develop a communications infrastructure by building bridges, roads, canals, and port facilities linking newly established commercial houses with large agricultural plantations built on the Ceylon and Penang models. Provincial officials floated even more ideas, identifying factors that had stymied profitable development for Spain. By the late 1880s, though, time had run out. The colonial treasury was "flat broke." As economic and political clouds gathered, it became evident that implementation of meaningful reforms was beyond the government's capability.[32]

The agricultural and commercial revolution had any number of consequences, but the one that most increased the probabililty of contact with infective human and animal hosts was the resulting mobilization of the population. A sedentary population had served colonial interests for at least two centuries. Pacification, conversion to Christianity, and consolidation of administrative authority went most smoothly when the people were settled and engaged in wet-rice cultivation. Few Filipinos had any reason to leave home, in any case, given the official neglect of the internal economy. The radical shift in economic development policy during the 1770s changed that. Exploiting the land's riches could not possibly have been successful unless people were in motion. Focusing narrowly on the removal of impediments to the movement of products, the proyectistas did not anticipate the long-term risks to colonial rule and to the public health. Father Martínez de Zúñiga's program for development of the interior was representative, calling for vigorous military action against upland peoples, Moro raiders, and outlaws together with a system of new settlements, canals, dikes, and roads. The administration followed that basic blueprint for the entire century.[33]

Driving the Moro raiders from interisland waterways was essential. Their depredations on the coasts of Luzon had peaked in the 1750s, but so long as they maintained bases on Mindoro (where they held captives for ransom or for shipment to Jolo), they could roam the Sibuyan Sea and choke commerce between Manila and the Visayas. The government mounted an expedition against the stronghold at Mamburao on Mindoro's northwest coast in 1772 and others followed, but Father Martínez de Zúñiga explained that "because [the Moros] had always easy access to the mountains, our expeditions did not accomplish the desired effect." Still, the navy kept the pressure on, and he was able to say at the turn of the century that "these corsairs could no longer undertake the piratical expeditions of yesteryears, nor could they rob anymore to their heart's content." Some pioneers from Luzon had begun to establish fortified settlements on Mindoro's coasts, and the government was using that foothold to establish security in the region by populating the island with Christian immigrants. To advance the project, Governor-General Rafael Maria de Aguilar sent a magistrate to Mindoro with powers to exempt the settlers from tribute, labor service, and monopolies so as to induce them to stay until regular towns could be erected. Father Martínez de Zúñiga thought that if the magistrate and the officials who would follow him could refrain from their "usual wanton tricks" of extorting profit from the settlers, the "project may prove useful to the Philippines and rid the provinces immediately close to Manila of the grievous injury" caused by the Moros.[34]

The government had as yet neither the money nor the means to project its naval power as effectively in areas more distant from Manila, but it began to take a more active role defending towns in Luzon's Bikol region and in the Visayas. Moros launched their most devastating raids on Samar poblaciones in the 1770s, with frontal attacks by as many as 220 boats with up to fifty warriors on each. The colonial administration provided some armaments for town defense, but Cruikshank gives primary credit to the priests and townspeople for building and sailing pueblo-based boats to intercept and pursue the raiders before they could land. That strategy forced the Moros to begin downscaling their forays to hit-and-run attacks against outlying visitas and abductions of fishermen and traders. Martínez Cuesta notes an improvement in community morale in eastern Negros during the first decade of the nineteenth century that seems to have resulted from the government's new interest in supporting local defense plans. The towns, under priestly leadership, organized a system of forts, early warning signals, and municipal patrol outrigger boats that encouraged the people to fight rather than flee to the hills. By around 1820 the Moros were subdued throughout the entire region and life immediately stabilized. In Sorgoson, for instance, former coastal residents returned from the interior, providing the initial impetus for the "phenomenal growth of towns and population" that followed, according to Luis Camara Dery.[35]

Manila had carried the war to the various sultanates of Mindanao and the Sulu Archipelago periodically from the start, mainly as a containment measure. A garrisoned fortress was established at the southern tip of the Zamboangan peninsula in western Mindanao as early as 1635. A century later it was the most important of six strategically situated frontier outposts. Hostilities did not preclude trade, but during the eighteenth century, Zamboanga languished commercially, gradually becoming an economic dependent of the increasingly powerful Sulu Sultanate, which was centered on Jolo island. Spain's decisive advance south in the mid-nineteenth century to clear the sea lanes and to establish de facto control in Mindanao can also be seen as part of the dynamics between the European powers to consolidate areas of commercial influence and to maintain stable trade conditions in Southeast Asia. Nicholas Tarling points out that while the rivals generally left each other alone, nothing prevented any of them from extending influence where no one stood in the way. The Sulu group presented such an opportunity, and so it was the fear of British or Dutch inroads there that evoked preemptive action. Steampower made it successful. In 1848 the Spanish navy, led by three steampowered warships just purchased from England, attacked and defeated the Samals at Balangingi, the island that served as the sultanate's principal slave-retailing center. Control of the southern seas passed to Spain as a result, and its steam gunboats were on regular patrol after 1860. Southern Filipinos were never brought under effective control, but the military eventually established a toehold on Mindanao firm enough to allow the beginning of limited migration and colonization from the northern islands in the early 1880s. Although the colonial advance fell short of its goals, the Muslim Philippines were quickly eliminated as an impediment to the agricultural and commercial development of the northern two-thirds of the archipelago.[36]

Two other categories of people presented obstacles to the exploitation of island interiors. Non-Muslim infieles of one ethno-liguistic group or another lived in the hill regions of most islands and not only resisted conversion and consolidation but were also generally hostile to pioneering on the slopes of those upland areas. Scott has explained the process by which groups that refused to submit to Hispanization had long since been transformed by the "magic of colonial alchemy" from Filipinos into cultural minorities—at least in the Spanish (and lowland Filipino) mind. The Ilocanos and Ibanags, two of the three linguistic groups that the Spaniards encountered upon arrival in far northern Luzon, eventually accepted foreign domination and over the years relinquished much of their own culture to assimilate that of the conquerer. "In the process, they became more and more like each other and less and less like their ancestors. The Isnegs, on the other hand, preserved more of the culture of their ancestors and so came to look less and less like their acculturating neighbors." Thus those who had changed most became "Filipinos." One result of this transformation was that when groups like the Isnegs seemed to impede progress in the nineteenth century, their differences invited merciless treatment by Spaniard and Christianized Filipino alike. Military expeditions were sent into mountains throughout the century. If the hill peoples were rarely conquered by force of arms, they were most often pushed back to make way for pioneering and subsequent town formation in the interior. They also suffered greatly from diseases the soldiers brought with them, especially smallpox. Late in the century, the "savage races" could still retard the pace of frontier settlement, as they did in western Nueva Ecija, "coming down from the impenetrable forest under cover of darkness to ambush hacienda workers"; but they could not prevent development.[37]

Bandits were the other group that the authorities needed to take action against. The colonial construction of "banditry" as comprising a wide range of officially disapproved behavior is notorious, but whatever the basic causes and rights and wrongs of unlawful activity in the Philippines, the bandits certainly presented a barrier to the flow of commerce. In Father Martínez de Zúñiga's time they made any overland travel hazardous, but the government had neither the capability nor a compelling reason to take effective measures. A corps of municipal police, the Cuerpo de Quadrilleros, was established in 1846 to provide more security in the growing towns. As the transformation of the economy took place, more and more persons were dislocated, and some took to various kinds of banditry. Bands of brigands "perpetrated acts of extraordinary daring," and some military units were "regularly engaged in the service" against them by 1860, according to Jagor. A decade later a government circular stated that banditry was causing "serious damage to persons, agriculture and commerce." In response, the Civil Guard (Tercios de Guardia civil) was created "for the conservation of public order and the protection of persons and property." Two regiments covered the provinces north and south of Manila, and a third was divided and headquartered in Cebu and Iloilo. Governor-General Valeriano Weyler sent them after bandits who had attacked pioneers settling the interior valleys of Negros in 1889, declaring that he would not tolerate "a situation that occasions so much harm to the development and agricultural wealth of said island." The increased police and military presence in the colony, along with the settlement of the uninhabited areas between towns, improved security and offset the growing rural lawlessness that Greg Bankoff has documented. Outrages of one kind or another remained common enough, but as in the case of the Moros and hill peoples, government action diminished the threat to movement of commerce and people.[38]

The intractable physical environment presented immense difficulties. The government understood the need for a transportation infrastructure, and indeed Enrile made improved communications one of his highest priorities in the early 1830s. He also decided to finance the program by having the municipalities administer it as a personal service. Thus generations of nineteenth-century Filipinos served their forced-labor obligations building roads and bridges and then repairing them. Progress was slow. In 1869, Keyser pointed out the disparity between a half-century of legislation mandating road construction and the actual accomplishment. Most of the relatively few roads remained deeply rutted and dusty in the dry season and virtually impassable during the rains, which washed out the flimsy bridges. All official reports from the provinces deplored the situation, especially after 1883 when a royal decree reforming the forced-labor policy had the unintended consequence of bringing public works projects almost to a halt, resulting in a marked deterioration of roads and bridges. Weyler asserted (with some hyperbole) in 1888 that in the whole archipelago "there is not a single kilometer of road that is in passable condition." Nevertheless, the network of rivers, roads, paths, trails, and fords was sufficient to tie población to sitio and pueblo to pueblo, both economically and epidemiologically. In 1892 the Manila-Dagupan railroad opened. Long anticipated as the key that would finally unlock Luzon's riches, within a decade the line was hauling more than 165,000 tons of freight and 1.1 million passengers a year between Lingayan Bay and the capital.[39]

Developing the public wealth meant opening new land. The Philippine frontier should not be imagined as a straight line dividing the country between settled and unsettled territories and moving inexorably forward. It is more accurate to speak of Philippine *frontiers* that ran at haphazard angles, opening and closing at different times in different places. Generalizations are particularly hazardous with respect to the Philippines, which John Larkin once described as "a collection of integrated societies developing at different rates and subject to diverse stimuli." The best-documented examples of the frontier process are from Luzon's central plain and Negros, areas that became "developed," but it is well to bear in mind Cruikshank's observation that most of the archipelago developed at a slower and less revolutionary pace. What all the frontiers had in common, however, was their assault on island interiors, which spurred unprecedented human mobility and the consequent spread of disease.[40]

The central plain frontier was opened much earlier than most of the others. Thus San Miguel de Mayumo, in the northwestern corner of Bulacan, had long been settled when restrictions against foreign commerce were removed. Thereafter, the pueblo functioned as a jumping-off point for movement into the interior when the colony was drawn into the world trading system. Around the beginning of the nineteenth century, according to Brian Fegan, merchants who had already accumulated some capital "devised new ways of combining capital and labor in order to procure crops for the world market." One method was to foster agricultural settlements on the frontier beyond the estates owned by the religious orders. In the previous century, some of the resident Chinese-Filipino mestizo families in San Miguel had acquired substantial tracts of forest and uncleared plains to the north of town. As cash cropping became profitable in the 1820s, they leased blocks of unsettled land to tenants under various sharecropping arrangements for clearing and cultivating indigo, sugar, or rice. While the frontier stayed open, a temporary mutuality of interest bound the capitalists, who received crops for export, and the peasants, who were able to establish themselves as cultivators under better conditions than existed in the settled areas they had left.[41]

Migrants from the Ilocos region helped settle the Cagayan Valley and the central plain as far south as Tarlac. The elements of merchant investment and rent capitalism were less important there, according to Marshall S. McLennan. Scarcity of land due to population growth began to push some Ilocanos out of their homeland in the second decade of the nineteenth century, and wagon caravans took large groups south to the unoccupied interior of Pangasinan. Their settlements became magnets and then springboards for subsequent waves of immigrants who, by the 1840s, had moved on into Tarlac and Nueva Ecija. Upon arrival most people joined relatives as sharecrop tenants or dependent laborers until they could clear land for themselves or accumulate enough money to purchase a lot from a settler. Other groups skipped the intermediate stage and went directly to the frontier, founding a settlement on uncleared land. Under the leadership of a headman, the new community functioned as a kind of cooperative as it prepared the land for the first rice harvests several years hence. Late in the century, many Ilocano families left home each year after the November rice harvest to work the later harvest on the plain. Some of those migrant workers stayed on.[42]

The settlement of Negros was more sudden and ruthless. Most of the island was unpopulated before the 1850s. During that decade, as Alfred W. McCoy has explained, the decline of Panay's weaving industry propelled emigration from depressed villages across the Guimares Strait to Negros. Some new-comers set off inland from coastal settlements to clear the forest and establish smallholdings. The governor authorized military action against resisting non-Christians to open the way, and the infieles were pacified amidst great slaughter and driven further into the mountains. Chinese-Filipino mestizos, who formed the urban merchant elite of Jaro and Molo on Panay, sensed the potential profits in sugar and, through a combination of power, money, and corruption, quickly dispossessed many of the original Negros pioneers. Backed by foreign capital, they consolidated the land into plantations and by the 1880s were producing large amounts of sugar for export. Meanwhile, the population of Negros Occidental increased about ten times, not including the flow of seasonal labor across the strait each year.[43]

The colonial government increasingly sponsored settlement efforts. Initially officials were optimistic that deportation of criminals and social undesirables could be turned to account. Penal colonies had been scattered throughout the southern islands for years, but in 1870 the authorities conceived the idea of creating farming colonies and providing the deported with the necessary supplies for crop development. The results were disappointing, however, and a decade later such spontaneous and independent action was renounced in favor of systematic colonization in potentially rich areas where Spanish government control was purely nominal. Having had little success with deported people and their "vicious habits," the government began to recruit families as immigrants to the colonies, offering free transportation, daily rice rations, land, tools, seed, animals, and a ten-year exemption from tribute and contributions. The master plan for Paragua (Palawan today) was typical. The indigenous peoples were to be Christianized and brought under administrative control, the fertile land and forests exploited, and colonies established on the island's west coast and strung strategically south to Borneo to take advantage of trade routes between China and Singapore. No one doubted the potential payoff of the various settlement schemes.[44]

Before the economy was commercialized in the nineteenth century, only a tiny segment of the population had been on the move. Suddenly the trickle became a flood with currents and countercurrents flowing in all directions. Some of them can be identified. The most constant one ran between barrio and población. Women had always carried food and handicrafts to and from the market, but the volume of that kind of everyday foot traffic increased substantially as the population grew and local markets became more important due to diminishing household self-sufficiency. Jagor captured the color and motion in his description of the evening market in Daraga, Albay, around 1860: "The women . . . sat in long rows and offered their provisions for sale by the light of hundreds of torches; and, when the business was over, the slopes of the mountains were studded all over with flickering little points of brightness proceeding from the torches carried by the homeward-bound market women." He noted that "all the younger women were accompanied by their sweethearts, who relieved them of their burdens." No one seems to have measured the flow outside of Manila, but a couple of random statistics from that city give the impression of incessant and growing movement. Vehicular traffic between Manila and the market district of Binondo was said to have increased five times between 1858 and 1885. Later, during the American war when movement was officially limited, as many as 2,000 men, women, and children still walked past a handful of checkpoints carrying food in and out of the city each day.[45]

As local transportation networks slowly improved, people came to the larger poblaciones from farther away on temporary business. John Foreman reported that in the 1890s they came from "great distances" to attend the lively market in Calamba, Laguna, each Friday. His observation contrasts with Father Martínez de Zúñiga's lament at the beginning of the century about the hazards that prevented so many people in the same region from merely getting to church on Sundays. Dr. Ezequiel Delgado described the hustle and bustle in and out of Nueva Caceres (Naga today), Camarines Sur, in 1886, and marveled at the constant stream of people arriving to attend the weekly market, to deal with the provincial authorities, and to visit friends and relatives enrolled at the two schools. The great expansion of secondary education in Manila (and thus numbers of visitors) was an especially effective means of transferring disease from the capital's rapidly filling reservoir of infection to the provinces.[46]

Internal migration from rural to urban areas grew enormously during the century. As land became more valuable in an economy increasingly based on commercial agriculture, those with money, credit, and access to the legal system consolidated power as landowners, middlemen, or merchants. Many smallholders and tenants lacked those means and were swamped with debt. Most remained on the land in diminished status, but some migrated to regional magnet cities. Others were drawn to Manila, where the influx of wealth was creating employment opportunities as drivers, domestics, cigar makers, prostitutes, and other occupations that were scarce or nonexistent in the provinces. Daniel F. Doeppers has concluded that migrants made up more than a quarter of the city in the early 1890s. Two-thirds of the newcomers came from pueblos in neighboring Bulacan and Rizal provinces that had been "long directly involved in provisioning the city, in growing, making, carrying to, and marketing foodstuffs and handicraft products in the city." The new railroad and improved steamship service facilitated the arrival of a greater proportion of migrants from more distant provinces during the last decade of the century. Manila's population grew so fast that a counterflow developed as workers from the capital began migrating to prosperous provincial centers like Nueva Caceres.[47]

The continual movement toward island interiors produced its own backwash. The epidemiological significance of the Philippine frontiers is missed if the process is seen as unidirectional. Pioneers experienced abnormally high rates of morbidity and mortality, especially from malaria, but if they had simply disappeared into the wilderness and lived in isolation, the impact on the general population would have been negligible. In fact, pioneers were never out of touch with the people they left behind. For one thing, the frontiers were never far from the settled areas. For another, people went back and forth constantly, as in the case of land scouts returning to Ilocos to tell others of opportunities in Nueva Ecija or that of seasonal laborers in Negros recrossing the Guimares Strait to go home. Furthermore, frontiers closed. That happened on the central plain once the available tracts of land were rented to share tenants, cleared, and planted. As Fegan has explained, mutuality of interest evaporated at that point, and owners began to insist on a more intensive extraction from the land. As population pressure rose, some tenants returned to the settled areas, whether to home barrios or to one of the growing magnet towns. The most disadvantaged or oppressed often took to the hills, swelling a floating population whose role in the spread of infection became especially important after the abolition of internal passport requirements in 1884 removed a legal barrier to unrestricted migration.[48]

The two-way movement of male Chinese between the mainland and the Philippines, subject only to ineffective maritime quarantine procedures when epidemics flared in and around Asian port cities, represented the most important contact with outside reservoirs of infection. The volume of that immigration had always depended on shifts in colonial policy. After expulsion from the islands in 1766, the Chinese population stabilized around 5,000, who were mostly resident in and about Manila. Restrictions were relaxed in the 1830s and then again in 1850 in hopes of alleviating the agricultural labor shortage. As a result, almost 7,000 Chinese officially arrived or left in 1857 alone (not including movement of Straits Chinese along the southern Singapore-Borneo-Sulu axis), which was at least four times the number of official entrants from all the rest of the world combined. The movement on the Amoy–Hong Kong–Manila triangle surged after 1870 as traditional kinship-based immigration was supplemented by the efforts of coolie brokers to supply the demand of foreign firms for labor. As a consequence, the number of Chinese in the Philippines expanded from about 6,000 in 1847 to approximately 90,000 in the 1880s. About 68,000 Chinese offically came and went between 1889 and 1893, and around 92,000 did so in the five years beginning in 1899. The wartime figure is epidemiologically significant even in comparison with that of the larger movement to and from North America and elsewhere during those years.[49]

The steamship's appearance in Philippine waters in the mid-1800s caused a quantum leap in the volume and velocity of contact with internal and external reservoirs of infection. More disease was imported by more frequent arrivals of bigger vessels whose speed decreased the chances that the chain of transmission would be broken en route. The world seemed to contract as travel times decreased by at least two-thirds. In 1869, the opening of the Suez Canal reduced the time and distance from Europe even more drastically, cutting the former three-to-six-month voyage to thirty-two days. Contacts of all kinds multiplied. Almost immediately Australia became a major market for Philippine sugar, and port openings in the Philippines, Java, and Cochin China spurred commodity exchange, especially in rice. By the 1890s it was commonplace for European theatrical companies to include Manila on their Asian tours; they usually arrived from Hong Kong on one of the two or three weekly steamers. Such developments caused Dr. Gomez to reflect on the process that had shrunk the world during his three decades in the islands and to account for the epidemiological consequences: "The ease and constant communication plus the commercial fever of modern times has established—if I am permitted the expression—the socialization of pathology between the separate continents."[50]

The Philippine microworld contracted, too, as steampower drew the islands together and sped the circulation of domestic and imported infections. Early in the century, communications between Manila and Cebu took place just "in the months of March and April and sometimes also in May," and an entire year could pass without direct contact between the capital and Negros. Letters from the bishop of Cebu took up to two years to reach some of the parishes in the diocese. Interisland commerce was still limited and slow enough for John Bowring to assert in 1859 that "the different islands have little or no intercourse with one another," and he cited instances of maritime districts with famine while neighboring islands had food surpluses. The steamship rapidly changed the situation, as McCoy's analysis of Iloilo City's shipping pattern shows. Before 1865, small sailcraft carried local produce at irregular intervals directly to Manila and ports on other islands from more than a dozen towns on Panay's coast. With the advent of steam shipping, sailcraft were relegated to a coastwise feeder role, carrying increasing amounts of rice and bagged sugar from ports on Panay and Negros to Iloilo City. There the rice was consumed and the sugar warehoused pending direct export abroad or shipment to Manila on twice-weekly steamers, which brought back imported cloth, farm implements, and luxury goods. The sailcraft returned home with domestic and imported finished goods or in ballast. In 1861, twenty-six boats had entered the port of Manila from Panay—one steamer from Iloilo City and twenty-five sailcraft from coastal ports. Two decades later just two of seventy-two arrivals were sailcraft. Meanwhile, arrivals in Iloilo from both the capital and Negros increased more than 500 percent.[51]

More peripheral islands underwent less sweeping transformations, but the patterns were similar. Before the ripples were felt from the commercialization of the Philippine economy, Samareños subsisted on a few major crops, plus forest and sea products, according to Cruikshank. A small number of ambulatory traders from Catbalogan and Guivan collected small amounts of various crops—principally coconut oil, rice, and forest products—and took them to Albay, Cebu, and Manila. Trade was small-scale and intermittent. Expeditions to Manila felt their way cautiously with advance boats scouting for Moro raiders. After midcentury, abaca emerged as the new cash crop, and by 1875, Chinese traders and urban mestizos were in place, a sure sign of commercial activity. As abaca grew to account for 92 percent of Samar's exports by value in 1893, the island became a net importer of rice. To handle the increased commercial activity, Catbalogan and Calbayog were linked to Manila by regularly sched-uled steamships, and arrivals and departures of both sailcraft and steamers in a number of ports more than doubled during the last quarter of the century.[52]

The steamship increased the pace and altered the rhythm of interisland trade. Speed was as critical to the diffusion of infection as was the growing volume of contacts. The faster the voyage, the less need for successive transmis-sions aboard ship to deliver disease successfully. More infections could make the trip in one generation. Before steam, the best class of square-rigged vessels made the run from Iloilo to Manila during the northeast monsoon from Novem-ber to March in ten to fifteen days, returning in four to six. By the 1890s, the mail steamer made the trip in less than thirty-six hours in either direction. In Bowring's time, trading vessels took seven to eight months to make the round trip between Manila and Jolo. Four decades later, the regularly scheduled mail steamer made the entire journey, including eight intermediate stops, in eight days. The steamer's indifference to tides and prevailing winds regularized com-munications within the archipelago as well. Outbreaks of imported disease must have become less seasonal and as a result, the intervals between them shorter and of more equal length as the new commercial rhythm took hold.[53]

The struggle for political control of the Philippines at the end of the century accelerated population movement even more, but this time under crisis condi-tions, which multiplied the probability of contact with infection. To think of the unrest from late 1896 to mid–1902 simply as two successive wars of indepen-dence against Spain and then the United States oversimplifies the chaotic mix of political, economic, and social forces at work. The wars provided the occa-sion for and the framework within which violent struggle occurred on many levels. Class conflict, local power contests, banditry and lawlessness, settling of old scores, and millenarian religious movements all proceeded contemporane-ously with the resistance against the two foreign powers. Some of those intra-mural struggles bore little relation to the fight for independence, and indeed Filipinos were divided on that issue.[54]

Civilian response to the approach of armed invaders at the end of the nine-teenth century was the same as it had always been in the Philippines—whole-sale flight. It began in Luzon's Tagalog provinces in late 1896 and continued whenever and wherever war approached during the next six years. The wild yearly fluctuations of births, deaths, and marriages in parish records suggests the scope of the temporary migrations. In Batangas, residents left their homes by the tens of thousands during those years, as Glenn A. May has shown. U.S. Army reports from Tanauan, Batangas in early 1900 described one example of that process. When the occupying soldiers entered the town, they found only one scared resident out of a population of 20,038. At the end of a week, 512 persons had returned, stores began to open, and the market resumed. Most of the others trickled back thereafter once hardships in the hills became unbear-able and the town appeared safe.[55]

Wartime movement was more complex than the Tanauan example of imme-diate flight to the nearest hills and relatively quick return home. The American military command restricted everyday mobility to some extent with a pass system, but four other general migration patterns are evident. First, many people sought security from war, starvation, bandits, or reprisals by going to Manila (where the inner-city population may have doubled), to other urban centers, or to towns garrisoned by U.S. soldiers. Second, the American army temporarily "reconcentrated" the population in various areas—Albay, Marinduque, and Batangas, for instance—as a means of combating guerrilla warfare. A third pattern was panic flight from disease (and often with it), usually to more remote barrios, as happened throughout the archipelago during the 1902 cholera epidemic. Finally, once the invading soldiers had occupied the towns and pacified the hinterlands to a greater or lesser extent, civilians and Filipino soldiers shuttled back and forth incessantly between poblaciones, the outlying settlements, and the hills. Much of that activity involved the transport of food.[56]

The foreign armies and their followers posed the greatest external threat to public health in Philippine history. After fighting broke out in August 1896, Spain rushed more than 25,000 soldiers to its colony. An influx of soldiers and civilians on a much grander scale began with the American intervention less than two years later. Prostitutes "from every corner of the earth" literally raced the army to Manila and upon Spain's defeat in August 1898, "emigrants from all parts of the world flocked thither like flies in search of honey." Some 122,000 U.S. soldiers arrived between 1898 and 1902. Their epidemiological impact was twofold. First, like earlier colonial troops arriving from Spain or Mexico or Filipino soldiers returning from Indochina, they brought disease from foreign reservoirs—this time from North America and to a lesser extent from Cuba, Hawaii, and China, where some units had either recently served or stopped over. All regiments carried a wide range of infections before they ever sailed from San Francisco. Second, and more important, the Americans contracted disease after arriving in the Philippines, and like all soldiers before them, transported and distributed it throughout the islands. At the time of its capitulation in 1898, almost one-sixth of Spain's soldiers were in Manila hospitals, a situation that suggested the potential for transfer of infection by military forces. The U.S. Army was a far more efficient instrument of diffusion than its Spanish (or Filipino) counterpart, however, due to its size and greater mobility.[57]

No convincing evidence exists to suggest that the North Americans imported diseases previously unknown in the Philippines. For a time, it was suspected that typhoid was new, but Spanish medical records make it clear that American proponents of that view were misinformed. Unfamiliar strains of various infections like variola minor smallpox were certainly introduced, however, further burdening an already debilitated population. A possible but less likely candidate for a wholly original importation is a species of hookworm, *Necator americanus*, which was prevalent in the southeastern United States. Hookworm was common in the eastern Visayas, but the American variety was unreported (or probably just undifferentiated) prior to the war. In any event, the soldiers contributed to what became a severe health problem by the beginning of the second decade of the century. Dr. Weston P. Chamberlain stated in 1910 that for more than ten years, "a continuous stream of men infected with the American hookworm" had entered the Philippines. He estimated that at least several hundred such cases, "entirely unsuspected on ordinary physical examination," had arrived each year and added, "Perhaps we may facetiously call this one of our many ways of 'Americanizing' the islands."[58]

The longest chain of disease transmission that I have been able to follow leads from northern New York State to central Panay. Typhoid fever was prevalent in the civilian population in Plattsburg, New York, in the summer of 1899. Some members of the Twenty-sixth U.S. Volunteer Infantry, training at nearby Plattsburg Barracks, contracted the infection through the water supply that the military and civilian populations shared. The infection was kept alive in a number of companies as the regiment crossed the United States by train, staged at San Francisco, and sailed directly to the Visayas, bypassing Manila. After disembarkation late in the year, the disease flared up as the soldiers prepared to sweep north from the Iloilo City area. They subsequently carried it with them as they pushed north into the interior of the island in early 1900. No direct evidence survives of a serious typhoid epidemic among residents of Iloilo province, but transmission presumably occurred because that infected regiment was one of the examples in the heated debate that later raged among American military and civilian health officials as to whether the army had been responsible for introducing typhoid into the islands for the first time. Although the disease had in fact long been known in the archipelago, it is worth noting that the detailed lists of prevailing diseases in central Iloilo province prepared by Dr. Bernardino Solivellas just six years earlier had not mentioned typhoid fever.[59]

More important were the infections that the soldiers picked up *after* arriving in the Philippines and then spread throughout the archipelago. Health records document in detail the fact that every regiment of the U.S. Army had large and often astounding sick lists almost from the moment of arrival until departure a year or more afterward. Every unit was heavily infected with malaria, dysentery, and venereal disease at all times, and some had intermittent or continuing trouble with typhoid and smallpox as well. Individual soldiers presented the entire range of tropical disease, which accounted for 3,693 deaths among U.S. troops in the Philippines during 1898–1902. More significant from the standpoint of disease transmission were the nearly half-million reported cases of illness in the army—four times more than the number of soldiers who served. Those figures grossly understate true infectivity since most asymptomatic and convalescent carriers did not seek treatment. Many victims of venereal disease either treated themselves or went to Filipino doctors. Even allowing for a certain percentage of malingerers, each man on average was infective—and highly ambulatory—for a substantial part of his stay in the islands. Rotation policies meant that any given company might serve in several widely separated regions during its tour of duty and carry the infections from one area to another, thus bonding theretofore discrete disease environments.[60]

Equally well documented are the mobility of the various units and the extent of personal contact between soldiers and civilians. The war presents many peculiarities but none more striking than the close day-to-day interaction between American soldiers and Philippine civilians. Once it was evident in late 1899 that Philippine resistance forces were going to rely on guerrilla warfare, the U.S. Army countered with a garrison strategy. Groups of twenty-five or more soldiers were eventually quartered in more than five hundred towns throughout the archipelago "to protect life and property during the unsettled condition of the country consequent on the dispersion of the insurrectos." Garrison life was tedious, although in retrospect the "hikes, fights, and [dances]" stood out. Strategies to pass the time usually involved personal contact with Filipinos. The troops were generally quartered in the rectory and other principal buildings in the town center, although they sometimes lived in houses scattered throughout the town with Filipino families or with *queridas* (sweethearts). A considerable number of soldiers entered into some sort of formal or informal marriage but readily left when their tours of duty were up—a practice that led one outraged officer to write some years later that "were an authenticated list of these marriages published in the United States, a wide field would be opened to prosecutions for bigamy, to say nothing of abandonment." Others resorted to prostitutes. No evidence exists as to the number of mixed-race offspring born during the war, but the Wood-Forbes Mission in 1922 was told that about eighteen thousand such children had been born since the beginning of the American occupation. Drinking and gambling were the next favorite pastimes. Both activities sometimes led to trouble with local townspeople and occasionally to serious crime. Usually, however, soldiers merely killed time. One wrote that "you can see soldiers anytime going into these little nipa shacks, where they drink, eat bananas, and hobnob with the natives to their heart's content, and in their way get to see real native life here." They hung around the market bantering with the sellers who "love to chaff the soldiers [and] have learned American rejoinders that are not in the dictionary." Under the circumstances, many townspeople were content to have the soldiers there, not only for security but for the money they poured into the local economies.[61]

Because U.S. military authorities were well aware that "the health of the command depends on the health of the inhabitants," sanitation ranked only below military security as a daily concern. The Americans often boasted of "literally washing up the Orient" and cleaning the Augean stables of hundreds of years of filth, but improvements in the garrison towns were primarily cosmetic, limited to regulations requiring householders to keep their yards clean and the dusty streets watered down. Little was done that had the effect of inhibiting the spread of infection, and the Regimental Health Records make it abundantly clear that the slovenly sanitation of the garrisons themselves actually facilitated the diffusion of disease. The command was plagued by constant diarrhea and dysentery so that soldiers throughout the land shed the archipelago's full spectrum of pathogenic microparasites with every bowel movement. Despite continual directives from the U.S. Army medical department about proper feces disposal, most units dumped their daily accumulation of excreta into the nearest water source—usually the river in which the towns-people bathed and from which some of them and others downstream took their drinking water. One army doctor later recalled that residents were constantly in the rivers, wading in and dipping their containers directly into the stream. When the depository was the sea, the detritus immediately washed back up onto the beach, from whence flies carried the microbial burden to the nearby dwellings. The cumulative effect was to aggravate the already seriously inade-quate Philippine waste disposal system and to add to existing gastrointestinal problems.[62]

The American war was simply the final and most violent stage in a centuries-long process that realigned the variables determining the probability that Fili-pinos would encounter disease. The most important threads running through the web of causation were those most closely related to population growth and mobility. Together, those factors acted to reduce the number of archipelagos within the archipelago. One can imagine an epidemiological map of the Philip-pines in 1903 that makes it seem as if the islands had drifted together since Legazpi stepped ashore, as if millions of years of geologic activity had been telescoped into a few centuries. So too can one envision a time-lapse photo-graphic record of the period accelerating movement in the islands over time until pioneers, vagabonds, soldiers, and ships are seen racing throughout the shrunken archipelago at manic speed. Still, none of that would have had epi-demiological significance if few of those hurtling figures had been susceptible to disease.

Susceptibility

SUSCEPTIBILITY results from the interplay between any number of variables, but the state of the host's defenses (rather than the virulence of invading micro-organisms, for instance) ultimately determines that individual's place on the continuum of health. Considerations of genetic inheritance, age, sex, ethnic group, prior immunologic experience, preexisting or intercurrent disease, and a wide range of human behavior influence the strength of the defense, or im-mune, system. Susceptibility in past populations is difficult to gauge. Our knowledge of what compromises the immune system and how it responds is still in its infancy today, so even if individual measurements of factors like nutritional intake, microbial burden, and stress had been recorded in the Phil-ippines, much guesswork would remain. It is even harder to substantiate changes over time, but it is clear that most nineteenth-century Filipinos in-creasingly faced the kinds of challenges that seem to promote vulnerability to disease. If factors linked closely with population growth and mobility were most critical to probability of contact, those responsible for poverty, debilita-tion, and malnourishment determined susceptibility.[1]

No precondition of disease is more basic than poverty. Those at the bottom of the socioeconomic scale in any society are at excessive risk for infection and have the least access to the health care system. Centuries ago a dynamic de-veloped in the Philippines (as elswhere) in which poverty was reinforced by undereducation, malnutrition, and disease. Each element is both a cause and a result of the others, but poverty is central. As nutritionist Philip R. Payne ex-plains, anything that "add[s] to the burden of the poorest . . . increases the risk that some irreversible downward step will be taken." The nineteenth-century transformations caught many Filipino families in that spiral, and relatively few have been able to escape since. Today, a nearly unbridgeable gap separates rich and poor. Recent studies have shown that more than half of the population live in "absolute" poverty. More than two-thirds of families are too poor to purchase and consume a nutritionally adequate diet, and about 80 percent of the school-children are undernourished. Filipinos as a group rank near the bottom of Asian peoples in per capita caloric intake and close to the top in the rates of many preventable diseases.[2]

No similar statistical estimates exist for the nineteenth century. Indeed, the historical dimensions of Philippine poverty are almost wholly unexplored. Modern measures would not be entirely satisfactory even if adequate raw data were available. Trying to establish a poverty line based on income would be difficult in a cash-short economy where many were paid in kind and where subsistence farming was still common, even if progressively less so. Wage scales are available for the end of the century, but they are of limited utility since most Filipinos still lived outside the salaried economy and subsisted on what they could grow, pick, catch, or make. Such information tells little about debt anyway. Although contemporary foreign observers routinely asserted that even the poor could live comfortably in the islands, few did. A variety of inescapable expenses, both public and private, forced many families to borrow money sooner or later. Debt was usually the first "irreversible downward step."[3]

Poverty, however it is defined, was not general across the spectrum of society. Pockets of relative affluence had always existed, and the nineteenth-century economic expansion drew an influx of wealth into the colony that became the basis of some substantial family fortunes. Contemporaries distinguished between the well-off and the poor, at least in the poblaciones, but rarely made proportional estimates. A bipolar picture of late-nineteenth-century Philippine socioeconomic structure is misleading in any case, however, since both classes were scattered along a continuum, as May has pointed out. Together the truly rich and the truly indigent at either end of the scale probably did not exceed 5 percent of the population. Thus, Reynaldo C. Ileto is undoubtedly correct in warning historians against viewing Filipinos as a people forever mired in grinding poverty. The colonial eye was myopic, but the American official who reported from Abra that Filipinos were nowhere "plunged in the poverty that brutalizes the poor in the great cities of Europe" may have been right. Still, poverty need not be the world's worst in order to have epidemiological significance. It was sufficient that the rising level of impoverishment had left a substantial and growing segment of the population without adequate defenses against infection.[4]

The concept of poverty has little meaning for this study unless it is related to susceptibilty to disease. It is not enough to know who was poor because the many facets of poverty interact with other variables in order to produce disease. When and where Filipinos were poor is more important to an understanding of the dynamics of health. The group that could be defined as poor grew both relatively and absolutely over time during the century, but individual and community exposure to imported infection, epizootics, crop failures, typhoons, floods, earthquakes, fires, locusts, and war varied widely. The wartime experience on Romblon is illustrative. Remote and virtually without roads, the island had been planted almost entirely to coconuts by fiat of an autocratic Spanish governor some years before, and the people were left vulnerable to all of the uncertainties and risks inherent in monoculture. By any socioeconomic measure, the proportion of poor people was well above the Philippine average. Yet because of port closures and the island's relative isolation from the major trade routes, it registered the lowest death rate in the archipelago during the cholera epidemic in 1902.[5]

Whatever the exact dimensions of Philippine poverty may have been, the contemporary evidence of the relationship between want and ill health is conclusive. All the médicos titulares pointed out the connection in their annual reports. Dr. Ricardo Terramon Caballero stated flatly that most tuberculosis deaths in Zambales were caused by poverty. In Camarines Sur, disease was primarily an affliction of the poor, who experienced "unheard of indigence and misery," according to Dr. Ezequiel Delgado. During the 1882 cholera epidemic, Dr. Guillermo Rebelo noted that the poor in Capiz suffered and died with much greater frequency than those who were well-off, an impression Dr. José Amide Castro corroborated in Pangasinan at the same time, explaining that the poor had no resources to ward off or to cure disease. Dr. Eulogio Raquel claimed that the poor in Ilocos Norte could not pay for medicine and simply died as a result. In Abra, it was difficult to arrest the spread of whooping cough among poor children, Dr. Agustín Llanera reported, because their crowded living conditions precluded isolation. And in 1888, a special commission of three médicos titulares and the colony's chief health officer reported its conclusion to the governor general of the Philippines that poverty and malnourishment were the determining factors not only in the spread of cholera around Manila but also of ill health in general.[6]

Poverty widened and deepened as the program to develop the public wealth started to take hold around 1840. The transformation of an economy based on subsistence agriculture and locally produced handicrafts to one driven by cash-crop exports did not help most Filipinos, however much certain individuals and groups prospered during the fits and starts of short-term prosperity. According to Jonathan Fast and Jim Richardson, the communal production of a variety of foodstuffs with a rough equality of distribution that had characterized the traditional Philippines was gone forever in developed areas by midcentury. Entire regions and islands were largely planted, overnight it seemed, to cash crops— tobacco in Luzon's Cagayan Valley, rice and sugar on the central plain, abaca on the Bikol Peninsula and the eastern Visayas, sugar in the western Visayas, and coconuts on Romblon. Governor Carlos Peñaranda of Pangasinan would later bitterly lament the consequences: "Agriculture has fallen considerably in this province, which used to be called the granary of the Philippines. The crop diversity that provided a firm base of wealth and a guarantee of well-being for aggrieved regions has passed, with hardly a transition and without the least forethought, to monoculture."[7]

As land values rose, many *indios* (those Filipinos not of mixed Chinese or Spanish blood) lost out in the ensuing scramble for good crop land. Using the legal apparatus to dismantle communal ownership of land and usufruct tenure, a new landlord class comprising primarily Chinese-Filipino mestizos rose on the backs of the disenfranchised. Those who retained smallholdings were increasingly drawn into crop specialization and usually had to borrow money to stay afloat. In the absence of agricultural banks, they fell victim to a wholesaling network that soon dominated the economy. Great merchant houses, both British and American (but mainly the former) financed exports, operating in the countryside through resident Chinese who distributed imported merchandise and collected local crops. The middlemen took on debt to the foreign firms but more than compensated for it by charging the indios high prices for goods and services and by exacting usurious rates for loans.[8]

As the new economy overtook old ways of living, indio smallholders were caught in the disjuncture. Few of them knew or cared much about written contracts, surplus production, intermediary crops, or saving money. From Peñaranda's point of view, the Filipino farmer was "anchored to his customs like ivy to a sheltering tree in a passive tenacity and silence that constitues both his principal virtue and essential defect; inalterable, indifferent, cultivating his small field, sowing what he can with the help of his wife and children and getting only what is strictly necessary for his family's life while leaving extensive lands, easy to work, unproductive." Without access to information or advice, they borrowed money from traders on disadvantageous terms, "contracting the most onerous obligations on the security of anticipated crop sales without heeding the conditions of the agreement," according to the governor of Cavite. Thereafter they failed to exercise prudent caution, he said. "They do not limit their expenditures to hopes of sale income, and when they can not meet their contract obligations, they pledge the subsequent crop. Finally the property is what is pledged. The result is that here very few farmers own their land anymore." They slipped into various tenancy and sharecropping arrangements or some other dependency relationship, often "voluntarily and perpetually enslaving themselves."[9]

Labor-control systems, all of which were increasingly oppressive, evolved to meet regional needs. Rent capitalism, in which fixed rent gave way to share tenancy, characterized the process in the sugar and rice bowl on Luzon's central plain. The partnership system, as sharecropping was euphemistically called, was sensible enough in theory but inequitable in practice. Governor Joaquín Rajal y Larre explained that in Nueva Ecija the landowner accepted as "partners" however many he judged necessary to cultivate his fields, providing the land, carabao, tools, seed, and even money at a high price, which were deducted from the fruits of their labors. Because share tenants customarily asked for and received cash advances (with a surcharge) for their many necessities, like marriages, baptisms, food and clothing, they fell into inextricable debt. Offering the following representative example, Rajal declared that share tenants were no better than debt slaves. A family that produced enough palay, tobacco, maize, and livestock to realize Pfs 37.50 per year would find that income more than offset by taxes at Pfs 4.69, food at Pfs 36.50, and clothing at Pfs 3.00, for a total of Pfs 44.19 in annual expenses. Hidden duties such as forced-labor service, illegal impositions, and all manner of abuses by minor government officials and agents of the landlord/partner were not calculated, nor was any amount estimated for sickness, ceremonial occasions, or fiestas. The poor were so demoralized by their state, Rajal said, that most simply submitted to oppression in order to avoid trouble. Many ran away, however, and thus created a shortage of agricultural labor that the developing province could not afford.[10]

The development of Negros drew seasonal migrant workers from Panay and Cebu, and their relation to capital quickly degenerated from share tenancy to wage labor to debt bondage. Working conditions on the sugar haciendas were more onerous than anywhere on Luzon. The former Bacolod judge Robustiano Echaúz unwittingly revealed why landowners (with whom he sympathized completely) had such difficulties assuring a reliable labor supply. He wrote that the workers cleared the forest by hand, subsisting on fast-growing root crops they planted, leaving the land ready for them to work twelve-hour days "in the scorching sun and unbearable heat." Millwork required sixteen-hour shifts. Then when locusts threatened, the owner "protects himself through persever-ance and hard work, organizing the workers, and sending them to the places invaded without considering the hours of work or the obstacles to be faced." Not surprisingly, many deserted the labor gangs. (What is surprising is that the owners were surprised. Echaúz could hardly believe it either, but assured his readers that "things like this happen today in Negros.") Many of the fugitives became vagabonds, joining the colony's increasingly large floating population. Since few had received official permission to leave their home communities on other islands in the first place, they were illegally undocumented persons as well. Some were driven to theft and brigandage. Echaúz's proposed solution to the "evil" of workers fleeing during the night, "which if it spreads, can put an end to the work of many years," was a law prohibiting vagrancy coupled with a grant of extraordinary enforcement powers to the authorities.[11]

Life became more precarious for most in the last third of the century due to an oversupply of agricultural products on the international markets and the increasingly volatile yearly fluctuations of world prices. Trapped in a restruc-tured economy, Filipinos suddenly found themselves at the mercy of decisions made thousands of miles away. Export earnings of both abaca and tobacco de-clined during the 1870s. Sugar was stable until 1884, when the price fell in the face of increased sugar-beet production and recessions in the West just as the world market for abaca picked up again. Good years alternated with bad, but the general direction of Philippine net export earnings was down. By the end of the century, only abaca, tobacco, and copra exports were improving. Sugar, cotton, and indigo were in decline. Rice exports were moribund, and those of coffee had ceased entirely. In the meantime, the internal demand for land had led to a decrease in the proportion of acreage planted to rice relative to poten-tially more profitable crops. Since the production of rice for export expanded around the rim of the South China Sea at the same time, the Filipinos became net importers of their staple food after 1870. One result of the new cash-crop economy was a declining access to food, as we shall see. For now it is enough to note that hunger crises occurred on the sugar-producing island of Negros in 1856, 1864, 1865, 1878, 1887, 1888, 1889, 1894, 1895, 1896, and 1897.[12]

Increased living costs, which Filipinos felt by the late 1860s, were another effect of the economy's integration into regional and international markets. The value of the Philippine currency subsequently declined against the U.S. dollar and the pound sterling as the price of silver dropped. The exchange rate of the

Philippine peso lost more than half its value on the international market in the mid-1890s as it dipped below Pfs 1.00 to the dollar for the first time and then bottomed out at Pfs 0.50. The ordinary person, who had come to rely more and more on imports of essentials like rice and cloth, paid for the peso's decreased purchasing power in world trade. Governor Peñaranda affirmed that everyone was losing ground to increased prices. Manila-based trading companies and middlemen took advantage of the colony's position as a rice importer, realizing windfall profits at the expense of the increasingly hard-pressed poor. The cost of imported rice at local markets in the Philippines continued to rise even though the price charged to Manila buyers at the external source decreased or stayed about the same. The price of rice in Saigon, Hong Kong, Bangkok, and elsewhere in Southeast Asia averaged $1.81 per *picul* (136 lbs) in 1885 and was virtually the same twenty years later. The price trend described a U-shaped curve in the intervening years, reaching a low of $0.78 in 1895. The Manila wholesale price, by contrast, rose 14.3 percent from 1890 to 1895, despite the 56.9 percent drop at the source. As wholesale figures jumped another 37.4 percent from 1897 to 1898, the cost to the consumer rose even more rapidly, increasing 50.0 percent.[13]

Prices generally continued to rise throughout the 1890s, while wages remained stagnant along with the economy until 1898, when the U.S. Army's arrival created an instant demand for labor and other services. However, only a relative few Filipinos bettered their actual economic positions during the ensuing war. Most of the new jobs in support of the occupation force were in and around the capital, where the cost-of-living increase matched the higher wages. People without war-generated employment lost more ground, and Manila's poor were in truly desperate straits for years to come. Many of those who were better off lost houses, belongings, draft animals, family members, or personal health to the war and found themselves impoverished, at least temporarily. It is true that American soldiers injected unprecedented amounts of money into local economies throughout the archipelago. The effects, which must have been substantial, have never been studied, but it seems safe to assume that for most Filipinos the miseries of the war years far outweighed the temporary economic benefits a military garrison might have brought.[14]

Debilitation was an inevitable consequence of impoverishment, leaving more Filipinos with fewer defenses against disease. The prevention and cure of an infectious process almost always depends upon whether the patient's immune system can mount an effective defense in time. Any factor that retards or suppresses that response thereby contributes to an unfavorable outcome. How the process works is imperfectly understood, but immunologist Philip Y. Patterson has concluded from what we know that "*any* diminution in *any* host defense system 'opens the door' to microbial invasion and disease." A heavy burden of pathogenic microparasites is one circumstance that lowers resistance and increases susceptibility to secondary infection. Once such an opportunistic infection becomes established in the immunocompromised host, it can quickly progress and easily disseminate. Disease with a high mortality rate may produce microorganisms too rapidly for the response, overwhelming the already enfeebled defenses and resulting in death.[15]

It is vital to include intestinal parasitism in any estimate of the burden of infection in a population group. Intestinal helminthism (or infection with parasitic metazoal worms) and intestinal protozoal infection were almost universal among Filipinos. A distinction needs to be made at the outset, however, between the helminthic and protozoal intestinal diseases themselves, such as ascariasis or amebiasis, and the far more significant role of such parasitism in preparing the way for secondary infection. Parasitism as frank disease was less important than might be supposed for two reasons. First, the identification of parasitic infection does not necessarily measure the extent of morbidity from intestinal disease accurately, as modern surveys in endemic areas of the world have shown. A parasitic infestation, as opposed to mere infection, may be necessary to produce pathogenesis. Second, some resistance can be acquired against intestinal parasites, so reinfections in an endemic area like the Philippines usually result in milder manifestations than occur in those initially exposed. In other words, because the level of exposure to intestinal parasites was high, ordinary Filipinos developed a corresponding level of tolerance.[16]

Moderate parasitism of a degree insufficient to produce serious intestinal disease can play an important role in compromising the immune system, however, especially when it operates in tandem with other debilitating factors, like concurrent infection, malnutrition, or severe psychological stress. All animal parasites, whether metazoal or protozoal, derive nutrients from their host. Although mutual tolerance is achieved in most cases, the host must protect itself with an abnormally high level of blood-forming and tissue-repairing activity. Anything that interferes with that defense mechanism results in a nutritional drain on the host and greater susceptibility to opportunistic infection. As parasitologists Henry Masur and Thomas C. Jones explain, "protozoa and helminths that cause mild or inapparent infection in normal patients may cause devastating disease in immunodeficient patients." That process has become familiar since the beginning of the AIDS pandemic. It also becomes easy to understand why Filipinos succumbed to disease so readily during the American war.[17]

Unfortunately, the earliest evidence on the extent of parasitism in the population that is of any use to us comes from early twentieth-century surveys, which themselves were too rudimentary to measure true incidence. The earlier generation of Spanish physicians knew little about microparasites or their role in the complex of poverty, hygiene, sanitation, and disease, so the late-nineteenth-century sources contain only the occasional vague reference to those infections. Filipino and American researchers conducted the first helminthic surveys in 1908, but reliable statistics did not exist until the 1920s, when testing had advanced beyond the "hit and miss methods" used at first. By 1925, surveyors had established that more than 98 percent of all persons living on Cebu harbored one or all of the four common soil-transmitted roundworms: *Ascaris lumbricoides*, *Trichuris trichiura* (whipworm), *Ancylostoma duodenale* (hookworm), and *Necator americanus* (hookworm). A high prevalence of fecal-oral and fecal-percutaneous worm infections is itself a strong indicator of a poor standard of living and hygiene. *Ascaris* and *Trichuris* are the first and second most common parasites of man in the Philippines. Prognosis depends on the intensity of the infection. Death is rare, but anemia is not, and there can be little question that some of the apathy and listlessness the médicos titulares reported so often, as well as increased vulnerability to secondary infection, was a proximate result of those two intestinal parasites.[18]

With the hookworms, which have the same general consequences, the extent of the infection depends largely on the iron reserves of the host, and thus poor Filipinos in endemic areas were especially susceptible due to their iron-deficient diets. *Ancylostoma* and *Necator* are slightly less common than the other two roundworms, only because they are more generally restricted to rural areas and especially to those regions (especially the Bikol Peninsula and the eastern Visayas) where rainfall is more evenly distributed throughout the year. Researchers were therefore astonished by a finding in 1922 that about 80 percent of the "laboring classes" of Manila were infected with hookworm. Such is not the case today, so if that study can be trusted, it would seem to provide indirect evidence of the poor nutrition of rural migrants to the capital at that time. In any event, hookworm infestation throughout the various rural areas of the archipelago was estimated to range from 40 to 90 percent the following year.[19]

The surveys taken between 1908 and 1914 all revealed the presence of four other metazoan agents of disease: the soil-transmitted threadworm (*Strongyloides stercoralis*), dwarf tapeworm (*Hymenolepis nana*), and pinworm (*Enterobius vermicularis*, formerly *Oxyuris*), along with the food-transmitted pork tapeworm (*Taenia solium*). None appeared to be prevalent, however, as only 3.1 percent of the persons examined were found positive for one of those worms. More recent studies seem to bear out that conclusion for the first two worms, but better testing procedures would have shown a greater incidence of the others. It is now clear that well over half of all Filipinos harbor pinworms today. Human taeniasis was also more serious than the early surveys suggested. As long ago as 1903 a study showed that 4 percent of Philippine pigs were severely infected with the metacestodes of *T. solium*, which have been shown to be transmissible to humans.[20]

The 1908 Bilibid Prison survey also found three forms of flatworms: the food-borne lung fluke (*Paragonimus westermani*) and liver fluke (*Opisthorchis japonicum*), as well as the waterborne blood fluke (*Schistosoma japonicum*) in a small number of subjects. Schistosomiasis is the most serious of the three infections and was far more prevalent than the survey indicated. According to Adel A.F. Mahmoud, its chronic and complex nature "expose[s] the host immune and defense mechanisms to a myriad of challenges," causing considerable morbidity and mortality in humans. Not until the 1950s was the full extent of the problem in the Philippines realized, when it was found in sixty-nine towns in Mindoro, Sorgoson, Samar, and Leyte and in most of the provinces on Mindanao. By 1975 schistosomiasis had been identified in twenty-two provinces with an average prevalence of nearly 16 percent. About two of every five persons on Bohol were infected.[21]

The surveys on incidence of intestinal parasites also established the presence of the four protozoal genera—*Amoeba, Lamblia, Balantidium,* and *Cercomonas*—but surveyors cautioned that the stool samples were often too old to allow for an accurate estimate of the prevalence of protozoal parasites. Nevertheless, the 1908 Bilibid Prison survey showed 23 percent of those examined to have motile amoebae in their stools and an equal number with the ciliates or flagellates. Amebiasis was considered a serious danger to public health in the islands at the time, and much research was done on the problem. The organisms were suspected to be lurking in the Manila water supply, until researchers in 1911 were able to derive only nonpathogenic amoebae from it. The true reservoir is the human host. A greater concern should have been infestation of *Giardia lamblia,* which has recently come to be recognized as more dangerous than previously assumed because it so effectively suppresses the immune system.[22]

Metazoal and protozoal infection was sufficiently extensive to be an important determinant of increased susceptibility. In 1916, a sanitary commission in Pasay examined 1,036 persons and found intestinal parasites in 94.7 percent of the stool samples. The most important fact about animal parasitism, however, was that most persons had multiple infections. Even the crude 1908 Bilibid survey discovered 7,636 infections distributed among the 3,447 infected subjects, an average of nearly 2.25 different infections per infected individual. The actual incidence must have been substantially higher. Two parasitologists have stated that "the pathologic effect of the multiple infections . . . is the sum of the individual effects, to which an underlying state of malnutrition must frequently be added as an important contribution to the total disease picture." Although a person harboring only whipworms (*Trichuris*) might be mildly debilitated, the additional burden of hookworms, *Strongyloides stercoralis,* and *Giardia lamblia* would, as Seraphim E. Macaraig put it, "sap the vitality and prepare the victim for almost any disease." It has also been established that communities with a high incidence of multiple infections are at far greater epidemiological risk than ones infected by a single species.[23]

While geofactors like climate, topography, and soil structure determine whether particular helminthiases can exist in a given area of the Philippines, human factors determine whether or not the diseases become endemic in an area. Erhard Hinz says that "since the great majority of helminths involve species whose eggs or larvae are passed out with the stool, defecation habits—and thus the hygiene behaviour of man—are of special significance." Various behaviors determine the occurrence of the different infections. He explains that soil-transmitted helminthiases are determined by hygiene, schistosomiasis by behavior concerning contact with water, foodborne helminthiases by eating habits, and insectborne helminthiases by the distance of dwellings from vector breeding places. The living conditions and behaviors of most Filipinos a century ago favored transmission of all forms of helminthiases. Dr. Philip E. Garrison thought in fact that "it would be scarcely possible to establish more ideal conditions for the spreading of intestinal parasites throughout the islands."[24]

Again the best evidence postdates the war. The Spanish physicians all lamented the sorry state of hygiene and sanitation, but the earliest attempt to study living conditions in the Philippines scientifically was not made until 1909. Then a team of Filipino and American scientists, physicians, and medical students from Manila went to nearby Taytay, Rizal, (formerly Morong province) and conducted a medical survey of the town. Taytay had an unwarranted reputation as an unhealthy town because the cholera epidemic two decades earlier was believed to have originated there, but in 1909 it presented more healthful living conditions than most Philippine municipalities. Situated on the eastern edge of the fertile Mariquina valley, Taytay had easy access to Manila yet it was virtually self-provisioned and was not dependent on imported rice from Saigon. Amidst the tranquility and rising prosperity of the postwar years, its residents were far better housed and nourished than most Filipinos had been late in the previous century. As the researchers noted, "The poorer people do not suffer any hardships." Still, the data on daily living conditions make it plain why that segment of the Philippine population carried such a heavy microbial burden.[25]

The 6,094 inhabitants received their water supply from twelve wells and a small spring situated about two hundred meters beyond the eastern limit of the town. The townspeople preferred the relatively unpolluted spring water but were deterred by the onerous and time-consuming task of hauling it from outside of town to the jars on their porches. Also, the spring was virtually dry for part of the year. The five wells that were within the town were not used for drinking water, which the women hauled from the more distant wells. Those were in the fields surrounding the town and were sometimes dug in the stream banks or in the streambed itself. Even though the mouths of the streambed wells were above the level of the water, "they received filtrations from the stream channels which in places contain carabao wallow and stagnant water covered with green scum." None of the others had curbs or walls sufficient to prevent surface contamination as splashing water washed dirt from the user's feet back into the well. Bathing and washing clothes were usually done together, preferably at the margin of a stream, if one was convenient to the house, or otherwise at one of the wells near the plaza. The researchers found that "the people . . . have the idea that wells near houses are apt to be dangerous sources of supply and so they generally prefer to bring water from the wells outside the town." Actually, chemical tests showed little correlation between location and water purity. All of the water was judged to be unsafe due to high concentrations of albuminoid ammonia and nitrites, which indicated pollution with sewage or drainage from refuse animal matter, and unacceptably high numbers of microorganisms that included coliform bacteria, vibrios, amoebae, and flagellata.[26]

The houses usually had two rooms, one of which served as the bedroom for the entire family. Meals were taken in the other, and washing hands before eating was not considered necessary unless they were visibly dirty. Boiled rice was accompanied either by a seasoned soup of fish and vegetables or vegetables alone or by a dish of dried fish. The meal was usually served in two common dishes—one for rice and the other for soup. Each person took a small portion of rice with the fingers, worked it into a bolus, dipped it into the stew, and then placed it into the mouth. "From time to time a piece of fish or other tidbit is taken from the stew." Afterwards, hands and mouth were wiped on a rag, and the kitchen waste was tossed onto a rubbish pile for the family hog. What it left was burned at regular intervals. The liquid kitchen slops were poured through the interstices of the split-bamboo-lath floor, creating and perpetuating a noisome puddle of mud under the house.[27]

A variety of arrangements for the disposal of human excreta were utilized. Almost half of the houses had no formal provisions at all. Family members either used a vessel inside the house and emptied the contents early the next morning in a convenient place, or they defecated in the bushes if they lived near the edge of town. Urination was often done through the kitchen floor. About a quarter of the houses had separate raised bamboo and nipa structures separated from the house by eight to ten meters and which served as outhouses. The user squatted over a hole in the floor, and the feces dropped to the earth beneath. An opening was left in the enclosure for the pig to enter and scavenge, and thus no excreta accumulated. The remaining houses utilized what was potentially the best method—simple pits, many of which had been constructed that year in response to a directive from the local health officer following a minor outbreak of cholera in nearby Cainta. Unfortunately, however, only the eighty-one pits in which the feces were covered with earth, ashes, or rice husks and occasionally disinfectants were satisfactory. These were judged to be the only sanitarily adequate disposal systems out of the 1,299 dwellings in town. Nonwaterborne transmission of infection from feces to humans was facilitated by the proximity of dwellings and their disposal arrangements to the breeding sites of the eighteen species of flies found by the survey team, including many of the Muscidae that were abundant in decaying vegetable and animal matter under and about the houses.[28]

Poverty was the underlying cause of the dangerously unsanitary way of life in the Philippines. The problems of water purity and feces disposal were insuperable for the poor. Filipinos did not drink bad water by choice or through ignorance—the money was just not available for individuals or communities to invest in a system of deeper wells, or best of all, artesian wells. The people went out of their way to get the best water they could, but the daily haulage of water over even relatively short distances was burdensome. As a result, families used the least amount of water possible. A research team on Cebu has recently pointed out that an insufficient quantity of water is almost as serious a problem as poor quality. The latter assures the spread of waterborne diseases like cholera and typhoid. An inadequate volume of water usually results in poor personal hygiene, which creates conditions favorable for the spread of water-washed diseases like scabies, yaws, leprosy, and the whole range of intestinal infections. The inability to dispose of feces in a sanitary manner was the biggest stumbling block to improved public health. A water-carrying sewer system was much too expensive to be considered for a moment. The earth-closet system and the simpler pit system, the best alternatives, were also too costly and would have required a degree of community supervision that did not exist. Given the time and expense inherent in the various improved methods, few persons would have thought them worth the trouble anyway when they already had an efficient scavenger on the premises that could be fattened in the process.[29]

Malnutrition is another consequence of poverty. One expert says simply: "Undernutrition and malnutrition commonly arise from the lack of resources to buy or grow adequate food; that is, from poverty." How the more complex connection between inadequate nourishment and disease works is not as clear, but we can be certain that it involves a weakening of resistance. Thomas McKeown explains that "response to any infectious disease depends on the state of health of the individual, and the state of health is influenced powerfully by nutrition." His formulation is useful as a general proposition so long as it is not taken as suggesting that well-nourished persons are always better protected against disease. The relationship is evidently far more complicated. It is more accurate (based on the state of knowledge today) to say that inadequate nutrition increases susceptibility to *some* infective agents and increases the severity of *some* infections once contracted, especially in children. On the one hand, it has been shown that the phagocytic cells (which search out and destroy invading microorganisms) of a malnourished host only function at 10 to 30 percent of normal efficiency. On the other, it is also clear that malnutrition is sometimes antagonistic to certain infections, meaning that the agent is weakened more than the infected host. Viruses, for instance, depend on cellular nutrients for their own survival, so it stands to reason that the better nourished the host, the better the pathogens would thrive. Different viruses behave differently, however, and it is not even likely that the same virus would interact identically with two equally nourished persons. Still, synergism (which results in weakened host resistance) is the norm. Nevin S. Scrimshaw summarizes the evidence thus: "Malnutrition is almost always synergistic with infectious diseases due to bacteria, rickettsia, intestinal helminths and intestinal protozoa, [but] with systemic viral, helminthic or protozoal infections, malnutrition is equally likely to be antagonistic or synergistic."[30]

The importance of nutritional intake in past population groups has received insufficient attention from historians. McKeown's provocative argument that improved nutrition (rather than advances in medical science) was principally responsible for falling mortality rates in the pre-twentieth-century industrialized world should go far to remedy that neglect. The World Health Organization's experience in developing regions gives credence to his speculation. One WHO expert has pointed out that until vaccines were developed, most children became infected with the measles virus, but death rates were up to three hundred times higher in the poorer countries. The explanation, he supposes "was not that the virus was more virulent, nor that there were fewer medical services; but that in poorly nourished communities the microbes attack a host which, because of chronic malnutrition, is less able to resist." P.M. Newberne and G. Williams have surveyed the scientific data and conclude that malnutrition influences infection "(1) by effects on the host which facilitate initial invasion of the infectious agent; (2) through an effect on the agent once it is established in the tissues; (3) through an effect on secondary infection; or (4) by retarding convalescence from infection."[31]

The médicos titulares were unanimous that Filipino diets were the direct cause of the pervasive anemia, digestive tract diseases, and general debilitation of the people that they all reported in the population after 1876. Dr. Mariano Cervantes's report from Samar about "unnutritious diets producing anemia and disentery, both acute and chronic, illnesses that resist treatment and are so difficult to cure" was representative. The somber tone sharply contrasts with earlier accounts, by nonphysicians to be sure, that described Filipinos preparing three meals a day in houses surrounded by fruit trees and vegetable gardens, the children running down to the river to catch the fish "only the minute the rice is put on the fire." The qualitative evidence is not comparable over time, however, and finally it is as impossible to establish conclusively that the nutritional intake of most Filipinos deteriorated during the last part of the nineteenth century as it is to prove by direct evidence McKeown's assertion that it was improving in Europe. Data on per capita food consumption or clinical evidence of nutritional state do not exist, and McKeown notes that the question is too intricate to be resolved even if they did. We can deduce an overall decline in nourishment from the increase in morbidity and mortality, and we can understand the process, but the hypothesis probably can not be proved inductively from the historical record. The only comparative data I know of are indirect. The Philippine Civil Service Board and the U.S. Public Health and Marine Hospital Service administered physical examinations to 1,169 Filipino prison guards, policemen, government employees, and seamen in 1904–1905. The 892 seamen, aged nineteen to sixty-four, were described as typical of the laboring classes. When average heights are calculated by age cohort, the tallest group proves to be that born before the mid-1860s. Furthermore, the ninety civil servants, who may be assumed to have been from the well-off class, were almost an inch taller than the seamen on the average. The intriguing, but hardly conclusive, implications are that diets were less nutritious in the last third of the century than immediately before and that a substantial socioeconomic differentiation in nourishment existed.[32]

The point has to be argued circumstantially, but still the Philippine case presents formidable problems. For instance, it is more difficult than one might suppose to know precisely what ordinary Filipinos ate. Contemporary descriptions by foreign travelers, doctors, and soldiers are not lacking, but they are usually vague and often dismissive—"rice, fish, and little else." The problem is that the observers rarely specified what the "little else" comprised, remarking only that the people supplemented their rice and fish by adding "some few herbs" or "the leaves of certain plants" and making it into a stew. Occasionally it would be noted that the natives planted banana trees around their dwellings, but fruits of any kind are rarely mentioned as a regular part of the diet. Perhaps the writers thought it too self-evident to mention. As Father Juan Francisco de San Antonio wrote around 1740, "To list all the fruits which Divine Providence has given the Indian on this land for his subsistence, as well as for his enjoyment and good appetite, will require a lot of paper because they are innumerable." The sources indicate consistently that when rice ran short, people lived on root crops, whether planted or wild, and they agree that most Filipinos did not eat beef, poultry, or eggs (except at fiestas) because they were too expensive. Cane sugar, where it was available, and sugar-based sweets were consumed between meals.[33]

Even if the descriptions are taken literally, it is still difficult to calculate the food value of a rice-and-fish diet. The nutritive value of rice is reduced to the extent that milling removes the husk, which contains thiamine (vitamin B_1). Most of the rice grown in the islands was homepounded and thus not highly milled, but the varieties imported in large quantities from Saigon and elsewhere after 1870 were. Thiamine deficiency causes beriberi and ultimately death. We shall see that beriberi became a major health problem in areas that became dependent on imported rice. Fish, too, vary widely in their nutritional compositions. The researchers in Taytay found that the residents had seventeen kinds to choose from when the day's catch arrived at the market in the early evening. For three centavos (in 1909) one could buy forty-three grams of protein in *tiguiti*, but the same amount spent on *dalag* purchased only sixteen grams. A recent study of 166 kinds of fish, crustaceans, and mollusks available in the Philippines underlines the nutritive differences. One hundred grams edible portion of *tilapia* provides 76.54 milligrams of calcium whereas the same amount of *tilamosak* yields 621.29 milligrams. The FAO-WHO recommended daily intake is 400–500 milligrams. Since rice is low in calcium, the choice of fish (and the Taytay data make it clear that poor and the well-off purchased different kinds) could determine whether or not a rice-and-fish diet contained adequate calcium. The Taytay researchers were satisfied that the rice and fish provided the people with enough calories and protein. It was not appreciated at the time, however, that rice and fish alone are insufficient in vitamin A, vitamim B_2, vitamin C, folic acid, iron, calcium, and magnesium and are low in fat.[34]

What the "little else" comprised then becomes crucial because the islands produced food that would have remedied all the defects of a fish and highly-milled-rice diet. The list of foodstuffs available in the Taytay market shows that a well-balanced diet was possible. The addition, for instance, of regular but modest portions of mongobeans, bitter melon, eggplant, chili peppers, sweet potato shoots and leaves, bananas, papayas, and pineapple would have provided a nutritional intake meeting all modern minimum daily requirements, though its fat content would remain low. Unfortunately, while the researchers were quite precise about rice and fish intakes, they found no way either to observe or measure fruit and vegetable consumption, concluding finally that it was "in relatively small quantities." Because they were interested in calories and carbohydrates, the surveyers lumped fruit, vegetables, and sugar-based foods together and estimated an average individual daily intake of 500 kilocalories. Since sugar was cheap—two centavos bought almost twice as many calories in candies as it did in fruits and vegetables—or free, if a sugarcane field was near, it seems safe to assume that the diets of the poor contained a high proportion of "empty" calories.[35]

The estimate of overall intake of 2,700 kilocalories for the "average person" and 3,100 for the "hard-working man" in Taytay needs to be approached with caution. As already mentioned, the residents were relatively well nourished and can not be taken as representative of the population throughout the archipelago late in the previous century. That aside, the caloric intake was not as adequate as would appear from the total itself. More than 70 percent of those calories came from rice alone, and a significant proportion of the rest were nutritionally worthless—the poorer the resident, the greater the proportion of the latter. Since it is not possible from the data to differentiate dietary food values by socioeconomic status, the average figures that the researchers calculated tell little about the nutritional state of those most susceptible to disease. Furthermore, the numbers overlook the seasonal nature of rice farming. A 1957 study concluded that Philippine farmers spent only 4.7 months of the year working on their farms, about 2 months in off-farm jobs, and 5 months in virtual unemployment. Nutrition researchers later found a mean individual energy expenditure of 3,307 kilocalories and a mean intake of 2,471 kilocalories among Laguna rice farmers during the active farming period. Whatever the actual figures may have been in any given region before the turn of the century, it is clear that many persons spent at least part of the year in caloric deficit. Prolonged caloric imbalance is common in rural parts of the world, and during the period of subminimal intake, susceptibility to infection is increased.[36]

After two years in the islands (1859–1861), Jagor informed his European readers that "of all countries in the world, the Philippines have the greatest claim to be considered a lotus-eating Utopia." The interesting question then is why so many Filipinos were anemic and malnourished. The answer lies not in the availability of food, though it is clear that some towns were better provisioned than others and that almost all areas experienced periodic scarcities. Dr. Solivellas reported from Pototan, Iloilo, in 1894 that the food there was abundant and varied. The pueblo produced much rice, and the surrounding rural area provided excellent beef and pork for public consumption. There were plenty of chickens to eat, doves and pigeons too, and the ducks were excellent. Especially delicious were the various fish that were frequently brought in from the east coast. Some vegetables and good fruits, especially mangos, were cultivated. Yet, he said that "with such good food the inhabitants do not eat as well as they could." Most of them only ate rice and some few herbs in a stew. They also ate dried fish with some frequency. "This diet, which is certainly insufficient, is mainly responsible for these people not being as strong and robust as they could be." The answer to the historical problem lies in the *access* to adequate nutrition. Amidst the conjunction of demographic, economic, and political transformations, an increasing number of Filipinos were losing the ability either to grow, gather, or purchase food. Some facets of this process are discernible.[37]

First, town formation and population contraction toward poblaciones resulted in an ever larger proportion of Filipinos who no longer regularly gathered at least some of their food from the forests. Such a rude diet might appear inadequate and even savage to the Spanish eye, but it was far more nutritious than what replaced it for many people. The fruits, tubers, and other forest products that Filipinos had traditionally gathered to supplement their rice and fish yielded a diet high in starch but one that was generally sufficient in nourishment. The ability to utilize the woods also gave people a nutritional hedge against rice shortages. It may be that the loss of foraging skills was one reason for the terrible suffering among población residents who fled at the advance of American soldiers three decades later and tried to subsist in the hills. If that is so, then it also becomes a factor in the collapse of the resistance. Unable to live on what the forest offered, most people had no choice but to return to their homes and make an accomodation with the occupying force.[38]

The accompanying changes in land tenure also affected family plots of fruits, herbs, and vegetables. All the early reports and travel accounts of the islands mention them, although it is often unclear if the observers literally meant that "every house . . . has its own orchard." It is likely that some of the more bucolic descriptions referred to the life of well-off inhabitants. It does seem to be true, however, that kitchen gardening was never as common in the Philippines as elsewhere in Southeast Asia. Father Juan Francisco de San Antonio claimed that it was unnecessary since "Divine Providence has given their land so many roots that can be used as food without any need of cultivating them." However that may be, as the agricultural revolution progressed, a declining proportion of the population had the means to maintain a small grove of fruit trees and garden around the house. Tenants had a right, at least in custom, to a lot on which they could stable animals, pursue sideline occupations like carpentry, and grow fruits and vegetables, but the increasing number of landless persons had no such security. They became dependent on what they could buy, and poverty (coupled with scant knowledge of nutrition) led them to spend as little of the shrinking family budget as possible on food. Instead, they substituted cheap stimulants that killed the appetite, like betel nut, tobacco, or sugar. Jean Mallat de Bassilan said that "[the indio] stands for days the heaviest and most fatiguing work . . . as long as he has tocacco; he either chews or smokes it; one would say he draws new strength from it: men and women, boys and girls, young and old, everyone uses it, from morning to night."[39]

Second, the growing disparities in wealth removed food that the poor in the producing areas could have consumed. As early as 1806, pueblo officials in Guiuan, Samar, complained to Manila of a food shortage caused by Chinese-Filipino mestizos who advanced crop loans to farmers and then shipped the harvested foodstuffs to Manila, via Cebu City. The flow of food to the cities increased and picked up speed as urban clusters grew. Dr. Regino Fariña y Tabares called attention to the problem in the early 1880s on Leyte, pointing out that diets were more nutritious in Tacloban than in the areas of the island that provisioned it. The process by which that situation occurred is not mysterious. In the late 1880s, for instance, Masbate cattle and carabao sold for an average of Pfs 8.33 an animal locally, while Manila buyers offered Pfs 25.00 for each. Consequently more than 70 percent of Masbate beef was exported to Manila. Food chased money, whether from rural to urban areas or from the poor to the wealthy within any community. Poor families had no choice but to raise poultry for sale rather than include chicken and eggs in their diets. Thus, most of the laying hens (and much else) produced in Zambales were sent to Manila for sale. When, in 1895, the province experienced food shortages due to bad weather and epizootics, the Junta de Sanidad (Board of Health) in Iba urgently petitioned the authorities in Manila to ban the export of food from the province, pleading that it was crucial to satisfy the necessities of life of the local people. The petition was rejected.[40]

The flow of nutrition away from the poor reached critical proportions after 1896 as the food supply became subject to the needs of three armies during the following six years. The U.S. Army was the richest purchaser in Philippine history. From the moment it arrived in mid-1898, it proceeded to buy rice, eggs, chickens, local fruits and vegetables, fresh fish, and any meat to be had. (When the islands' meat supply finally ran out, American soldiers were provisioned by beef brought in from Australia on refrigerated ships.) The transactions were sometimes contracted out to resident foreign firms like Warner Barnes & Company, whose purchasing agents scoured the countryside, but local commanders soon came to rely on enterprising Filipinos. As shortages of foodstuffs got more acute, the army simply paid a little more. Producers and local suppliers benefited financially (as did the thieves and rustlers who supplied the suppliers), but the effect on most people was a gradual nutritional constriction, since there was no possibility of outbidding the United States government.[41]

Third, ecological changes also aggravated the problem of food access for the poor. Although no one realized it at the time, the deforestation of Luzon's interior foothills (as new land was cleared for agriculture) was producing gradual aridification of the lowland environment, silting of riverbeds, and more extensive flooding. Local and regional food shortages had always followed periodic crop failures due to locust infestations, flooding, drought, or incapacitation of workers, but late in the century such disasters increased in frequency and severity. The flooding problem was serious enough to merit study in 1876. An investigator noted that the riverbed capacities of both the Agno and Cayanga in Pangasinan were insufficient to contain the volume of water produced by heavy rains. The effects were widespread. In the big floods, "it is not only the crops that suffer; the roads are blotted out, the bridges are destroyed, most of the cattle and draft animals are drowned, commercial articles in the warehouses are spoiled, coastwise vessels grounded on the river banks are swept away by the current, as are trees and houses (with or without their inhabitants), and great areas of land are stripped of their covering vegetation, rendering them barren for a long time to come." The problem contined to worsen. In 1888, Governor Luis de la Torre registered his concern about flood damage in Pampanga. He pleaded that the government pay attention to the province's many rivers, "especially the Rio Grande because it has so much water and because its bottom has been rising for years by constant deposit of silt." He said that something should be done "not only because of the interference with commerce on the river but because of crop loss due to the ease with which the water rises over the low banks and covers the plain, destroying everything in its path." The economic and dietary consequences of natural disasters became increasingly intertwined as a result. Although typhoons and severe storm damage have always been a seasonal fact of life in much of the Philippines, McLennan points out that subsistence farmers traditionally mitigated the hardship by hunting and gathering. Such temporary survival strategies became more difficult as cash-crop practices took hold and pushed back the forest, thus destroying the natural watershed.[42]

Locusts found the drying environment favorable for breeding. One observer early in the century asserted that a locust plague could be expected every fifteen years or so. The rhythm accelerated along with agricultural change. The files of the Inspección general de Beneficencia y Sanidad (Department of Beneficence and Health) become jammed after the mid-1860s with yearly appeals from provincial governors for emergency relief from the "complete misery" and "horrors of hunger" caused by locusts. Municipal authorities and large landowners (like Echaúz's hacienda owners on Negros) mobilized brigades of farmers to attack the insects in their larval stage and drive them into ditches where they could be burned before developing wings. If the locusts got airborne first, however, communities in their path were utterly helpless. The areas hardest hit seemed to be those that had recently been deforested. Following a three-day squall that hit Negros's northeast coast around Bacolod in 1867, "the sun and moon disappeared for twenty-four hours as an immense band of locusts came down from the mountains, inundating and lashing the sugarcane fields, which had all just been sown and in just three days are ruined." During the respite between the two great epidemics of disease in the 1880s, the central plain on Luzon suffered the first of a succession of general locust infestations. The governor of Tarlac reported that "the oldest residents have no recollection of ever seeing or hearing of such a huge calamity." According to an eyewitness in Pampanga, "an immense cloud of locusts came to Apalit, descended on the beautiful corn and sugarcane fields on the banks of the Rio Grande, and stayed there four days causing considerable damage and depositing their eggs over two leagues of ground."[43]

After rinderpest killed most of the draft animals on Luzon in 1888–1889, the ecological process was accelerated as unplanted fields provided the insects even more extensive breeding grounds. When war ended the agricultural recovery of the next decade, the cycle resumed. Not only did areas under cultivation contract significantly, but cooperative measures against the larval insects were often impossible because of temporary local emigration and general upheaval of life. The losses to crops in 1903 from drought and locusts were so great that the new colonial government declared a public emergency in August and passed legislation requiring everyone to assemble en masse to repel the pests. By then, however, the towns were so poor and ill-equipped that the administration had to approve a special outlay to finance the purchase and distribution of the galvanized iron sheets needed to trap and drive the insects to the prepared ditches.[44]

The fourth factor affecting the people's access to adequate food was the U.S. Army's tactic of fighting the resistance forces by controlling the Philippine food supply, thereby making life unsustainable for many. After war broke out in February 1899, the American command promptly instituted a pass system that restricted civilian movement from town to town and thus severely disrupted the everyday, small-scale traffic in foodstuffs that was such an integral part of Philippine life. Further orders were issued in May to prevent coastal vessels from carrying rice, other food, and munitions to the Philippine army on Luzon. Many of the sixty-three open coastal ports and subports were closed in order to freeze unauthorized interisland commerce, but as an American officer explained in a letter home, even the "friendly islands" would have to suffer in order that the insurrection on Luzon could be quelled: "War is a terrible thing. Is it not? The actual killing and wounding of men is a small part of the misery caused by it. However if this war can be ended by even such strong measures as starvation or others equally severe, why of course they must be used." By July 1899, Las Pinas, Cavite, had been occupied for a month. Its inhabitants were confined to the town and were "in absolute want of nourishment," according to a petition to the American command for passes allowing townspeople to go into Manila "to buy foodstuffs for subsistence." Since provisions could not move without military permission, towns and entire regions soon became substantially dependent on the U.S. Army for their food supplies. The command was not slow to use that power to reward or punish civilians according to their perceived sympathies and willingness to collaborate. Even those who were favored sometimes had to work on roads in exchange for rice. Another officer wrote from Dagami, Leyte: "It gives one a queer feeling sometime to think of the number of men, woman, and children dependent for food on his permission. Of course, they are not grateful at all."[45]

Once the resistance forces adopted guerrilla tactics in 1900 and proved elusive, the U.S. Army developed a policy that went beyond merely interdicting and controlling the movement of food. All palay, rice, and storehouses clearly for use by enemy soldiers were to be destroyed. That plan would have caused hardship for the people even had it been implemented as intended, since guerillas and civilians often depended on the same rice stockpiles, but the food-denial program got out of hand. Increasingly unsure who was enemy and who was friend, American soldiers on patrol did not agonize over such distinctions. They shot and burned indiscriminately, engaging in an orgy of destruction throughout the Philippines. As resistance persisted, anything from food to fishing nets that could either sustain the "insurrectos" or enable the populace to support them became military targets. In some commands it was standard practice to shoot the few carabaos and cattle that had survived the most recent rinderpest epizootic. Not only would the guerrillas lose a potential food source, but the civilians might stop aiding them if faced with a total collapse of agriculture.[46]

Official reports of detachment commanders document the following *partial* enumeration of the destruction on Marinduque in a period of less than three months after December 11, 1900: 71 tons, 2,708 bushels, and 352 sacks of palay; 62 tons, 2,083 bushels, 171 sacks, and "much" rice; 2½ tons and 428 bales of hemp; 1,800 pounds of tobacco; 1 acre, 70 bushels, and 3 sacks of corn; ½ acre of sweet potatoes; 3 sacks of peas, carrots, and onions; 150 bolts of cloth; "considerable" timber and "a lot of" lumber; 45 boats; 1 shipbuilding yard; 10 fishing nets; 11 storehouses; 230 carabaos; 396 cattle; 519 horses; 1,703 houses, "all the houses in Catmao barrio," "all houses in three barrios," and "all houses found seven miles northeast of Gazan." With one-fifth of the population homeless, the food destroyed, agriculture and fishing crippled, and the island ports closed, it is not surprising that the parish records show an abrupt jump in civilian mortality coinciding precisely with American operations. Monthly burials continued to increase, and by early 1902, mortality appears to have been almost 700 percent above the average annual rate on Marinduque during the 1890s.[47]

The American policy was absolutely calculated. Ileto has pointed out that a similar strategy had been successful a few years earlier for the Spaniards, who also knew that sympathy for a cause would quickly evaporate in the absence of food. Filipino civilians either fled food-scarce regions in search of sustenance or they remained and collaborated with an enemy who could provide it. As Ileto puts it, "The need to eat . . . sets certain limits to a people's hopes and will." The American program proved even more effective. Whereas in 1897 western Batangueños could flee their devastated province for areas that still had food, like Cavite and Mindoro, agricultural production was so generally crippled during the American war that food-surplus regions hardly existed. Port closures, the pass system, and population reconcentrations further restricted interregional migration. The alternative of collaboration was correspondingly more attractive as a result.[48]

General Robert P. Hughes developed the policy of "gradually pinching the insurrectos" on Panay in October 1900. Mounted detachments moved about the island with "roving commissions" to do what was necessary to stamp out the insurrection. One soldier described a raid for his local newspaper in Michigan: "We burned every house, destroyed every carabao and other animals, all rice and other food." The secretary of war customarily dismissed such letters home as "but the vapid utterances of overtalkative soldiers who are more anxious to see their names in print than to pay strict attention to the truth." However, the surviving field reports not only detail the wholesale and wanton destruction visited on the countryside but also show that Hughes, at least, was fully aware of what was happening, despite his later congressional testimony. Colonel J.T. Dickman wrote in his field report about a foray he led against Dumangas: "I burnt up the whole town, completely destroying the homes of 4,000 people." One episode captures the people's frustration, anger, and despair in the face of American savagery. Captain Edwin F. Glenn led a platoon in a raid on Pavia, arriving during the siesta. Glenn said that "the people were completely surprised except a few in the center of the place *who were aroused by the crackling of the bamboo around them* and who attempted to strip the nipa and in-flam[m]able material from the frames of their houses before we could reach them" (emphasis added). The soldiers discovered one man who had torn down his own house and was setting fire to the ruins. He said "with some spirit" that he preferred to burn it himself, whereupon the corporal ordered him to desist, saying that "it was not a matter for him to decide whether his house should be burned or not." Glenn concluded his report by noting that "in spite of numer-ous showers which made the burning difficult, Cabugao and its neighboring barrios were left as memories." Hughes eventually lost control of his operation. On December 14, he received a succinct telegram from Captain A.A. Barker, who was leading a detachment that was "working" the Janiuay-Calinog road in the area where the island's three provinces met: "The territory covered every-thing destroyed." Fires were suddenly reported everywhere. As the burning got out of control, Hughes became frantic at having lost touch with most of the detachments because he had changed his mind about the wisdom of razing the island. The rampage continued through January 1901, however, and the sol-diers destroyed much of the populated part of Iloilo province before he could rein in his marauding command.[49]

The implications of such devastation had been clear to Colonel Dickman almost a year earlier: "The result is inevitable; many people will starve to death before the end of six months." His prediction was not far wide of the mark. Conditions were already desperate in some parts of the island by October 1900, that is *before* General Hughes began "pinching" the population in earnest. Lieutenant-Colonel W.H. Van Horne described the famine prevailing in the district surrounding Sara, Iloilo. The people had not been able to plant that year, he said, due to the war, grasshoppers, and drought. Since the Americans had closed all ports to the north, the people had nowhere to go, and so the poor from throughout the district had crowded into Sara. "Yesterday, market day, there were fully three hundred people in this town without means of subsis-tence and several have died in the market place and on the streets from sheer starvation. These people are now in such a condition that they could not work, even if work could be found for them."[50]

The U.S. Army applied "strong measures" efficiently and thoroughly every-where that resistance seemed particularly stubborn. One cavalry officer re-ported that his troops "often were sent off the road mounted or dismounted to burn a house or barrio, or kill animals, while waiting for the infantry to rest." No one could have been surprised at the consequences of a war waged against the civilian food supply, either directly by destroying food or indirectly by burning houses, smashing fishing boats, and shooting carabaos. Outright starvation like that in Sara shows how really desperate the situation sometimes became. More commonly, death resulted from the infections and epidemic diseases to which malnourishment had made people more susceptible. It is important, however, to contextualize the wartime mortality within processes begun centuries earlier (and still ongoing today). The cumulative effect of the various transformations in Philippine life had heightened vulnerability to disease well before the American intervention. The fighting only added to the burdens of an already debilitated population, putting the youngest and oldest most at risk. One American medical officer surveyed the just-occupied region south of Manila only a few months after the hostilities began and reported that malnutrition among children was so pervasive and severe that the use of easily assimilated foods, like malted milk, was equivalent to medical treatment. Shortly after that, in August 1899, Lieutenant James A. Moss led a scouting patrol from Manila just across the San Juan River to a barrio of San Francisco del Monte, Morong. On his return, he reported: "With apparently just about enough food to sustain life, the natives seemed in great poverty. An inspector of the cemetary showed eight comparatively fresh graves, mostly, judging from their size, those of children."[51]

The complex of factors that had produced the late-nineteenth-century health crisis was rearranged as relative tranquility prevailed after the war ended in mid-1902, and some of the uncertainties of day-to-day existence dissipated. As the new colonial goverment took control with substantial Filipino cooperation and participation, serious political unrest and revolutionary upheaval ceased. The more vigorous and better-funded administration in Manila was able to proceed with public health programs, like smallpox immunization, that reduced mortality from infectious disease. As the panicked population movements gave way to settled life in the towns, malaria subsided. So did the extreme psychological stress of wartime. The first postwar decade saw great advances in knowledge about how to prevent and treat malaria, beriberi, cholera, and rinderpest. Most important, perhaps, is that as life stabilized and land was put back into cultivation, more people ate better. The result in epidemiological terms was that the probability of contact between infectious agents and susceptible hosts declined. Death rates declined dramatically, and population growth accelerated once again, as it had when the hardships of life eased after the end of the Dutch wars two and a half centuries earlier.

PART TWO

Venereal Disease: Evolution of a Social Problem

SOMETIME in November 1897, sixteen-year-old Faustina Trias left her home in Calumpit, Bulacan, and moved with her husband, Candido Ramos, to Manila, where they entered the domestic service of a certain Doña Ladislana. After about a month, seamstress Martina Rafael and her husband, Pedro de los Santos, a day laborer, offered to employ the couple. Despite their less-than-lofty social status, Rafael and Santos somehow convinced Trias and Ramos to transfer to their service. Doña Ladislana had already advanced Ramos twenty-three pesos, however, so it was arranged that Rafael would pay the debt in full, and Ramos would reimburse her by going to work as a coachman for another Spaniard, Don Catalino Sevilla. With the young husband out of the way, Rafael took Trias for a walk a few nights later and delivered her to a house of prostitution run by Alejandra Umali. There Trias was locked up and held as a virtual slave for a month and a half and forced to have sexual relations with those who came to the house. After experiencing genital bleeding, she became frantic but could not escape because the other inmates helped keep guard over her. She finally slipped away one night when Umali was sleeping and no one else was watching. She found her husband in his lodgings at a rice store owned by a barrio captain, and together they went to the tribunal and told their story to a judge. An action was brought in early 1898 against Rafael, de los Santos, and Umali. A médico titular testified that Trias could not attend the preliminary hearings because of the serious venereal disease that she had suffered for more than a month. Umali had disappeared, and the authorities were still searching for her when Admiral Dewey sailed into Manila Bay, throwing the colonial administration into disarray and effectively terminating minor legal actions like this one.[1]

This case provides some insight into the workings of a sex trade that had grown enormously during the previous several decades and became more corrupt and vicious as opportunites increased for profiting from it. Its byproduct, venereal disease, was one facet of a general health crisis that was itself an outcome of growing disparities in wealth. Although most people stayed close to home and coped as best they could with escalating living costs, the increasing stream of poor and landless migrants included many who were drawn to urban centers by jobs that the new agricultural export economy had created. For young women, employment as domestic servants, laundresses, seamstresses, and tobacco-factory workers represented a means of helping their families, and many left for Manila or one of the provincial capitals. Once there, some found their way into prostitution, which seemed to offer more money. One of its many trade-offs was a high probability of venereal infection, however. Sexually trans-

mitted diseases (STDs) were not yet among the worst Philippine health problems, but the sex industry infrastructure that has helped make them so today
was in place before the first American soldier ever stepped ashore. Its formation underlines the socioeconomic dimension of the late-nineteenth-century
disease system.

Venereal diseases do not figure significantly in the early Philippine record.
It is clear that STDs existed in the population, but references prior to the late
nineteenth century are sporadic and generally lack urgency. Postconquest
transmission was propelled by prostitution, which came to exist on the periphery of the indigenous culture wherever soldiers, sailors, and foreigners congre-
gated with money to spend. Writing in 1921, Spanish scholar Enrique
Rodríguez-Solís concluded that "the history of prostitution in the Philippines is
a copy of what we caused in America—the same fleets with equal consignments
of soldiers, functionaries, and harlots." By 1740, infection among the troops
moved the colonial government to establish a hospital in Los Banos, Laguna,
"for the convalescent soldiers, on account of the specific properties of the waters of that district, particularly for venereal diseases." A couple of decades
later, the British occupation force was said to have left at least four hundred
prostitutes behind when they sailed away from the islands. Most observers
were unconcerned, however. Guillaume Le Gentil said in 1766 that venereal
disease was "very common [in Manila among Spanish families] but no one dies
of it." He claimed that "people who are suffering from it marry without hesita-
tion; and the disease thus passes to the children by succession—it is a kind of
inheritance of which but few families there are free." At the turn of the nineteenth century, Father Martínez de Zúñiga acknowledged the presence of "a
few wayward women" in Manila. He thought that the cause of such looseness
was "the foreigners, Spanish bachelors, and the unhappiness and misery of a
certain group of persons." Mallat was equally nonchalant, noting in 1840:
"Syphilis is very slow and is easy to treat, no matter what our pathologists say:
in the hospital it never resisted for more than fifteen or twenty days. The natives cure it by the simplest methods some of which are very strange."[2]

The threat to public health was certainly more serious and extensive. Since
the clinical consequences were not as obvious as those of the diseases that
killed tens of thousands each year, venereal infection would have been all but
invisible to most foreign observers once infectives left the military posts and
the port of Manila. Filipino soldiers and sailors returning home must have
imported venereal infections into their barrios and transmitted them to their
contacts there, usually wives or queridas. Father Antolín's comments in 1739
indicate as much. They are exceptional for his recognition of the potential for
rapid diffusion of STDs and social damage. Road building from Cagayan at
the northern tip of Luzon had brought the first cases of syphilis south through
the valley to the priest's mission of Ituy and Paniqui. He said that the disease
had been unknown previously but had become quite common. Plenty of
men and women were sufferers, with consequent harm to the fecundity of the
population.[3]

Which infections existed and in what proportions is not known. Both syphilis and gonorrhea were undoubtedly present, and although observers almost always wrote only of "sifilis," it should be noted that gonorrhea cases usually outnumber syphilis cases in a population by as much as ten to one. The distinction was not made until 1879 in Europe, yet the Spanish physicians in the Philippines seem not to have applied it even thereafter. Some proportion of the reported disease surely comprised less serious infections like chancroid, lymphogranuloma venereum, and granuloma inguinale as well, but those differentiations were not always made either. Another uncertainty results from the frequent confusion of STDs with nonvenereal infections (especially yaws) that present similar symptoms. In any event, effective treatments of gonorrhea and syphilis were not available until the development of specific penicillins in 1937 and 1943, respectively.[4]

Syphilis has been called a "destroyer of life" and is the most serious of the venereal infections. The causative agent is the spirochete *Treponema pallidum*, which is usually transferred from one human host to another through sexual intercourse. Three stages of the disease exist: the primary and secondary stages, which occur early in the course of the infection, and a tertiary stage that follows a long latent period when infectivity declines. After about two years of latency, the infection is no longer sexually transmittable. All patients develop some resistance to their own infection, and the degree to which they do so determines whether the disease terminates in a spontaneous cure, remains latent, or progresses to the tertiary stage. Latency is the most common outcome. Patients acquire a resistance sufficient to destroy enough spirochetes to prevent tertiary syphilis but not enough to overcome the infection. About a third of all untreated patients eventually move into the third and most dangerous stage of the disease, in which the most serious manifestations are inflammatory reactions of the heart and vessels or of the central nervous system. Almost one-half of all tertiary syphilitics die from those late complications. Survivors normally acquire lifetime protection against reinfection after six months but continue to suffer from irreversible tissue damage. Since fully effective treatment was lacking before the 1940s, it is reasonable to assume that perhaps 5 to 10 percent of all Filipinos contracting syphilis died as a result and that those fatalities were subsumed in other categories on lists of mortality by cause. The number of fetal deaths is impossible to know. A pregnant woman with latent syphilis can transmit the disease to her unborn child, which can cause death in utero. About half of the pregnancies in women with primary or secondary syphilis result in stillbirth, perinatal death, or premature delivery. Surviving infants are weak, develop poorly, and usually die at an early age.[5]

Gonorrhea, by contrast, has been labeled a "preventer of life" and is perhaps the most common bacterial disease of humans. Infection is almost always transmitted by sexual intercourse. Systemic reactions are not extensive, and spontaneous recovery usually occurs. The quick responses to treatment that Mallat observed and that doctors in Manila would later report among registered prostitutes indicate the prevalence of gonorrhea. However, complications of untreated gonorrhea can be serious and debilitating if the infection does not remain localized. Gonococcal arthritis, for instance, is a suppurative and destructive disease of the joints. Although mortality from gonorrhea is negligible, urethal stricture in males and, more commonly, pelvic inflammatory disease in females often lead to sterility. Gonorrhea is particularly persistent since acute infection in either sex may become virtually asymptomatic for months or years without the bacterium's disappearance. Further, the disease carries almost no immunity to reinfection, so the pool of susceptibles is never depleted. In the Philippines, most victims probably sought and received herbal treatments of varying effectiveness from local healers, as Mallat has indicated. Since the magnitude of the problem there will be forever hidden, we can only assume that complications from untreated or partially treated gonorrhea were not uncommon.[6]

By the 1870s, Spanish physicians and others had come to perceive STDs as a rapidly worsening and potentially grave problem throughout the archipelago. Syphilis was never listed as a specific cause of death in the *Memorias médicas*, but it appeared in the ten leading causes of morbidity on each of the three statistical lists that survive in those reports. As usual, we are dependent on impressionistic evidence. In 1876, Dr. Gregorio Martín Blanco reported the alarming spread of syphilis in Ilocos Norte and deplored the casual attitude of the people, who neither treated nor feared the disease and did not avoid sexual intercourse when one partner was infected. Dr. Farina wrote the same year that "syphilis claims its own contingent on Leyte," remarking that although the doctors and provincial officials were much occupied with the problem, the inhabitants seemingly were not since they treated the infection with an infusion of sarsaparilla at most. Bad hygiene then caused cases to progress rapidly to the tertiary stage with grave results. In 1887, Dr. Enrique Lopez de Séneca reported that syphilis in Albay was "becoming more general every day," with cases ranging "from the most simple chancre to gangrene in its highest grade."[7]

The epidemiology of STDs in the islands is reasonably clear, though the lack of detailed evidence invites guesswork. Manila was the principal port of entry for imported venereal diseases and the main port of reentry for domestic ones. After recycling through the medium of prostitution, the infections were taken from port to port throughout the archipelago by crews of coastal trade vessels. (Dr. Farina strongly urged the authorities to prevent infected sailors in the coastwise trade from leaving Manila.) Further remixing occurred in the port towns, after which their sexual contacts passed the infections to men who came there for markets, fiestas, and other occasions. They then "distributed syphilis to other pueblos with great prodigality." Such importations were apparently responsible for the few cases of the disease in Pototan, Iloilo; otherwise the infection would be unknown in that interior municipality, Dr. Solivellas said. Army and navy personnel also diffused STDs effectively, and their camps served as foci of infection. As one observer noted in the 1880s, "In every place where Spanish military posts stood or have stood, one encounters syphilis, and moreover, in its most loathsome forms." Once the infections took hold in the barrios, lack of a fully effective treatment and the people's relative indifference to the disease (if the médicos titulares can be believed) perpetuated the problem. We cannot begin to quantify the prevalence of venereal diseases, which varied substantially from place to place, but incidence anywhere in the archipelago was proportional to the volume of its traffic, direct or indirect, with Manila, Iloilo City, and Cebu City.[8]

Mobility and prostitution were essential to the spread of STDs, and both increased in response to the colony's growing commercial activity. Evidence is scanty on sexual exchange in the provinces, however. The physicians almost never said that prostitution was a problem (or indeed that it even existed) in their poblaciones, either because it was not or because it was a subject best left officially unacknowledged. References do crop up here and there. Dr. Martín blamed prostitution along with casual attitudes for the increasing number of venereal diseases in Ilocos Norte. A partial record exists of criminal charges brought in Bangued, Abra, against Mariano Navarro and Ciriaca Domasal in 1885 for prostituting a minor, Fragides Navarro, perhaps the codefendant's daughter. One advocate of government regulation asserted in 1896 that "clandestine or hypocritical prostitution exists in the big Philippine towns with the gravest harm resulting to the public health and morality." The *Gaceta de Manila* regularly printed the names of women arrested for prostitution in the provinces, though the lists were indeed small, and an American court-martial transcript refers in passing to a prewar house of detention for prostitutes in Calapan, Mindoro.[9]

Fortunately, we have a brief description of prostitution in the port town of Capiz (today Roxas City) on Panay's northern coast. In the mid-1880s, Dr. Cornelio Mapa y Belmonte alerted Manila to the rapid spread of syphilitic infections in Capiz province, especially in its administrative center. He attributed the worsening situation to unregulated prostitution, poverty, lack of education, and what he termed "seduction." He described one aspect of the system: "Young girls, scarcely pubescent, earn their daily sustenance thanks to the few small commodities they bring to the market for sale. There they come under the influence of other women, usually older, who are depraved and given to vice [i.e., prostitution]. Uneducated and eager for money, the young girls follow the lead of their new companions and so little by little the custom spreads. Once delivered into the vice, they go from house to house without protection of any kind—as if they were looking for venereal or syphilitic infection. When they are finally infected they go about propagating it unknowingly, causing grave harm to the public."[10]

Lacking even approximate numbers of prostitutes and contacts in the port towns, it is impossible to gauge the magnitude of the STD problem in the provinces. Dr. Mapa's description of the initial contacts at the market is somewhat ambiguous because it is not clear whether the older women were actively looking for young prospects. His further observation, however, that the prostitutes operated on a freelance basis (rather than living together and working in brothels under someone's control) does suggest that the town did not have the system of cold-blooded recruitment and debt peonage (and sometimes worse) that was developing in Manila at the same time. A fair reading of the historical record, combined with what we now know about the diseases themselves, indicates that by 1870 venereal infections outside the capital were only a moderately serious health problem, but one fast becoming a legitmate cause for concern. More important though, the infrastructure for widespread dissemination was operational when tens of thousands of foreign soldiers arrived several decades later.

Records of prostitution in Manila for the last part of the century do survive. The files themselves document the persons, almost all of them female, who were arrested for prostitution-related offences and imprisoned pending resolution of their cases. The papers represent the results of investigations into the background of each detainee and the circumstances of the case. Also, the final disposition of the matter—by release from prison, deportation to the southern islands, or permission to return home from those colonies—sometimes, but not always, appears. It is possible to compose a statistical profile of the prostitutes from the information scattered through the official files, but the shortcomings of the data are substantial. Only a small fraction of the original records remain. They span the years from 1858 to 1897 but contain great gaps within that period. In addition, the individual case files vary widely from mere notations to detailed depositions. Consequently, the profile is based on substantive information about only a third or so of the 412 women who turn up in the records. We know almost nothing about the others except their names. Notwithstanding those limitations, the *Prostitución* records provide the richest primary source of information on any one aspect of nineteenth-century Philippine public health.[11]

The data permit a remarkably clear look at the social and economic context in which STDs flourished and spread. What emerges is a picture of a burgeoning sex trade fueled by rural want and metropolitan money—a proximate result of the colony's new relationship with the global trading system. In the process, prostitution had become one of a handful of late-century urban growth industries, like tobacco processing, that were tied to the Philippine agricultural revolution. Because of its ambivalent position as a tolerated (and eventually regulated) segment of the underworld, prostitution in Manila presented opportunities for gain through extortion, bribery, exploitation, and abuse that were not common spinoffs from wholly legitimate and socially approved industries. The primary beneficiaries were officials, police, landlords, and brothel proprietors. Substantial part-time employment for ordinary people was also created. Life for many in the Philippines was increasingly catch-as-catch-can, and the sex trade provided a way for a wide range of peripheral figures to pick up a peseta here and there. Thus a second stratum of individuals—watchmen, runners, tipsters, recruiters, coachmen, volunteers, and assorted hangers-on— profited. Few of the prostitutes did. Most were unable to do more than sustain themselves for a time as they shuttled back and forth between brothel, prison, and hospital, hoping to avoid deportation to the agricultural and penal colonies in the south.[12]

The extent to which Manila's increasing affluence acted as a magnet to the impoverished in the cash-poor provinces is highlighted by the fact that almost two-thirds of the women who worked as prostitutes had migrated to the capital to make a living. Of 143 women whose home towns appear, 91 came from twenty-one different provinces. Almost all came from Luzon. Manila's attraction became weaker as distance from the capital increased, and growing urban centers in other regions exerted their own influence. Initially, few prostitutes were actively recruited or tricked into coming to the city, at least until the last decade of the century. The records have little to say about the specific reasons the women had for moving to Manila, but it is clear that the capital functioned in the provincial mind as a place one could go for a time and earn enough, by one means or another, to help out the family. How aware young women were that the sex trade existed or was an option would have varied among the individuals. It certainly would have been a desperate choice. Dery has emphasized that in the Philippines, "society's worst opprobrium is reserved for the prostitutes." In any event, no one envisioned getting rich. Most of those who went to live temporarily in Manila had participated in a family decision that they could help out more by working there than by staying at home. As parents aged and needed physical assistance, or if emergencies arose, the daughters would return home to live. The migration was extremely fluid anyway. Homes in the provinces were not far away, and for some the trip back by steamboat (or by train for others in the 1890s) was reduced to a few hours, so it is safe to assume that many of the women went home for short visits whenever they could.[13]

To understand the historical development of STDs in the Philippines, on its own terms and comparatively, it is important to realize that a daughter's move to Manila was a culturally sanctioned strategy for families in real need. The degree of tolerance depended on the extent of need, the daughter's age, the observation of outward proprieties, and other variables, but the basic attitude represented a cultural "go" signal for venereal microparasitic traffic, to use Morse's metaphor. Most of the young women stayed, at least initially, with a relative or family acquaintance while they looked for a way to make some money. After a time, a small proportion of the women drifted into prostitution by one route or another, often by some variation of Dr. Mapa's example from Capiz. Once in Manila, it would have been plain to all that cash for sex was available, and some women must have started to consider it after hearing talk while cooking, sewing, washing clothes, or rolling cigars.[14]

Those who became prostitutes did not represent a cross section of female migrants or of those who had lived in the city all along. They were the truly powerless, utterly without standing or prospects for advancement in life. Three-quarters of those we know about (at least 70 of 92, or 76.1 percent) had lost one (36 cases) or both parents (34 cases). The actual proportion may be as high as 84.4 percent because the information for six of the women is ambiguous or illegible. So long as a single daughter remained subject to paternal authority in a two-parent household, it was unusual for a young Filipina to leave the house. When one or both parents died, the family structure shifted and the need to help support siblings or any remaining parent drove some daughters to the urban areas. Their families had been poor even in the best of times. The occupations of the prostitutes' parents, listed in 34 instances, were in every case at or near the bottom of the wage scale. Those of the 18 listed fathers included farm laborer (9), day laborer (1) boatman (1), coachman (1), fisherman (1), carpenter (1), shoemaker (1), and buttonholer (1). The occupations of the 16 listed mothers were economically and socially comparable and comprised seamstress (8), laundress (3), cigar maker (1), shopkeeper (1), and ricebagger (1). Assuming that small sample to be representative, it appears that the families were overwhelmingly landless. That, of course, is the precise group that was dying at increased rates and was generally the biggest loser in the transformation to cash cropping.[15]

The prospects of the young women, unsurprisingly, were no better. More than 85 percent of the 117 whose occupations were recorded at the time of arrest were described as seamstresses (44), cigar makers (36), or laundresses (20). The fact that the tobacco processing factories were in Manila rather than in the countryside accounts for the greater proportion of cigar makers among the daughters than among their mothers. The remainder were domestic servants (9), shopkeepers (which does not imply that they owned the shop) (5), laborers (2), and midwife (1). They were almost uniformly illiterate. Of the 77 women about whom such information appears, 72 could neither read nor write, 2 could read but not write, while the remaining 3 claimed to be literate. Most were on their own financially—only 7 of 132 were married and apparently living with the spouse when jailed. The great majority, as one would expect, were single (113). The rest were either widowed (10) or separated (2).[16]

It looks as though the "typical" prostitute entered the trade at about sixteen years of age and worked actively for seven or eight years. We can not actually derive the average age of the women upon entering the profession, however, since the files simply record the age of the detainee as of that particular arrest. Many of the women were arrested year after year, and some only appear in the records on their way to prison for the sixth or seventh time. The previous histories of some are not given or are incomplete. Given those limitations, the records show 136 women ranging in age from thirteen to forty-one. More than half (75) were twenty years old or younger, with the largest concentration (21) at eighteen years of age. Even then, the wide age spectrum is deceptive. Many of the women continued on after their teenage years, but the sex trade in the Philippines has always thrived on very young women. Few of the 18 women who were listed as aged thirty and older were active prostitutes. They were representative of the small percentage of former prostitutes who had found the means or connections to remain in the industry as proprietors (*amas*).[17]

Once "given to vice," a prostitute entered an underworld inhabited by men and women who were as desperate as they and for whom arrest and imprison-

ment—usually for theft, fighting, or scandalous behavior—was a common occurrence. The papers in the 1877 case of Maria Robles, alias "Batallon," give
the flavor of that world. Forty years old at the time of this arrest, she had
presumably been an active prostitute in her younger days, though the file does
not say so. In any event, she was a well-known lowlife character and had served
time in Bilibid just two years previously for fighting and scandal, offenses usually connected with prostitution in some way. Since her release, she had been
in league with her boyfriend, Brigildo "Gildo" Ramirez, and his gang of boat
thieves, giving them a refuge and a hiding place in Navotas for their loot, stolen
from barrios around Laguna de Bay and destined for sale elsewhere. The outlaws, who were from Cavite province, had became increasingly arrogant, recently committing a number of robberies and thefts in Navotas and Tambobo.
Their activities were common knowledge, but Batallon's neighbors were afraid
of their vengeance, especially since the robbers had apparently paid off some
officials. The terrorized residents finally reached the breaking point, however.
They worked up the nerve to denounce her to the local official in charge of the
mestizo population as "a bad seed in this pueblo" and to request her deportation to "the new establishment of Jolo where they need women to be useful
while there are too many malefactors here." She was arrested and charged with
prostitution and receiving stolen goods. Whether she was deported to the south
or released with a stern warning after a short jail stay does not appear.[18]

The prostitutes could expect to be jailed more than once. The files indicate
the presence or absence of previous prison records in 106 instances; of these,
there were 66 cases of at least one prior incarceration. That number understates
the incidence of multiple arrests because some of the files are incomplete and
because many of the first-time detainees were undoubtedly jailed later in their
careers without appearing again in the surviving records. Repeat offenses were
officially considered evidence of incorrigibility, but they say as much about the
powerlessness of those detained. Arrests could usually be avoided by the payment of a small bribe, but the women were almost always at the mercy of forces
beyond their control. If, for instance, one had the misfortune to be picked up
at the time (or because) her ama had become tired of the demands for higher
payoffs and had determined to resist them, no bribe would be offered and the
prostitute could count on at least a couple of weeks in jail. Thus Maximiana de los Santos appears in the records in 1877 for the seventh time in two
years. Alejandra Rejes was jailed for prostitution each year between 1879 and
1884. Nineteen-year-old Benigna Raymundo turns up in the files in 1887 for
the first time as a result of her eighth stay in Bilibid, and Filomena de la Cruz
was picked up and imprisoned five times in as many months that same year.[19]

The official response to prostitution evolved along with perceptions of the
social harm it occasioned. The institution itself was never the problem. Initially
civil authorities were most concerned with "public scandal" and the consequent outrage to society. Prostitution led too often to drunken brawling, which
could be tolerated so long as the trade was confined to the immediate port area,
but by the 1870s, the potential for profit had grown to the point that landlords

were establishing amas and prostitutes in small nipa bungalows throughout the city. The houses were still located within reach of sailors and soldiers, but as encroachment on residential neighborhoods began, ordinary citizens pressured the authorities to maintain peace, tranquility, and public decorum. Hence, thirteen-year-old Victoriana de la Rosa was arrested in front of her brothel because she "served as an attraction and inducement to the continual procession of sailors and soldiers that on certain days and at certain times passes in front of the parish house on its way to the outlying neighborhood of San Jose." Likewise, Juana Rodriguez, a nineteen-year-old seamstress, was picked up along with three companions in front of their house of prostitution in San Nicolas, Binondo, for "making scandal with soldiers and other people [that was] clear to all passers by."[20]

The classic scandal occurred not in Manila but in nearby Mariquina, where Placida Javier pushed community tolerance too far in 1874. Local passions eventually became too inflamed for us to trust the testimony entirely, but it was alleged that years earlier the laundress had abandoned her husband, left their home in Mariquina, and run off with one Damasio Samson. Sometime after her husband died, she returned home without her paramour to take care of her son and aged father, for whom she was the sole support. She then "entered into various illicit relationships." Older (she was in her late twenties), more experienced, and far more brazen than the teenage prostitutes, she embarked upon "the most scandalous mode of living," entertaining married men and even Chinese. Not surprisingly, the commander of the local civil guard began receiving complaints from various families. She then astounded the community by taking up with former cabesa de barangay Don Faustino Guevara, a family man with political enemies. She was jailed. Upon her release, she audaciously drove to her lover's house, whereupon Don Faustino, "in the presence of his wife and children got into the horse-drawn carriage with her, and they rode down the road in triumph with loud voices celebrating her release." The outraged residents had her rearrested for prostitution immediately.[21]

Prior to the mid-1870s, the standard punishment for prostitution (or rather for the accompanying breach of public decorum, since no one was actually arrested for prostitution itself) was deportation to a penal or agricultural colony on one of the southern islands, usually Paragua, Balabac, or Mindanao. The solution made some sense at the time. Since the affront to public sensibilities seemed the biggest problem, exporting the most offensive visible manifestations of the vice was thought sufficient to appease church and society. Hard work in the south would reform the women as well. Thus, legislation provided that prostitutes were to be deported "for the benefit of society in general," a principle cited by the authorities when twenty-eight-year-old Rafaela Mesa was sentenced to exile in Puerta Princesa, Paragua, in 1872 because of her "disordered and harmful life." The policy also fit nicely with the larger impetus to develop the public riches. As the governor of Paragua later explained, Mesa and the other twenty-five women who were deported with her had been sent "under the concept that as farm laborers and seamstresses they could render useful services to the colonies." Exile was for one or two years, and in practice, petitions for release were routinely granted upon evidence of the deportee's good behavior and correction of her vices.[22]

In the mid-1870s, the rising incidence of venereal disease could no longer be ignored, and official policy was changed. The files contain no specific directive, but it appears that examinations for venereal disease were mandated around 1875 in all cases of women arrested for prostitution. About the same time, detainees who previously would have been sent south straight away were instead jailed, examined (and treated if infected), and then released after a short stay in prison. The case of the eighteen-year-old laundress Matea San Juan illustrates the transition in policy as well as any other. Daughter of a farm laborer and a laundress, both deceased, she left her home in San Pedro Tunasan, Laguna, and went to Santa Cruz, in Manila. Arrested with others in 1875 for prostitution, she was examined by the Bilibid physician and found to have venereal disease, whereupon she was immediately remitted to the Hospital de San Juan de Dios for treatment. She was hospitalized for a week and then went back to jail for two more weeks before her release. Less than a year later, she was arrested with three other prostitutes in Binondo after a fracas in front of the house where they worked. The women had allegedly refused admittance to an artilleryman from the Peninsular regiment, which resulted in an uproar and her arrest. San Juan was jailed, examined for infection, and after an investigation of her background, remitted to the provincial authorities in Laguna.[23]

Deportations continued until the end of the Spanish regime, but decreasingly so. It became standard practice to release detainees after two weeks of incarceration with a warning. After an individual's third or fourth arrest, she would usually be sent, like San Juan, back to her home province. Whether the women were sent home or deported, they usually returned to Manila as soon as possible, like Braulia Esquerra, who was transported to the south on the steamship *Patina* at age fourteen and was back in Bilibid three years later. The authorities seem to have concluded that the social problem was not exportable and that the task of individual reformation was increasingly irrelevant in face of the more important disease problem. By 1881 women were being arrested on suspicion of venereal disease, a charge separate from prostitution, and sent immediately to the infirmary at Bilibid for examination.[24]

Such ad hoc procedures would never suffice, however. By around 1880 the colonial government determined that systematic regulation was needed. Plenty of Spanish and other European examples were available, and in the end it was decided in 1883 to use Madrid's regulations except where it was necessary to introduce others. A statement formalizing that decision was partially drafted but left unfinished, apparently because the writer quit the civil service. When his superiors looked into the matter, they were dumbfounded by such bureaucratic sloppiness, but getting the legislation drafted and proclaimed was not the main problem. The more serious obstacle was the staunch opposition of both the church, in the person of Archbishop Payo of Manila, and a powerful segment in the higher echelons of Manila society that saw in regulation a sanction and protection of vice. In 1887, however, the liberal interim governor, José Centeno y García, was presented with evidence that prostitution (and implicitly, venereal disease) was far more pervasive than generally thought, or perhaps acknowledged. He used this startling evidence as the occasion to order a program to control it, and the Madrid regulatory regime (or something like it) went into effect before the end of 1888. Regulation was apparently not extended beyond Manila (and perhaps Cavite City), undoubtedly because of the expense it would have entailed, despite calls for it from provincial physicians like Dr. Mapa. The perception in Manila that the threat to the public health was much less serious in the provinces probably served to validate official inaction.[25]

The *Prostitución* files do not contain a copy of the first regulations, but a later version that took effect in mid-1897 is included. It mandated registration of houses of prostitution and their inmates, both amas (or amos, the male counterparts) and the prostitutes. The latter were subject to the law whether or not they actually lived in the houses or even worked there. An official was charged, on paper at least, with the duty of consulting with the woman and her family prior to registration in order to assess the prospects for her reclamation and to warn her of the consequences should she persist in her conduct. It is hard to believe that anyone took that regulation seriously, but it well illustrates the gap between the underlying assumptions of the program and the reality of prostitution in the Philippines. Few of the women had a family with whom the authorities could readily consult, for one thing. Equally illusory but more serious was the erroneous idea that prostitution was the fault of depraved women who had a free choice to change their ways. In fact, they were victims of economic forces well beyond their control, and far from being free agents, moral or otherwise, most had already become entangled in a form of debt slavery.[26]

The heart of the program was the provision for regular medical examination and treatment. Each inscribed woman was subject to twice-weekly checkups by the corps of medical inspectors from the health department's new public hygiene section, and the results were recorded on individual health identification cards. Those infected were to be immediately hospitalized. Both amas and prostitutes were obliged to report changes of residence or domicile of the latter within forty-eight hours. Strict punishment was threatened against amas who held women in their houses against their will, whether for indebtedness or not—claims for monies owed were to be resolved in the judicial system. Amas were also warned against concealing unregistered women in their houses. If they did so and contagious disease resulted, the penalties would be more severe. Medical inspectors were given substantial power to revoke permission for the houses and amas to stay in business. The system was to be financed by a schedule of fees for registration, examination, and treatment as well as by various fines and penalties for infractions of the rules.[27]

The quantitative evidence does not allow a firm judgment as to whether compulsory examinations reduced the incidence of venereal disease. We have no idea how many women worked outside of the regulatory system (or within it, for that matter) and thus avoided medical examinations. The one roster that exists shows thirty-seven brothels under the control of thirty-one amas and six amos and employing 123 prostitutes in 1893. Other testimony from that period said to be based on information from Spanish and Filipino officials asserted that 1,693 prostitutes were living in Manila. Whatever the number of those officially registered, it is clear from the more detailed case files and the 1897 regulations themselves that amas hid women and imprisoned others and that many women worked as casuals, making themselves available for occasional work. Others worked independently. An anonymous Spaniard who had lived for some years in the Philippines said that they "roved freely in all the streets, promenades, and plazas, mostly at night in closed coaches, which are truly ambulatory brothels." Prostitutes and their customers also coupled "behind houses or against a wall, like dogs and beasts, with neither modesty nor shame." For an agreed-upon favor or monthly payment, the various guardians of public order were usually willing to give the women "a complete guarantee of tranquility and peace so that they would not be interrupted in their nocturnal recreation."[28]

Also, the results of examinations only appear, and then sometimes ambiguously, in about a quarter of the files, and only nine such notations (all positive for infection) exist after regulation began in about 1887. Nevertheless, in the 108 cases in which an outcome is clearly recorded during the period 1872–1890, the tests were positive for infection in 66 instances. That proportion agrees with a statistic from the early 1890s offered by the anonymous Spanish writer, who claimed that of 857 women presenting themselves for registration, 571 were found to be infected. Undoubtedly examination and detention of infectives until "cured" was of some help, if only because they could not transmit the disease while in the hospital, but the overall rate of infection does not seem to have been reduced. Considering that two-thirds of the women were infected at all times and that their sexual contacts used no prophylactic means against infection, the scope for transmissibility becomes evident. Indeed, more than one-quarter of the soldiers in the Peninsular Artillery regiment were said to be regularly in the military hospital for syphilis and venereal diseases.[29]

Qualitative evidence is more useful in sounding the depths of what was a rapidly worsening social and medical problem. By the time regulation began in the late 1880s, effective control of STDs in Manila was already doomed. The few detailed case files that survive reveal a progressively complex, corrupt, and brutal system in which the basic elements of the far more serious situation that exists today are already visible. The increasing numbers of needy and helpless young women, combined with the growing opportunities for others to milk the trade, ensured that prostitution would thrive, regulations would be evaded, and venereal disease would spread. An 1890 case involving mutual allegations of extortion by two Spanish hygiene officials shows how the new regulatory system increased the possibilities for graft. The truth of what actually happened is anyone's guess, but the overall picture of shakedowns and rake-offs is clear enough. Don Mariano Zabala and Don Pedro Simon were enemies. Zabala was twenty years younger, and it looks as if Simon resented him as an upstart who was encroaching on his territory. They eventually clashed over who would control prostitution in the Quiapo–Santa Cruz area. Besides demanding sexual favors from the prostitutes, both men collected money and gifts from the amas; anything would do—money, rings, furniture, and even a horse in one instance. Any refusal was met with fines, physical abuse, and threats of legal trouble. The proprietors were willing to tolerate the exactions of one official but not two, and someone, probably Maxima Macalinao, an ama, finally filed a complaint.[30]

Zabala, accompanied by the watchman Dionicio Encarnacion, went to Macalinao's house one evening and demanded protection money against being shut down. She had a lucrative business that catered to well-heeled Spaniards rather than to the usual run of soldiers and sailors. Not only could she afford to pay Zabala, but she was especially vulnerable to his threat. Just two months earlier her house had been the site of "a terrific scandal" when Don Cipriano Subrido Fernandez, Don Angel Prensado Lojo, and Don Estanislao Corral Perez had engaged in a drunken brawl that destroyed most of the furnishings. The men were fined, but her house became notorious. Accordingly, she did not demur when Zabala came by. She paid half on the spot and subsequently met him and handed over a diamond ring worth 100 pesos. Macalinao later told acquaintances that she had not been bothered since paying Zabala off. Simon apparently learned of the transaction from Encarnacion, who had since lost his job for some reason. Seizing the chance to get even with his rival, Simon went to Macalinao's house and demanded that she sign a sworn statement against Zabala for his extortion of the ring. When she balked, Simon threatened her with deportation and beat her up.[31]

The investigation revealed another layer of corruption that is important to an appreciation of how prostitution meshed with the larger economy and why once established, the trade could only grow. The watchman Encarnacion and a partner, Mariano Bolinao, were also found to have regularly extorted gifts from many amas for overlooking various infractions of the hygiene regulations. Payments were usually in kind—most often in the form of "guinea hens, pigs, ducks, socks, undershirts, handkerchiefs, and embroidery of various kinds." The nature of the last of those items makes it clear that it was the young inmates of the houses who bore the high cost of doing business for their employers since, it will be recalled, most of the women were seamstresses by trade. Many spent their days producing handiwork that could be used to pay off watchmen and other petty functionaries, who in turn could sell the merchandise just as their immediate superiors could sell the rings, furniture, and horses. Sidelines, however small and in whatever form, have always been important as supplemental sources of income in the Philippines. Prostitution flourished because, among other things, it increasingly generated such employment and money. Manila's attraction accordingly grew stronger in the cash-scarce provinces, where the cost of living and personal debt were rising. As prostitution became enmeshed with the legitimate economy, those with a stake in the activity's continuation became a more formidable barrier to anyone who would get rid of it or even contain it.

As a result of the investigation, Zabala and Simon were both relieved of their positions and ordered to make restitution. The final report solemnly stated that the offenses were extremely serious. Sensitive to the reality that the new hygiene section's work was unpopular among powerful segments of society, the writer said that it was absolutely imperative, whatever the cost, for the smallest abuse to be eliminated so the benefits of regulation would be evident. One need not doubt the sincerity of the investigating commission, but nothing in the record indicates that substantial change occurred thereafter. Two footnotes to the case turn up in the files three years later. One of the amos registered on the 1893 roster, who was running a house with three inscribed prostitutes in Tondo, was none other than Dionicio Encarnacion. By that time, Macalinao was the ama of two brothels. Just two weeks after the registration list was compiled, however, she was arrested after a knife fight in one of the houses over a stolen wristwatch. The head of the Guardia Civil Veterana (the Civil Guard unit created specially for Manila) requested permission to close her houses. Deportation papers were drawn up, but the record stops at that point.[32]

Payments to officials were not always coerced. One of the infractions that the amas were willing to pay the inspectors to overlook was the employment of unregistered women. That infraction must have been more and more common, since a growing proportion of the youngest women who appear in the later files had been tricked or forced into prostitution and held unwillingly. Such noncompliance with the regulations seriously compromised the effort to control venereal disease as the following case demonstrates. Venancia David appeared before a municipal judge in 1892 to make a complaint on behalf of her young cousin, Florentina Caulas. The year before, Caulas, then fifteen years old, had met with one Gregorio Sarmiento and agreed to be a *criada* (domestic servant) in his household at a salary of two pesos a month. After a week, however, Sarmiento "began to make a business deal of her honor." In effect, he sold her to Silvestre de la Cruz, amo of a house of prostitution on the Calle Iris near Sarmiento's residence. Caulas's opposition was to no avail, "owing to her youth and feminine weakness." She continued to live and work as a servant at Sarmiento's house while also working as a prostitute for de la Cruz. That arrangement lasted for a year, presumably outside the registration system, "until yesterday when she took action to leave her master's house because she could no longer stand the shame, and went to live with her cousin, to whom she told all."[33]

Sarmiento's role as a wholesaler or supplier of women reveals yet another level of profit in the system. Such suppliers became a regular feature of the cases from the 1890s. Some worked on an informal basis, tipping off an acquaintance in the trade when a young women came to his or her attention. Once money passed between supplier and proprietor, the hapless victim suddenly found herself in debt (legally or not) with little chance of working her way out of it. Irene Atienza's plight illustrates the process. She was the fourteen-year-old daughter of a widower in San Miguel de Mayumo, Bulacan, and had left home in 1897 after an altercation with her father's querida. Shortly after the girl arrived in Manila, a prostitute named Martina Ramos was tipped off by an aunt about "a youth who wanted to be a prostitute [and who] turned out to be Irene." They took her to Ramos's ama, Maria Cruz, the wife of a municipal guard who lived behind the church in Sampaloc. Cruz paid twenty-five pesos, "so Irene was indebted to her," as Ramos later put it. The girl was then installed in the brothel with little chance of escaping since Cruz's policeman-spouse was undoubtedly part-owner of the enterprise. Atienza remained a hostage of Cruz for four months until a chance remark by an acquaintance enabled her uncle to find her and take her away.[34]

As demand increased in Manila, other wholesalers began to operate more systematically, ranging through the neighboring provinces offering young women various incentives to come to the city. The most common one was the promise of a position as a domestic servant with a good family. (One observer of this "criada system" claimed that the parents were "often indifferent or deceived as to the real service for which their daughters were intended.") Numerous variations of the basic pattern existed, but after reaching Manila the young women were lured, pressured, or forced into prostitution sooner or later. The Manila-Dagupan railway made recruiting easier, as fourteen-year-old Apolonia Mojica's experience shows. She fell into conversation with a friendly stranger, Victorina Garcia, late one morning outside her house in Guiginto, Bulacan. Garcia had been sent that day by her employer, Martina Navarro (a registered ama) "for the purpose of finding young girls to work in her house." Learning that Mojica was lonely for her father, who was in Manila for a few days, Garcia offered to take her there on the railroad to meet him. Mojica eagerly agreed. She got a ride on the train and another in a horse-drawn cart before finding herself in Navarro's house late that same afternoon. Much longer-range recruitment developed when the arrival of the Spanish and then the American soldiers opened up unprecedented opportunites for profit at the end of the decade, and the system quickly expanded in response. By the end of the American war, brokers were recruiting women from the farthest reaches of the archipelago and shipping them to the capital.[35]

The U.S. military had its own perspective on the problem of venereal disease, of course, eventually viewing the "diseased woman" as the army's worst enemy in the islands. However that may have been, the diseased soldier was a far graver threat to public health. More than 120,000 American soldiers arrived in the four years after mid-1898, and the conjunction of their money and mobility with poverty, both preexisting and war-created, caused a quantum jump in the incidence of Philippine venereal infections. Explaining that increase entails using more indirect sources of evidence. The American military was far less concerned with Philippine public health, except as it threatened the army's operational capability, than was the former civil administration and therefore kept few records on the subject. Thus the extent to which Filipinos suffered from venereal disease (and indeed from almost all diseases) during the war years must be inferred from the health records of American soldiers and their units.[36]

The U.S. Army was already heavily infected with STDs before it left North America. The soldiers came from a civilian population in which the problem was not inconsiderable, and as a result, seventeen of every thousand candidates for enlistment were rejected because of venereal infection. Rates soared as soon as volunteers and regulars began training, thanks to the "dives [that] sprang up like mushrooms" around all encampments and staging areas. Shortly after the Third U.S. Cavalry got to Fort McKenzie in Georgia, for instance, one of the regimental physicians reported that it was difficult to treat the venereal diseases in the division hospital since the wards were so crowded with infected soldiers. Once the troops reached the Presidio in San Francisco for final staging, men who reported gonorrhea or chancroids were routinely examined, given medicine, and immediately returned to duty. Syphilitics were normally hospitalized until considered cured. The Regimental Health Records show some exceptions, however, and even men with secondary syphilis were occasionally returned to duty. An issue arose, though apparently not until 1900, as to whether or not to send men infected with venereal disease on to the Philippines. The official decision is missing from the files, but it is plain that the policy had been, and continued to be, to ship all soldiers who were expected to be fit for duty by the time they reached the archipelago five weeks later. An anonymous army official who sailed with one of the first regiments to embark in mid-1898 stated that 480 of the unit's approximately 1,300 men had been "registered for venereal disease" in San Francisco. Since no completely effective treatment yet existed for either syphilis or gonorrhea, the policy, even if sound militarily, represented a serious hazard to public health in the islands.[37]

Venereal infection ranked near the top of the U.S. Army's list of concerns when the first men sailed from California. Since the cumulative historical experience of armies in both war and peacetime indicated that the problem was inevitable, the challenge was to minimize it rather than to prevent it entirely. The contemporary experience of the British army in India did not give cause for optimism: statistics for 1895 showed a rate of 522 cases of venereal disease per 1,000 soldiers. Syphilis accounted for almost half of those cases, and most ominous of all from a military standpoint, 8,000 of 70,031 soldiers were found to be useless for field operations. Rumors of a Philippine superstrain of venereal infection fed the near paranoia in the army's medical department. Chief Surgeon Henry Lippincott wrote Washington in July 1898 just before disembarking from the *Newport* in Manila Bay that "It is believed that Syphilis of a most virulent type exists in these islands and that our men are bound to be affected unless stringent measures are adopted by Commanding Officers to prevent the men visiting houses of ill fame or associating with lewd women." Predicting that a system of examination might become necessary after the anticipated fall of Manila, then still in Spanish hands, he warned not only of the loss of time on active duty through disability but of "the terrible consequences that may result in the United States by the arrival there of men poisoned by Asiatic Syphilis." It goes without saying that the havoc the poisoned men might cause amongst the Filipino population never crossed his mind.[38]

If no super-syphilis was ever found, some of Lippincott's fears materialized after the troops came ashore. Although, as the adjutant general of the army admitted, "a not inconsiderable part of such [venereal] disease is imported with the troops from the United States," the incidence leaped after their arrival in the islands. About 25 percent of all cases on sick report in 1898 for one brigade of some 4,000 volunteers were for venereal disease, and it is clear that the sick lists did not begin to reflect the actual extent of infection. Even the surgeon general acknowledged that the disease was much more common than would seem from the official health records. Separate wards had to be established in all the Manila hospitals for the "rough riders," as infected soldiers were called. One veteran later recalled that he had seen times when 50 percent of a company was infected, adding that the men took no preventative precautions whatever, prophylactic measures being entirely lacking.[39]

Once Manila was taken from the Spaniards, Philippine and American leaders acted together to head off venereal disaster. On August 13, 1898, Emilio Aguinaldo and Leandro Ibarra signed a decree authorizing the continuation of the Spanish administration's regulatory system "in order to prevent the contraction of syphilitic and venereal diseases." Chaos reigned for a couple of months, however, before the U.S. Army and the new board of health could reimpose some order on the sex trade. Many of the American soldiers were quartered in Sampaloc. Although Alejandra Umali and others had run houses in that section previously, the character of the predominantly residential area now changed overnight. One observer reported that "the orgies became so frightful that the Spanish families of the districts began to lock up their houses and rent residences in other parts of the city." Soon few respectable families remained, and according to him, "two whole streets are filled with drunken soldiers, rioting, yelling Americans and half-naked women." Houses of prostitution appeared everywhere. On Calle Alix, a street in the northwest sector, "these houses occupied both sides of the way for three-quarters of a mile, the windows filled with soliciting women in garbs too scandalous for description."[40]

Foreign prostitutes and pimps stampeded "from every corner of the earth" towards a rendezvous with the American army in Manila. One American newspaper reported that "abandoned women poured into the new and active market" from Vladivostok, Yokohama, Hong Kong, Singapore, Calcutta, and other treaty ports. Many of the first arrivals were Russians, Austrians, Romanians, and other eastern Europeans who had been working in colonial Asia when the situation in the Philippines erupted. The STD rates among British soldiers in India suggests that "this flood of cosmopolitan harlotry" must have added new strains to the suddenly augmented pool of imported infection in the islands. The newcomers were soon joined by American and Japanese prostitutes, the latter quickly becoming the largest single foreign contingent. Estimates of the scope of the influx vary. One outraged observer alleged that eight hundred foreign prostitutes sailed into the Port of Manila the first year, each paying a fifty-dollar "tip" to customs officials, usually through one of the ship's officers. Another witness claimed that three hundred prostitutes had arrived on one steamer. The flow never ended. Some women were refused entry, some were apprehended subsequently and deported, but many others kept slipping through in the guise of circus performers, nurses, teachers, and "wives" of legal entrants. In the meantime, the ranks of the domestic prostitutes were swelled by a floating group of Filipinas anxious for a stake in the new Klondike.[41]

The board of health took the first regulatory steps in October 1898 by setting aside a wing of San Lazaro Hospital for diseased women. Known prostitutes were detained and examined by army medical officers and sent to the hospital if infected. Gradually the old inspection system was reinstituted throughout the city. Examination fees were two dollars at the houses and one dollar at the hospital for whites and half those sums for Filipinas. Most of those detained were the latter, since infected foreigners usually stayed away from the houses at inspection time and sought private treatment instead. A few months after war erupted, the American military government took over the supervision of prostitution in Manila on June 1, 1899, as a "military necessity." When bubonic plague appeared briefly in late December 1899, brothel inspections were intensified and the system tightened. Because the women had become adept at exchanging inspection books, a photographic identification system was introduced. Thereafter, each known prostitute was registered on a card by name, number, and picture. Information about the regulations was posted in each establishment in three languages. New inspectors were added as the houses proliferated and frustrated the effort to confine prostitution to certain areas.[42]

Regulation could do little against runaway venereal infection. During two and a half months in early 1900, 435 women were detained and treated. The highest number in hospital at any one time was 161. Since 542 prostitutes were on the register, it seems that up to 80 percent of all registered prostitutes contracted some form of venereal disease at sometime during that short period. In contrast, the incidence of gonorrhea among modern-day prostitutes is about 20 percent. Many women worked outside the system, at least occasionally, and their infection rate must have been high. The usual procedure in Manila brothels was to send to a neighbor for additional help whenever the number of soldiers outnumbered the inmates. Those "reinforcements" were available on call, not as regular prostitutes but as casuals willing to work now and then. Prostitution had become a genuine sideline. At an even lower level of organization, many women worked outside of the houses altogether. The trade became more informal as poor Filipinos scrambled for a share, however small, of the American money that rained on Manila. Soldiers found that many men, women, and children, upon receiving payment of a peseta, were willing to conduct a woman to a designated meeting place for sex. The epidemiological potential of the new situation was explosive, especially in the provinces where neither the regular nor the part-time prostitutes were systematically examined. That potential became real as soon as the U.S. Army fanned out from Manila in early 1899.[43]

Prostitution was not officially licensed and regulated outside of Manila. Manpower and resources to police the system and to conduct the necessary physical examinations were lacking in most places. Beyond that, regulation was a heated issue in the United States just as it had been in Spanish-colonial Manila, and the army faced the same sort of opposition that Governor Centeno had. In Europe, municipally regulated prostitution districts under police control and medical supervision had existed in some of the major cities for years. By contrast, regulation of prostitution had not been politically possible in the United States (except briefly during the Civil War) due, in the army's view, "to all the obstacles that pious ignorance could put forth." Influential moral reform organizations such as the Women's Christian Temperance Union and the Association for Philanthropic Labor argued generally that government "superintendence" of prostitution was nothing more than "an effort to make vice safer for young men" and was demonstrably immoral, cruel, and futile. The main effect, they contended, was not to reduce the incidence of venereal infection but instead to promote vice and to produce "a traffic in girlhood and hopeless slavery." The spectre of a loose political alliance of convenience between such groups, anti-imperialists, and the Democrats (then out of power) was sufficient to induce circumspection in the Philippines. Regulation in Manila was accomplished with as little publicity as possible, and indeed when the army later came under criticism for "licensing" prostitution, General Arthur MacArthur issued a statement in which he carefully justified the measures by conceding that prostitution was *regulated* in Manila but denying that it was *licensed*. In such an atmosphere, Secretary of War Elihu Root was unwilling to push his luck by allowing the military to manage prostitution throughout the entire colony.[44]

Some local commanders organized the trade on their own, however. Lieutenant Owen J. Sweet did so on Jolo and became embroiled in controversy for his trouble. Whether he had found a chaotic situation there with hundreds of prostitutes of several nationalities that he simply regulated, as he subsequently insisted, or whether the institution had been unknown in the region before he began to run an elaborate prostitution service "on the canteen plan," as his enemies charged, is in doubt. He claimed that he had been concerned that assaults on the local women would provoke a more violent reaction from the Muslim Filipino population than similar incidents had done on Luzon. So three houses were rented, two for enlisted men and one for officers, and about forty women were procured from overseas—most were Japanese brought in from Borneo and Singapore. The women and men were examined regularly, and the latter had to show their medical certificates to enter the houses. Each soldier had a running account that he settled on payday. Lieutenant Sweet's system seems to have run smoothly, although the enlisted men's houses were occasionally closed, as when three heavily infected companies of the Twenty-third U.S. Infantry arrived from the north to take up station on Jolo.[45]

Since most foreign women chose to stay in Manila, Filipina prostitutes would have had the Christianized provinces to themselves were it not for competition from local women who became queridas of the soldiers. It is not surprising that most men preferred having steady girlfriends—they were usually faithful and were less likely to be infected, at least initially. Love matches existed, but the practical aspects of the relationships are understandable. From the woman's point of view, a private's monthly pay of $15.60 made him appear fabulously wealthy. When he offered half of it, which was enough for her entire family to live on for a month, some women found the temptation sufficient to "overcome the will and moral conscience, as well as priestly injunctions," as one soldier put it. The Philippine church had traditionally attempted to make single men marry their queridas, but such illicit relationships had been on the rise as clerical influence declined in the turbulent late nineteenth century. That moral and religious scruples persisted, however, is clear from the fact that many soldiers agreed to go through some sort of marriage ceremony even though they had no intention of taking their "wives" with them when they left the islands. It is plain that most of the men considered the liasons a temporary convenience. For example, on leaving Tayabas City, one soldier wrote home to his brother in Ohio: "The boys all hate to leave their senoritas, but they will find plenty others in Candelaria or Tiaon." Estimates of the prevalence of such relationships varied. One soldier pointed out that some of the men garrisoning Bauang, La Union, "were not lucky in making local alliances," but another report from a town south of Cebu City said that "the lieutenant and nine-tenths of his men had their native queridas." That did not necessarily preclude them from sexual relations with prostitutes at other times, of course.[46]

Indeed, the military-based sex trade was sufficiently profitable for houses of prostitution to be established in the largest garrison towns. Such brothels initiated the spread of venereal disease in many areas. Once prostitution was in place, it spawned official and unofficial networks of profiteering that have proved resilient ever since. Formal prostitution did not take root in towns and barrios where the American garrison was small and likely to be temporary. Instead, the soldiers there encountered women who moved thoughout the region in groups of two to four. The medical officer in Binalonan, Pangasinan, described them as "a transient class of native women who are infected [and who] travel from one post to another spending a few days at each garrison." The potential for disease diffusion from the sexual transactions at those subposts was strong because military physicians were generally not stationed there and because the women and men were so mobile.[47]

Medical officers were generally pessimistic about the prospects for lowering the incidence of STDs in the command since it was manifestly impossible to keep the men and women apart. Occasional calls for "stringent measures to prevent the further intercourse of men with native women" were unrealistic. One surgeon in Baliuag, Bulacan, pointed out that "consorting with native women can not be controlled when the troops are stationed in scattered town quarters." The experience on Siasi in the Sulu group illustrates the hopelessness of control measures. Venereal disease seems not to have existed there when a company of the Twenty-third U.S. Infantry first occupied the island in

September 1899, but it was rife just nine months later "due to the fact that many enlisted men are coming here from Cebu and Jolo where they have not had medical treatment or have failed to report the fact that they were diseased." The situation continued to deteriorate as infected men were transferred to Siasi from all over the Philippines. Those from Luzon, predictably, presented the worst problem. Since the men did not change their habits upon arrival, the epidemic was soon out of control. The medical officer finally despaired as he reported his lack of progress in venereal disease prevention: "The only effectual means under the sun would be to kill the women, or to castrate the soldiers."[48]

Two incidents illustrate the potential for the exponential spread of infection. The first was the subject of a sworn statement that Private Fred F. Newell signed upon his return to the United States about a gang rape he had witnessed in Naga, Cebu. The victim was a fourteen-year-old girl who had been seduced by a soldier in his company while she was employed as a servant to another soldier's querida. While on guard duty shortly after that incident, Newell saw the first soldier bring the girl into camp and take her into a bell tower where "twenty men had carnal intercourse all night with her." He asserted that "six or seven men out of the twenty caught venereal diseases from the night spent in the bell tower" and that later he had seen them treating themselves. The girl subsequently went to Cebu City and entered a house of prostitution, he said, where she undoubtedly continued to transmit the infection. The second incident led to Private Phineas Foutz's court-martial trial for murder. Testimony established that prior to his arrest he had been continuously infected with venereal disease and had undergone unsuccessful medical treatments in Liloan, Mandaue, Cebu City, and everywhere he had been stationed. He spent most of his time in brothels, flirting with young Filipinas, who "he liked better than our American women," or with his fourteen-year-old girlfriend, Geneviva Torres. An acquaintance described him as "the most passionate man I ever saw." He was arrested for killing Torres by repeatedly stabbing her with a blade concealed in the end of a cane. At the time of the attack he was still under care for venereal disease at the hospital in Cebu City, but the attending physician testified at trial that the patient was not getting better. The doctor suspected that the accused was either a masturbator or was having sexual relations during the course of his treatment. In either event, Foutz's sexual career ended abruptly when he was convicted and executed.[49]

Some American officials were alarmed about the consequences for the indigenous population, and though the concern manifested itself rather late, the rapidly deteriorating situation had made it genuine. In May 1901, the president of the Manila Board of Health, Major F.A. Meacham, formally reported that it was indisputable that syphilis was now "spreading among the native population of these islands, with what ultimate results we are fully informed in the past history of this disease among primitive peoples." Another board member cited the recent deaths of thousands of Hawaiians as an example of the potential harm to the Filipinos. During the same month, Chief Surgeon Charles R. Greenleaf said that the time had arrived for concerted measures to be taken "lest our forces become seriously crippled and an irreparable injury be done the people of these islands by those whose object is to help and elevate them." He pointed out that although the problem had always existed in Manila and the seaports, native women outside those centers had been free of infection as a rule. Recently, he observed, much venereal disease had been imported by women from Europe, America, and Japan, and by soldiers and sailors. The infections were currently spreading beyond Manila into the provinces, and since amicable relations between Filipinos and Americans were "nearly universal at the present time," it was likely that a large number of women would be infected with little prospect of cure. Official army statistics underscored the growing seriousness of the problem—while the rate of admissions among the soldiers for gonorrhea had declined 9.4 percent between 1898 and 1901, the rate for syphilis had increased by 103.6 percent.[50]

General MacArthur responded to the board of health report by issuing General Orders No. 101, which mandated twice-monthly examinations of the men and immediate treatment of those found infected. Medical officers were also specifically charged with placing all women suspected of being infective under surveillance so as to stop the further spread of disease. To do so, the officers were directed to invoke the aid of the municipal authorities. By then most towns had been returned to civilian government and had Filipinos in charge. Since those officials had been chosen for their apparent loyalty to the new regime, MacArthur may have expected them to cooperate with the program. To make sure, the army physicians were to stress that cooperation would result in improved health of Filipinos. The advice was sound but disingenuous since the army, as always, was only concerned with its own state of readiness. A 1937 study by the U.S. surgeon general's office concluded that MacArthur's order had been aimed at "detecting and giving early treatment to concealed cases of venereal disease" among the troops. It emphasized that General Orders No. 101 "was not intended primarily as a method of controlling the prevalence of the venereal diseases from the viewpoint of preventive medicine, but [was] a purely military measure for the purpose of increasing the efficiency of the Army."[51]

The surviving records are not nearly complete enough to allow an accurate estimate of the extent to which the soldiers were infected at the time of General Orders No. 101. Rates of 20 percent at Santa Rosa, Nueva Ecija, and 30 percent at Bugason, Antique, were reported at the first inspection thereafter, and it is probable that the overall incidence of infected men was within that range. Whatever the precise rate, it presented a clear peril to Philippine public health, given the intimacy of the soldiers and women. The program seems to have lowered rates of infection among the men at first, but the initial successes did not continue. Since hostilities had ended in most areas, local commanders were less and less likely to see the problem in the light of "military necessity," and vigilance was relaxed. Nor was it ever feasible to keep the men and women apart, so the twice-monthly inspections did nothing to prevent the men from becoming infected and perpetuating the disease in the interim. Most important, however, the medical officers never established any control over the women.[52]

The U.S. Army underestimated the difficulty of the problem. In earlier experiments with regulation during the American Civil War, the standard procedure had been for an infected soldier to report his contact to his commanding officer, who would then take steps to have her arrested and examined. That method did not work in the Philippines, despite scattered claims of success by some medical officers. The detection and disposition of infected females proved to be "difficult and unsatisfactory." As early as October 1901, for instance, it was obvious that the new regime was not working in Tuguegarao, Cagayan, as "considerable" syphilis and gonorrhea were reported. The medical officer explained the problem: "The attempt to locate the women has been unsatisfactory as the men insist they wouldn't know the women if they saw them again." In Tayug, Pangasinan, nearly 50 percent of all sickness among the soldiers at the beginning of 1902 was venereal.[53]

The control program could not succeed without the full cooperation of local officials, who alone had the ability to identify the women and the power to detain or expel them. Such help was often not forthcoming, and without it, as one American medical officer pointed out, "the treatment of the soldiers is only temporary." The "non-cooperation of the civil authorities" was specifically blamed for the failure to contain the syphilis contagion among the troops in Tuguegarao. The stated reason for the lack of official energy was usually "a lack of funds and material," which was always true but masked other considerations. In some cases, plain inefficiency probably played a part, along with the short-sighted view that STDs were an American military problem. Moreover, non-compliance with American desires on this and other matters was a manifestation of what Ileto has called "resistance-through-inaction." The American need for help presented Filipinos with an easy and natural way of retaliating for the accumulation of slights, humiliations, and resentments built up during the war, but different cultural and practical approaches were most responsible for the lack of support. Filipinos were more likely to understand the complexity of the problem, whereas the Americans tended to see only its medical aspects. From their point of view, the situation could be resolved if everyone would simply cooperate. The Philippine socioeconomic context, including the fact that the war and the American presence had created a dependency on U.S. dollars by the women and their families, was lost on them. Filipinos in power have never been known for extraordinary sensitivity to the tribulations of the poor, but many must have balked at the idea of arresting or harassing needy people simply to suit the convenience of the American army. From their standpoint, a crackdown on prostitution had as many drawbacks as advantages. Tacit toleration, on the other hand, accomplished a number of things aside from irritating the Americans. Most important, it left the money flow and possibilities for profit undisturbed. Prostitution had become too important for too many people for any municipal official to be too energetic about rooting it out.[54]

The threat to Philippine public health from cholera, malaria, beriberi, tuberculosis, and some of the other turn-of-the-century diseases has diminished. Smallpox no longer exists. STDs, by contrast, have soared into an appalling social and medical problem, and the emergence of HIV/AIDS has added a more tragic dimension. A century and a half ago, the Philippines were wrenched into the world economy as a society bottom-heavy with poverty and without serious cultural obstacles to sex-for-money. Increasing venereal infection was unavoidable, especially in the absence of effective medical treatment. But it is conceivable that more efficient and honest regulation could have held STDs to manageable levels and restricted prostitution largely to its traditional (albeit rapidly growing) foreign clientele. Confinement of the sex trade to enclaves in Manila and a few other port cities might have kept venereal disease from the general public throughout the islands. If that was ever a possibility, however, the American intervention in 1898 precluded it.

Smallpox: Failure of the Health Care System

No viable smallpox vaccine reached Bangued, Abra, in 1884 from the Central Board of Vaccination in Manila, and as a consequence, no vaccinations were administered anywhere in the province that year. Nor did any fresh lymph arrive the next year. Nor the next. Then in 1887 smallpox struck, attacking many people, according to the provincial governor. After six years without successful immunizations, Dr. Llanera tried to circumvent Manila by ordering vaccine directly from the vaccine institute in Gifón, Spain. Despite letters from the institute's director confirming that payment had been received and the vaccine sent, nothing ever arrived. Resigned to accepting whatever the central board in Manila would send, the médico titular awaited delivery. The crystals that finally came proved not to contain any lymph at all when he tried to reconstitute them. At the end of his patience, Dr. Llanera angrily absolved himself of all responsibility for future smallpox deaths and predicted that the critical situation in the province would continue "until God knows when." In 1891, he attempted once more to go outside of normal channels, ordering from the English pharmacy in Manila, but again received nothing. Utterly exasperated, the physician again warned his superiors at the Department of Beneficence and Health of impending disaster and asked sarcastically if the authorities in the capital imagined that all children in Abra were protected by immunity. He implored them to have the board send good vaccine immediately, but what was delivered during the next three years was worthless. His fears were realized in early 1894 when smallpox "with alarming characteristics" erupted again in a barrio of Bangued. The epidemic raged for three months with 50 percent mortality among those attacked. Residents later recalled that huts had been built next to the cemetery as temporary hospitals. So many died that almost all were buried without the priest's prayers. Dr. Llanera reminded Manila that no successful vaccinations had been given for over a decade. He ended his 1894 report on a skeptical note, expressing the "not infinite" hope that the newly opened vaccine institute in Manila along with a proposed system of universal vaccination and rigorous enforcement would rid the archipelago of the great evil.[1]

Smallpox vaccine was a recent accretion to the complex of beliefs and practices with which Filipinos approached the question of health. Their late-nineteenth-century conceptual model was an amalgam of three others. It comprised centuries of traditional beliefs and practices overlaid with a thick layer of Christian teaching and a thin crust of modern (i.e., Western) medical concepts. Filipinos have shown a remarkable ability to absorb exogenous ideas, often seemingly contradictory ones, and rework them into functional patterns. Their approaches to health and illness were no exception. The result was a culturally integrated belief system that, while not seamless, offered satisfactory explanations for one's state of health and various prescriptions for responding when it was challenged. The system worked as well as any other in the world under noncrisis conditions. Unfortunately, it was practically useless in the face of infectious epidemic disease. Filipinos had little protection other than natural resistance and a relative isolation from outside reservoirs. When those defenses became significantly impaired during the course of the nineteenth century, many were left almost helpless.

Indigenous beliefs and customs varied from region to region, but most Filipinos understood health to be a state in which individuals enjoyed a harmonious relationship with their environment, both natural and supernatural. That condition was manifested by physical vigor and freedom from incapacitating discomfort. Illness, by contrast, was thought to be the consequence of a negative relationship that caused a lack of ease, or "dis-ease," whether physical, mental, emotional, or spiritual. A wide array of nondisabling disorders that Western medicine classifies as disease, and thus treatable as such, were considered as *non*-health (as distinct from *ill* health) in the traditional scheme. Some, like insanity and leprosy, were thought to be innate or inherited and not treatable, and therefore lifelong sufferers were allowed to live in the pre-twentieth-century Philippine community unmolested, but also untreated. Other conditions, like venereal disease and measles, were annoying or troublesome but usually not incapacitating, and though their unpleasant symptoms might be alleviated, they were generally not thought to be worth bothering about.[2]

Causation, in the traditional view, was either natural or supernatural. If the former, little could be done since it was idle to attempt to control the course of nature. Natural happenings occurred in their own time and would pass away in like manner. The Filipino concept of time, like that in most agricultural societies, was geared to the rhythm of the seasons. Most Filipinos "believe that time functions as the *link* between nature and man," anthropologist F. Landa Jocano has written. Certain diseases tended to predominate at certain times. Malaria's appearance each harvest season in many areas, for instance, was explained not as a result of fetid emanations from the ground (miasma) or because the end of the rains created optimum breeding conditions for *Anopheles* mosquitos, but because it was *time* for it to appear. Colds and skin rashes were inevitable when it was time for the seasons to change. Bronchitis arrived when the winds shifted. It was natural that gastrointestinal complaints would be common as soon as the rains became heavy. Measles and smallpox could be anticipated with confidence in the dry months. So long as those seasonal and thus naturally caused diseases did not take epidemic form, no particular cause for concern arose; however, when they did, supernatural agency was apparent.[3]

Conditions that seemed to be caused by spirits of the earth, sorcery, and witchcraft demanded prompt attention lest they became incapacitating or fatal.

Even a headache, if supernaturally provoked, could develop into a dangerous condition if simply ignored. Thus, it was prudent to go to a healer for an appraisal of ill health or even non-health because only a specialist could determine the nature of its causation. Each community had its own traditional healers, who Jocano divides into two categories—major specialists and minor curers. They have always been highly respected. The residents trusted them (and still do) because they came from the community, worked within the local cultural framework, and drew their curative materials from familiar objects. They thus ministered to the psychological component of well-being more effectively than any outsider could. The primary physician was the herbalist, who diagnosed the ailment, at least preliminarily, and decided who could best deal with it. Five general kinds of treatment existed—herbal medicine, fumigation (sweating), and massage for physical manifestations, along with countersorcery and propitiation of supernatural beings for the spiritual aspect of the complaint. If the first kind were indicated, the herbalist would apply an expert knowledge of the medicinal properties of local plants, either by poulticing or rubbing the affected area of the body with plants in raw form, by smearing it with a liquid juice or sap extracted from the plants, or by having the patient drink a brew made from them. If one of the remaining types of treatment was needed, the sufferer would be referred to the appropriate specialist (usually a diviner, masseur, or sorcerer) or to one of a number of persons with ability to cure certain conditions. Medicinal and magico-religious treatment might proceed sequentially or together with the aim of restoring equilibrium or harmony between the patient and the environment.[4]

Christian beliefs were not seen as incompatible. Indeed, that model of health, as understood and absorbed into the existing cultural system, offered a second line of defense against the most serious conditions. The Church, in the person of the local padre, tended to ascribe them to the will of God or to the work of the devil. The priest knew which verses to chant in order to summon the help of the appropriate saints. Like the healers, he was respected, the more so the deeper his roots in the community. He was also the direct agent of God. As the two models blended over time, the Christian God came to be viewed as the one who ultimately dispatched saints and benevolent, non-Christian environmental spirits alike to help healers combat the panoply of demons and devils who were Satan's agents on earth. Filipino healers ascribe much of their power to religion, according to Jocano. "Even sorcerers reinforce their powers by having their paraphernalia blessed in the Church or at least drenched with Holy Water. The healer's most potent antidotes for serious illnesses are religious prayers, Holy Water, and sacred objects, possibly taken from the altar." All of the authority and power of healer and priest were needed when disease became epidemic. "The common folk consider epidemics as visitations from heaven or scourges sent by God," says Jose P. Bantug. Many believe that "the devil himself comes down in person to announce the epidemic, assuming the form and dress of a man, but with the feet similar to that of a cock." He appears in the guise of a familiar acquaintance, and whoever first answers him dies instantly. When such calamities struck, proper ritual was the only recourse. During the 1888–1889 cholera epidemic in Albay, for instance, the padres sought to alleviate the heaven-sent punishment by requiring the people to recite the "Tara Santa Mariang Hade" (Come Let Us Go to the Blessed Mother) each afternoon. When smallpox broke out in the same province, the healers sent parents to the river each afternoon to shout to the spirits, *Apo, dai man cami pagkuhac* (Spirit, please do not get us).[5]

The Spanish physicians imported the developing Western biomedical model of health during the nineteenth century. Most of them were torn between contempt for traditional healing and a realization that Western practitioners had much to learn from the herbalists about the properties of medicinal plants, which Dr. Martín noted "have a legitimate place in therapy." The best of the doctors would have welcomed a fusion of the various models, which in fact was happening but escaped notice because "superstition" continued to dominate. Aside from vaccination against smallpox and those principles of hygiene and sanitation that people could afford to practice, concepts of Western medicine made little headway in the Philippines prior to the twentieth century except among the socioeconomic elite in Manila and the other major urban areas. The Spanish médicos titulares rarely ventured outside the población except during epidemics, and their medical practice was limited to a tiny clientele who came to their clinics and could pay for the prescribed medicine. In 1877, the University of Santo Tomas in Manila began graduating Filipino médicos titulares who were trained in modern medicine, and those who were skilled in combining Western and indigenous practices were far more instrumental in melding the new approach to health into the Filipino cultural framework than were their Spanish counterparts. By all accounts, however, the most effective agents were those padres, Filipino and Spanish, who were able to mediate all three models by dispensing Western medicines in the barrios along with expertise in local pharmacology and guidance in invoking saintly assistance. The cumulative impact of Western medicine on popular beliefs was limited in the nineteenth century, however, principally because it was not demonstrably superior to the competing approaches. Although neither oil of *manungal* (coconut) nor prayers ever arrested epidemic disease, neither did flannel, camphor quills, or opiates. Too often the promise of smallpox vaccine proved empty as well.[6]

We do not know to what extent the Filipinos suffered from smallpox prior to the Spanish conquest. The disease had been endemic in parts of India, China, Korea, and Japan for at least a millennium, and regional trade contacts must have made periodic outbreaks unavoidable in the Philippines. The lack of a general demographic disaster on the heels of Spanish intervention may be circumstantial evidence that the population had long had reasonably frequent exposure to the virus. On the other hand, smallpox attacks were explosive in formerly isolated regions when it was introduced by Spanish contacts, so the fact that the experience in the Americas was not repeated may simply underline the low probability of contact throughout the archipelago. Fenner and his colleagues have accepted reports of early Dutch and Portuguese mariners, however, to the effect that smallpox was endemic in the sixteenth century on the larger islands of the Indonesian and Philippine archipelagos. Whatever the case may have been in the former group, it is most improbable that the virus was endemic in the sparsely populated Philippines. Smallpox cannot maintain itself in population groups of less than 100,000 to 200,000, and no island was that populous except perhaps Luzon. Even there, settlement was thin and communication irregular, and the likelihood of contact may not have been high enough to sustain the virus permanently.[7]

Indeed, the early evidence indicates that smallpox was not endemic. In a 1574 letter from Manila to the Viceroy of New Spain, Martín de Rada wrote, "A general epidemic of smallpox has raged here this year, which has spared neither childhood, youth, nor old age. I believe there are very few who have not had it (that is, of the natives), and many people have died of it." Although that description is hardly precise, it does not describe a reaction to an endemic infection. Once endemicity is established, smallpox becomes a disease of childhood, and outbreaks become less explosive across the entire age spectrum. Since the virus is constantly present, most adults will have contracted and survived it in their own childhoods and are thereby rendered fully resistant to subsequent attacks. Historical experience shows that a century or more is needed for that age-specific pattern to become established in a population. We would have to know just what de Rada meant by "many people" to judge how close to a "virgin-soil" epidemic it was. A case-fatality rate among adults under about 25 percent, for instance, would be evidence of previous importations within their lifetimes, as we shall see.[8]

The pattern of explosive outbreaks against a nonendemic background persisted throughout the archipelago. How devastating the eruption was in any community was largely determined by the periodicity of importations. Spanish control of Manila, which quickly became the principal port of entry for infections, increased the volume of contacts between that settlement and others. Beginning in the mid-1590s, Nueva Segovia (Cagayan) and the offshore islands experienced a series of smallpox epidemics during the pacification that were undoubtedly sparked by virus imported from Manila. The initial contagions were general throughout the populace, "attacking practically all of them and being very fatal." After four decades of repeated outbreaks, Diego Aduarte described smallpox there as "almost like a plague among the Indians." During the military pacification of Bohol more than a century later, "a contagious epidemic of smallpox showed and declared itself, which had stealthily and slowly gained a foothold in the city and spread through the villages in its environs, without escaping little or big of the very great population of the natives." In the Sulu group, smallpox apparently "made fearful ravages, and most of the inhabitants fled from the scourge" in 1608. Whether the introduction of the virus was connected with the "desultory war" the Spaniards had been waging there for several decades is unknown, but the disease was still not endemic two and a half centuries later. Charles Wilkes reported in the 1840s, before vaccination had been introduced in those islands: "The smallpox has at various times raged with great violence throughout the group, and they speak of it with great dread. Few of the natives appear to be marked with it, which may have been owing, perhaps, to them escaping this disorder for some years." Juan Antonio Tornos reported living through an epidemic on Leyte and Samar in the early 1760s in which "over thirty thousand people died; that is to say almost a third of the population, and in that proportion they must have died in the remaining islands." In 1789, the infection was imported on a vessel from China into the Ilocos region. Soon it was relayed to Manila and thereafter "spread desolation" in neighboring provinces.[9]

Those reports describe violent outbreaks that occurred at random intervals in generally susceptible population groups and resulted in high mortality across all age cohorts, thus indicating the absence of smallpox between importations. Where smallpox is constantly present in an unvaccinated population, however, epidemic waves become regularized, and uneven, age-specific susceptibility causes fatalities in the youngest and oldest cohorts and produces a progressively lower case-fatality rate in the others. Moderate eruptions at regular intervals punctuate the general pattern of low-level but constant smallpox mortality. By the mid-eighteenth century, most regions fell somewhere in between the poles of virgin soil and endemicity. Still unable to support the virus continuously, their traffic with other areas was sufficiently extensive to ensure regular importation, which modified early epidemic patterns. The evolution toward more frequent but less devastating outbreaks is evident in Pedro de San Francisco de Assis's remark during an outbreak in the población of Cagayan in 1756 that "the scourge of smallpox" had formerly been much greater in the Philippines.[10]

The point is relevant because the historical memory of the explosive early outbreaks served as the benchmark by which nineteenth-century officials judged the success of their vaccination program. They had no way, of course, of knowing about evolving patterns of epidemic waves, but they were intuitively correct when they asserted that the situation had been more horrible in the distant past. When they wrote, most Philippine communities were no longer virgin soil, so when smallpox erupted, fewer deaths occurred among persons over about five years of age, and case-fatality rates were generally lower. Unlike the other principal nineteenth-century diseases, smallpox (along with malaria) had been a major cause of mortality at least since the conquest. As patterns of infection shifted over the centuries in response to the changing total environment, mortality from smallpox relative to deaths from other causes declined, especially after the introduction of vaccination at the beginning of the nineteenth century. The more important issue is why Filipinos continued to suffer and die from the disease in huge numbers for a full century after the means were at hand to prevent infection.[11]

Smallpox is caused by the variola virus, *Orthopoxvirus variola*, and two subgenera of smallpox exist—variola major and variola minor. All cases of smallpox in the Philippines were of the former variety until the American troops brought the other. Five clinical types of variola major (or classical smallpox) are commonly recognized and are classified according to the nature and development of the rash—haemorrhagic, flat, modified, noneruptive, and ordinary. Case-fatality rates vary from nearly 100 percent in the haemorrhagic and flat types to almost zero with the modified and noneruptive types. The great majority of cases (88.8 percent in A.R. Rao's 1972 study of hospitalized patients in Madras, India), however, are of the ordinary type, with its characteristic raised pustules. Rao found that case-fatality rates among its three subtypes varied markedly—62.0 percent for confluent, 37.0 percent for semiconfluent, and 9.3 percent for discrete—with an average of 30.2 percent for all cases of ordinary type smallpox.[12]

Data unfortunately do not exist on the distribution of cases among the five variola major smallpox types in the nineteenth-century Philippine outbreaks. Information on how that distribution changed during periods of food shortage, war, or other stress would be even more helpful, but that too is unascertainable. The most severe cases—haemorrhagic, flat, and ordinary confluent—seem to correlate with an inadequate immune response, so if it could be shown that case-fatality rates increased in the late nineteenth century, we would have compelling evidence of a progressively debilitated population. But that is not possible. It is not even clear just what suppresses the immune response (both humoral and cellular) to the smallpox virus. Nor is much known about the effect of the various nonspecific mechanisms that form part of host's defenses. Age is certainly a factor, since immune systems function less effectively in the very young and the very old, and case-fatality rates are accordingly the highest at the extremes of the age spectrum. Hormonal changes also are important. Pregnant women have a much greater incidence of haemorrhagic smallpox, due to elevated levels of a chemical that results in impairment of the immune response. It is clear that malnutrition interferes with host defenses, but despite a few scattered indications that smallpox and malnourishment may be synergistic, the latter connection has never been proved. Nothing is known of the effects of multiple infection nor of the psychological stress of wartime conditions. Notwithstanding the lack of empirical evidence, few immunologists would be surprised if it were shown that either susceptibility to or gravity of smallpox increased as a consequence of the myriad of late-nineteenth-century assaults on Filipino host defenses.[13]

Smallpox infection is usually accomplished by the entry of particles into the nose or mouth, either by inhalation or by contact with contaminated fingers. The virus then multiplies within the mucous membranes of the upper respiratory tract, after which it spreads to the reticuloendothelial cells throughout the body and continues to multiply during the nine-to-fifteen-day incubation period. At the end of that time, the virus escapes into the bloodstream and infects the skin and mucous membranes. As the epidermal cells are invaded, the characteristic lesions are produced on the skin, and the virus is shed from them. At the same time, lesions form and ulceration occurs in the mouth, releasing the virus into the saliva. Depending on the type of smallpox, the pathogenesis covers the entire spectrum from a toxemia so overwhelming that the patient dies before the usual signs appear to an infection so mild that it goes unnoticed by either patient or doctor. Most cases, which are of the ordinary type, are biphasic, however, and have an acute febrile stage (comprising two successive but distinct fevers) that overlaps slightly with an eruptive stage. Together they last about thirty-three days. In about a third of those cases, the patient emerges permanently scarred from the eruptive phase but alive. In the others, sleeplessness usually passes into delirium, the second fever does not abate, and death results eleven to fifteen days after the appearance of the rash.[14]

Transmission of the disease normally results from direct interpersonal contact (contact infection). Dr. Gaudencio Ares was correct in 1884 when he attributed the prevalence of smallpox on Cebu to the close proximity in which the people lived. Modern investigators in Asia have established that almost all propagation occurred as a result of close family contacts, particularly between those who slept in the same room or bed. Transmission between persons living in the same house but who did not share sleeping quarters was the next most frequent method. The disease rarely spread between inhabitants of different houses, even when they were in the same compound. Filipino dwellings, most of which had but one room for sleeping, averaged five to six persons in each. In periods of upheaval and especially during the American war, when many people fled to the urban areas and hundreds of thousands had their houses destroyed, the average densities of living units increased significantly. Also facilitating transmission was what Ileto has variously described as the culture's "insistence that death and dying remain a social event" and its "refus[al] to dissociate . . . disease from the network of social relationships in which it appeared." Filipinos generally regard illness as a condition requiring the support of others, which takes the form of the physical presence, day and night, of relatives and friends. Western physicians noted disapprovingly that the stream of visitors tended to increase in direct proportion to the seriousness of the disease. When death arrived, it was observed by nine days of mourning, which included a feast lasting several days in which all who came to pay respects lived together in close quarters. Unfortunately, prevention of smallpox transmission and epidemic spread requires strict isolation of the patient, effective vaccination, surveillance of contacts, proper burial, and disinfection of the premises, bedding, laundry, and personal items. However socially useful the Filipino approach to death and dying was (and is) in most instances, it functioned as another of those "go" indicators for infectious traffic.[15]

Host resistance is the most important epidemiological aspect of infectious disease. It can be conferred by genetic inheritance (and then compromised as we have seen), but it can also be *acquired* either passively or actively, the distinction being whether or not the individual synthesizes his or her own antibodies. Passive resistance means that the host, usually a newborn infant, has antibodies but cannot produce new ones when the old ones are destroyed. The short-lived exemption from diseases to which the mother is resistant is acquired by the transmittal of her antibodies through the placenta and the milk. For Filipino infants a century ago, such passively acquired resistance was often diminished due to the debility of so many mothers. Resistance is actively acquired either naturally (by contracting the disease itself and surviving) or artificially (by vaccination). Both methods of actively acquiring resistance came into play with smallpox, so it alone among the major infectious diseases was vulnerable to control, if not eradication, in the nineteenth century.[16]

Each disease confers its own measure of actively acquired natural resistance on its survivors. Smallpox grants absolute, lifelong protection against reinfection. That fortunate circumstance reduces the number of susceptibles in the population and makes subsequent outbreaks less devastating than if the virus were introduced into a completely nonresistant society. Hence, the epidemiology of smallpox changes as the virus establishes endemicity in a population group. Resistance acquired by previous infection is vital to an unvaccinated community because it assures that smallpox epidemics cannot be an annual occurrence. Intervals between pre-nineteenth-century contagions varied according to the volume and frequency of community contact with external reservoirs, but the high birth rate replenished the pool of susceptibles so quickly that Filipinos could expect the next outbreak sooner rather than later.[17]

Vaccination was the great hope. Smallpox was the only infectious disease that was preventable by actively acquired artificial resistance during the nineteenth century. Complete protection rarely exceeds ten years, but an efficient revaccination program overcomes that problem. Furthermore, control does not depend on every last person being immunized. Rather, it is a matter of keeping the pool of susceptibles permanently below the level at which the virus can sustain the chain of infection. The concept of *herd immunity* explains why that is so and is the theoretical basis for modern eradication programs. It is a measure of the cumulative resistance of the group, which varies from disease to disease. Just as individual resistance decreases the probability that a person will contract an infection, so herd immunity reduces the chances that an epidemic will develop in a larger segment of the population. That is because the susceptibility of the group is less than the sum of the individual vulnerabilities of its members. Group resistance is the product of the number of nonresistants and the probability of their exposure to infected persons. Because not every susceptible person comes into contact with an infective, the probability of contact is the intervening factor that makes group resistance greater than would be expected from the total of individual susceptibles. Vaccination's promise lay in its ability to reduce the number of nonresistants in the population below a critical threshold under which the probabilty of contact is so low that epidemic spread is highly unlikely.[18]

The introduction of smallpox vaccine into the Philippines in 1805 and the vaccination program that followed has long been touted as Spain's finest accomplishment there. Following Dr. Edward Jenner's experiments with the cowpox virus and his development of a vaccine in the late 1790s, the Spanish court physician, Dr. Francisco Xavier de Balmis, brought the vaccine to Manila after first delivering it to New Spain and Guatemala. By transfer from arm to arm among twenty-five small children, the vaccine retained its potency during the ocean crossings. A smallpox institute and vaccination board were established by the end of the next year, and immunizations were being administered throughout the colony in 1808. Fifteen years later, Dr. Fernando Casas stated that the vaccine "was in use in all the towns of the thirty provinces of the country," but his claim was undercut by an admission that the program was not running smoothly. The government, he said, "having seen that nothing came out of the hints, advice and other mild means of persuasion, ultimately resorted to force, imposing punishments and punishing severely the justices and sub-alterns when they did not aid its beneficial intents." Others have been more credulous. Dr. Jose P. Bantug, a modern physician and historian of medicine in the Philippines, has likened the Balmis mission to "an epic poem worthy of the proudest years of Spain when the scepter of Castile lorded it over a vast colonial empire in which, as it has been truly said, the sun never set." Contemporaries talked the same way. One effused in 1838 that Balmis and his companions had the glory "to deposit in these Islands that inexhaustible source of health, prosperity, and growth of population." In 1876 Dr. Martín praised the vaccination program "for its perfection, for its results, and for filling a censurable lack that exists even in more advanced nations." Another observer said a year later that "nothing demonstrated the loving interest with which Spain regards the inhabitants of its overseas provinces more than bestowing on them this means of health . . . doing away with epidemics of such a terrible disease."[19]

Taken at face value, the archival record seems to support those rhetorical flights. It shows an apparently zealous and efficient vaccination apparatus, headed by the Central Board of Vaccination, which operated pursuant to detailed regulations issued in 1851, 1873, and 1893. In Manila was "a central house charged with keeping the vaccine viable in the children of the surrounding neighborhoods and of sending incessantly and in abundance crystals and tubes to the provinces where houses of vaccination have been established in the government or parish house of the towns." One or two Spanish general vaccinators worked in each provincial administrative center, backed by more than a hundred Filipino vaccinators scattered throughout the provinces, and numerous Filipino assistant vaccinators in the various pueblos and their outlying barrios. The files are choked with reports and statistics of numbers of children vaccinated and adults revaccinated throughout the colony each year. Statements by vaccinators, médicos titulares, and provincial governors attest to the efficacy of the program.[20]

The evidence belies the claims, however. The record does not tell us much about the period before the 1870s, but it is clear that the vaccination program functioned sporadically and ineffectively during the last quarter of the century. Whether that represented a sudden breakdown is uncertain, but Martínez Cuesta has taken a look at the evidence for Negros and concluded that vaccination had failed early in the century: "The authorities of the archipelago took no notice of the progress of vaccination, which they had introduced with commendable zeal." He points out that until about 1870, a single person was responsible for maintaining the vaccine supply and administering vaccinations for all of Negros and that just three years earlier, "a despicable attempt" to suppress his position entirely had nearly succeeded. The situation did not improve afterwards, either on Negros or in most other places. Dr. Felix Martín in Antique admitted in 1886 that "smallpox wears out all the provinces year after year," and five years later the journalist Pablo Feced lamented the "regular recrudescence of deadly epidemics." The new vaccine regulations of 1893 were met with withering sarcasm from an anonymous physician who saw them as a typical product of an Overseas Ministry bureaucrat who had no idea about Philippine conditions. The regulations proceeded on the assumption that the vaccination program was functioning with reasonable efficiency. Such was not the case, the doctor asserted, in a country where roads and bridges hardly existed and rains shut down movement altogether. Did the ministry suppose, he wondered, that the few vaccinators each had their own steamship to go to the various coast pueblos and a *globo aerostático* (balloon) to reach the ones in the interior. He picked out Article 31 of the regulations, which required that leftover vaccine be remitted from the provinces to Manila, as a representative piece of "silliness" born of ignorance about provincial towns and the service itself. "Leftover vaccine! With this system what is left over in the Philippines is smallpox."[21]

Data in the *Memorias médicas*, the *Calamidades públicas* (Public Disasters) files, and other archival sources compel the conclusion that Filipinos had little protection by way of vaccination. After 1870, scarcely a year passed without a serious epidemic breaking out somewhere in the archipelago. A partial list begins with the contagion that followed in the wake of successive typhoons that battered Manila in 1871. The parish priest of Binondo stated the next year that scarcely a fifth of those on the census roll for the San Jose area had survived. Cotabato had a serious epidemic in 1871–1872 as did Lepanto three years later. Leyte was hit hard in the early 1880s as was Pangasinan in 1883. Bad outbreaks occurred in Nueva Viscaya in 1883–1884, in Cagayan de Misamis and Capiz in 1886, and in Antique during the middle years of the decade. Contagion appeared in Abra in 1887 and in Camarines Sur and Davao during 1890. Dr. Gomez stated that the epidemics of 1872, 1880, and 1891 had killed a total of 45,000 persons in Iloilo province, and Ticao and Ilocos Sur were struck in 1891 as well. Bulacan, Pampanga, and Abra had epidemics in 1894, and Zamboanga did the next year. Numbers the U.S. Army recorded when it attempted to vaccinate the entire population during the war tell much the same story. More than a third of the 600,000 persons who presented themselves for vaccination on the central plain of Luzon early in 1900 had already had smallpox. The administrative officer there estimated that "50 percent of [the] living population have had the disease." The American medical officer in Aparri, Cagayan, reported that about 25 percent of the people there had previously acquired immunity from the disease. Army physicians turned away 2,200 of the 3,900 persons who came to be vaccinated in Pandan, Antique, for that reason. Those figures suggest that perhaps from 35 to 45 percent of all Filipinos contracted smallpox during the late nineteenth century.[22]

The official rhetoric should alert us to what historian Onofre D. Corpuz has called the "vast discrepancy between the paper regime and the working regime of Spanish colonial administration." The vaccination program, in fact, was notable not for its "perfection" but rather for its imperfection. The truth is that the effort to control and eradicate smallpox fell far short of the progress achieved in Europe, North America, and even on Java. Still, it would be a mistake to hold the Spanish bureaucracy entirely accountable, as Martínez Cuesta does. The difficulties of controlling smallpox in the Philippine total environment were a good deal more formidable than even the officials realized. The obstacle to success was a compound of popular attitudes about disease, a shortage of colonial finances, inadequate means of enforcement, administrative ineptitude, lack of technology, and the sheer difficulty of carrying out any program in an island world so far-flung and inaccessible. Ironically, the methods and resources the Americans later employed underscore the impossibility of the task the Spaniards faced.[23]

The popular enthusiasm that Filipinos have shown for various aspects of Western cultures, including medicines, suggests that the belief system would have accommodated smallpox vaccination long before it did had it only worked. Since it was not self-evident that vaccination was beneficial, however, many avoided it whenever possible. For one thing, they thought the procedure unnecessary. In accordance with their understanding of causality, smallpox inevitably arrived after the dry weather came and would just as surely disappear with the rains. In unusually bad years, appeals to the roving spirits responsible for the affliction seemed to have the best chance of success. Vaccination was apparently ineffective, given the fact that the disease always reappeared, and beyond that, it seemed positively foolhardy since it was thought to predispose infants to other skin ailments. Worse still, many were convinced that the procedure transmitted the smallpox infection itself, which would "carry them to the grave." Though Dr. José Amide Castro railed in 1883 against those who died "intractable to any rational treatment," one may wonder who was the more rational in light of his further statement that some Pangasinan residents who had been vaccinated were later attacked more severely than those who had not been immunized.[24]

Neither the delivery system nor the vaccine itself were adequate. On paper, the Central Board of Vaccination appeared equal to the task. Unfortunately, it lacked the financial resources, the personnel, and the powers of enforcement necessary for success, especially in the face of popular resistance. Like all branches of government, the board was chronically short of funds. Given the sorry state of the colonial treasury, the administration's highest priorities included public health only when a cholera epidemic was raging out of control, and it was unrealistic to expect increased funding for ongoing noncrisis programs. One consequence was that the service was seriously understaffed. Beyond that, local vaccinators were paid almost nothing and were unreliable as a result. Cutting costs at that level was shortsighted, as medical officials in the provinces understood. Dr. Llanera reported in 1887 that the assistant vaccinators in Abra were so underpaid that they could not be counted on to carry out the program in the outlying rancherias in the hills where the various non-Christian peoples lived. He pointed out that as long as the infieles remained unprotected, the entire province was at risk, and he asserted that disaster had so far been averted only because of the dispersed settlement in those districts. Similarly in Cavite, Dr. Juan Peres stated that the vaccinators were so poorly compensated that they commonly abandoned their jobs and that it was often impossible to hire replacements. Others stayed on the payroll, such as it was, but did nothing. Instead they regularly submitted padded or wholly invented totals of vaccinations and revaccinations, thereby making the official statistics almost useless as a measure of the extent of prophylaxis in the population. The problem may have gone further. In 1884, Dr. Octavio Janay reported cryptically from Nueva Viscaya that the vaccinators were "misusing" their positions and as a result it was impossible to "root out the deplorable superstition" that prevailed among the people and prevented rational treatment. Various other malfeasances were common enough for the governor-general a decade later to order all provincial governors to "pursue such abuses with zeal and energy, punishing those culpable with full rigor under the law." The one that occasioned the decree was "the pernicious custom of inoculation by substituting for vaccine the pus produced by persons with cases of smallpox more or less benign." The reform proposals that the médicos titulares routinely submitted always included urgent appeals for higher pay for all vaccinators. That recommendation, like most of the others, remained unimplemented, and smallpox control was impossible as a consequence.[25]

The immunization procedure was regularized, in theory at least. In the towns a public crier announced that vaccinations were going to be administered under the direction of the general vaccinator and that parents, school principals, and government officials should take themselves and those in their charge to the municipal building. Those who preferred vaccination at home could be accommodated for a standard fee. Immunizations in the barrios were accomplished more informally if and when an assistant vaccinator arrived. Adult revaccinations were often neglected, but when they were administered, more women than men were vaccinated, undoubtedly because it was they who brought in the infants and young children. Women were also more likely to be in and around their houses when the vaccinators came to the outlying neighborhoods. Even so, the authorities always complained that too many mothers hid their children and thus presented the constant risk of epidemics. Martínez Cuesta thinks, for instance, that perhaps a third of the children on Negros were vaccinated. Many men simply made themselves inaccessible.[26]

Since the central board had no actual enforcement power, it had no means of ensuring that all, or even most, susceptibles got vaccinated. In effect, vaccination was optional. Mandatory legislation complete with fines for noncompliance was on the books late in the century but had little practical effect since no punishment was prescribed, and attempts to carry out the law were not successful. Suggestions for reform were always predicated on the necessity for making vaccination truly compulsory and for punishing recalcitrant parents. Spain's relatively light military presence in the colony probably rendered that scheme impractical, even if the civil administration could have been convinced that the effort was worth supporting. The program's success thus depended on the willingness of local Filipino officials to pressure residents into getting vaccinated and helping to conserve the vaccine by volunteering for arm-to-arm propagation. Indeed, Batangas governor Manuel Sastrón conceded in 1893 that without some kind of compulsion to force mothers to bring their children to the local tribunal or the doctor's office, no one would get vaccinated. Some officials obviously cooperated, but it is understandable that many would have seen little reason to push such a controversial and unpopular program on the community. Dr. Peres claimed, unsurprisingly, that local officials were indifferent to the vaccination program, and as a result, apathy prevailed outside of the provincial capitals. Whatever the truth of that assertion, the subsequent American experience suggests that the Spanish campaign was bound to fail in the absence of actual coercion.[27]

Even had the entire population embraced vaccination without qualification, smallpox would still not have been defeated because the vaccine itself was often attenuated or even inert. Insufficient quantity and poor quality plagued control efforts everywhere in the world during the nineteenth century, but the difficulties involved in delivering potent and uncontaminated vaccine over distances in tropical conditions were almost insuperable. For most of the century, the board used human repositories to transport vaccine and to preserve it once there, as the Balmis mission had done. A susceptible recipient, usually a child, was vaccinated, and when the lesion (vesicle) was sufficiently developed by the ninth or tenth day, a portion of lymph was extracted therefrom and inserted into the arm of a second susceptible. That obviated the climatic problem but presented others. The vaccine could be conserved indefinitely by the unwieldy process of successive transfers, but in practice the vaccine source was usually lost as the chain was broken by immune reactions, accidental destruction of the vesicle, or by local administrative negligence. Arm-to-arm propagation also presented the risk of transferring other infections, particularly syphilis, from subject to subject.[28]

Increasingly, the usual method was to transport active virus in either liquid or dry form, especially after midcentury, when the use of animals to produce substantial amounts of vaccine was perfected in Italy. A vaccine farm using carabao calves in the production of lymph was established in 1850 in Manila. Although much simpler than the arm-to-arm method and without the risks of source loss and infection transfer, transportation in both dry and liquid states proved unsatisfactory. Each form was subject to extreme bacterial contamination and often left a scar that mimicked a successful "take" but provided no immunization. The provincial doctors found it difficult to reconstitute the dried lymph prior to use as vaccine, and development of an improved air-drying process would have to await the twentieth century. The liquid vaccine required refrigeration to remain viable, but ice plants did not exist in the Philippines until the Americans established them. Late in the century, glycerol was usually added to the preparations as a diluent and stabilizer. Glycerol proved to have antibacterial properties as well, but it also accelerated the inactivation of virus in above-freezing temperatures. Glycerolated lymph retained potency in the Philippines for no more than ten days in the absence of refrigeration. Thus the longer the trip from Manila to the provinces, the less the chance that enough viable virus remained to raise a pustule and provide a measure of protection.[29]

Dr. Llanera's reports from Abra, summarized earlier, provide the best insight into the true state of the vaccination program. Médicos titulares in Lepanto, Nueva Viscaya, Pangasinan, Cavite, Camarines Sur, Romblon, Antique, Capiz, and Iloilo had similar experiences. In areas more remote from Manila, the program seemed not to function at all. At the end of 1871, smallpox spread by boat from Zamboanga to Cotabato via Basilan and Pollok and set off a serious epidemic. The official correspondence between Zamboanga and Cotabato during the following months contained much advice on prevention and treatment ranging from sanitary measures to drinking tea and warm milk. Vaccination, either past or prospective, was never mentioned. The distribution of deaths equally among all age groups strongly suggests that Cotabato residents were unprotected by vaccination. The next year Governor-General Rafael de Izquierdo admitted to the Overseas Ministry in Madrid that "the vaccination is not done as it should be for lack of knowledge among those in charge of performing this function and the absence of a medical professor to whom to entrust the supervision of this most important service in the majority of the provinces."[30]

In most instances the vaccine proved useless, as in Abra. Some of the physicians were honest, frustrated, or angry enough to acknowledge the true state of affairs. In 1886, vaccinators in Antique could manage only a 5 percent success rate on children after two rounds of immunizations. Vaccinations were discontinued thereafter as the majority of pueblos ran out of vaccine and no viable lymph arrived in 1888. Dr. L. Villamil blamed the situation on the "incompetence of the service." In neighboring Iloilo, Dr. Gomez asserted that during the period 1890–1893 "the practice of vaccination here has been completely discredited." Thus it may be that virtually no viable smallpox vaccine was delivered to the island of Panay for at least seven years. Matters were the same on Luzon, even though the provincial doctors were much closer to the distribution center in Manila. That Abra's case was not exceptional is shown by Dr. Monserrat's angry charge in 1888 that the hard work of many people in Pangasinan had produced no results because the central board had failed to send good vaccine despite his repeated requests. Consequently, vaccination had been totally abandoned and the prestige of the program was almost nonexistent. The people "judge by what they see," he remarked acidly.[31]

The 1891 epidemic in San Fernando and San Jacinto on Ticao occasioned no such outburst from Dr. Bibiano Nolasco, whose almost identical yearly reports attest to the ineptitude of his superiors in Manila who tolerated them. Fortunately, the only three changes that he (or his clerk) made each year in his reports—vaccination statistics, numbers of births and deaths, and notation of epidemics—provide data that reflect either on the quality of the vaccine or on the efficiency of the immunization program, but probably on both. Throughout the 1880s, the annual vaccination reports, compiled from numbers submitted by the vaccinators, duly indicated that an average of about 200 children a year were vaccinated in each of the two pueblos, in addition to the adults revaccinated. Since only about 150 babies were born each year, some of whom must have died without having been vaccinated given the high infant mortality rate in the islands, the figures may have been inflated. The other possibility is that many young children (here and in other provinces where numbers of reported vaccinations exceeded the number of available children) were revaccinated again and again and counted in the vaccination column each time, presumably as a result of the low percentage of successful takes. Whatever the truth, in 1889 for some reason that Dr. Nolasco did not reveal, the vaccinators outdid themselves, allegedly vaccinating 598 children in San Fernando and 1,112 in San Jacinto. Numbers of immunizations returned to their usual levels during the next two years, by which time both pueblos should have had nearly absolute protection. Nevertheless, smallpox erupted in 1891, attacking a total of 430 persons and killing 92 of them.[32]

As Dr. Llanera had suspected, the new vaccine farm did not improve matters substantially after 1894, but the experience in Zamboanga raises the possibility that unsettled conditions in parts of the colony presented more of an obstacle than did shortcomings at the new production facility. Smallpox epidemics appeared throughout the islands that year, creating a serious enough situation for the colonial administration in Manila to appropriate Pfs 10,000 for emergency relief with unwonted speed but with little effect. Early the next year, a troop ship from Iligan imported two cases into Zamboanga and set off a deadly outbreak there. The doctor's subsequent silence about the quality of the vaccine he received almost daily from Manila suggests that what arrived was satisfactory. Certainly the frequency of shipments indicates a great increase in quantity. Unfortunately, the new farm never had a chance to realize its potential since vaccination was virtually abandoned during the revolt against Spain that began in late 1896. We can expect that systematic work in the parish records will show abnormally high levels of smallpox mortality, at least in Luzon's Tagalog region, during the period of fighting in 1896–1897. The high proportion of scarred persons that the American vaccinators met on the central plain a few years later not only included the survivors of that episode but presented a living record of the failed vaccination program.[33]

To demonstrate that the immunization campaign did not work well is not necessarily to conclude that it was wholly useless. Owen has speculated in passing that vaccination may have substantially reduced smallpox mortality in the nineteenth-century Philippines. Fenner, on the other hand, seems to contend that vaccination had little effect. The truth, I think, lies somewhere in between, but the available data will not tell us exactly where. The information on smallpox in the *Memorias médicas* is overwhelmingly descriptive rather than quantitative, except for numbers of reported vaccinations. Common sense says that vaccination must have had a beneficial, if limited, effect. After all, if the vaccine had *never* worked, the doctors would have said so. Some percentage of the population obviously presented positive reactions, and even a dismally low take rate would have served to lower the pool of susceptibles and the case-fatality rate, if only slightly. Even Dr. Llanera said in the 1880s that epidemics were not as frequent as they had been in the distant past. Yet it is also plain that various regions were completely unprotected by vaccination for periods of up to a decade, at least after the mid-1880s. Dr. Ares claimed that in certain years Cebu had pueblos in which "scarcely 10 percent were free from the sufferings of the affliction." By the time American soldiers landed, the reservoir of nonresistant Filipinos had been filling for years. The explosion of smallpox thereafter indicates that the population had hardly more protection in 1898 than in 1805 when the royal expedition had landed.[34]

It should be possible to devise a statistical tool to help interpret more closely the existing data and any that may come to light. Studies in Asia during this century have shown that in populations unprotected by vaccination about 25 percent of those attacked died. The rate could fall as low as 15 percent in groups containing some vaccinated persons. On that basis, the 21.4 percent case-fatality rate on Ticao in 1891 indicates that the thousands of immunizations provided some, but not much, protection. Records of Philippine case-fatality rates would go far toward solving the problem, but the médicos titulares almost never reported those statistics, undoubtedly because they were either unavailable or unreliable. Still, let us assume that the average smallpox case-fatality rate was between 15 percent and 25 percent and that between 35 percent and 45 percent of all Filipinos contracted smallpox. That means that between 5.25 percent and 11.25 percent of the population died of the disease. In other words, 88.75 to 94.75 percent of all Filipinos died of some cause other than smallpox. In any statistically average year, then, smallpox mortality could be expected to fall within that 5.25 to 11.25 percent range as a percentage of total mortality. To get total numbers of expected smallpox deaths in any year, we need the total population counts (the Christian population increased from about 5.5 million in 1876 to about 7 million in 1902) and the average annual death rates (the best estimates for the 1870s, 1880s, and 1890s are 3.05 percent, 3.61 percent, and 3.20 percent, repectively). Death rates obviously fluctuated wildly from year to year, but taking 1876 as representative, 167,750 persons died that year. Smallpox should have accounted for some number of deaths between 8,807 and 18,872. That rough method can be used to derive the expected range of smallpox mortality for each year. The high end of the scale would be about 25,200 at the end of the century.[35]

Those calculations yield some benchmark figures by which to gauge, however imprecisely, the effect of vaccination. At the outset, the fact that from 35 to 45 percent of the population apparently got smallpox is strong evidence, standing alone, that the effect was minimal. That observation aside, it is safe to conclude that a community or other population group in the Philippines was unprotected by vaccination whenever it appears that (1) smallpox deaths as a proportion of total mortality exceeded 11.25 percent or that (2) the case-fatality rate among those attacked by smallpox exceeded 25 percent. An ambiguity arises, however, when smallpox deaths are within or below the normal range of proportionate mortality because the indicated protection might have been conferred by a recent epidemic instead of or in addition to vaccination. Thus, the formula should be seen as a measure of acquired resistance, not simply vaccination prophylaxis. The necessary data that have so far come to light are sparse. In the first category, it appears that smallpox deaths in Ilocos Norte never exceeded 3.4 percent of total mortality in any of seven reported years between 1876 and 1891. In Cavite, however, smallpox represented 14.0 percent of all deaths in 1876, and more significantly, five of its pueblos recorded proportions of between 30 percent and 45 percent. Iloilo province must have registered even higher proportions if Dr. Gomez's figure of 45,000 total smallpox deaths in 1872, 1880, and 1891 is credible. In the second category, a few examples of case-fatality rates exist. Nueva Viscaya and Antique reported rates of 8 percent and 3 percent in 1884 and 1886, respectively. On Ticao in 1891, as mentioned above, 21.4 percent of those infected succumbed despite seemingly total prophylaxis. The rates were much higher in areas where we know that vaccinations were not being administered—more than 40 percent in central Iloilo province in 1895, more than 50 percent in the Tayum, Abra, epidemic the previous year, and 54.5 percent in Minlagas and Medina, two barrios in Cagayan de Misamis that the vaccinators had not reached in 1886.[36]

Applying the foregoing to Owen's calculations from the parish records of Tiagon, Camarines Sur, and interpreting them in light of the qualitative evidence suggests that it will be possible to improve our understanding of what happened. In that parish, deaths from all causes averaged 160 per year in the 1880s and 151 per year in the 1890s before jumping to 443 per year during the war years and shortly thereafter, 1900–1905. No smallpox deaths were recorded between 1882, when the full series of records begins, until 1890, which reflects either extraordinary good luck in avoiding imported virus, a devastating epidemic just prior to 1880, an efficient vaccination program, or merely incomplete record keeping amidst the confusion of the two cholera years. The rest of the province may not have been so fortunate during the 1880s, however. In his annual report for 1888, Dr. Delgado said that the death rate in Camarines Sur remained stable from year to year so long as the normal diseases prevailed, but when cholera or smallpox appeared there were "great calamities." He may have had a premonition of what was coming next as well because he noted that the vaccine he was receiving was not good, due to the sea voyage and local humidity. Predictably, epidemic conditions prevailed two years later, at least in Tiagan. The parish statistics indicate that smallpox as a proportion of total mortality there in 1890 and 1891 was 29.4 percent and 22.6 percent, respectively. Two more outbreaks occurred, at about five- or six-year intervals, between which the pool of susceptibles was replenished. In 1896, 13.5 percent of the deaths were due to smallpox, which indicates a minimal level of prophylaxis, although the widespread immunity acquired by the survivors five years earlier may have done more to limit the epidemic than any sudden improvement in the vaccine. But the disarray in vaccination after 1896 is evident in the 26.4 percent proportional figure registered in 1902 amidst the great cholera epidemic.[37]

From the available evidence, then, it appears that the effectiveness of vaccination varied widely from region to region and from year to year. (In interpreting the fragmentary data, it should be kept in mind that every area had its own epidemiological rhythm, which depended on the frequency of its contacts with external reservoirs, the timing and extent of its last outbreak, and its birth rate, among other variables.) Owen is probably right to suggest that vaccination was beneficial over the entire nineteenth century. The dangers of colonial rhetoric have been noted, but José Montero y Vidal's assertion that the introduction of vaccine in 1806 initially "had a marked effect in diminishing the effects of smallpox" seems plausible. That would accord with the experience elsewhere in the world, where for some decades mortality declined significantly and epidemics were less severe. But Fenner and his colleagues point out that after the first successes, all countries experienced a resurgence of smallpox, though only to a fraction of the previous levels. They attribute the setbacks to contamination of the cowpox material, shortage of lymph, theological and philosophical objections, and the failure to appreciate the necessity of revaccination. It seems reasonable to assume, until we know more, that a similar but more extreme pattern occurred in the Philippines. The early successes, though real, were probably not as great, especially in areas distant from Manila. The fact that the people distrusted vaccination so thoroughly late in the century is some evidence of that. If it had ever been clear that the vaccine worked, some measure of popular faith in the process would have been still evident just two or three generations later. Then when smallpox resurged, it probably returned to levels not far below those in the pre-Balmis era, at least in those areas where the vaccination program collapsed altogether.[38]

The possibility exists that despite all the setbacks, the vaccination program functioned well in some places. The case of Ilocos Norte is intriguing and suggests that the determining factor of success or failure was the quality of the local administration rather than time and distance from Manila, climate, or efficiency of the central board. Médicos titulares and governors in that province consistently reported that smallpox was not a major health problem. Only one minor flareup is reflected in the (incomplete) set of reports between 1876 and 1891. All the officials attributed the province's good fortune to the careful conservation of lymph and the "zeal" of the faithful and competent vaccinators. It is certainly conceivable that they were exaggerating or even lying, but a cover-up of any significance seems unlikely. Of the *Médicas memorias*, the Ilocos Norte reports contain the most complete statistical data, and nothing suggests that smallpox deaths might be hidden in other categories. The most plausible explanation is that the province really did administer the immunizations with care. The impressive numbers of reported vaccinations and revaccinations may be reasonably accurate, and officials probably took pains to ensure that what potent lymph they did receive from Manila (whether in human repositories or not) was preserved by arm-to-arm transfer. The ability to propagate the vaccine's potency *after* it reached the provinces is almost certainly the key to understanding why the program was more successful in some places than in others. Protection would have been substantial in the best-administered municipalities. It is likely that in Ilocos Norte success fed upon itself over time and that the people there came to have more trust in the process than elsewhere. Unfortunately, however, the experience there seems to have been the exception that demonstrates the general rule.[39]

Filipinos paid dearly for the herd immunity that they were acquiring actively and naturally during the last part of the century, as attested by the many smallpox survivors the U.S. Army vaccination teams later turned away because they were already fully resistant. That protection probably averted utter disaster when the war broke out, however. What happened was bad enough, and it could have been of little solace to the families of the thousands who died of smallpox during the war that the Americans were eventually able to confront the disease more effectively than their predecessors. Smallpox was one of the diseases the U.S. Army's medical department particularly feared. Army regulations required that all recruits be successfully vaccinated, but medical officers took further preventive action after the expeditionary force mobilized in San Francisco. All soldiers were vaccinated there or aboard ships disembarking in the islands. Vaccine was more reliable in the United States than in the tropics, but serious problems of quality plagued control efforts. One private in the Thirty-first U.S. Volunteer Infantry had been vaccinated on five occasions in Kentucky, where he had resided during three epidemics since 1892, before finally getting smallpox after enlisting in 1899. Those who developed the infection before leaving California were detained on Angel Island and eventually vaccinated eight times. Despite all the precautions, however, smallpox cases arrived in the Philippines.[40]

The relationship between imported smallpox and outbreaks throughout the archipelago during the war is uncertain. On the one hand, it is doubtful that a great many undetected carriers crossed the Pacific. For one thing, the incubation period only averages twelve days, while the voyage took five weeks (if no time was spent in Hawaii) and thus afforded substantial opportunity for detection and isolation of infectives. The absence of explosive outbreaks among units with clinical cases indicates that the vaccination of the troops was generally if not completely successful. Nevertheless, transmission among the soldiers continued all the way to the islands. That such a long chain of transmission was possible was shown much later in the Intensified Smallpox Eradication Programme after 1967, where it was determined that villages in India and Bangladesh were not to be considered free of infectives until six weeks after the onset of the last known case. In the Philippines, the relatively few carriers who did slip through may have caused substantial damage. It is clear that the variola virus differs from continent to continent so Filipinos would have been highly susceptible to whatever North American isolates did arrive. Indeed, something analogous had happened less than a decade earlier when serious epidemics were set off on various islands, especially Panay, by smallpox imported from Spain to Manila and from there disseminated throughout the archipelago.[41]

Certainly the potential existed for harm. A substantial reservoir of the variola virus existed in the United States in the late 1890s. Variola major had resurged during the 1860s in many parts of the country, and epidemics had occasionally swept through the civilian population in the vicinity of military posts. After those explosions, though, variola major resumed its gradual decline in the mid-1870s. Then in 1896 variola minor smallpox was imported into the United States for the first time at Pensacola, Florida, via a case of unknown origin but probably from the Caribbean or southern Africa. By the time the first troops assembled in San Francisco two years later, infected areas included all of the country east of the Rocky Mountains, except for the upper Midwest, New England, and the southeastern Atlantic seaboard. During 1899, variola minor spread to those regions as well. Because the new strain was unfamiliar and presented such relatively mild symptoms, doctors were initially confused, and thus army health records do not distinguish between the two forms among Philippines-bound soldiers. We know only that smallpox continued to arrive with the troop trains in Oakland throughout the war. Private Joseph Estes enlisted in the Eleventh U.S. Cavalry in Oklahoma City in early 1901, about the same time that Private Joseph Kelly signed up in Minneapolis. Smallpox prevailed in both places. Estes afterwards claimed that he had often met cases in the street on his way to and from work. The infection, though widespread, was so mild and so few fatalities resulted that people did not think it worthwhile to take to bed. By the time Estes and Kelly reached the eruptive stage, they were bound for Manila on the *Kilpatrick* and had already infected Sergeant Claude L. Long. Variola minor has almost never appeared anywhere in Asia except for the Philippines, and it is certain that U.S. soldiers from places like Oklahoma City and Minneapolis were the means of introduction. Despite its low case-fatality rate, Filipinos were ill-equipped to carry any additional burden of disease.[42]

However, many more smallpox deaths resulted from the spread of virus contracted in the Philippines than from direct North American importation. Epidemic smallpox erupted initially amidst the confusion in the besieged capital as American and Filipino forces prepared to attack the Spanish-held city in August 1898. Shortly after Manila was occupied, two cases developed among the Thirteenth Minnesota Volunteers and were traced to a laundress who was discovered fondling her infected child with hands wet from washing the regimental laundry. Chief Surgeon Lippincott saw little cause for alarm, though, and reported in October that no contagion among the troops need be feared. Matters became more serious the next month when cases continued to appear in the army, and others developed among the two thousand or so imprisoned Spanish soldiers awaiting transportation home. One U.S. soldier later recalled that it was about this time that "the spread to the American troops caused the

Army Medical Corps to view the general health and living conditions of the civil population of Manila as being pertinent to the well-being of the American command." The new board of health reopened the Spanish vaccine farm so as to end dependence on unreliable vaccine from San Francisco and Yokohama. All American and Spanish troops were promptly revaccinated, a corps of six city vaccinators was hastily organized, and as many as eighty thousand civilians were immunized.[43]

Still, there was no real sense of urgency until late December, when cases among the Twentieth Kansas Volunteers were traced to twelve infected residents across the street from batallion headquarters in the Binondo section of Manila. The army medical department promptly revaccinated the entire regiment, but ten Kansans died within the month. By then every American soldier had been revaccinated at least four times since arriving in the islands. Nevertheless, it was reported that the disease "still hangs on," and the medical officers admitted to "much trouble and anxiety." With tensions rapidly building between the erstwhile allies, no one was taking the smallpox threat lightly any longer. The contagion smoldered in Manila until the outbreak of war on February 4, 1899, after which "the density of the populations in the central portions of the city increased probably 100 percent, due to the burning of the suburbs and the terror existing among the people living in suburbs not burned." Smallpox suddenly erupted again, killing seventy-five civilians, and for the next three years the disease flared throughout the Philippines wherever anticipated invasion created fear and set the population in motion. The huge pool of young children who had not been vaccinated due to the collapse of the delivery system after the beginning of the revolution made epidemics inevitable.[44]

In the western Visayas, for instance, smallpox preceded the occupying forces during 1899. Erupting initially on Guimares Island in January, the disease was epidemic when the Sixth U.S. Cavalry reached the La Carlotta–Valladolid area of Negros Occidental in July. No record exists for that year, but 522 cases and 193 deaths were reported during the first half of 1900, when the outbreak was presumably subsiding. The typhoid-carrying Twenty-sixth U.S. Volunteer Infantry landed on Panay in November 1899 and discovered more than 50 smallpox cases within a half-mile radius of the main road in Molo. As the soldiers pushed inland, the epidemic peaked in Pototan but was still claiming ten victims daily when they arrived. Early the next year, they found 384 cases and about fifteen to twenty funerals a day in Barotac Nuevo and a raging epidemic around Banate and Anilao, with every house reportedly infected. The disease was so general among the poor fishing families that the medical officer deemed it impractical to isolate cases or to destroy houses. Similar conditions greeted the occupying army on Luzon north of Manila. Smallpox was either epidemic or subsiding from recent outbreaks in every pueblo. It was so prevalent on the northern edge of the plain that medical officers anticipated some infection among the command, noting ominously that a substantial proportion of the people had never been vaccinated. One report explained that transmission was facilitated by "the free mixing of troops with the natives in their homes, in numerous vino [palm wine] selling places, and in gambling resorts." American soldiers and the operational capability of the command suddenly seemed to be at serious risk. Urgent measures were needed.[45]

Since it was impossible to prevent soldiers and civilians from mixing, a different approach was required, especially as the Filipino army's developing guerrilla strategy made it likely that American troops would be living among the people for an indefinite period. The new policy was based on a report by Major L.M. Maus from Bautista, Pangasinan, in February 1900 in which he noted that smallpox was prevalent in every town because the people had been unprotected for some years, and the disease was "not rare among our troops as a consequence." It would "not [be] possible to stamp out this disease among our soldiers, in spite of the frequent and careful vaccinations practiced among them, until the natives are themselves protected." Although smallpox was "quite fatal, [it] appears not to be dreaded," and that casual attitude among the people and their refusal to isolate infectives left the army no choice, he contended, but to inaugurate a rigorous and wholesale immunization program. Orders were promptly issued to vaccinate all people within the limits of the division, which included the seven provinces immediately north of Manila. Within five months, 606,697 persons were either vaccinated or certified as protected by previous infection or vaccination. The army then undertook mass vaccination in all occupied areas. In the Visayas, where the disease was extensive, vaccine shipped on ice from a new farm in Iloilo after May 1900 ended reliance on lymph that was attentuated by the time it arrived from Manila. American medical officers were ordered to cooperate with Filipino doctors, and vaccination was made compulsory in some places, like Iloilo City.[46]

Even where American occupation was not extensive enough to enforce mandatory vaccination, the medical officers were pleasantly surprised at the lack of popular resistance. One line officer wrote from Pototan that "a good many submitted freely to vaccination—which was unexpected." During a three-day period in early 1901, 3,990 residents presented themselves voluntarily at the hospital in Pandan, Antique (population 12,162). Why people suddenly came forward after a century of avoidance is unclear. The presence of the U.S. Army was surely seen as a potentially effective means of compulsion, but maybe smallpox had been disastrous enough during the war to overcome some of the traditional antipathy to vaccination, or perhaps people associated the power of the army with the effectiveness of its medicine. In any case, the combined effect of pacification, a nearly empty pool of susceptibles, and immunization provided the population with effective acquired immunity. Mortality statistics for 1902 and 1903 bear that out—no smallpox fatalities were recorded during those years out of the 3,632 deaths in Potatan and Pandan. The successful immunizations there and elsewhere may have provided a radical discontinuity with past experience sufficient to impel changed beliefs and behaviors. As popular resistance to vaccination began to break down, the cultural groundwork for future control efforts was laid.[47]

Popular acceptance of vaccination was obviously not total and unqualified, however, since some degree of coercion was deemed necessary if the army was to be protected from smallpox by immunizing the entire population. Vaccination was forcibly imposed during General J. Franklin Bell's Batangas campaign in late 1901 and early 1902. There, as a means of antiguerrilla warfare, the army confined all residents to twenty-eight towns designated as "reconcentration zones." To prevent an outbreak of smallpox among the American troops engaged in the pacification effort, eighty Filipino vaccinators were hired and put to work in parties of two, accompanied by a detail of U.S. soldiers. Orders were given that "the party should enter first the most crowded houses and drive the inmates to the farthest room, then working at doorway natives are led out singly and each of any age not showing pock-marks, vaccinated." The board of health provided plenty of glycerolated carabao virus, and about 300,000 persons were vaccinated in two months with successful takes ranging from 30 to 80 percent in the various zones.[48]

No statistics exist on annual smallpox mortality for the Philippines prior to 1902, in which year 14,106 deaths were recorded as part of the far greater mortality from cholera and malaria. By then fighting had ended in most regions, although life remained unsettled. The official figure increased to 20,359 the next year before receding to 10,146 in 1904. The high number in 1903 represents 6.2 percent of all deaths that year, which only indicates that several years of epidemics, along with vaccination, had almost depleted the pool of susceptibles. Just how much higher smallpox mortality had been in the preceding years we can not know. One clue may lie in Dr. Victor Heiser's much-quoted statement that smallpox had claimed more than 40,000 lives annually "during the Spanish regime and for some years after the American occupation." Dr. Heiser tended to use overly high round numbers, and his figure is certainly wrong if he intended it as an average annual toll for the whole of the Spanish era or even for just the nineteenth century. Nevertheless, his access to officials in the former administration and their records, such as they were, made him the best-informed American about the state of public health as it had existed in the 1890s. His numbers seem perfectly reasonable for the war years. I am inclined to accept them tentatively as additional evidence of the complete breakdown of vaccination between 1896 and 1900 and as further testimony about the inadequacy of the immunization program in general. Heiser's estimate puts the 1902–1904 totals into perspective as the tail end of prolonged levels of abnormally high smallpox mortality. Deaths continued to fall thereafter as American and Filipino civil officials continued to administer a coercive smallpox control program that eventually achieved the successes that the Spaniards have long claimed for their campaign. It had taken a full century, capped with a spasm of death thanks to two colonial wars, but as peace returned to the islands the promise of the Balmis mission began to be realized.[49]

CHAPTER 5

Beriberi: Fallout from Cash Cropping

THE YEAR 1882 became the most disastrous on record in the Philippines as epidemic cholera ravaged the archipelago from end to end, trebling the average annual death rate. The disease arrived in Manila from Zamboanga during August and killed one out of every ten persons before abating in October. Just after the contagion peaked, a severe typhoon battered the city and left most families temporarily homeless. The flood waters that submerged low-lying areas for weeks and the high cost of scarce construction materials prevented many from rebuilding their houses immediately. In the midst of such misery, according to resident German physician M. Koeniger, "an illness appeared among the natives that was new to them and at the beginning carried off its victims without exception in a few days or weeks." In the epidemic's first stages, the mortality rate was higher than he had ever observed with any disease. The terror already prevailing increased even further when health authorities officially acknowledged the new outbreak, and word spread that its malignancy and occasional glandular swelling indicated bubonic plague. Dr. Koeniger quickly recognized the disease as beriberi, identical to an affliction prevalent in Japan and known there as *kakke*. He persuaded the Spanish medical administration in Manila to publish that somewhat reassuring information, "which successfully calmed minds agitated by the widespread belief in the appearance of the plague." The disease nevertheless "spread quickly across the province of Manila and the neighboring districts along the coast and raged with the same intensity through November and December before gradually diminishing from January on."[1]

Although no one understood the implications at the time, the appearance of beriberi provided dramatic evidence of the interrelationship between the public health and changes in the total environment. Observers like Dr. Gomez in Iloilo who had watched the commercialization of the world economy extend the range of various agents of infection were not surprised in the least by the cholera epidemic, but they missed the closer association between the evolving pattern of crop specialization in Southeast Asia and the deadly new affliction. Experts outside the Philippines in the early 1880s focused attention on the disease itself. They were divided as to whether beriberi was caused by a nutritional disturbance or a specific poison of miasmatic origin. Dr. Koeniger was correct in rejecting the latter hypothesis, but since vitamins were unknown and thiamine had not yet been isolated and synthesized, neither he nor anyone else understood that victims were suffering from a noncommunicable disease resulting specifically from a deficiency in the dietary intake of vitamin B_1.[2]

Two years after the Manila outbreak, Dr. Kanehiro Takaki developed effective preventative measures following a nine-month Pacific Ocean voyage of the Japanese naval vessel *Riujo* on which 169 of the 276 sailors had contracted kakke and of whom 25 died. Suspecting an imbalance in the ratio of carbon to nitrogen in the navy's diet, Takaki performed a famous experiment in which he added meat and dry milk to the stores of another warship about to make the same voyage. Only fourteen crew members of the latter ship were attacked. His remarkable findings were published in leading Japanese and English-language medical journals by 1887. Unaware of Takaki's work, Dr. Christian Eijkman, a Dutch physician working in Java, found in 1890 that feeding a diet of polished rice to fowl produced a fatal polyneuritis, or paralysis, accompanied by histological changes in the nerves resembling those in human subjects afflicted with beriberi. He also discovered that both rice bran and rice germ had preventative effects. Further progress was made after the turn of the century, but even though the miasmatic theory had been eliminated as an explanation of disease in general, the experts continued to disagree on whether the causative agent of beriberi was a bacillus, a nonbacterial toxin, or a dietary deficiency. The latter explanation eventually was proven, of course.[3]

Unfortunately, all of the foregoing breakthroughs were academic with regard to the Philippines. Despite the fact that enough knowledge was available in the late nineteenth century to prevent and cure beriberi, physicians in the islands apparently remained oblivious to the findings in Japan and Java. It seems surprising in retrospect how slowly such discoveries became known even to those with the expertise to apply the new knowledge. We find, for instance, a U.S. Army medical officer in Zambales during 1901 who was worried about what he supposed to be the infectious nature of beriberi. He had discovered two cases in the local hospital and immediately gave orders that they be "treated in isolated quarters [with] every precaution possible being taken to avoid its spread." More startling, given the known effect of the Japanese discoveries on the spectacular performance of its navy during the 1904–1905 war against Russia, is that the American and Filipino health experts who conducted the 1909 Taytay medical survey were still not positive about what caused beriberi, though they tended toward the "rice theory."[4]

Even if Spanish health officials had grasped the implications of what Takaki and Eijkman had found, effective action would have been difficult. The commercialization of the Southeast Asian economy, a process under way for at least a half century by then, had set irrevocable economic forces in motion that altered Philippine dietary habits, reduced thiamine intake to dangerously low levels for many, and thus prepared the way for the emergence of beriberi. Unless the government was prepared to provide meat and milk for the people as the Japanese navy had for its sailors, no solution was possible, since those items were scarce and far beyond the budgetary reach of most families, and it was not yet realized that legumes and leafy vegetables would also suffice. In any event, the problem persisted long after the secrets of the disease had been fully revealed and assimilated by all health providers. Beriberi ranked among the five leading causes of death in the Philippines as late as the 1960s, a statistic that illustrates as well as any other the relentlessness of poverty.[5]

The change from subsistence to cash-crop agriculture determined subsequent patterns of Philippine impoverishment more than any other historical factor. The transformation must be understood in the wider context of the regional and global economies, of which it was a small part. Following Robert Clive's procurement in 1763 of the revenue collection in Bengal, inputs of both British and Indian merchant capital started a flow of agricultural commodities, including rice, from eastern India to the West. Thereafter, improved ship and sail design, lower insurance costs, and better port services conjoined with restructured Western supply and demand to incorporate Southeast Asia into the world market. A "loosely integrated international trading system" developed, according to Peter A. Coclanis, in which "European merchant capital, supported when necessary by state power, succeeded during this period in regularizing and routinizing such trade and in shifting its emphasis from high-value preciosities to bulk commodities, of which rice was one." By the mid-nineteenth century, exports from Bengal, Lower Burma, and the Dutch East Indies had established Asia as the West's principal source of rice. The rich valleys and deltas of the Irrawaddy, Chao Phraya, and Mekong rivers had long produced some rice for export, but as Owen has written, the trade was "characterized by frequent government interference, limited volume, and low prices." Fearing famine, each kingdom had traditionally sought to ensure adequate domestic reserves, so at times export was banned altogether, and at others it was subject to royal permission or special license. Then in the 1850s, Western pressure to remove trade restrictions became irresistible. The seminal event was the British seizure of control over the Irrawaddy delta and the opening of Rangoon to world commerce after the second Anglo-Burmese War in 1852. King Mongkut had begun the process in Siam the year before and eventually made concessions to the British in 1855, permitting rice exports at a set duty. After an unsuccessful attempt to intervene in Vietnam at Da Nang towards the end of the decade, a Franco-Spanish force attacked again further south and accomplished "the opening of the port of Saigon to the commerce of the world" on French terms in 1860.[6]

The Southeast Asian rice-export industry grew dramatically thereafter. Steam power and the Suez Canal helped tie European markets to the supply at Rangoon, Bangkok, and Saigon/Cholon. Mills were built in those port cities, and total paddy acreage expanded about threefold between 1850 and 1914. To ensure a continuous supply of rice from cultivator to miller-operator, "a complex network of rice brokers, agents, market towns, credit, and internal transportation" developed. The governments generally were facilitators of the rice trade rather than active participants. By keeping restrictions on commerce to a minimum, the rulers allowed private traders a relatively free field. During the four decades after 1863, exports of rice from Burma, Siam, and Cochin China grew more than seven times. The result was more complex than a one-way drain to the metropolises, however. A shift in commercial relations within Southeast Asia occurred that was based on a division of labor whereby the lowland-delta regions of the mainland (themselves extended or opened with Western investment) were used to grow rice to feed the inhabitants of insular Southeast Asia, who produced cash crops like sugar, hemp, coffee, coconuts, hardwoods, and tin, not only for the world market, but for a fast-growing, intra-regional Southeast Asian trade. The 4.8 percent annual growth rate in rice exports, which probably quadrupled the rate of population increase throughout Southeast Asia, was sufficient to cover any rice deficits that the island societies might incur by devoting their energies to the production of other crops.[7]

Demand was worldwide. Each mainland producer had its own favored markets, but together they exported rice in substantial amounts not only throughout Southeast Asia, but to Hong Kong and China, India and Ceylon, Africa, Latin America, and Europe. Smaller quantities reached Russian Asia, Australia, and Oceania. A number of trends are evident from Owen's statistics for the period 1872–1911. The most striking is that exports to Southeast Asian ports grew at the expense of those destined for more distant locations. The opposite might be expected, given the continuing advances in long-range sea transportation, but Southeast Asia's rapidly growing population and its new regional system of crop specialization created a huge need for rice. The proportion of rice going to Europe declined steadily over time, falling from 54 to 35 percent. At the same time, destinations on the periphery of Southeast Asia—India, Ceylon, Hong Kong, China, and Japan—increased their collective share from 30 to 40 percent, while Southeast Asia proper recorded the largest proportional growth as mainland exports to Singapore, the Straits Settlements, Federated Malay States, Netherlands East Indies, and the Philippines rose from 16 to 25 percent of the total. The rapid growth of that internal sector was largely due to Singapore's development as the region's major entrepôt. Operating on the basis of what W.G. Huff has called *bookkeeping barter*, the city's Chinese traders provided the link between rice-producing and rice-consuming areas on the western rim of the South China Sea. Crop or commodity specialization and export expansion, the engines of regional economic development, were promoted because Singapore gave the three rice basins "access to a growing regional market for food." At the same time, producers in Malaya and Netherlands East Indies "could exchange tin and tropical produce for rice, obtain finance, and reach new and growing markets in the West."[8]

The systemic and cooperative aspects of the intermeshed economies are clear two centuries later, but Spain's liberal economic reformers did not recognize those facets as the era of agricultural commercialization dawned in eighteenth-century Southeast Asia. The competitive aspects were more evident, and the Philippines seemed to be in a particularly favorable position. The archipelago's regional diversities promised to make the Spanish colony the most successful producer of the widest range of crops. It lacked easily extractable minerals, but proyectistas thought that none of the other political entities in Southeast Asia could match its agricultural potential. Tobacco, indigo, coffee, coconuts, fibers, sugar, and lumber were each perfectly suited to one or more regions of the Philippine island world. So too rice. Filipinos traditionally had little interest in producing more rice than they consumed, and if the locusts and miasmatic fevers (i.e., malaria) did not come, there was usually enough. Then amidst the zeal to exploit the land, the colonial administration decided to promote the expansion of rice production so that it too could become an exportable cash crop. Early in the nineteenth century, work was begun on a system of ditches, irrigation canals, and dams that, with the later introduction of waterwheels, permitted double cropping and established Pangasinan as the granary of the Philippines. In 1836, just after officially opening the Port of Manila, the government authorized free commerce in rice, as long as the grain's domestic price did not exceed that fixed by decree at the beginning of the decade. Free traders managed to do away with that safeguard against shortages two decades later. The royal order of 1856 declaring "completely free the commerce and exportation of rice and palay" went on to state that the new policy was based on the conviction that "to facilitate agricultural production no more powerful vehicle exists than freedom in agricultural transactions."[9]

The results were gratifying. One observer later wrote: "The production of rice increased to a truly wonderful extent from the moment exportation was permitted. Its value increased accordingly, and all of this with a crop that the natives previously would not grow [in surplus amounts] without the threat of severe punishment." Soon Pangasinan was not only supplying much of the Philippines (through Manila) but was also exporting substantial cargos directly to China from Sual as early as the 1830s, two decades before that port was officially opened to overseas trade. The production of rice for export drove development on the northern part of the central plain. Immigrants from the Ilocano provinces helped push the frontier east, opening rice lands in the newly formed pueblos. An internal exchange system quickly developed, as Mendoza Cortes explains. Towns on the Lingayan Gulf coast sent small boats carrying salt, nipa palm wine, and nipa leaves (for house construction) south on the Agno River to Camaling, where those products were exchanged for rice brought in from interior towns on horseback and by water. Chinese and mestizo traders in Lingayen, the commercial center of the gulf, then arranged for the export of rice not consumed by coastal residents. By the late 1850s, ships loaded with rice made about two hundred departures from Sual each year bound for Manila while another sixty ships went directly abroad. After the American war, a Filipino official in the Bureau of Agriculture recalled those days: "There were years when the crop was so abundant that there was not sufficient labor to carry it from the field, even though each laborer was given one-third of the amount which he could cut per day, and the rice was abandoned in the fields for lack of labor."[10]

The logic of free trade compelled one final legislative step. In mid-1857 it was decreed that importation of foreign rice and palay would be permitted through the end of the coming harvest season. Then late in the next year, another royal decree announced that such shipments would be permitted thereafter at all times. Rice imports commenced immediately and actually exceeded exports in 1858, but that was an aberration, since during the next decade and a half the Spanish colony sent out almost eleven times as much as it brought in. By the 1870s, however, the economy's problems became evident as the other Philippine cash crops were affected by violent price fluctuations in the world market. The archipelago's agricultural potential was still unquestioned, but Spain clearly did not have the financial, technological, or administrative resources to compete successfully under such unsettled conditions. Concessions to reality had been made since the beginning, the most important being that of allowing foreign interests to take the lead in facilitating the development of the public riches. To maximize the share of the profits that would remain in the Philippines, it now seemed necessary to encourage the fullest possible expansion of the more lucrative cash crops despite the increasingly unpredictable world market. Thereafter, newly opened lands throughout the archipelago were more often planted to sugar or hemp, and later tobacco, than to rice. Although acreage devoted to paddies increased absolutely throughout the islands, it began a relative decline as its share of the cultivated land dropped from about 50 percent in 1870 to 45 percent by the end of the century.[11]

The move toward regional crop specialization had disastrous effects everywhere. Even in Pangasinan, which continued to rely on rice production for export, it was "the competition of foreign rice in Manila [that was] the original cause of the rapid impoverishment of this province since 1870," according to Governor Peñaranda. Even though the value of its rice exports had remained at about the same level, "standing still is a decline," he insisted. In the meantime, no effort had been made to diversify crops, with the result in Pangasinan, for instance, that indigo and coconut cultivation was neglected, no coffee or cacao was produced—"not even for consumption by a group of families"—and farmers showed no interest in planting an intermediary crop of corn. Because the Port of Manila had become the focus of the external rice trade, nothing remained of the Lingayen Gulf factories and shipyard, "where once sailed first-class ships like the *Bella Vascongada*." Other manufacturers had not picked up the slack; in fact, "industries, properly speaking, don't exist." The process in the abaca-producing Bikol region was representative of areas that developed an exportable cash crop other than rice. Owen has concluded that while rice production there may have actually doubled during the nineteenth century, the number of those who had to be fed increased more rapidly yet. The problem was first addressed by rapid expansion of the existing interregional Philippine rice trade in which production on the Bikol plain around Nueva Caceres supplied deficit areas in neighboring Camarines Norte and Albay. The trade was accelerated "as the region's population growth showed a distinct shift toward upland areas suitable for abaca cultivation and coastal towns accessible to trade—both lacking self-sufficiency in rice." By the 1870s, however, that solution no longer sufficed, and the region became a net importer of rice from Pangasinan at first and then increasingly from Saigon. "Kabikolan, though it continued to feed a majority of its own inhabitants, remained a chronic grain-

deficit region thereafter." Two decades later a government agronomist there
noted that rice yields had declined and concluded: "The usual harvests of 10–
25 hectolitres per hectare leave no hope that the Philippines can feed itself.
They remain tributaries to neighboring countries for their people's primary
necessity."[12]

Little concern was evident initially, however, as substantial foreign imports
began to supplement domestic production. In fact, the new commercial pattern
seemed more rational. Profits from the real cash crops would buy external rice
for less than it would cost to devote valuable land at home to ensuring absolute
self-sufficiency. Frederic H. Sawyer, an Englishman who lived in the islands
from 1878 to 1892, expressed the point as clearly as did any of the colonial
officials, declaring his opinion "that the cultivation of rice is the lowest use that
the land and the husbandmen can be put to." He argued that it was generally
a sign of progress when former rice-producing areas could begin to discontinue
its cultivation because "it is probably an indication that the cultivators are raising some more profitable crop, and earning money by exporting valuable produce, wherewith to import rice from countries in a lower stage of civilization."
Because the world market for agricultural commodities was increasingly uncertain, Sawyer should have been able to see that his idea was better in theory than
in practice. That aside, what neither he nor anyone else could know was that
the loss from the nutritional tradeoff would in any case more than offset the
benefits expected from the restructured trade configuration.[13]

The Philippines became a net importer of rice in 1873, and imports exceeded
exports in every year thereafter save 1874 and 1876. The transition was abrupt
and the reversal of the recent eleven-to-one export-import ratio complete. For
the period 1875–1902, imports of rice exceeded exports by a factor of eighty-
three, and by 1902, the American colony was purchasing more than 300 million
kilos of foreign rice annually and selling none of its own. Philippine transactions were made outside the Singapore bookkeeping-barter entrepôt system,
with virtually all of the imported rice coming directly from Saigon/Cholon in
Cochin China. In part, that was because Southeast Asia's integration into the
world rice market was a "sequential process," as Coclanis has explained,
"wherein insular areas (Java and areas along the Bay of Bengal) . . . were incor-
porated rather early, and the areas on the South China Sea (Siam and Cochin
China) rather late." In addition, most Philippine traders looked not to Singapore, but to Hong Hong, which "played a similar, if far lesser role" as entrepôt
in the area west of the Malacca Straits. Thus, Manila's purchases at Singapore,
Rangoon, and Bangkok were negligible, amounting to less than 1 percent of
exports from those ports. By contrast, Philippine merchants bought 10 percent
of Cochin China's exported rice during the two decades beginning in 1882.
Statistics for Philippine purchases by source do not begin until 1899, but during the next five years about 88 percent of all imported rice came from Saigon/
Cholon. The amount purchased varied widely from year to year, but extraordinarily high import-export ratios correlate with poor harvests in the Philippines
resulting from drought in 1878–1879, the end of the tobacco monopoly in 1881,

cholera in 1882, drought in 1885, epidemics and an epizootic in 1888–1889, and war, drought, and disease during 1899–1902. No statistics exist for the years of revolution in 1896–1897, but since we know that a food crisis existed in at least part of the Tagalog region, imports may have been substantial.[14]

After a quarter-century of such troubles American officials could still conclude that crop replacement had represented a net gain. The director of industrial information pointed out that until 1895, increasing rice imports had been paralleled by rising total exports of other products and that in any event "the net returns from raising exports and importing food are greater, not only to the landlord but to the laborers and to the Islands, than the returns from producing the food itself." The authors of the 1903 census stated more generally: "It may be said that, as a rule, the falling off in the production of rice has not resulted in any great loss to the population." They were absolutely wrong.[15]

The deficit in domestic rice production affected the population adversely in at least two ways. The first was an increasing dependence on a network of private buyers and merchants who controlled the supply and cost of imported rice. During times of crisis—that is, when local rice harvests failed for some reason—the obvious problem had always been how to provide immediate, short-term famine relief. Food shortages in the Philippines were traditionally limited in both area and duration, and sufficient rice always existed somewhere. The challenge was getting it to the affected area quickly and then ensuring effective distribution. The crucial factor was the power to control the various elements of the relief program—purchasing, transport, distribution. As the Philippines became integrated into larger trading systems, local Chinese merchants took over all stages of the relief process, and they often responded to considerations of profit rather than human need. As a consequence, those who needed the rice the most were not the ones who received it. In the old era of local subsistence production, in which there were no significant surpluses, the people in rice-consuming regions left themselves little margin for shortages due to locusts, storms, or sickness. The government could arrange emergency shipments to deficit areas from those that were untouched, but the meager production, inadequate storage facilities, and slow sailcraft hindered its efforts. If rice failed, the inhabitants fell back on secondary crops like corn or sweet potatoes, which they supplemented with whatever fruits, vegetables, and fish were available. In desperate years, they lived poorly on roots, tubers, sugarcane shoots, reeds, the inner portion of banana-trees, and anything else that grew wild and could be gathered. As the agricultural and commercial transformations limited access to a variety of foods and new town-centered living patterns eroded foraging skills, proportionately fewer people were able to endure periods of hunger.[16]

During the few decades after the 1830s, when free trade had produced rice surpluses and before the population outgrew them, more effective emergency food relief should have been possible. The response to a subsistence crisis in Kabikolan in 1845–1846 suggests that although the means for relief did exist, the necessary resolve did not. The main impediment in that case, according to

Owen, was the administration's insistence that the program pay for itself. Because the poor could not afford their own relief, they consequently received none of the rice the government shipped in. It went to the well-off instead. Private merchants quickly sized up the situation and concluded that it was not worth their while to arrange for grain shipments. Local civil administrators who had their own surpluses did not release them, and neither church nor private charity was adequate. While some mortality could not have been averted, the deaths that occurred after the rice arrived were preventable.[17]

The conjunction of the steamship with the evolving Southeast Asian commodity-exchange system increased both the amount of rice to be tapped and the speed with which it could be delivered to stricken areas. Those gains were offset, however, when the colonial government lost control of the relief process to the transnational Chinese network of purchasers and suppliers. The Americans encountered that system in late 1902 when war-induced food shortages were exacerbated by a sudden price increase throughout the colony due to the attempt of a "syndicate of Manila and provincial merchants" to corner the market and control the cost. The civil government attempted to purchase rice at its nearest foreign source, Saigon/Cholon, but found itself stymied by the syndicate, which had already bought up the supply. As a makeshift alternative, "first-class famine rice" was obtained at Calcutta, but it turned out to be "an inferior quality of red rice, which soon developed weevils." The administration tried to break the organization's stranglehold by selling most of the rice to a firm that had a fleet of small coastal steamers and could deliver it throughout the islands. Once it reached the various ports, however, the best of the lot was bought up by wealthy landowners, and the rest was distributed by local Chinese merchants who mixed it with even worse rice and sold it to the poor for just under the price of the syndicate-controlled variety. Officials claimed victory, but the advantage to the ordinary person does not appear to have been significant. Since the American administration had the means to act far more vigorously than its predecessor, it is a fair assumption that during the last three decades of Spanish rule, the Philippine poor had been entirely at the mercy of the various private intervenors who could acquire and control foreign rice in times of scarcity.[18]

The more important consequence of the Philippine imports was the substantial loss of vitamin B_1 from the diets of many Filipinos because Saigon rice was thiamine-deficient. Rice in its raw form contains more than enough vitamin B_1 to prevent beriberi even if no other source is consumed. Thiamine is located beneath the grain's outer husk in a skin known as the pericarp and in the germ. It is the milling process that is a fundamental determinant of beriberi. First, the husk is removed, but the grain retains both the pericarp and the germ, and hence the vitamin B_1. How much of it is lost subsequently depends on how thoroughly the milling is done. Virtually none remains once the rice has been highly milled, and any that does is gradually lost during storage. The rice can be processed even further to improve its appearance by rubbing the grains with talc to produce polished rice, which is favored by most consumers but is utterly bereft of vitamin B_1.[19]

Most rice grown and consumed in the Philippines before the twentieth century was only partially milled and retained sufficient thiamine to forestall beriberi. The crop was cut by hand and the grain then separated from the straw by one of several crude threshing techniques: tramping it by carabao or pounding it by hand, either by striking the bundles against a stone or pounding the straw in a large wooden mortar. It was then stored in the husk and hulled as required. According to Mallat's description in 1860, "The indian of the countryside . . . pounds it himself with the aid of his wife in his mortar or *losong*, each time he needs rice for his meals." The rice, still containing most of the vitamin B_1, was then cooked and eaten. A small but growing proportion of Philippine-grown rice was milled somewhat more thoroughly in crude mills, with motive power sometimes provided by animals or water, but most Filipinos who ate domestic rice at the end of the century still prepared it as their grandparents had. Unfortunately, more and more people were eating imported rice.[20]

The mainland rice-export industry diversified its milling and marketing capacities during the late nineteenth century so as to maximize profit and meet regional preferences. Rice had traditionally been shipped in paddy, or palay, form because it kept well on long voyages with the husk still on the grain. With the advent of faster sea transportation, exporters were quick to eliminate much of the bulk—and thus half of their freight expenses—by milling at the port of departure, though exporters would sell to specification. For instance, India was indiscriminate as to type, buying the cheapest available rice at the least expensive source. Europe imported a middle grade of rice, remilling and polishing it on receipt. Some was then sent on from Hamburg, Liverpool, Amsterdam, and other European ports to Cuba and Puerto Rico. (Spanish port cities like Barcelona and Seville were shut out. Domestic legislation to protect Valencian rice growers had produced the "shameful spectacle in which Spain participated [either as shippers or processors] neither little nor much in this flood of rice," from Southeast Asia to its own colonies in the Antilles.) China received shipment in paddy form, then milled it, consumed some, and reexported the rest to Japan. The Philippines would only accept highly milled and polished rice.[21]

Saigon rice was generally considered less desirable than that exported from Rangoon and Bangkok due to poor quality control and inferior milling machines. Cholon-based Chinese merchants bought directly in the up-country fields from a variety of cultivators. Palay from the various sources was mixed before being bagged and sent on junks to the mills in Cholon. If the palay got wet in transit, additional mixing occurred when it was set out to dry on arrival. As a result, according to Charles Robequain, "rice arriving at the factories varies widely in color, size, hardness and adherence of the husk." Since the husking, bleaching, and polishing machines could only be set for one type of grain, "a mediocre heterogeneous product containing large amounts of broken and waste rice" was turned out. To the extent that it retained some thiamine, it was healthier rice, however. Poor Filipinos would have been even worse off had the colony been integrated into Singapore's barter-exchange system, which would have provided access to the better-milled rice from Rangoon or Bangkok.[22]

The construction of the Manila-Dagupan railway line in the early 1890s stirred interest for the first time among foreign investors in the possibility of revitalizing rice exports from the central plain. By this time, the granary had moved east from Pangasinan to the newly opened lands of Nueva Ecija, but the railroad would be able to transform the relatively inefficient system of shallow interior waterways and poor roads into a transportation infrastructure that could make Philippine rice competitive on the international market. Western entrepreneurs had not been attracted by rice, as Owen points out, so long as "at any given time some other commodity was enjoying far more spectacular profits." By the 1890s, however, profits from Philippine cash crops were uncertain, and the more modest but steadier returns on rice suddenly looked attractive. Accordingly, steam-powered mills with high milling and polishing capacity were built along the Manila-Dagupan railway line at Calumpit, Geron, Moncada, and Bayambang. Governor Peñaranda wrote in 1891 with great anticipation about the "magnificent steam machine" that was going to be installed soon in Bayambang and would revolutionize rice production on the plain. His prediction was correct, but its fullfillment had to await the new century.[23]

The trade statistics are equivocal because the establishment of the mill coincided with agricultural recovery from the rinderpest-malaria-cholera years of 1888–1891 on the plain, but it looks as though the new steam-milling capacity may have had an immediate, but short-lived, impact on production. Annual imports had averaged about 70 million kilos since the dramatic jump from an average of 15,000 kilos in the early 1880s. Exports had dwindled to nothing. Then in 1893 imports suddenly dropped by more than 40 percent, to about 41 million kilos, and exports resumed, reaching in 1894 their highest level since 1876. Imports still exceeded exports thirtyfold, but had the trend continued, a less unfavorable trade imbalance would have eventually resulted. War and rinderpest foreclosed that possibility, of course. Statistics break off for a few years, and when they resume in 1898, rice was no longer being exported and imports had begun an 800 percent leap that would peak at over 300 million kilos just a decade after the aborted recovery had begun.[24]

Filipinos consumed three types of rice, according to E.D. Kilbourne, a member of the board for the study of tropical diseases in the Philippines: "that grown at home and pounded out by hand in large wooden mortars; that grown at home and submitted to milling of varying degrees of thoroughness; and the imported rice, all of which has been milled and polished abroad." Writing in 1910, Kilbourne reported that the first kind was eaten by residents of the rural areas and about one-half of those in the coast towns. The second and third varieties were consumed in the coast towns and their immediate riverine hinterlands. Most of the rice eaten in the islands late in the nineteenth century was thus still homegrown and handpounded, especially in rice-surplus areas. Eyewitness testimony by two American soldiers, W.B. Wilcox and L.R. Sargent, who traveled through Nueva Ecija during the harvest season on the eve of war, shows that the new mill at Bayambang had had little effect on local diets as of 1899. They noted the existence of the modern steam mill but reported that the people throughout the province still prepared their rice "very primitively, with implements that resemble on a large scale the mortar and pestle of the chemist." Everyone seemed to be engaged in threshing, often in groups of three and four with a musical instrument to mark the cadence. The two observers remarked that "we seldom in this district got beyond the muffled sound of the rice beaters."[25]

Consumption of the second kind of rice (more completely milled domestic rice) was increasing rapidly during the 1890s, however. Foreman reported that the new steam-powered mills "supply large quantities of cleaned rice to Manila and other provinces, where it is invariably more highly appreciated than the imported article." He also said that the Spaniard Don Manuel Pardo had opened a mill at Nueva Caceres and had commissioned the construction of a steamer in Hong Kong built specifically to carry Bikol rice to provincial markets. Because Pardo and his partners (or perhaps another group of Spanish investors) soon came under fierce competition from Chinese hand-mill operators, Owen has inferred that the market for milled rice "had developed to the point where it was worth disputing." The polished domestic rice aggravated the thiamine deficiency in Manila and other pueblos of rice-deficit regions by adding to the stock of nutritionally empty food, but the scale on which Saigon rice was imported after mid-decade suggests that the output of Philippine steam mills could have accounted for only a small fraction of total consumption before the end of the American war.[26]

Beriberi is not contracted by eating highly milled rice. If thiamine intake from other foods is adequate, eating polished rice is utterly harmless. Though various minimum daily requirements have been proposed, most experts would agree that intakes ranging from 0.3 milligrams for infants to 1.3 milligrams for very active males and pregnant and lactating females is sufficient to prevent beriberi. Since some of the vitamin is lost in storage, washing, and cooking as well as from the antagonistic activity of the enzyme thiaminase, which is contained in some commonly eaten raw fish, the daily Philippine thiamine requirement has been established at 1.94 milligrams and 1.71 milligrams for a very active man and woman, respectively (or 0.38 milligrams per 1,000 kilocalories). In addition to unmilled grains, the principal dietary sources of vitamin B_1 are fish, meat, eggs, legumes, and leafy green vegetables. Modest amounts will easily satisfy the daily requirement, but poor Filipinos ate little of those foods, except for fish. Still, beriberi is an extraordinary state, and victims in the Philippines have traditionally been those who for some reason have had to subsist for a few months on highly milled rice and almost *nothing* else. Inadequate intake need not last any longer than that for the disease to develop. The body does not store thiamine readily, and depletion of reserves can be experimentally produced in humans within twelve to fourteen days. Clinical symptoms usually appear between eighty and ninety days after the start of a thiamine-deficient diet. Thus, the recurring disasters that increasingly visited the Philippines late in the century, together with the growing reliance on highly milled rice, created the necessary conditions for the development of beriberi among the population, especially the urban poor.[27]

Dr. Koeniger's report of the beriberi outbreak in Manila that followed on the heels of the cholera epidemic, the typhoon, and the flooding in 1882 is an example of the process. He noted that neither the Europeans nor the Chinese were affected by beriberi. They ate a diversified diet that included large quantities of meat and fats. The former group, he asserted, consumed more meat in Manila than they would have done had they been in Europe. The indios and most of the mestizos, by contrast, lived year in and year out on "dry rice boiled in water and a little fish, as well as fruits and a few vegetables." But even that diet had not been available during the last half of the year because the cholera had arrived during the rainy season, a time when not much fishing took place and little fruit was eaten. Koeniger's remark that that interval was always the unhealthiest period in the islands is not surprising. And 1882 was extraordinary. The rivers and canals were polluted by the sewage of cholera patients so the water was considered to be poisoned, and no fish were available at all. Terror prevented the people from venturing outside their homes or daring to eat anything but rice. The majority of those most acutely affected told the physician "that they were so afraid of the cholera that for as much as two months during the raging of the disease they had not left the house." Under those circumstances, the thiamine reserves of even the better-off classes became depleted. Dr. Koeniger reported that "the rich Mestizos, Indian clergy, and others who later on suffered from beriberi confessed to me that for months they had lived solely on rice out of fear of contracting cholera."[28]

In the form of the disease that is manifested in adults, beriberi presents a range of clinical symptoms dependent on the degree of cardiac involvement. That, in turn, seems to be largely determined by the extent of the deficiency, combined with any number of stress factors (like physical exertion, pregnancy, lactation, alcohol consumption, and perhaps fear) that increase the victim's metabolic rate and hence the need for vitamin B_1. Three distinct types of the disease predominate in tropical Asia, each of which is apparent in Dr. Koeniger's description. The terminology can be confusing, but they are, in ascending order of gravity: (1) *dry beriberi*, otherwise called atrophic, neurological, paraplegic, or paralytic, (2) *wet beriberi*, variously referred to as subacute, dropsy, edematous, hydropic, or cardiac, and (3) *fulminating beriberi*, also known as fulminant cardiac, or Shoshin (named for the region in China where it was studied). In all its forms beriberi is the same disease, and a mixture of its characteristic edematous (swelling), neurologic, and cardiocirculatory symptoms is usual, though they vary in intensity and one predominates. The onset is generally insidious, but occasionally the first symptoms are acute and death ensues within hours, unaccompanied by the usual neurological engagement. Beriberi is absolutely preventable by the consumption of a diet that is thiamine-sufficient. The only cure for the disease is thiamine.

All three forms are potentially fatal. Dry beriberi develops in people subsisting on a diet containing 0.2 to 0.3 milligrams of thiamine per 1,000 kilocalories per day, just under the 0.38 milligram Philippine minimum daily requirement. Such individuals become depleted of vitamin B_1 and develop peripheral neuropathy of a mixed motor and sensory type. Degeneration of the nervous system is marked initially by the gradual onset of weakness in the lower limbs, followed by an inability to coordinate muscular movements. Beginning with foot and toe drop, the weakness gradually spreads to the thighs and to the arms, leaving the victim unable to button a coat or to walk without a cane. Wet beriberi is the consequence of an even lower intake of vitamin B_1. Persons consuming a diet that includes less than 0.2 milligrams of thiamine per 1,000 calories per day experience some of the neurologic manifestations of the dry form, especially as the disease advances, but cardiovascular signs are more prominent and more serious. A generalized puffiness develops, digestion is disturbed, and anorexia results. Circulatory changes begin, and the heart is often enlarged, having an altered beat that becomes rapid with the slightest exertion. Death is a not uncommon outcome in both the dry and wet forms if intake of thiamine is not increased. The fulminating form of beriberi can develop in those with either the dry or wet type of beriberi or in those without prominent symptoms of either. Fulminant cardiac failure—sudden and fatal—is apparently precipitated by a variety of physiologic stresses that increase the rate of metabolism, but the Shoshin form has an unpredictable aspect as well, since most who succumb are men who are otherwise healthy and have shown few signs of thiamine deficiency. Patients die fully conscious and in extreme agony.[29]

Most of the clinical manifestations of the adult form of beriberi are evident in Dr. Koeniger's account of the 1882 outbreak. Much of what he did not understand is clearer today. His report, for instance, of a far higher case-fatality rate among those who were attacked early in the epidemic was to him simply evidence that the disease naturally evolved from "pernicious" forms towards the weaker atrophic and hydropic ones as it spread in the community. What actually was taking place was that those who were the most thiamine-deficient developed beriberi first and died before vitamin B_1 could be returned to their diet. Lactating women, unsurprisingly, were especially vulnerable. "The most endangered group predisposed to beriberi seem to have been women in childbed. They fell victim to the disease at such a high rate that it was almost impossible at the beginning of the year to find wet nurses, and their price went up significantly." Those whose thiamine intakes were barely insufficient exhibited symptoms later, lingered longer, and usually recovered once life returned to normal—when the dry season arrived at the end of the year, fishing resumed, fruits became more abundant, and vegetables began to appear in the markets. The physician found that "after a duration of the disease for several weeks, often for months, most hydropic and atrophic cases improved slowly, with a gradual decrease of all symptoms." By mid-March of 1883, beriberi had almost disappeared.[30]

It is difficult to believe that Shoshin beriberi was not prominent in the Manila outbreak, but even the cases Dr. Koeniger describes as pernicious, as distinct from the milder atrophic and hydropic types, seem not to have ended in sudden cardiac arrest. Those who eventually died apparently did so quietly and only after the steady onset of the full range of usual symptoms, especially stomach discomfort and heart palpitations. "The patients were continuously restless and could not keep food down for days, being plagued by choking and vomiting. The body and heart weakened steadily, and finally the pulse could hardly be felt. In the end the patients lost consciousness and death came without a fight." That is not a description of the abrupt terminal stage of Shoshin. So far as it appears, the doctor's pernicious, or acute, cases seem simply to have been the most serious of the dry and wet types—those patients whose vitamin B_1 stores were depleted by October and had no chance of improving their diets before death.[31]

The German physician noted that no statistics on case-fatality rates were available, but given the lack of such data in the modern literature, his remarks are worth considering. "In the beginning, the general impression among doctors and laymen was that the disease was almost absolutely terminal. I treated a number of patients, however, who were stricken right at the start and still made it through alive." While hardly discounting the terrible ravages of the disease, he concluded that the common estimate in Manila of 60 percent mortality among those attacked in the first stages of the epidemic was "almost certainly too high." He said that his only reliable statistic was on absolute numbers of deaths. In Malabon, a pueblo of about 25,000 inhabitants seven kilometers from Manila (but he may have just been referring to the población), more than 300 succumbed from beriberi in less than two months. He hastened to add that Malabon was probably the worst afflicted of all the surrounding towns, an observation that is significant because of the town's traditional role as the trading junction that linked inland commerce between Manila and much of provincial Luzon. By the 1880s it had also become a major processing center for tobacco and sugar exports. Malabonenses had provisioned the capital with upcountry rice for a century, and the epidemic suggests that they were now the conduit for (Saigon) rice flowing in the opposite direction as well. In any event, Dr. Koeniger drew the conservative conclusion that "surely ... the overall number of victims in the capital and the surrounding province was several thousand." The scale of the Manila outbreak was matched in Iloilo, where 5,000 persons died from beriberi, according to Dr. Gomez. When it is remembered that the beriberi fatalities occurred during the worst cholera epidemic in Philippine history, we can glimpse the outlines of a real catastrophe. Recordkeeping was in absolute disarray that year so the usual sources of mortality statistics are generally silent, but the pattern was undoubtedly the same everywhere as beriberi followed cholera into the rice-importing towns, along the coasts, and up the connecting rivers throughout the islands.[32]

Dr. Koeniger's assertion that none of the physicians in Manila were familiar with beriberi when it appeared in 1882 is probably accurate. Prior to the introduction in the early nineteenth century of milling machinery that could remove the husk from rice, and with it the vitamin B_1, the disease was relatively rare in Southeast Asia, although it was beginning to appear with increasing frequency after the early seventeenth century. In fact, beriberi has existed in Asia for about four thousand years. References to kakke appear in Japanese documents in the early ninth century, but scholars conclude that the disease appeared infrequently since only a tiny privileged segment of society ate white rice. Ordinary city dwellers did not begin to eat the highly milled variety until sometime in the seventeenth century, and in 1691 a terrible epidemic resulted in Edo. Edema was said to be the characteristic symptom, but the fulminating cardiac type prevailed as well. Preference for the new rice spread to the Japanese populace in general around 1870, and for the next half-century, beriberi was one of Japan's major public health problems. Its course is less clear in Southeast Asia, but references to the disease in the Western medical literature begin with reports of an outbreak on Java in 1626 and become frequent enough in the nineteenth century to indicate a developing health problem.[33]

The history of beriberi in the Philippines is even less certain. In 1658, Father Francisco Colín wrote of a common disease (caused by the southeast wind blowing over the top of some volcanos, he thought) in the Malay archipelago "that they call Berber, which in some numbs the trunk and extremities, is accompanied by swelling and paralysis of the joints, and when the numbing reaches the chest and touches the heart, the patient dies suddenly." That description is strikingly similar to what we know of the epidemic in Edo at the end of the century. In a footnote, he said that "in the Philippines it is called *Beriberi*," so it is probably safe to assume, with Bantug, that Father Colín had been familiar with the disease during his many years as a missionary in the Philippines. Several other seventeenth-century sources refer to beriberi among sailors in the Manila-based naval fleet. One writer in 1619 referred to an outbreak during a campaign in the Dutch East Indies, calling the affliction "a common disease of the legs." The first nineteenth-century reference to beriberi concerns cases in Zamboanga, where a physician reported that "many people consulted me because of Beri-Beri" in 1852.[34]

Beriberi was thus not making its initial Philippine appearance in 1882, but no evidence has appeared to indicate that it had been a serious health concern before the last quarter of the century. Until then, the islands had been able to provide a sufficient quantity and variety of food along with unmilled rice to spare their inhabitants the worst effects of deficiency diseases. Traditional subsistence strategies and fallback diets afforded enough nutrition to see most people through local food crises until better times. By the 1870s, however, the growing dependence on imported rice began to increase the risks presented by lean years. The first signs appeared almost immediately. In his yearbook for 1877, Ramón Gonzalez Fernandez included something known as "berbu" in an informal listing of the nine or ten most common diseases in the Philippines, describing it only as "a considerable swelling of the stomach." Gonzalez was just compiling information, having no medical expertise himself, but it seems likely that the garbled report is an early harbinger of what was about to happen.[35]

The experience of 1882 illustrates a new conjunction of factors in Philippine life that could for the first time alter diets drastically enough to produce beriberi in its full-blown and fatal forms: urbanization, increasing poverty, cholera, and highly milled rice. The interaction was crucial. The first three elements had been present less than two decades earlier during the cholera epidemic of 1865 in Manila, but beriberi did not occur because the urban poor had not yet begun to eat Saigon rice. During the following decade the dietary change was made, but still no fatal outbreak of beriberi occurred. The missing element was the cholera. During the nonepidemic conditions of the 1870s, even the poorest urban consumers of Saigon rice could also eat adequate amounts of fish to keep their thiamine intakes at the minimum level to ward off deficiency. Cholera removed that safeguard not only by terrorizing people into refusing any food but rice, as Dr. Koeniger noted, but also by restricting cholera convalescents to a rice diet. Without knowing it, Foreman made the latter connection when he noted that "many who have recovered from Cholera become victims to a disease known as Beri Beri, of which the symptom is a swelling of the legs." Writing in the 1890s, he had seen the more recent 1889 cholera epidemic, so it is evident that the process then was the same as it had been in 1882 and as it would be again in 1902.[36]

The fact that beriberi is seldom mentioned explicitly in the *Memorias médicas* is frustrating but less puzzling than it might seem initially. First, the reports that survive tend to be clustered in noncrisis years when the disease would not have been a serious cause of mortality in the provinces, so except for Dr. Gomez's retrospective remark about the five thousand Iloilo fatalities in 1882, little discussion appears. The new affliction had occasioned lively debate in other forums, however. Dr. Mapa noted in 1887 that the "great sufferings" caused by beriberi were absorbing the attention of the public and press in both Iloilo and Manila while everyone searched for its cause. The newspaper debate focused on current theories that had narrowed the probable causative agent to poverty, mud, or Saigon rice, though he said that recent events in Capiz showed that the last, at least, could be eliminated from consideration. The failure of the 1886–1887 rice harvest in the province had necessitated the importation of a two-month supply of Saigon rice, and not one case of beriberi had developed. Unwittingly revealing why, he stated that many people had eaten vegetables, fruits, and roots until the rice arrived. The physician conceded that two months was a relatively brief period but was sure that it was sufficient for the disease to have appeared. Having seen cases in Manila in 1883 and 1884, he was positive that the agent of disease resided in the marshy, low-lying ground surrounding the houses of the victims.[37]

Second, little was known about beriberi in the provinces. Few of the médicos titulares had any direct experience with the condition since their patients were precisely those whose nutritional intakes were sufficient. Nor did any of the various people who gave information about specific deaths to the parish priests recognize in its symptoms a distinct disease. As a consequence, listed causes of death where they appear are of no assistance in trying to assess the role of beriberi. The data from Ilocos Norte and Cavite, for instance, contain the apparent cause of some twenty thousand deaths, and not one is specifically attributed to beriberi. Some clues exist, however. In 1876, Dr. Martín produced a detailed list of all known ailments in Ilocos Norte, and two of his categories— diseases of the circulatory and nervous systems—may include some beriberi cases. He thought the two systems were intimately linked, especially in the tropics, where the "dominance" of the nervous system and lack of education among indigenous peoples had left their intellectual faculties undeveloped. As a result, he thought, "palpitations" (of the heart) were extremely frequent, and nervous disorders with accompanying convulsions were present throughout the archipelago "in a considerable proportion." Dr. Peres was less given to theory. He merely listed the prevailing diseases in Cavite by season without comment, placing cardiac diseases second in the rainy months. Deaths from beriberi that did not fall into the foregoing categories were undoubtedly subsumed under catch-all rubrics like "other frequent diseases," which in the case of Ilocos Norte accounted for a little more than a quarter of all deaths (3,961 of 15,739) during the cholera year of 1889 and its immediate aftermath.[38]

Cholera did not reappear until 1902, but the war became a precipitating condition in the meantime insofar as it drove people to urban centers where dependency on Saigon rice became almost total because domestic rice production was crippled. Those who fled to the hills were at no greater risk of beriberi than if they had remained in their villages, but that was little consolation since they encountered malaria, dysentery, and malnutrition instead. Beriberi is more difficult to document than other diseases that occurred during the war because the American army was not worried about it except to the extent that their Filipino auxiliaries, the Philippine Scouts, might be affected. Westerners did not seem to contract the disease, so it posed no threat to the combat readiness of the American troops. Nevertheless, there are scattered references indicating that the civilian population suffered greatly. After the lowlands of northern Luzon had been pacified in 1900, Major Maus's report of the state of things there mentioned that "beriberi is frequent in the rainy season." In a report on U.S. Army medical department operations in the Visayas at about the same time, Major L.W. Crampton stated that although no beriberi existed in the command, it was prevalent among the civilians. On Panay, Colonel Dickman paused long enough during General Hughes's "pinching campaign" to note in a letter home that beriberi was one of three diseases that "decimate" the people.[39]

The postwar census confirmed the existence of beriberi in every province. Despite what was almost certainly a massive undercount, 5,666 and 4,766 deaths were attributed to beriberi in 1902 and 1903, respectively, making it the sixth leading cause of mortality behind malaria, cholera, tuberculosis, diarrheal diseases, and smallpox. Amidst the backwash of war and cholera, some people hid from the census enumerators, so the mountains of numbers contained in the four-volume survey are more impressive than they are precise. The data on beriberi are particularly suspect since methods for determining the cause of death were no better than they had been before the war, and the disease was not yet understood. Much of the beriberi is concealed in other categories. Writing a few years later, Dr. Maximilian Herzog identified malaria, tuberculosis, and dysentery as the most common complications of beriberi in the Philippines. When they were implicated, the prognosis was grave. Otherwise, patients usually recovered. Since each of the three complicating diseases were more familiar to most Filipinos, witnesses would naturally ascribe death to them, thus obscuring the actual prevalence of beriberi in the islands.[40]

Something much worse lies partly obscured beneath the haze of incomplete understanding and misleading statistics in the historical record. It is infantile beriberi—the hidden tragedy of Philippine cash cropping. Medical awareness of the type of beriberi that presented in babies lagged behind advances in understanding the forms that attacked adults. It was not even suspected that the manifestations in adults and infants were related until after Japanese researchers asserted in the 1890s that a mysterious disease in infants might somehow be connected to lactation in mothers with beriberi. Since infantile beriberi was not fully understood until 1920, no one in the Philippines had any insight into the affliction prior to the end of the American war. The disease usually occurs in infants who have breast-fed for at least one month from mothers whose milk contains inadequate amounts of vitamin B_1. The illness generally appears during the second or third month of life, especially in the ninth, tenth, and eleventh weeks. Nursing babies whose mothers subsist primarily on highly milled rice and who show clinical signs of thiamine deficiency are clearly at risk, but most of the affected infants nurse from mothers who exhibit only slight symptoms of beriberi. Thus, mothers who were never seriously affected by beriberi themselves, seeming instead merely anemic, actually carried nutritive deficiencies severe enough to ensure that their babies would die within four months of birth.[41]

Symptoms of the infantile form resemble those of the adult type, though the acute form (involving engagement of the digestive system), short duration, and grave prognosis of the former are significant enough differences to explain why no one associated the two types. Also, the onset of clinical signs and the subsequent course varies among infants. Some apparently healthy babies suddenly succumb from acute cardiac failure, whereas in others, development is more gradual and can run through the entire edematous, digestive, neurologic, paraplegic, and cardiovascular progression. Infants with beriberi are initially restless, querulous, and exhibit a generalized puffiness. Unlike the case with most adults, loss of appetite, vomiting, and excretion of green feces are usual. Paralysis proceeds not from the peripheral nerves, as in adults, but from the cerebral nerves. The first sign is a characteristic hoarseness and aphonia, or silent crying. Loss of reflex activity in the peripheral joints then follows, although that is not immediately evident to the untrained eye. Cardiovascular symptoms herald the gravest phase of the disease. Rapid heartbeat is more prominent than in the adult form, but the cardiac enlargement, venous engorgement of the neck, and collection of edema are similar. Such pressure on the circulatory system brings on the Shoshin state, wherein the intervention of a new element, like an infection of any kind, can result in death from cardiorespiratory failure within twenty-four to thirty-six hours. One research sample in Hong Kong during the 1940s indicated that intercurrent diseases were present in most instances and caused a significant proportion of the 95 percent death rate in untreated cases.[42]

It was clear to contemporaries that familiar diseases like malaria, smallpox, tuberculosis, cholera, and a variety of afflictions of the gastrointestinal and respiratory tracts accounted for a large proportion of Philippine mortality. Enough was known about the adult form of beriberi that some knowledgeable physicians included it among the most serious threats to the public health as well. The médicos titulares were less sure of the exact causes of infant mortality, however, and that uncertainty left a gaping hole in contemporary knowledge about public health in the colony, since infants had by far the highest death rate of any age cohort. Data are insufficient for certainty, but probably one out of every five Filipinos died before reaching one year of age. Some mortality was due to smallpox, which there was no mistaking, but physicians tended to distribute the bulk of deaths among various gastrointestinal and respiratory ailments (like enterocolitis, infantile cholera, nonfebrile influenza, and bronchitis) and a mysterious affliction they called "eclampsia," which simply denotes a convulsive state and is thus a symptom rather than a disease. The descriptions in the annual reports, together with contemporary circumstances, leave little doubt that a significant proportion of that mortality was actually a consequence of infantile beriberi. The experiences in Ilocos Norte and Iloilo, provinces with growing population pressures, and thus rice deficits, make the point clear.[43]

The first hint that beriberi was involved appeared in Dr. Martín's 1876 catalogue of nervous and circulatory disorders when he said, almost in passing, that the convulsions he had mentioned were especially predominant in infants. After a decade of Saigon rice and a cholera epidemic, his successor in Ilocos Norte, Dr. Raquel, reported that "a considerable amount of eclampsia" had occurred in 1886. He had personally attended a number of infants in the last stages of the disease after parents came to him as a last resort. Correlating what he had learned from them about the onset of symptoms with what he subsequently observed, Dr. Raquel described the disease. The infants initially appeared unhappy, slept fitfully, and had a profound look of discouragement. When they began to cry, breast feeding was of no avail in stemming the flood of tears. Palpitations and convulsions were manifested by twitching in the extremities, heightened breathing, a pallid expression, and a frenzied gaze. Body temperature began to fall, and the pulse became fast, but faint, as the death throes began. The eyes rolled so that only the whites could be seen, the trunk muscles contracted, the extremities became rigid, and the jaw clenched. An anguished and rattling breathing heralded the end. Dr. Raquel noted that informants in the other pueblos of the province had reported the same clinical course in cases there. He sadly admitted that "no success whatever crowned our forceful efforts to save the infants [since] eclampsia is a fatal disease for babies of that age."[44]

The cholera epidemic at the end of the 1880s had no Dr. Koeniger, so the dimensions of the beriberi that followed in its wake are harder to discern. The annual reports from Iloilo province provide strong evidence, however, that its infantile form was the hardiest among the evils of those bad years. Physicians there developed a succession of hypotheses to explain the high infant mortality rate that persisted after the cholera had disappeared, but it is evident today that infantile beriberi was primarily responsible. Dr. Gomez, the leading theorist among the Spanish medical corps in the Philippines, attributed the epidemic of infant deaths in 1891 to "lingering understrength cholera germs." Noting that the bacterium had recently extended its range throughout the world, he elaborated the theory that cholera had been endemic in the Philippines since the epidemic of 1865. As proof that it had never completely disappeared, he cited sporadic outbreaks of suspicious cases among infants in the years between the three major epidemics. He speculated that the germ had remained dormant in a weak form that was not virulent enough to affect anyone except babies. He conceded that his theory was not exact, but he thought it accounted for the infantile form of the disease.[45]

In 1892 he offered a different explanation for some puzzling aspects of a severe influenza outbreak that had caused considerable mortality among both adults and infants. A distinct form of the disease seemed to prevail in each group. Vomiting, anorexia, cerebral engagement, and eclampsias were prominent among infants, but what was exceptional was that some babies developed a fever and others did not. The former group proved easy to treat, but in the nonfebrile patients, the course of the disease was more insidious and resulted in death. Since he had no way of recognizing infantile beriberi in the grave cases, Dr. Gomez concluded that the discrepancies "sufficiently demonstrated the diverse forms that the same disease can take." He traced the phenomenon to the recent "socialization of pathology between the separate continents." He pointed out that grippe had originated in the cold regions of the world, where it was characterized by pulmonary symptoms, but carried to the tropical countries, it presented differently. "Today the influenza of the torrid zone, yesterday the black vomit of Europe." The process was merely the most recent example of the historical evolution of disease.[46]

During the following year, Dr. Gomez reported that beriberi had not claimed too many victims. He was speaking, of course, of adults, and said the cases that had occurred were invariably among the poor and were almost all of the hydropic form. Of the four patients he had personally attended, two had died. The others he claimed to have successfully treated with a combination of quinine and strychnine. Turning to the general state of public health, he sadly reported that despite all the recent successes of medical science and the progress against miasmas and germs, mortality in Iloilo was "disastrous." During the last half of the year, infant mortality had reached the highest levels he had ever known in a normal (i.e., nonepidemic) year. At least 176 infants had suddenly died of eclampsia that had no apparent cause. For some reason "the central nervous system was producing a constant reflex action in the young creatures," and for the first time, he could not explain the phenomenon.[47]

Dr. Solivellas arrived in Pototan, in the central zone of Iloilo province, in 1894 and reported that cases of what he thought was either infantile cholera or enterocolitis were "extremely abundant," due perhaps to insufficient caution that parents took with their babies. He did not elaborate further. By the end of 1895 he was genuinely alarmed. He stated flatly that enterocolitis among infants was the leading cause of mortality in the province and killed more babies than did smallpox, which appeared only sporadically. The affliction started with indigestion caused by defective lactation and premature weaning of infants whose mothers were "not robust because of their scarce diets" and had an inadequate quantity and quality of breast milk. The babies got worse each day, becoming weaker and developing intestinal catarrh or enterocolitis. They started vomiting and the gastric symptoms generally relented, but diarrhea then ensued with the feces eventually turning green. Swelling of the abdomen was followed by stupor, and the disease either remitted and became subacute with intermittent symptoms, or death followed quickly. To his report Dr. Solivellas appended mortality statistics for the previous fourteen months in the población, where, he believed, records on cause of death had some reliability. Infants accounted for more than one-half (54.1 percent) of all deaths in Pototan. We can see today that of the 679 deaths, almost half (333) were ascribed to conditions that showed symptoms characteristic of infantile beriberi: enterocolitis (194), eclampsia (52), gastric catarrh and gastritis (46), and intestinal catarrh, enteritis, and disentery (34). Undoubtedly, some of those deaths were diagnosed correctly. Most of them were not, however, and it is certain that a substantial proportion of infant mortality not only there but throughout the Philippines was due to infantile beriberi. Indirect confirmation came two decades later.[48]

In 1910, two American researchers, Dr. Allan J. McLaughlin and Dr. Vernon L. Andrews, were moved by the "appalling infant mortality" in the Philippines (48.8 percent of all deaths at that time were infants as opposed to 18.3 percent in the United States) to "determine accurately what diseases really constitute the greatest factors." They decided to verify the official mortality statistics for Manila for the fiscal year 1908–1909. (By then infantile beriberi was recognized as a specific disease even though it was not yet completely understood.) The causes of death had been certified in the 4,542 infant deaths as follows: infantile convulsions (1,615), congenital debility (596), infantile beriberi (595), acute bronchitis (569), acute meningitis (287), acute enteritis and other diarrheas (286), and all other causes (594). The two physicians analyzed the pathologic findings by necropsy in a series of 219 infants. The actual causes of death were infantile beriberi (124), cholera (33), pneumonia (18), meningitis (6), enterocolitis (6), other diseases (20), and undetermined (12). They concluded that about 70 percent of all certified causes of death in Manila were erroneous and that the failure to recognize infantile beriberi accounted for greatest share of that massive misdiagnosis. Whereas it was the officially recorded cause of only 13.1 percent of the 4,542 infant deaths in Manila, the necropsies suggested that the actual figure was at least 56.6 percent. The researchers declared that "infantile convulsions" was unacceptable as a cause of death because they were a symptom of some specific disease, which they found to be infantile beriberi in thirty-one of forty cases. They also determined that breast-fed infants accounted for 73.7 percent of all infant mortality and 87.0 percent of those babies whose cause of death was certified as either infantile convulsions or infantile beriberi. The findings of the study indicate that at least three-quarters of the eclampsia the Spanish physicians spoke of was actually infantile beriberi, as was a substantial proportion of what they assumed to be infantile cholera, enterocolitis, and bronchitis.[49]

What had originally caught the researchers' attention was a postwar infant mortality rate in Manila so high as to be nearly incredible. It was the proximate result of a war the Americans had waged on the dwindling food supply of an already undernourished population as a means of pacification. Intuitively we know that substantial movements of impoverished people to urban centers that were wholly dependent on Saigon rice must have increased the incidence of beriberi in both the adult and infantile forms. Vital statistics for the war years are not available, but in 1903, according to the Manila Board of Health, 3,387 births were registered versus 3,872 deaths of babies under one year of age. The following year was nearly as bad, with 6,341 births and 6,029 deaths. It may be that births (and not deaths) were underreported, but if so, the reason is not apparent. Infant mortality in immediate postwar Manila thus appears to have been by far the highest recorded in the world. Even if we arbitrarily double the number of births, not on the basis of any evidence but out of sheer incredulity that infant mortality could approach 100 percent, it would still retain first place. Physicians in Manila during the first decade of the century were aware that rates in the city had reached unheard-of levels and accepted such birth-death ratios as believable. Whatever the actual figures may have been, the McLaughlin-Andrews findings six years later make it almost certain that more than half of those babies had died of infantile beriberi.[50]

It was estimated earlier that smallpox accounted for something like 6 to 12 percent of Philippine mortality in a statistically average nineteenth-century year. (The proportion would have been higher before 1800.) By contrast, virtually no one died of beriberi until the archipelago's economy was fully integrated with the regional and world systems in the 1870s. Once it was, beriberi developed rapidly into at least as serious a threat to the public health as smallpox. The pattern of death differed, however, since beriberi could only follow the trail blazed by Saigon rice, whereas smallpox was ubiquitous. Thus, mortality from beriberi was not as widespread in the islands as that from smallpox and ranged from virtually nothing (in statistical terms) in interior areas where domestically grown, handpounded rice was eaten to at least 25 percent, and perhaps a good deal more, of all mortality in Manila in its worst years. Where beriberi deaths in any locality during those three decades fell along that spectrum depended first, on the proportion of highly milled rice consumed, and second, on the presence of objective factors (poverty, natural disasters, agricultural pests, seasons, epidemics, war) that acted to deprive diets of nonrice sources of vitamin B_1. It is obviously impossible to know beriberi's share of overall mortality from 1873 to 1902, but my assumption is that it accounted for 5 to 10 percent and that the overwhelming majority of those deaths were among infants. Those statistics represent a terribly high human cost to the Spanish colony for its role in Southeast Asia's emerging division of labor and to the American colony for the opportunity of being set "in the pathway of the world's best civilization."[51]

CHAPTER 6

Malaria: Disequilibrium in the Total Environment

IN HIS REPORT to the 1876 Universal Exposition in Philadelphia, Ramon Jordana y Morera informed the world that the richness and variety of Philippine flora was "beyond praise." As inspector general of mountains, forests, and lands, he had worked almost nonstop for six months organizing the collection of forest products to be sent to the international fair. It was the perfect occasion to advertize the islands as the principal Far Eastern market for timber and to hasten the day, not far off in any case he thought, when China and Japan would build their railroads and ships out of Philippine wood. Rumors were already heard of impending orders from Spain and California for shipments of lumber "by the ton." Jordana went on in his presentation to point out that even on Luzon only a very small proportion of the land had been reduced to cultivation and that most of the island was still covered with extensive forests. Entering them for the first time, he wrote that "one's spirit is suspended" in the presence of gigantic trees with trunks two and three meters in diameter. Under their spectacular canopies of verdure, the fertile soil nurtured a first layer of vegetation so thick that a machete was necessary to clear the way. When the wind suddenly agitated the tops of the colossal trees, "one realizes his insignificance before the grandeur of Nature that surrounds him, and afraid of having surprised its secrets, there surges an irresistible impulse to abandon such dark and mysterious places." He did not mention that anyone who did not flee those woods was likely to come away with malarial fever.[1]

The forested uplands that loomed over the inhabited lowlands throughout the archipelago had always been forbidding and inaccessible. They had long been the home of despised hill peoples and a shifting population of lowlanders who had fled there whether, as Ileto says, "to avoid the payment of tribute and forced labor, to escape from the clutches of the law, or to live as a hermit and ascetic." For most Filipinos, however, the uplands were a place to avoid. Prior to the nineteenth century, the one month of forced labor cutting timber in the mountains had been the most dreaded of all colonial obligations. Not only was the work onerous and dangerous, but the woods were full of fever. Everybody knew that the forests were unhealthy, but no one understood exactly why until the early twentieth century, when it was finally realized that malaria was transmitted by the mosquitos that inhabited those regions.[2]

Until the eve of the twentieth century, malaria was assumed to be somehow produced by fetid emanations, or miasma, that rose from decomposing vegetation or from the soggy earth itself. Dr. Amide's report for 1883 is typical. "Marsh fevers" prevailed constantly in Pangasinan, but that year had been much better, he said, because of "the abundant rains with which we have been favored, which flooded everything, fields and creeks, impeding the fermentation of decomposing vegetation in the womb of these malarial emanations." The disease's various names reflect the misunderstanding. The word "malaria" comes from the Italian *mal'aria*, meaning "bad air," and "paludism" (*paludismo* in Spanish) derives from the Latin *palus*, meaning "marsh." Drainage of marshes had long been the standard weapon against malaria wherever government or private resources permitted, and it had some effect in lowland malaria countries since mosquito-breeding sites disappeared along with the miasma.[3]

Confusion persisted even after Sir Ronald Ross's work made it clear in 1897 that the infection is transmitted to people by mosquitos. Some American army medical officers had heard of the discovery, but others were completely ignorant of it. Shortly after arriving on Siasi in September 1899, the physician ascribed malaria to the "predisposition to sleeping in damp clothing by not changing clothing when coming off from fatigue and drill as the men have generally been perspiring freely." An outbreak among the troops garrisoning San Pablo, Laguna, the next year was severe enough to occasion a special report. The men had been busy cleaning up the town, hauling away "many wagonloads" of filth, refuse, and dead animals to be burned. The doctor explained that "removing so much filth and opening ditches caused an outpouring of malarious germs." When fever plagued the soldiers in Ilagan, Isabela, during the hot months of 1901, the medical officer stated confidently that "the cause doubtless is to be found in the season and in the necessary exposure to the sun on the march." Captain George K. Sims fell back on more traditional theory as late as November 1901 to account for malaria among the garrison at Maasin, Leyte. It was the rainy season, he said, and pinpointing "the mists that arose from the ground after a hard rain," he explained that the cases had developed from those vapors.[4]

The late-nineteenth-century discoveries about malaria bionomics thus had virtually no effect in reducing transmission in the Philippines before the end of the American war. A further misunderstanding existed that caused health workers to spend two decades stalking the wrong mosquitos even after their role was finally recognized. Though malaria is a disease of the lowlands in most countries of the world, Philippine malaria is normally contracted in the uplands. Governor Rajal had come as close as anyone in realizing the cause—that even though malaria seemed to be a miasmatic disease, it was the wooded high country where fever lurked. Noting in the late 1880s that lots of paludismo existed in the northern pueblos of Nueva Ecija near the Cordillera (the mountain range in northern Luzon) from November through January each year, he reasoned that it was "caused by the action of the winds that are saturated with miasmas of the forests." But of course he, like everyone else, overlooked the mosquitos. Six varieties of Philippine anopheline mosquitos are capable of infecting humans with malarial parasites, but *Anopheles minimus flavirostris* is the principal vector and the only one capable of sustaining the disease in the absence of unusual transmission factors. It inhabits shady areas along the banks of slow-moving streams at altitudes between 800 and 2,000 feet, concentrating at 970 feet. The other varieties are too inefficient to sustain malaria above or below that zone unless epidemic conditions prevail.[5]

Cornelio M. Urbino said in the 1950s that Filipinos have been comparatively lucky in that most live below the endemic region. It is hard to quarrel with that judgment as it applies to the prepioneering era or to recent decades. Prior to the nineteenth century, few went into the upland areas and brought plasmodia back to the populated lowlands—too few to constitute a high probability that enough of the weak lowland vectors would bite them and live long enough to transmit the infection by biting someone else. Twentieth-century movement between upland and lowland regions has been constant, of course, but understanding of transmission mechanics, screened windows, mosquito nets, and antimalarial drugs have given the general population a fair measure of protection. That was not the case, however, during the nineteenth century, when population pressure, poverty, and the fever to uncover the colony's "germs of wealth" set unprecedented numbers of persons in motion. Many of them, unarmed with prophylaxis of any kind, began penetrating the endemic zone and were infected. Enough returned to lowland communities from time to time that even the inefficient anophelines could sometimes transfer enough of the parasites into the full reservoir of susceptible blood there to set off epidemics.[6]

To see why the situation would have been better had Filipinos and *A. minimus flavirostris* lived together and why (since they did not) malaria was the biggest killer in the late-nineteenth-century Philippines, it is helpful to understand a little about the disease and its epidemiology. From one point of view, malaria is simply the background, and it is the plasmodium that is the principal actor. As Norman Taylor has written: "Man, the mosquito, and malaria are mere incidents in the life history of an organism that needs our blood for food, uses the stomach of a mosquito to complete its sex life, and in the process causes the most devastating disease known to science." All human-infecting strains of four species of malarial parasites (two of which, *Plasmodium vivax* and *Plasmodium falciparum*, are significant in the Philippines) are transmitted globally by about sixty species of anophelines in a cycle in which insect and human act as successive hosts. The female adult mosquito requires blood meals to produce fertile eggs, and if the meal is taken by biting an infected human (rather than an animal), it may also ingest malarial plasmodia. The parasites migrate throughout the mosquito's body, and those that reach the salivary gland are injected into another human host when the mosquito takes its next human blood meal. There they eventually enter the blood stream, and as the infected red cells rupture (causing malaria's characteristic febrile response in humans), the parasites move to other red cells where some of them continue their maturation and await ingestion by a mosquito, thus beginning another round of the process. Others remain in the blood stream, proliferating until their life cycle is broken by the infected person's immune response, antimalarial drugs, or the death of the human host.[7]

From an anthropocentric standpoint, the effects of the parasite's odyssey on human beings are what is important. Although malaria lacked some of the drama that surrounded the more horrible or terrifying epidemic diseases, the Spanish physicians reported marsh fevers as the leading cause of mortality and morbidity year in and year out late in the nineteenth century. Its most significant consequence lay in helping to perpetuate the cycle of poverty. Survivors of malarial attacks experience either relapses or recrudescences for periods of up to about five years, depending on the species of plasmodium, and the anemia resulting from the destruction of infected red cells can seriously impair the ability to earn a living, especially among those (farmers and fishermen, for instance) who do hard physical labor. American physician Fred B. Bowman seems to have understood that when he observed in 1910 that mortality from malaria in the Philippines was less important than the "neuroses and indefinite conditions met here [that] are due to latent malaria or to succeeding attacks over the years." The catalogue of effects (acute and chronic physical disability, a high infant-mortality rate, contribution to adverse outcomes of other diseases, reinforcement of malnutrition by activation of the poverty cycle) is all-encompassing and ensures a deteriorating standard of living. "Indeed," concludes epidemiologist Robert H. Black, "it may be said with assurance that any facet of the life of the indigene in a malarious country must be viewed against a background of chronic malaria."[8]

The individual's prior immunological state largely determines the course and severity of the disease. Though an attack of malaria only confers limited and varying degrees of protection on its survivors, the resistance thus acquired is a significant transmission factor, the more so the higher the level of endemicity in the community. When the disease is constantly present in an area, infants experience their first attacks at four to six months of age. Subsequent infections become more severe until the third to fifth year of life, when those who have survived begin to develop a homologous resistance (that is, to the same strain of parasite) that progressively reduces the effects of later attacks so long as the victims do not migrate from the region. A low level of heterologous resistance to other strains within the same species (but not to other species) results, and repeated infection with several strains can produce heterologous resistance to all of them. Nevertheless, it is obvious that the strain-specificity is a major limitation on the scope of acquired resistance to malaria. Thus individuals from a highly endemic area can develop severe infections when exposed to different strains in or from another community. Still, homologous resistance is crucial, as Black explains: "Adult tolerance, which is an expression of immunity, is secured at the price of much sickness and death in childhood. Thus it is possible for a community to survive despite the presence of malaria which would prove fatal to a nonimmune adult coming from an area where there is no malaria."[9]

Filipinos and their communities had little acquired resistance. Most settlements were in the lowlands so individuals had little chance to build tolerance actively because they were not constantly reinfected. What resistance they might have acquired from contracting the infection in the endemic area or by being bitten while an epidemic temporarily prevailed in their communities was soon lost. The next outbreak would inevitably result in high death rates with mortality spread more evenly along the age spectrum than would occur in endemic communities, where deaths cluster mostly among children under five years of age. Nor did Filipinos have real access to passively acquired resistance in the form of antimalarial drugs. The properties of the Andean fever bark tree (*Cinchona*) as a febrifuge had long been known, but crude infusions of the crushed bark had limited effect against malaria. The isolation of quinine from cinchona bark in 1820 gave medical science its first modern antimalarial drug, though its effectiveness is only partial. Philippine malaria was hardly touched by quinine in any case. After long effort, the most effective species of the plant, *Cinchona ledgeriana*, was successfully brought to Java and cultivated there in commercially profitable quantities by the last quarter of the century, but the Philippines continued to be entirely dependent on imported supplies until well into the present century. Quinine could be purchased at drugstores in some of the principal urban areas (where little malaria existed), but ample testimony from the médicos titulares makes it clear that its price placed it well beyond the reach of the poor, and everyone agreed that the poor suffered disproportionately from malaria as a result. Governor Camilo Millan claimed to know of an "indio ilocano in the throes of death" who received a free visit from a doctor who prescribed quinine. The pobre chose not to spend a peso for the remedy, "which would surely have saved his life," explaining that since he only had eight pesos, all of which were saved for his funeral, he was resigned to dying since he could not afford the medicine. The particular incident sounds fictitious but the evident mix of poverty and skepticism about the Western conception of health rings true. It appears again in the observation of a doctor in Albay that "victims of malaria put themselves entirely in the hands of Providence, waiting with a resignation without equal for the outcome of the attack."[10]

The extent to which malaria pervades the life of a population group is inversely proportional to the stability of various interconnected factors in the total environment. Anything that alters even slightly the ecological balance between man, mosquito, and parasite can dramatically increase malaria in a community, and the unstable Philippine island world of the late nineteenth century therefore favored its prevalence. Whether the disease can sustain itself, and at what level, depends on the complicated interplay of numerous factors associated with host (both human and anopheline), agent (the plasmodium), and environment (physical, biological, and socioeconomic). The important transmission factors for humans include (1) level of parasite infestation, especially in children, (2) recovery and mortality rates from the disease, (3) extent and kind of resistance in the community (herd immunity), and (4) personal habits and living conditions. Factors associated with the mosquitos are (1) availability of water for breeding, which depends on climate and season, especially as they determine temperature and rainfall, (2) longevity and hibernation habits, (3) efficiency as vectors, including relative preference for humans or animals as a source of blood meals, (4) dose of parasites inoculated in human host per bite, and (5) availability of humans as donors and recipients of parasites. Aspects relating to the parasites are (1) virulence and (2) persistence and tendency to cause relapse in humans. The interaction of all these factors is so complex that any organizational scheme is necessarily oversimplified. Disease transmission in nature has no neat division of labor. Human availability, for instance, could be a host factor as well as a variable of vector capacity. Obviously it is both. Moreover, the major environmental factors—from atmospheric pressure to socioeconomic status—are interwoven through those three somewhat artificial categories.[11]

The relationship between the transmission factors in nature is extremely delicate. Malariologist George Macdonald has pointed out that "no engine however well governed runs perpetually at the same speed." Nor, by analogy, can those variables remain perpetually balanced so that malaria continues to prevail at the same level in the community. When something happens to upset the equilibrium, the level of transmission is determined by the rate at which cases reproduce themselves, which is potentially astronomical. Fortunately a number of natural constraints on the reproduction rate exist, but nature's balancing mechanism is imperfect because the stimulus (infection) and its reaction (acquired resistance) are not synchronous. Epidemics can be severe during the lag time (generally two months or more) before the brakes are applied, and the mechanism reverses. The number of primary infections then starts to decrease, the reproduction rate falls towards the point at which one infection is capable of reproducing an average of one new case, and malaria will eventually disappear from the community if nothing happens to reverse the decline. Since decreased transmission is accompanied by a corresponding loss of resistance, however, a new upsurge of infection is inevitable sooner or later.[12]

Thus transmission continually oscillates around true equilibrium. The degree of relative stability is critical because malaria can only be epidemic in communities where the balancing mechanism is characterized by wide deviations on either side of the mean. Narrow fluctuations occur in areas where malaria is endemic. Emiliano Pampana has stated the basic epidemiological principle: "A disease which, like malaria, engenders immune responses in proportion to the frequency of infection can be epidemic only in populations which experience it only marginally or not at all." Malaria in any region of the world falls somewhere along a continuum that reflects the relative efficiency of nature's governing mechanism, and in the lowland Philippines it tended strongly toward the unstable pole. Its features conformed to the general profile of unstable malaria worldwide—weak vector capacity, low to moderate (but fluctuating) endemicities, abrupt and severe seasonal epidemics, wide fluctuations in volume and area of infection, and highly variable community resistance.[13]

Macdonald emphasizes that in zones of unstable malaria where acquired resistance is unimportant (like the nineteenth-century Philippines), "very slight modification in any of the transmission factors may completely upset equilibrium." Mathematically small increases in transmission "may in the end produce grossly disabling epidemics." Those variables associated with the mosquitos are particularly important, and indeed, Macdonald says that "the degree of effect on the infection rates is determined solely by the total biting figure." A. *minimus flavirostris* is a relatively inefficient vector, because its normal human-biting rate is low. It can transmit malaria year-round, but its capacity fluctuates with the season, especially in areas where heavy rains flush the streams and disturb its breeding cycle. Although Philippine temperatures permit a fairly rapid completion of the extrinsic incubation cycle (the development of the parasite in the anopheline host), the mosquito is moderately short-lived. In addition, it stays away from civilization. Moreover it is zoophilic, meaning that if given a choice, it prefers to feed on cattle and carabaos rather than on humans. Precise analysis of the actual interaction between transmission factors at any time or place in the nineteenth-century Philippines is out of the question since little or nothing can be known about specific changes in parasite rates, local atmospheric conditions, anopheline longevity, and much else. We can, however, identify two crucial developments that upset equilibrium by increasing vector capacity. The unprecedented movement of people in and out of the endemic zones increased the ability of A. *minimus flavirostris* and the weaker vectors to transmit the infection. Superimposed on that process during the final fifteen years of the period was the disappearance of most of the bovine population, which multiplied the main vector's biting rate on human beings. Epidemic malaria inevitably followed.[14]

The many late-century migrants who penetrated the endemic zone did so for various individual reasons, but underlying all the major prewar movements was the fact that the land there was potentially productive. To stretch the point, it can be argued that the subsequent groups of war refugees and soldiers would not have been in that area had not the productive capacity of the Philippines seemed sufficiently promising to make the islands worth conquering. In any case, the engine of nineteenth-century development was the increasing profitability of land. Many of those who opened new lands, either for themselves or on behalf of others, had been dispossessed of their own holdings for just that reason. Contemporaries blamed the deficient title system, which was a fair enough charge as far as it went. The colonial administration had issued land titles, but like all other official initiatives, the program was never fully implemented. Keyser claimed in 1869 that not even 1 percent of rural properties were registered. Under the unwritten rules of customary land tenure, people considered themselves the owners of any land cleared by their forebears and farmed for generations by the family. Possession and use had always been sufficient, and since the authorities had never enforced the provisions on the books, few persons ever gave them a thought. Once land became a source of potential wealth in the cash-crop era, however, caciques (powerful local officials cum property owners) carefully acquired legal titles and used the legal process to oust the occupants. In practice, the registrant was the owner. Alert to the developing problem and the need for a rational functioning system, the government issued a decree in 1880 urging landusers to secure title. When that got no response, another in 1894 offered titles free of charge to claimants who filed within a year. Unregistered land would revert to the Crown after that. Few people took up the offer.[15]

Some of the dispossessed remained on the land as tenants, some went into the growing poblaciones, and others moved toward the frontiers, either as partners or on their own. Sancianco described the senseless process by which pobres were induced to abandon their cultivated lands so easily: "The prevailing influence of caciquism leaves the oppressed poor—debilitated and ignorant, unresisting and submissive—without any remedy other than resigning themselves to clear other lands since the usurpers always win in the courts." Keyser said that after "abandoning the homes in which they had been born, they build a hut either near the town center or on uncultivated land, which is abundant thanks to the fact that the population is very scarce in relation to the territory." Having become "inhabitants of the forest, where they do not have to fear the anger of neighbors, they clear enough land to provide for their necessities." The forested lands were invariably further inland and usually at higher elevations, so the involuntary migrants were close to or in the endemic malaria zone. Their rude huts, and especially the ones thrown up alongside a stream, functioned as acceptable nocturnal indoor resting places for *A. minimus flavirostris* and thus immediately became foci of malarial transmission.[16]

Had the planners in Manila or Madrid fully understood the ecological consequences of exploiting the land's wealth, they might have taken pause. The conjunction of humans, parasites, and mosquitos was one such outcome, and indeed malaria has since proved the main obstacle to agricultural development of the hill regions. Pioneering efforts at permanent (as opposed to shifting) cultivation require inputs of intense labor because of the necessity for repeated tilling, and malaria saps the energy needed for such work. Most Filipino migrants arrived from the lowlands without any resistance to the disease, and government settlement projects in the twentieth century have commonly succeeded or foundered on the ability of its medical staff to counter malaria. Nineteenth-century pioneers were far more vulnerable. Few Spanish officials saw the problem so starkly, but Dr. Nolasco at least glimpsed its contours, and he addressed it in one report. He was torn between his desire to eradicate disease on Masbate and Ticao and his conviction that it was imperative to develop the riches of the province. Malaria was evidently produced in the extensive forests, and although he identified the low-lying mangrove stands as the focus rather than the wooded hills, he knew the disease could be minimized if people simply avoided the unhealthy area. Therein lay a dilemma, however, since the province exported kindling and other wood products to Manila. He stated the essence of the problem in his annual report for 1886: "Every year the people pay a small but sad tribute to these fevers in exchange for the riches of the land they inhabit." After considering the factors, he concluded that it was wisest to develop the land, pay the necessary tribute, and leave the eventual solution to medical science.[17]

A fully informed debate would probably have finally weighed the costs and benefits in the same way, but adjustments might have been attempted. A dialogue of sorts was in fact taking place and had all the facts been known, the approach that prevailed might not have, and malarial transmission would have been reduced. At issue was how best to tap and then allocate the Philippine store of wealth, but the more immediate question was whether the government should step in and manage the exploitation of undeveloped land, and if so, to what extent. A perennially empty colonial treasury and increasing worldwide demand for tropical products provided context. Malaria was peripheral to the debate and was brought under consideration rather late by the wrong side and then almost as an afterthought. The outcome was determined more by the sequence of events than by discussion, decision, and implementation, but the entire process serves as an example of how factors in the total environment (in this case, economic) shape patterns of disease.

In 1855 a new government department, the Inspección de Montes, was established and charged with the scientific exploration and survey of mountains, forests, and lands. It did not begin functioning until Jordana came from Spain seven years later as chief engineer, but its importance was evident almost immediately thereafter when an 1863 decree ordered all provincial governors to remit to the Inspección all papers regarding land concessions in the mountains, wood cutting, new tillage, and profits from resins and other forest products. The measure was an early indication that the government intended the department to go beyond merely discovering and inventorying the colony's potential wealth. The Inspección would actively manage it, not only to rationalize forest exploitation but also to provide the state with income it would otherwise have lost. Two decades earlier, the governors had been deprived of their long-exercised and much-abused right to engage in trade and commerce, and this decree served as a warning against the temptation to profit by concessioneering. The plan took form in 1866 when another decree authorized the chief engineer to enclose the mountains of the state and to prohibit woodcutting. Henceforth, the government would decide how the forest riches were to be tapped, and it would grant permission to do it. As custodian of the Crown lands, it would sell forest products, rent or sell land, and impose fines for infractions of its regulations. What was not yet clear was whether the restrictions would apply to all the mountains of the state or just to some of them.[18]

The scheme aroused strong and effective opposition from those who believed that economic development required the widest possible extension of agricultural cash cropping. They feared that state management would impede the ability of private capital to have land cleared and put into cultivation. The newly created Junta de agricultura, industria y comercio, "whose principal mission is to propose reforms to remove obstacles and hindrances that impede the development of the country's riches," provided a focus for that view. That board received unanimous support from the provincial governors, and the fight began in earnest. A memorandum to the Sociedad económica de amigos del país in 1868 defended official policy on three grounds. First, unregulated exploitation had already depleted the forest wealth and caused a scarcity of light wood products that the ordinary people needed for construction and fuel but could no longer gather easily since what remained was far from the populated areas. Much of it was being sent to the productive, but unwooded, central plain. Prices had quintupled as a result, and the residents of the forested provinces were suffering especially. Second, limited access to the forests would not harm agriculture in any way and would in fact be beneficial since farmers had to have trees for rainfall, firewood, and construction. Those needs would be met by scientific conservation of the forests, which would include selective cutting and thinning. Third, although some of the goals might be met by enclosing only some mountains, state management of all wooded areas would ensure a source of income to the empty colonial treasury. And since "vegetation strangled man in the tropics," there would be enough riches for all.[19]

Despite that strong backing, the Inspección des Montes quickly showed a willingness to compromise. In an unsigned letter to the governor-general in 1869, the writer (probably Jordana) acknowledged that since newly cultivated lands are necessarily developed from the forest, the tie between the administration of each was close. The chief engineer took a decidedly conciliatory tone in his annual report for the fiscal year 1874–1875. Well aware that his position was delicate, Jordana carefully tempered advocacy with caution. He pointed to 30 percent and 83 percent increases in income from the sale of wood and from fines over the previous year, and although he admitted that the amounts received were not large, the results "demonstrated that the hopes on which the new organization had been founded were not illusory." Income would improve even further if the department was given more assistants and forest inspectors, he noted. (In other words, it was desperately short of resources and personnel. The few forest inspectors it did have had only worked four months during the past year.) He saw a promising future for Philippine timber exports if the Inspección was allowed to manage the forests in accordance with "sound scientific principles." Lest that strike the wrong chord, he hastened to assure the governor-general and the Overseas Ministry that in carrying out its mission "this branch rejects exclusivism and appreciates the forest question under the higher criteria of the general interest, never having tried to contain the spread of agriculture nor having opposed its natural and legitimate development by denying it the lands it needs."[20]

The expected boom in Philippine lumber exports was slow to develop, while the profitability of agricultural cash crops was amply demonstrated, making it easier for the Inspección's opponents to insist that the forests make way for cultivation. Then they advanced a new argument—forest clearing would promote health. The secretary of the agriculture board, Manuel del Busto, was one of the many who worried about the perceived shortage of farm labor and believed that European colonists were needed. In an 1884 propaganda piece designed to attract immigrants and approved for publication by the governor-general, del Busto conceded that colonists throughout the world had experienced difficulties with climate and disease, but he argued that people can change their environment. Citing various colonial sites like Sydney, Batavia, and the Cape of Good Hope as examples of places where "unfavorable conditions" had disappeared, he observed that "the province of Cagayan, in these islands, has been until a few years ago a focus of malarial fevers and today is one of the most healthy in the archipelago thanks to forest clearing and cultivation." Similarly, in the colony at Puerto Princesa, only six inhabitants had been free of those fevers as recently as 1877, but few serious cases existed there at present. "In sum, every hot country that is uncultivated and covered with virgin forest is insalubrious, and the Philippine Islands are not an exception to that rule, but human action modifies these natural causes, making healthy and habitable countries that were previously deadly."[21]

The creation of an agronomical commission in 1884 reflected the shifting weight of influence. It was handed a wide brief that gave it responsibility for virtually all aspects of agricultural research and development. (It was not handed enough money to carry it out, however.) José Guevedo, director of one of the commission's five new research stations (Daraga, Albay), used both developmental and health justifications six years later to urge that reserved forest lands be kept to an absolute minimum. Going further, he offered a bold plan for Masbate, which was the most undeveloped area in his station's jurisdiction. Whereas Dr. Nolasco had assumed that the island's prosperity was tied to exports of kindling and such to Manila and other urban centers, Guevedo thought in much bigger terms. Pointing out that sales of wood products (amounting to some Pfs 3,500 per year) did not even cover the salaries of agricultural service employees there, he claimed that Masbate's income could easily reach millions due to "the enormous creation of riches that would result from the almost total cutting of trees on this island." He would plant the cleared areas to abaca, and prosperity would surely follow. "The simple inhabitants of Masbate envy Albay and Camarines their abaca production and ask why it is not grown on their island." A secondary benefit, he contended, would be improved public health. He dismissed the old arguments that forested mountains "clean up the atmosphere and make more healthy the country in which they abound." He thought such theories scientific nonsense—it was self-evident that "the forest is the place where one is certain to encounter fevers of all varieties." He acknowledged that life was precarious for timber cutters and other virgin-forest dwellers but argued that once land was deforested and planted, health improved. "This is not the place," he concluded, "to explain the many reasons against the extensive conservation of forests. But in summary there is no reason in meteorology, hydrography, nor hygiene to conserve—and very much to gain in not doing so, and the economic reason is the strongest."[22]

By the last decade of the century, the forces that favored agricultural cash-crop development at the expense of the managed conservation of forested land had triumphed. The victory was manifested less in allocation of resources—Guevedo asserted that his station could not carry out any experiments because it had received "not one cent"—than in government inaction. Since it lacked the budgetary and human resources as well as the political will to impose the proposed restrictions on forest exploitation, land clearing and unregulated woodcutting proceeded as it had before without serious interruption. In practice, the forests had been turned over to private exploitation and were "managed" by private timber merchants, labor contractors, work foremen, and purchasers who bought up wood products to keep them off the market. When the lumber export boom failed to materialize, the cutters were blamed. It was claimed that pay advances were necessary to induce them to work and that they used a multitude of methods, chiefly negligence and escape, to avoid fulfilling their contracts. In the latter instance, the timber merchants were put to considerable expense to capture the fugitives, which was not an easy matter with "people accustomed to life in the forests and who received secure asylum and devoted protection from other indios." Jordana's earlier hopes for scientific conservation were dashed. In 1891, he lamented the fact that the species of trees "most punished" by the timber merchants were never replanted. The best slow-growth hardwood was disappearing from the sitios and was being replaced naturally by faster-growing but softer, and thus less desirable, invaders. One respected journalist concluded that Jordana's immense forests (and thus their potential usefulness and wealth) were a chimera because the good wood within the people's reach was already gone and what remained was locked away in areas inaccessible to current technology.[23]

It also seems that the government came to rethink its initial enthusiasm for enclosing and managing the forests when it gauged the resistance to the plan, the small benefit to the treasury, and the comparative figures of cash-crop and timber exports. Had the conservationists known more about malaria, they could have at least argued strongly that the unrestrained battle against the forests was one of the reasons that labor was debilitated and scarce. They might have found an articulate ally in Dr. Gomez, whose constant refrain was that with a healthier populace "the unending clamor about the day laborer should not exist and thousands of colonial projects would not be dead letters." As it was, he lamented, "nothing comes of these wandering ideas." And had the conservationists known more about ecology, they could have countered the argument about deforestation making regions more healthful by pointing out the pernicious effects of aridification. Since such knowledge has had scant effect in preventing the archipelago's ecological despoilation in recent years, it is unrealistic to imagine that the nineteenth-century government conservationists could have prevailed under any circumstances. The controversy is more significant as an example of how a past population group unwittingly contributed to the development of what became their greatest mortal enemy—malaria.[24]

By the 1950s, researchers had in fact established a positive correlation between vegetation and malaria in the Philippines and suggested that clearing forested areas eliminated the shady, remote breeding areas of A. minimus flavirostris and was thus an effective control method. It was acknowledged, however, that the first inhabitants suffered. Dr. Urbino explained in more scientific terms the process that del Busto, Guevado, and others had grasped intuitively, pointing out that when the first pioneers arrive and clear an endemic area, malaria soars because their nonimmune blood provides a new reservoir of infection. Once "a favorable micro-climate" is established, he said, the disease subsides and outbreaks become less frequent. However, given the immensity of the Philippine forests, the lack of tools, and the ignorance about the role of mosquitos, we can disregard the utility of forest clearing as a control technique as well as the further question of whether it could have been accomplished in the late nineteenth century. More relevant is the fact that development of the public wealth resulted in large numbers of nonresistant persons going into areas where malaria was constantly transmitted, becoming infected there, and then returning to areas where virtually everyone was susceptible. The only potential check on that process—restricted access to the forests—was never applied. Whether the benefits of exploiting the land justified the health costs may still be open to debate, but it is at least certain that those who paid "the small but sad tribute" were not the ones who received the benefits.[25]

As important for the spread of malaria as the direct assault on the forests to clear land were the extensive seasonal migrations through, near, or into endemic regions as people went in search of harvesting work. An American observer described the movement resulting from the practice of working on shares. "In well-populated sections of the Philippines during the harvest season there is an exodus to rice regions, sometimes a considerable distance away. Often whole families leave their homes. On returning they usually bring with them their share of the crop." A mid-1950s survey conducted in a number of areas throughout the Philippines demonstrated that such medium- and short-range migration is epidemiologically significant. The study measured the effectiveness of insecticide spraying along stream banks in stemming malaria transmission. Researchers found the control technique to be generally effective, and sometimes dramatically so, as long as the inhabitants remained within the sprayed areas. In one town under study—Santa Maria, Laguna—the local population shifted frequently as residents went for a week or two to their upland farms in preparation for planting. Such movement in and out of the protected area, the surveyors remarked laconically, "did not produce favorable results."[26]

Harvest migrations within Ilocos Norte provide a clear nineteenth-century example of short-range movements and effective transmission. By the 1870s, population pressure forced rice fields up against the hills on the eastern fringe of the narrow coastal plain. Anopheline density declines at the height of the rainy season (August-October) in northern Luzon as breeding sites are flushed, but by harvest time the rains have ended and density again swells, and sporozoite (plasmodia ready for injection) rates in *A. minimus flavirostris* reach one of their two annual peaks. Consequently, malaria increasingly became an occupational hazard of the harvest, and overall mortality in the province was highest at that time in epidemic years. (The death rate normally crests during the rainy months.) The winter of 1878–1879 was particularly bad. Dr. Martín ascribed the epidemic to the fact that the north wind and intense mists prevented the ground from drying out, but his own description makes the actual process clear. The entire province was severely affected, but he noted that fatal cases were most frequent in the eastern pueblos where the rice fields were situated. Their proprietors "are by and large residents of other pueblos and as a general rule in the months of December, January, and February they move to those fields for the harvest, but no sooner did they arrive this year than they were attacked by malaria and had to return to their true homes." Scarcities resulted because not enough healthy workers remained to bring in the crop, and "since almost everyone's well-being or misery depends solely on the rice crop," public health suffered in 1879.[27]

Soldiers performed the same epidemiological function as pioneers and harvesters but more efficiently because they moved in larger groups over longer distances. The Americans, who are the only ones we can follow through the records, brought various strains with them even though malaria had generally been in retreat since the 1880s in the United States. There, in contrast to the Philippines, the pioneering movement was coming to an end, large-scale drainage operations had been undertaken (and were effective since the main vectors inhabited the lowlands), quinine was in general use, housing was better, the livestock population had grown (providing more blood meals so as to decrease human-biting rates), nutrition had improved, and the malarial strains had apparently decreased in virulence. The southeastern region of the country was an exception to that pattern, however. Agricultural dislocation after the Civil War had facilitated anopheline breeding, and malaria actually increased there in the late nineteenth century. As a consequence, army regiments containing substantial numbers of recruits from the southeast were heavily infected with malaria even before they reached San Francisco. Rates reached 10 percent and higher.[28]

The Mississippi Valley in western Tennessee was the reputed malarial belt of the country, and the incidence of infection among the First Tennessee Volunteers was correspondingly high. The regiment mustered during the last half of May 1898 in Nashville, and by June the medical officers were attributing the prevalence of malaria to the unsanitary conditions at Camp Bob Taylor. By the time the regiment got off the train in Oakland, late that month, 104 cases of malaria had developed. Other southeastern-based units had the same experience. The Twenty-ninth U.S. Volunteer Infantry, comprising men from Alabama, Mississippi, Georgia, Tennessee, and Kentucky, had 112 malaria cases on the sick list at Fort McPherson, Georgia. The Thirty-second U.S. Volunteer Infantry was made up of Kansas and Missouri recruits, and it arrived on the West Coast with well over 100 cases. Worst of all was the Sixth U.S. Cavalry, which had served in Cuba during the summer of 1898. When it reorganized at Chicamauga Park, Georgia, in August, 240 of its 712 remaining soldiers had malaria. Some proportion of the plasmodia was transported along with the men to the Philippines, where the people had no acquired specific resistance against North American strains. In an era before air travel, it was the persistent features of *P. falciparum* and *P. vivax* malaria (caused by some of the parasites remaining in the red cells) that posed the main danger to susceptibles who were at least five weeks and almost half a world away. In addition, *P. vivax* can take as long as thirty-eight weeks to incubate if the infecting dose of sporozoites is small. The mechanism is not understood as yet, but two experts say "the result is that an infection contracted in the autumn may not result in parasitaemia until the following spring, when the hibernating anophelines become active in time to pick up the infection and pass it on." Thus, a man could have contracted a mild infection at home in the Mississippi Valley or elsewhere prior to enlistment and not have been a factor in transmission of malaria until venturing into the Philippines more than half a year later.[29]

As with the other diseases, the infections that the soldiers contracted after arrival and disseminated about the islands were more significant epidemiologically than the ones they imported from abroad. During their year or more in the Philippines, the troops were remarkably efficient vectors of disease, functioning as traveling reservoirs of infection. They were particularly effective participants in the malaria transmission cycle because they came without acquired resistance to indigenous strains. Once parasitized, they could increase the burden of infection among the residents of a community without intimate or even particularly close physical contact. Even allowing for the American tendency to diagnose malaria too readily, it is clear that all regiments became heavily infected with plasmodia right after taking up camp, usually somewhere on the outskirts of Manila. Since most of those sites were not in the endemic zones, the high rates of malarial infection provide a neat demonstration of epidemic potential when one transmission factor—in this case the availability of human recipients and donors—is suddenly increased. The Twenty-seventh U.S. Volunteer Infantry, for example, remained in the immediate environs of Manila, and yet 431 of its 1265 men were admitted to the sick list for malaria during the first three months in the country. The Thirty-second U.S. Volunteer Infantry, headquartered on the central plain in Angeles, Pampanga, registered 350 malarial cases (28.1 percent of total mean strength) in the first month alone. The Eleventh U.S. Cavalry outdid both. Stationed in Cavite province, 537 soldiers out of 1071 contracted malaria during the first two months.[30]

When the Twenty-eighth U.S. Volunteer Infantry began to form at Camp Meade, Pennsylvania, in July 1899, malaria was not the problem that it was in regiments from the Southeast since most of its recruits came from New York, New Jersey, and Pennsylvania, areas outside of the primary transmission zones. Nevertheless, sixteen cases of malaria were under treatment immediately. Following summer training, some 1,163 men (including the malaria cases apparently) boarded trains for the cross-country trip in September, and after three weeks at the Presidio, they sailed for Manila, arriving in November. The soldiers were initially divided among four stations within a few miles of Manila and well away from the fighting, but somewhat more than 20 percent of the men were admitted to sick list during the first month, mainly with fever and diarrhea. In early January, the troops undertook their first arduous and prolonged hikes up into the heart of southeastern Luzon's endemic malaria zone in pursuit of the elusive resistance forces and returned with more fever. Malaria immediately became epidemic among both soldiers and civilians in the vicinity of Dasmarinas, Cavite, where the regimental headquarters was established and one batallion was stationed. The pueblo is located in a hilly region, and the medical officer reported that "practically all the natives suffer from malaria, none being free." During February and March, entries on the battalion's sick list there reached an astounding 89 percent of total mean strength.

Since no improvement was expected unless headquarters was moved, the entire regiment was transferred for that reason in April and divided between three stations in Laguna and Batangas. The change may have been beneficial for the Dasmarinas battalion, but the regiment as a whole fared no better. One-third of the men were admitted to sick list at one time or another during the following month, mainly with malaria, dysentery, and diarrhea. May was worse, with regimental admissions climbing to 43.6 percent. The list gradually shortened as the soldiers settled into garrison life and plasmodial superinfection caused malarial resistance to build. They were recalled to Manila in November and sent south to Mindanao at the beginning of December. The consequences of the imported Luzon plasmodia are unclear because malaria was no longer epidemic in the regiment, and the medical officers thus had little to say on the subject. The epidemiological impact there would have depended on the new pattern of local transmission factors, of which we have no record. In any event, the regiment remained on Mindanao for just three months, its sick list growing slightly, before sailing for San Francisco in March 1901.[31]

The army's mere presence caused Filipinos to alter their behavior so as to increase human and anopheline transmission factors sharply. The wartime migrations of nonresistants from low-lying pueblos to remote barrios at higher elevations were more destabilizing than earlier population movements. Entire towns emptied. Many more people were on the move because unlike the prewar migrations of male seasonal workers, families fled the war together. Since infants and young children had the least amount of acquired immunity of any age cohort and the elderly had relatively low resistance levels, parasite rates and mortality were especially high in refugee groups. A medical officer with the occupying American force watched as the residents trickled back from the hills into Ligao, Albay, in early 1900 and reported that they "were in a very bad state of health; many of them being carried into town with fever, and reports of whole families dying with the disease in the mountains were brought in daily." Another officer visited four barrios near Lipa, Batangas, and observed a great deal of sickness among the residents: "I found them blistering their heads and necks for headaches caused by fever. Many had chills. I found all ages suffering with fever." Major L.M. Maus summarized the situation as of mid-1900: "As a result of the recent wars, a large proportion of the natives had become impoverished, run down in health, and greatly in need of medicines. . . . The only quinine available in the country was that supplied to the troops." He estimated that the "malarial parasite is probably responsible for at least one-half of all the sickness" on Luzon.[32]

Even after the survivors returned from the hills, the infestation level was high enough to allow lowland vectors to sustain the infection. In Indan, Camarines Norte, malaria was pervasive a month after the people came back in, and it was reported that they "die fast." As the five thousand residents of Mercedes on Mindanao began to rebuild their homes, a U.S. military surgeon reported that more than one hundred persons had died of disease in the past two weeks and that the people were on the verge of starvation. About 45 percent of the inhabitants were suffering from malaria and typhoid, and the crops were rotting in the fields for want of harvesters who were well enough to gather them. The continuing grip that outdated disease theory had on American minds aggravated the misery in Banate, Iloilo, in 1900. The commanding officer there identified the damp earth in the fields surrounding the town as the cause of the region being full of malaria. In order to prevent the ground from exuding miasma, he ordered a halt to cultivation of the soil near the town, thus crippling local food production without affecting the malaria.[33]

The second identifiable facet of increased vector capacity (after the increased movement in and out of endemic zones) was the loss of most of the Philippine cattle and carabao population to rinderpest twice after 1888, which diverted anopheline feeding to humans. Cattle plague, as the disease is also called, is highly contagious and usually fatal. The agent of disease is a virus that is transmitted from infected to noninfected animals by close contact, especially by rubbing noses, and most probably by inhalation. The sick animal excretes the virus for only two to three weeks after infection and acquires lengthy resistance, possibly for life, if it survives. Unfortunately, few did. The Southeast Asian carabao, or domestic buffalo, which was by far the most important source of agricultural power in the Philippines, is known for its poor resistance to rinderpest. The principles of the diffusion of this infection are essentially the same as those associated with the spread of human ones. The world can be divided into areas of low and high risk of rinderpest, and the Philippines fell into the former category prior to 1887, when the virus was introduced, apparently for the first time. Virgin epizootics in low-risk areas are explosive and result in high mortality. Researchers who conducted studies on anti-rinderpest serum in the Philippines after the American war asserted that mortality was from 95 to 100 percent among animals in a country previously free from rinderpest once they were brought into contact with the virus. Even in enzootic areas, from 70 to 80 percent might be destroyed. The disease was neither preventable nor curable during the nineteenth century, and although various anti-rinderpest serums were developed in Manila as early as 1901, no effective control or treatment was utilized in the islands until the 1930s.[34]

The importation of the rinderpest virus was arguably the single greatest catastrophe in the nineteenth-century Philippines. Contemporary observers and many historians since have naturally focused on events like typhoons, cholera epidemics, political executions, revolution, and war, whose effects on humans are direct. By contrast, rinderpest's connection with mosquitos and malaria was not known at the time and has not been generally appreciated since. When the carabaos died, the farmers lost their principal source of power, so they could not cultivate as much land as before. The consequent reduction in food supplies, in turn, aggravated malnutrition and debt. Untilled land that returned to scrub or vegetation provided favorable breeding conditions for both locusts and anopheline mosquitos, depending on the season, climatic zone, or elevation of the land. In lieu of its preferred blood meals, A. *minimus flavirostris* increased its human-biting rate, setting off seasonal epidemics that made it difficult for the labor force to work even the reduced amount of agricultural acreage. Malaria's relapsing and recrudescing features debilitated labor for years. In the absence of rinderpest, it takes about three years for the various transmission factors to return to the original equilibrium after epidemic malaria. In its presence, the period is extended because the bovine population needs at least five years to replenish itself fully, if the people are able to begin breeding draft animals immediately, which most Filipino farmers were not. As the carabao and cattle slowly replaced themselves, human-biting rates remained high and malaria continued to prevail. After restocking, equilibrium was precarious because the new animals had acquired no resistance to the virus. The next importation would begin a new cycle.[35]

The great cholera epidemic of 1889 was in a way merely an interlude during a temporary lull in an even greater outbreak of malaria, at least on Luzon. In fact, both epidemics were disastrous, all the more so since they coincided, but cholera's more dramatic explosiveness has long deflected attention from the one that had much greater long-term consequences. Rinderpest appeared in Taytay at the end of 1887. Where the virus originated is unknown, but it was believed to have come to the Philippines from Indochina with carabaos that were imported for breeding purposes. The disease had long been present in mainland Asia and seems to have been epizootic sixteen years earlier in Cambodia, where it was reported that "a terrible malady decimated the water buffalo [that are] so necessary for the labor of rice." Losses were so serious that the royal government prohibited rice exports. Wherever the actual point of origin in 1887, the Philippine epizootic spread rapidly from Taytay, paralyzing agriculture and commerce. The senior physician in Bulacan province wrote that it caused "terrible destruction, killing thousands and thousands of bovine creatures, disturbing the agronomy of entire provinces." He claimed that "the negligence of the pueblos was so extreme that the carcases were abandoned on the land or in the rivers." Steamship captains operating between Manila and Bulacan reported that it was impossible to enter the mouth of the river due to the multitude of dead animals floating in the water. The padre of Haganoy said that the detritus made it difficult for even the smallest boats to navigate.[36]

The provincial records uniformly show a sharp upsurge in malaria in the wake of bovine mortality. In Ilocos Norte, thousands of cattle and carabaos began to die in August 1888, according to Dr. Raquel, who was one of the first to suggest a connection between the epizootic and the malaria that soon followed. The physician was puzzled when malaria became general throughout the province instead of remaining contained in the eastern pueblos as it usually did. He concluded that "the putrefaction from the rotting carcases infested the atmosphere and stirred malarial activity." No other explanation accounted for the disturbance of the "equilibrium of salubrity" in the towns where the fevers were not endemic, he thought. Epidemic malaria prevailed through the 1888–

1889 harvest season and persisted until cholera broke out in July 1889 when the heavy rains began and made conditions ideal for the transmission of water-borne diseases and reduced anopheline density at the same time. No one understood those ecological dynamics, of course, but the appearance of cholera made it seem likely that all three diseases were somehow linked. Dr. Monserrat described how the epizootic had "spread like a spot of oil [all over Luzon] causing sufferings without number." Most of the dead animals were either flung in the rivers, preserved with salt and eaten, or simply exposed to the action of the sun's rays. A small number were buried or burned. He thought it self-evident that the quantity of decomposing animal substances had a deleterious effect on the public health. The fact that the cholera cases followed the path of the epizootic and malarial fevers "inclines us to believe in the genealogical unity of infectious germs and points to the epizootic disease as the origin of the malaria and the cholera." The latter subsided on the north central plain by October, just as the mountain streams began to subside and enable the anophelines to breed again efficiently. Malaria naturally resurged when the new generation of mosquitos found themselves with only humans as a source of blood meals.[37]

Bovine mortality was extensive, and as a result, agricultural output was set back for several years. The demographic statistics relating to livestock were as, or even more, unreliable than those for humans, but for what it is worth, official figures showed that in Pangasinan, for instance, 77,969 of its 93,244 carabaos and cattle died in the epizootic. That estimate was probably low, and indeed 90 percent mortality among Philippine bovines was the figure commonly cited by experts afterwards. Two years into the recovery, Pangasinan still had fewer than one-fourth as many draft animals as it had two decades earlier. Rice harvests declined sharply, necessitating emergency imports from Cochin China to make up the deficiency. Other provinces experienced similar losses as fields went unplanted, and what was harvested rotted for lack of transport to market. The governor of Morong, for instance, reported in 1892 that commerce was still nonexistent in that province. Twenty thousand carabaos had died from rinderpest in 1888, and four years later the farmers were just beginning to plant cane again for the first time, he said. The price of carabaos increased, of course. In Pampanga, the usual cost of Pfs 12–15 per animal jumped to Pfs 35–40 immediately in 1888, making it impossible for the ordinary family to replace the animal it had just lost. Luzon's agricultural production did not begin to rebound until about 1893, when carabao replenishment began to take effect. Until then, mortality from malaria continued to be excessive, and malnutrition increased as food production dwindled. Some areas experienced famine. Once the agricultural recovery got underway, it was cut short after three or four years by the revolt against Spain, during which the growth in the draft-animal population may have slowed or even reversed itself.[38]

Another major outbreak of rinderpest was impossible for some years after 1888 since the few surviving animals had acquired something approaching total resistance to the virus. Within a decade, however, replenishment with susceptibles by natural increase and by importation was sufficient to support another full-scale contagion once favorable transmission conditions existed. The virus was likely to arrive with animals brought in from Indochina or Hong Kong. By that time even the few Asian ports where uninfected or unexposed animals could be purchased were themselves adjacent to countries where the disease existed, so it was "only a matter of time before the disease appears in some of the export animals," according to a veterinarian familiar with the situation early in the new century. Animals arriving in Hong Kong, for instance, were held in a depot that was "thoroughly infected with both foot and mouth disease and rinderpest, which makes it almost impossible to select a ship load of cattle for the Philippines without some of them subsequently coming down with the disease." Chinese cattle dealers were allowed to mix healthy and diseased animals indiscriminately, so it was certain that some of those that reached Manila would be potential sources for an outbreak. The problem was compounded, he thought, because dealers in the Philippines "did not understand the significance of an infective disease and strongly opposed any action taken by the government which tended to interfere with the immediate sale of their animals."[39]

The revolt against Spain in the Tagalog regions of Luzon beginning in August 1896 provided the right conditions for the spread of rinderpest. Some of the refugees took their carabaos with them as they fled the fighting, the armies commandeered what animals they could find for haulage and food, and rustlers stole others. As with human movement, bovine mobility and mixing increased the probability that the animals would come in contact with the virus and pass it on through close contact. The disease may have reemerged as early as 1898. Ileto points to reports of complete carabao depopulation in western Batangas at that time and argues that even the combined effects of flight, forced conscription, and theft would not have produced that result. Whether or not the virus appeared that early, wartime conditions between 1896 and 1898 precipitated changes in other transmission factors. Human movement in and out of endemic malaria zones increased, and numbers of anophelines undoubtedly did too. A report from Balayan, Batangas, in 1898 said that because of the draft-animal scarcity, the untilled land "has now become a jungle." The provincial governor reported that at Tuy, Batangas, three years of neglect due to a shortage of labor and carabaos had turned all the land into a wilderness. Standing pools, irrigation ditches, and vegetated areas untouched by human activity would have provided secondary vectors with optimum breeding conditions. Subsequent studies support such speculation. A 1906 survey in Angeles, Pampanga, discovered that when the grass around Camp Stotsenburg was allowed to grow to any great length, mosquitos and malaria both increased. It has been shown since, for example, that *Anopheles balabacensis* thrives in shaded pools but disappears when the covering growth is removed. As vegetation reclaimed uncultivated fields after 1896, the increase in numbers of lowland anophelines was enough to overcome their normally feeble ability to transmit malaria.[40]

Thus, factors of transmission were already in disequilibrium when rinderpest broke out. It is unlikely that the U.S. Army was directly responsible for introducing the virus, but the invading forces certainly spread the epizootic, first on Luzon in 1899 and thereafter throughout the islands. As the army pushed north and south out of Manila, it requisitioned for haulage all the carabaos it could locate. Those animals traveled much greater distances than they would have normally, increasing their susceptibility through debilitation, and being in large groups, they easily spread the disease by nasal discharge. The usual consequences followed this second depopulation of draft animals, except that its conjunction with the other hardships of war made the suffering of a decade earlier pale by comparison. As it turned out, the Americans were hardly inconvenienced by the sudden disappearance of their bovine porters. Just as carabaos became scarce in late 1899, mules and horses began to arrive from the United States to fill the teamsters' needs. Quartermaster General Marshall I. Ludington was thus able to note in his next annual report that "the army has not felt seriously the loss of this animal."[41]

Reports from areas occupied after late 1899 increasingly mentioned rinderpest, which was so virulent that it had no difficulty surviving the dry season (during which time transmission normally abates) in the first half of 1900. It reached Aparri, Cagayan, at the northern tip of Luzon by May 1900 and was still killing large numbers of animals there a year later. Southeastern Luzon was also affected by mid-1900 as the disease moved north through Albay into Camarines Sur. Around Nueva Caceres, all of the cattle and all but a few of the carabaos succumbed. At Pili, "the Bicol River was lined in all shallow places with the carcases piled up and the air was foul all over the fields." The American medical officer at Buhi, in the same province, reported that the "stench from the carcases is unbearable at times." By January 1901 the cattle plague had spread beyond Luzon, and conditions were epizootic in Cagayan de Misamis. Soon the eastern Visayas were invaded, and by midyear the military surgeon in Palompan, Leyte, reported that no fresh beef could be obtained.[42]

Malaria followed of course. No one seems to have had any new insight into the connection, however. If they had, presumably the U.S. Army command would not have encouraged its malaria-ridden troops to kill the remaining beasts as part of the pacification program. Nor would it have been indifferent to those who killed livestock just for fun. The ecological process was inexorable once mosquitos were deprived of their primary blood meals. In Daet, Camarines Norte, for example, the medical officer reported in October 1900 that the animals were "falling dead all over town, blood running in a small stream from their rectums." As we would expect, his next monthly report noted that the townspeople were dying at a great rate, mostly due to malaria. By January, four to eight funerals were being held each day. On Marinduque, rinderpest and American soldiers had combined to eliminate the carabaos and the once-flourishing herds of cattle by late 1901. In November of that year, "considerable malarial fever" was reported, and conditions were epidemic three months later just as the cholera was about to arrive. That passed but since there was still "not a head [of cattle] to be seen" on the island in mid-1903, malaria continued to account for the great majority of death and disability there. The concurrence of war, rinderpest, and malaria crippled localities for years. The situation in Cabuyao, Laguna, was representative. That pueblo had once produced both rice and sugarcane in abundance, but those fields had not been tilled since 1896 and were said to be "now overrun with weeds" in 1903. Peace had come at last, but no draft animals were left with which to begin clearing the land and planting the crops for the next harvest. The extent of malarial infection among the farmers was not reported, but census data indicates that the human energy required for the (extra) work was substantially impaired. Death rates in the municipality for 1902 and 1903 were 116.5 and 47.1 per 1,000, respectively, and malaria accounted for 50.1 percent of the mortality.[43]

The postwar census concluded that 42 percent of Philippine carabaos died in 1902, mainly in the Visayas and Mindanao since the population on Luzon had already been almost completely wiped out. The enumerators hastened to add that since no statistics were available for the previous war years, the figure represented about half of the real death rate during the epizootic. Contemporary estimates for Batangas, which May accepts, were that from 75 to 90 percent of carabaos in that province had died by mid-1902. Though the years 1902–1903, like 1888–1889, are chiefly remembered in Philippine histories for the disastrous cholera epidemic that swept the islands, malaria killed more people. The census (again, for what it is worth) counted 211,993 deaths from malaria versus 200,348 from cholera during those two horrible years. What made malaria the much greater problem was its persistence and its effect on productivity. Cholera disappears in any given area after about three months. By contrast, malaria relapses or recrudesces in individual survivors, and transmission continues at abnormally high levels in the community after epidemics for at least three years until the original ecological equilibrium is regained. One contemporary study suggests the extent of malarial infection in the population during the war years. By 1906, malarial transmission was returning to its preepidemic levels, and yet the researchers found that 46.7 percent of the children tested were infected. By contrast, that proportion seems to have dropped sharply, to 13.2 percent, during less troubled times two decades later. And so, at the end of the war, its carabao population almost gone, its anopheline-mosquito population presumably increased, and much of its human population destitute, the Philippines faced a bleak short-term future.[44]

CHAPTER 7

Cholera: The Island World as an Epidemiological Unit

By ABOUT 1870 all the elements were in place for a lethal epidemic of Asiatic cholera that would scour the archipelago from end to end. Localized for centuries in India, the disease had become pandemic in the early nineteenth century and had spread to the Philippines three times since, most recently via Shanghai. That last outbreak, in the mid-1860s, had been serious, spreading beyond Luzon to Mindanao and some of the Visayas, and officials had scrambled afterwards to fix quarantine procedures in Philippine ports. Spanish legations everywhere went on alert. Then in July 1873, the consul in Singapore notified Manila that all ships arriving from Bangkok had been put under strict quarantine because of a cholera outbreak that had occurred "with alarming characteristics of intensity and propagation" in the Siamese capital. The Junta Superior de Sanidad (board of health) in Manila immediately imposed its own fifteen-day quarantine on all ships from Siam and reserved the power to decide on further measures should any changes in the health of those on board have occurred en route to the Philippines. Notice of the potential emergency, along with a directive to take appropriate measures, was sent to the local administrations of all open Philippine port cities, each of which sent back acknowledgments and reports. The military governor of Zamboanga, for instance, described plans to dock any ship from the infected area at Santa Cruz island, within sight but about an hour's distance from the port, where the vessel and the crew were to be quarantined until health officials determined that no danger existed. As replies continued to come in, the Spanish consulate in Singapore relayed word to the board of health in early September that the contagion in Bangkok had died out and that the quarantine against departures from that port had been lifted. The board in Manila proceeded to end its quarantine in accordance with newly-established procedures and sent out the appropriate directives to the other ports. Luck had held for the time being.[1]

Asiatic cholera was by far the most terrifying of the diseases that ravaged the Philippines. Its course was sudden, swift, virulent, agonizingly painful, and most often fatal. Popular fear was increased by the obvious helplessness of healers, priests, and physicians. The riots that exploded in Manila during the 1820 epidemic—after rumors circulated of a plot to poison the waters—were intensified when some foreigners gave cholera victims concoctions of cinchona and alcohol, which were "a thousand times more pernicious than the disease that they were intended to guard against." So were some of the prescriptions administered in the Philippines throughout the century, especially those containing opiates. Other remedies were less dangerous but no more effective. Infusions of manungal oil, betel-nut chewing, and prayers to San Roque were the most popular preventatives, and health officials urged the people to avoid fresh air, to wear flannel, and to burn smudge pots of lemongrass and tar. Other recommended measures, such as straining drinking water and observing personal and household hygiene, made more sense but had little impact in the face of widespread poverty and insanitation. By the 1870s, Spanish and Filipino doctors generally, if imperfectly, understood the conditions for the propagation of cholera, but the prevention of epidemics was impossible, and effective treatment of patients was not available in the Philippines until the twentieth century.[2]

Cholera follows an invasion of the small intestine by the bacterium *Vibrio cholerae*, which is ingested with contaminated water (or less commonly, food). The infection causes massive diarrhea and vomiting resulting in rapid and severe depletion of body fluids and salts. Patients either convalesce rapidly, undergo a fevered stage before recovery, or die. The case-fatality rate in Asia during the nineteenth century seems usually have to ranged between about 50 and 70 percent. Death is rare today when proper treatment is administered. Modern antibiotics shorten the duration of diarrhea (and thus the excretion of vibrios), and prompt intravenous replacement of lost fluids and salts brings rapid recovery. The latter procedure is the only cure, and although it had been tried in Europe as early as 1831, the first attempts at fluid replacement were not undertaken in the Philippines until 1909. Prior to that time, the disease was able to claim its victims virtually unhindered.[3]

Genetic and actively acquired resistance were the only defenses against cholera available to Filipinos and their communities. The first is not fully understood, but the great variance in individual susceptibility suggests that it may be important. Not everyone exposed to infection becomes infected, and many of those who do are asymptomatic. Although the severity of infection is clearly related to the number of bacteria ingested, individual differences in characteristics like gastric-juice acidity probably influence the outcome. Malnourishment compromises natural defenses readily, however, and that being so, acquired resistance is a crucial factor. When cholera vibrios secrete their toxin in the intestine, the host produces various types of antibodies that not only prevent multiplication of the parasite in the gut but also provide substantial, though not complete, resistance to subsequent infection, both homologous and heterologous. The duration of that protection is unknown, but the effect on the community is determined by the same epidemiological principles governing the state of herd immunity against other diseases that confer some degree of resistance. Thus, cholera is generally restricted to individuals under ten years of age in endemic areas, while all age groups are equally susceptible in nonendemic regions like the nineteenth-century Philippines.[4]

Cholera is transmitted by carriers, a fact of crucial importance in the epidemiology of the disease, and the one that doomed efforts to stop its spread in the islands. Robert Koch spelled out the problem as early as 1884: "We must consider that it is not only the individual who dies of cholera, or who has an unquestionable attack of cholera, that is liable to transfer infection, but that all possible transitions up to this most violent form of the disease, even slight attacks of diarrhea, take place, which are probably just as capable of giving infection as the worst case of diarrhea." Indeed, a large number of mild or symptomless infections exist for every clinically recognized case, especially in children, and it is those ambulatory patients who are primarily responsible for maintenance and transmission of the infection. Ironically, the more intense the infection, the less important is the patient in spreading the disease, since he or she will be bedridden. Acute carriers are those who have had asymptomatic or mild cases (the latter typically presenting simple diarrhea and malaise) and who pass vibrios for about a week thereafter. The spread of the disease is only limited by the distance the person can cover in that time.[5]

Lacking antibiotics and the technique of fluid and salt replacement as well as the means to improve sanitation and water supplies significantly, Philippine health authorities could do little to combat cholera a century ago. Isolation of infectives and their household contacts would have been the most effective weapon, as it was against most infectious diseases, but it was impossible as a practical matter. The cultural disinclination of Filipinos to separate those who are ill from their relatives and friends, along with the antagonistic nature of the colonial relationship and the inability to enforce isolation, precluded that means of control. Quarantines have never proved particularly effective anywhere since it is impossible to impede all movement from an endemic area. For cholera to become epidemic or even pandemic, all that is necessary is a high volume of infection in the endemic region and substantial movement into an area with a high proportion of susceptibles. Aside from the difficulty in detaining all suspected infectives, some carriers are intermittent excretors and will slip through any protective barrier. Advance preparation (such as the construction of temporary hospitals) could have reduced interaction between susceptibles and some infectives, but Spanish health officials in the Philippines rarely did more than react to epidemics that were already underway. An overcentralized administrative structure and the chronic shortage of funds worked together to impair the ability to anticipate emergencies at the provincial and local levels.[6]

If the money and will had existed, all municipalities could have organized permanent boards of health with at least partially effective powers of enforcement under noncrisis conditions. Preparations for possible disaster could have been ongoing. Dr. Gomez pointed out that the padres were the natural persons to take the lead since they lived amongst the people. They saw diseases begin, knew who had to be isolated, and could give succor to the poor, not only spiritually, but by distributing money and clothes. In practice, however, local boards (comprising the padre, local officials and administrators, and the médico titular, if one resided there) were formed only in response to crises and sometimes only after specific authorization from Manila. They were then allowed to lapse after the emergency had passed, which was usually long before the colonial administration granted any relief funds. Public health in the Philippines was unlikely to improve, Dr. Gomez said, so long as the various provincial and municipal boards created by mandate from Manila existed in name only, like those that the governor-general had created during the 1882 cholera epidemic, which, "having neither independence nor resources, died in their birth." As a consequence of such inadequate administration, temporary cholera hospitals were seldom built until after contagion had broken out, and in the ensuing chaos the authorities were too busy burying the dead to isolate those who were merely ill.[7]

Since cholera went unchecked after it appeared, the most practical option open to the health authorities was to concentrate energies on preventing its arrival in the first place. Each of the major nineteenth-century Philippine cholera epidemics was almost surely the result of imported infection, despite heated contentions by some contemporaries that the vibrio had established endemicity in the soil or in various water sources. The issue is unimportant, however, because any diffusion among the various islands represented an "importation," whether the initial outbreak occurred in Bengal or on Luzon. The only line of defense in the Philippines was the informal, international system of maritime quarantines, which was triggered by reports of outbreaks in ports from Aden to Nagasaki. Five years after the 1873 Bangkok scare, the alarm was sounded again, this time by the Spanish legation in Nagasaki, and quarantine procedures were activated once more. It too proved to be a false alarm. No record exists of the number of vessels detained in Philippine ports as a result of the alerts that decade, but it is likely that what saved the archipelago were the quarantines against departures from the infected ports. The localized outbreaks in Siam and Japan during the 1870s were contained, but when cholera became pandemic again in the next decade, the volume of infection in the affected areas and the amount of shipping bound for the Philippines was too great to be blocked in the ports of departure. And once the disease had crossed the Sulu or South China Seas, Philippine quarantines would prove to be of little use.[8]

Cholera continued to converge on the islands from all directions. In September 1881, the Spanish consul in Singapore again raised a cholera warning—this time from Batavia. Within a month, word arrived from Macao that new foci of infection had appeared elsewhere on Java and also in Japan. It was also reported that Singapore had as yet failed to take adequate precautions against eastbound shipping. The steamship *Catharina II* weighed anchor in Manila Bay in November after a voyage from Spain, via Gibralter, Port Said, Singapore, and Saigon. When the captain failed to produce a certification of good health from Singapore, the ship was promptly detained for a week's observation. The same precautions were taken with the *Diamonte* from Hong Kong, and when a cholera case was reported aboard the *Emuy*, also from that port, the quarantine was strengthened further. Then news of a cholera outbreak in Aden arrived the next month, and the Philippines went on full alert. The director general of the Junta Superior de Sanidad rushed a circular to provincial officials instructing them to take precautionary measures and warning that the colony was at increased risk "since frequent commerce between Europe and Asia has made propagation of the disease so easy."[9]

The precautions were of no avail. A devastating archipelago-wide epidemic was set off by the arrival of "the guest from the Ganges" into the Jolo group six months later, probably from Borneo and perhaps traceable to Mecca. Dr. D.R. Alba y Martín, director of health for the Port of Zamboanga, later published an account of how the epidemic had arrived and taken hold. His subtext, though tactful and muted, is significant for its recognition that economic development had a public health cost and for its contribution to the embryonic debate in the Philippines about how the two should be balanced. While acknowledging the importance of commerce to modern civilization, the doctor argued that its claim must be secondary to the ancient principle that the people's health is the supreme law. Safeguarding the public health required the government to recognize the necessity of enacting and then enforcing regulations that might well inconvenience commerce and trade. The cholera epidemic was a clear example of the consequences of failing to do so.[10]

Prior to 1882, according to Dr. Alba, official notices arrived from Manila each year announcing the appearance of cholera in one place or another in Southeast Asia, but the Philippines had so far been spared. During the first half of that year, however, it began to appear that the long-anticipated disaster might be at hand when he began receiving "extraofficial" reports in Zamboanga about outbreaks first on Sumatra, then on Java, and finally on Borneo. The threat arose from "the frequent communications between our subjects in the Jolo Archipelago and the Moros of Borneo, the Celebes, Tawi Tawi, and the infinity of other islands." Long- and short-distance commerce was conducted by a variety of fast Moro boats whose shallow drafts enabled them not only to sail the open seas but to enter estuaries and rivers and thus to penetrate island interiors directly. Regulation of such movement would have been beyond the means of any quarantine system, but the colonial adminstration in Manila was almost entirely powerless in this case because it exercised only token control over its southern islands and none over those beyond. The sultan of Jolo was still the ruler in the Sulu Archipelago, even though he had to suffer the presence of a military garrison near his residence at Maibung on Jolo island. One consequence of Spain's merely nominal rule over the southern entrance to its archipelago was that the movement of disease paid no heed whatever to formal political boundaries in that part of the world.[11]

When the mail steamer *España* arrived in Zamboanga on June 14, 1882, passengers who had boarded in Jolo reported the existence of cholera in Maibung and in other places on Jolo near the troops. Dr. Alba immediately notified the military governor of Zamboanga, who convened the board of health. Quarantine measures were put into effect to prevent passengers from disembarking and cargoes of commercial vessels from being unloaded in the port until the expiration of a five-day holding period, during which health clearances were given only after a medical examination of all persons and disinfection of clothes, cargoes, and animals. The board's decision to enforce a quarantine was not a foregone conclusion. The port physician's repeated references to the "many enemies" of the quarantine system who opposed its "grave inconveniences to the flow of commerce" suggest that every vote in favor of issuing a restrictive order as the crisis developed was a hard-won victory. He was also able to argue successfully that the quarantine should be extended to all Moro boats, no matter how small, with special attention to those that had sailed more than twenty-four hours to reach port. Accordingly, the port captain announced that no Moro boat of any description would be allowed to enter, nor could any Moro depart the port of Zamboanga without a physical examination and health clearance from Dr. Alba. Moro "mandarins" in the barrio of Magay and on the nearby islands of Sacol, Santa Cruz, and Tictabong were ordered to enforce the quarantine in their districts.[12]

Dr. Alba was not sanguine about the prospects for success of his cordon sanitaire. For one thing, it had been thrown together too quickly. "Cholera is a guest for whom one must prepare," he wrote. Quarantines on both land and sea could be effective, he maintained, but only if they were rigorous and thorough, and he was well aware that the one around Zamboanga was hopelessly porous. Reports of cholera on Sumatra or Java were alarming, and its appearance on Borneo presented a dire threat, but once it broke out on Jolo there was no chance of escape for the Philippines. In that island world, all roads led to Zamboanga, and as outposts of empire, Jolo and Zamboanga were in constant communication. The Spanish doctor claimed that "for the Moros, Zamboanga is Paris and Versailles." Because "they live for the day" and did not produce surpluses of necessities like rice and betel nut, Zamboanga functioned as the "indispensable storehouse for their existence." The innumerable Moro boats converging on the trading center at any time would avoid the quarantine by landing outside the reach of the port's one watchman, which was easy enough to do since "the *vintas* [boats] go wherever they wish." Anyone unlucky enough to be stopped could offer a small bribe and be allowed to land, transact business, and leave.[13]

Should the quarantine in Zamboanga fail, the potential consequences were clear. The historical record reflects for the first time the widespread understanding that the revolution in transportation and commerce had put all Filipinos at common risk to imported disease, wherever its original port of entry. Dr. Alba recalled that the governor-general in Manila was desperate to prevent the introduction of cholera into Zamboanga "because it could logically be presumed that having invaded this province, it would undoubtedly spread to the others." Although he did not allude to the epidemic of a decade and a half earlier, everyone was aware that cholera could survive the trip between Manila and Zamboanga. Dr. Alba put the problem this way: "Once cholera had invaded the Jolo archipelago, anyone with a little knowledge of the geographical position of those islands and the nomadic instincts of their inhabitants could be assured, without being a prophet, that they would spread the disease in all directions and that sooner or later it would enter Mindanao, and almost surely through Zamboanga, from where it would then spread throughout the entire [Philippine] archipelago."[14]

As Dr. Alba and the other junta members worked to institute the quarantine, notify Moro leaders, police sanitation in the public market, construct temporary cholera hospitals, and organize isolation procedures, they learned that the naval schooner *Sirena* had arrived from Jolo with sixty sick soldiers on board. They were being transferred, as was the routine practice, from the post hospital on Jolo to the larger and better-equipped military hospital at Zamboanga. The *Sirena* carried a health clearance from Jolo, but Dr. Alba was immediately alarmed and requested that the provisions of the quarantine law be extended to naval vessels. In Zamboanga, military interests were even more powerful than commercial ones, however. Receiving support from only one other member of the board, the prominent local merchant Eduardo Fargas, the proposal was rejected. His backing was enough, though, to secure Dr. Alba permission to examine the men on board prior to disembarkation. Finding the usual tropical diseases amidst deplorable hygenic conditions, but no cholera, the physician was somewhat reassured. Even so, the cases of dysentery were worrisome, and as a precaution he requested that the men be isolated for a time in temporary structures on a nearby island. Again the junta turned him down, but he and Fargas did win agreement that, without exception, all ships coming from the Celebes and Jolo would be detained for three days of observation.

A few days later, the gunboat *Paragua* arrived with fifteen sick cases on board, having stopped at Jolo where the sultan had personally confirmed to the commander the existence of a "very rare disease" that was characterized by vomiting, diarrhea and the death of most of its victims within 24 hours. It was said to have been imported on the steamship *Hong-Hang*, which plied between Batavia, Borneo, and Jolo, by a pilgrim who was returning from Mecca. The *Paragua* was promptly detained in the port of Zamboanga for the three-day waiting period despite the ship's health clearance and the commander's vigorous protests. When Dr. Alba discovered that the gunboat had neither a doctor nor facilities for the sick, he offered to treat the invalids, but the angry commander refused, and the military governor of Zamboanga declined to intervene. Just then, at the beginning of July, the warship *Legaspi* steamed in from Jolo with seventy-nine sick transferees and a request from the military governor of Jolo that ordinary quarantine procedures be waived. Despite assurances that the men presented only common diseases and had not had contact with Moros, Dr. Alba was able to have the ship held under observation for five days before landing. During that time, five deaths occurred on board, which the ship's physician ascribed to chronic malaria. He insisted that the men harbored nothing more dangerous, and with great misgivings, Dr. Alba allowed them to disembark. Deaths continued, however, and it soon became evident that the soldiers had carried cholera into Zamboanga.[15]

During the same period, a Moro named Agase had secretly brought his family from their home on Sacol over to Tictabong, just a few miles from Zamboanga. A colorful adventurer, Agase had once been a much-decorated Spanish agent who had led numerous missions to rescue prisoners held by the Moros. Later it was discovered that he had used those heroics as a cover for his own piratical activities, and Dr. Alba noted that his fall from official favor explained why he had taken care to arrive quietly and to evade the authorities. Feeling ill, however, Agase soon returned to Sacol, where he died of cholera. Deaths characterized by vomiting and diarrhea immediately followed on Tictabong and were officially reported by local Moro leaders as fever aggravated by the custom of bathing while sick and by the consumption of fruits and alcoholic beverages. Residents of the island knew better, however, and fled in all directions, moving undetected along the mangrove-covered estuaries on the main island.

The many other avenues of importation into Zamboanga are untraceable, but the hopelessness of Dr. Alba's task is clear enough. Whatever the precise chain of infection, Zamboanga's first known cholera death occurred on July 7 in one of the poorest barrios. The physician was called at nightfall to the house of Julio Bautista, who had just died after twelve hours of vomiting, diarrhea, and cramps. Diagnosing the cause of death as true Asiatic cholera, Dr. Alba ordered the body interred immediately. He intended to have Bautista's house burned but changed his mind when he learned that more than thirty persons had visited the decedent during his illness and had already scattered. Under the circumstances, the benefits of destroying the house seemed outweighed by the risk of fire spreading to the rest of the barrio, so he directed that only Bautista's clothes and other effects were to be burned.

Dr. Alba's worst fears were soon confirmed, however. Two days later he watched helplessly as a Chinese who had been transferred from the general hospital to one of the hastily constructed isolation structures died after a six-hour struggle. More deaths followed the same day, and one of the soldiers from the *Legaspi* was admitted to the military hospital with cholera. At that point, the physician conferred with his colleagues, Dr. Agustín Planter and Dr. Antonio Suarez. They pooled what they knew and concluded that cholera had indeed been imported from Jolo by several routes. Faced with the certainly that an epidemic was about to explode, neither the military governor nor the other board members continued to balk at recommendations from the medical community. The junta declared that the population was in a state of epidemic and imposed a total prohibition on all movement in or out of the port. The governor himself declared that a cholera epidemic existed at the military hospital, of which he was the director.

The board labored mightily to prevent further spread of the disease as the epidemic broke loose, but to no avail. It was already too late. Dr. Alba admitted that despite the frequency of worldwide cholera epidemics during the nineteenth century, medical science had made no major breakthrough against the disease: "Apart from isolation and incommunication, it can be said that we are in the infancy with respect to methods of prophylaxis." Then once a community was infested, "isolation is in most cases absolutely impossible, and not being rigorous, is totally useless." Still, methods such as prohibiting crowds from congregating, billeting soldiers well away from the populace, destroying structures, utensils, and clothes of the victims, and disinfection of latrines were at least theoretically available "to attentuate the havoc." His analysis shows that advances had been made in understanding the epidemiology of cholera. He pinpointed the latrines as the principal foci of infection, noting that the old methods of purifying the air "are as useless as they are ridiculous." Once the epidemic broke over Zamboanga, however, all of the attenuating methods seemed either impossible or futile, as the dispersal of Bautista's contacts had already shown. Primary attention had to be given to the patients in any case, but that was a losing battle as well. Dr. Alba explained that in epidemic conditions doctors are simply unable to work as fast as necessary and that truly "in those cases *time is life*."[16]

The subsequent death toll makes it plain that time had run out. The epidemic raged through the military district, including its offshore islands, for about two months, the last death occurring on September 15. Official statistics indicated that about one out of every six persons in the main pueblo died. Almost 40 percent of the 7,571 residents were attacked, and just under half of those succumbed. Contacts immediately spread the infection beyond the city. Whether the infection reached Basilan from the north or south is unknown, but mortality among the Moro population on that island was said to be severe, with half of the residents of Panigayan dying. Boatloads of food were taken out to sea and overturned so that evil spirits would let them live in peace, but to no apparent avail. Fatalities began to occur in the district's other Mindanao pueblos (Tetuan, Las Mercedes, and Ayala) within a week of Bautista's death. Mortality there, while high, was not as catastrophic as in Zamboanga. Still, more than a quarter of the district's 15,359 inhabitants contracted the disease, and 11.2 percent of the population (1,719) died of cholera in two months.[17]

In the meantime, the islands to the north awaited their guest. In Capiz City on Panay's northern coast, Dr. Rebelo had about a month to prepare after word arrived in mid-July of the cholera outbreaks in Jolo and Zamboanga. "Such frightening news, which was not long in spreading through the población, began to awaken alarm among the families," he said. As incoming reports continued to chart the disease's inexorable progress, the local board of health worked feverishly, not to prevent its arrival, which was considered a certainty, but "to prevent the epidemic from spreading in the pueblos or to minimize its effects and at the same time to remove permanent or accidental causes of poor health." Local boards were appointed in the various towns to work on preventing the epidemic's spread through the province. Capiz City was divided into eight administrative zones in which commissions of relief were to distribute food and medicine. A small structure that would function as a provisionary cholera hospital was to be built immediately. A commission was appointed to visit houses to investigate the causes of bad health, and it was recommended that the entire pueblo be cleaned—sewers, estuaries, roads, schools, and corrals. Prisoners were to be released from the jail to reduce crowding, it being further agreed that none but those committing serious crimes would be admitted thereafter. Regulations were issued to ensure that meat and fish would be inspected and that the air would not be polluted. Vigilance over the poor was to be increased to keep friends and relatives from overcrowding the small houses. Most important of all, beaches and boats were to be monitored closely.[18]

It is impossible to know how many lives, if any, were saved by the board's actions, but nothing in the record indicates that they made a great difference. Preparations went forward, but with "much difficulty and blunder," and effective implementation proved impossible. As Dr. Rebelo put it: "The Juntas initiated much, but not everything was realized." Underlying the futility was the impossibility of ameliorating "the abandoned state in which most inhabitants live." Manila was immediately petitioned for funds to carry out preventive measures, but the growing emergency had stopped all normal activity in the archipelago, including the mail service as well as the usually plodding bureaucracy. As a result, the board knew that "the grievous enemy would surely claim many victims before authorization came from Manila." Fears intensified as contagion seeped northward province by province, at the same time leap-frogging between ports that were in frequent communication. Tension became almost unbearable as first Negros and then the southern tip of Panay were invaded. Reliable reports of high death tolls in Iloilo City and Jaro followed. "No one could ignore them," the doctor said, and "even the parish priest began to show the strain in his appearance."[19]

Cholera came ashore on August 18 in Dumulug, a barrio on the beach north of Capiz City, apparently brought in at night by some fisherman coming around the northeast horn of Panay from Estancia, where the epidemic had just broken out. The governor instantly dispatched Dr. Rebelo to the area in a fruitless attempt to restrict the disease, which "exploded like a bomb." By August 23 it had appeared to the south of the población, and then to the east. When it "invaded the center of this perimeter" a few days later, he returned and worked heroically but by his own admission had little success. He treated only the smallest fraction of the victims, of course, many of whom were in their last throes when he saw them, and then he prescribed the deadly alcohol and opiate remedies in which some physicians still had faith. Ironically, he remarked with bitterness that most of his patients who did not die immediately "gave up the prescribed regime and handed themselves over to traditional healers, stupid and uncivilized people who are devoted to giving poultices and sticking plaster for all sorts of ailments, which pass among the Filipinos for an infallible method, but inevitably give rise to suffering in a terrible disease such as cholera."[20]

Within a few days of the outbreak, victims were already "dying too fast to keep up with the burials." The disease had attacked with "irresistible violence [and] those charged with carrying out the corpses frequently felt the first symptoms in the street." Death commonly came in a few hours. Dr. Rebelo noted that the poor were attacked disproportionately and that "those weakened and debilitated by preexisting diseases" were most likely to die. The epidemic peaked in September, seeming to fade thereafter, but it resurged in both Octo-

ber and November before disappearing from Capiz City in the first week of
December. The 1,626 deaths recorded for the town meant that about one of
every nine residents died. The only indication of case-fatality rates comes from
a notation that 115 cholera patients were admitted to the hospital and that 67
of those died. The available statistics for the entire province suggest that mortality was less in the interior, yet Dr. Rebelo said the situation was worse in the
other pueblos. If the health authorities in Capiz City were unable to deliver
medicine, relief, or even attention to most victims there, elsewhere no resources were available at all. Permission for emergency funding never did arrive from the central government. The frustrated physician credited the tireless
work of "those who strove for the public good" with averting utter disaster.
Pointedly, he also gave "thanks to heaven for being interested in the people."[21]

Manila is twice as far from Jolo as Capiz City is, but the capital had no more
time to prepare since shipping contacts were direct and regular. Despite the
reduction in volume of seaborne traffic after cholera invaded the archipelago,
the spread of the disease to the capital was still a certainty. The imported vibrios finally came via Zamboanga, perhaps on the *Francisco Reyes*, which had
steamed into that southern port around the first of July with the mail and orders
to take a doctor to Jolo and to bring all of the Sixth Infantry's sick back to
Zamboanga. Everyone agreed that the ship had brought the disease back to the
capital on its trip north, but Dr. Benito Francia y Ponce de Leon claimed that
cholera had arrived shortly before on another steamer. Writing five or six years
later, he said that the first verified cases had actually been some servants of a
brigadier general who was being transferred from Jolo. However it may have
arrived, the disease "fell upon well-prepared ground," as Dr. Koeniger put it.
The large numbers of migrants drawn to the city by the transformed economy
lived in miserably unsanitary conditions, and an epidemic was unavoidable once the infection was imported into that setting. Only the natural
interplay of transmission factors would determine when it would fade out.[22]

Still, the board of health immediately took all of the standard administrative
measures when the epidemic erupted around August 20. In addition, smudge
pots of lemongrass and tar were burned throughout the city to counter infectious miasma, and medical officials advised the people to protect themselves
even further by keeping camphor-filled quills in their mouths. The sale of fruits
and certain other foodstuffs was prohibited. For community morale, the authorities prohibited the tolling of bells for the dead and dying, and regular band
concerts were given in different parts of the city. Once the epidemic had burst
upon the population, however, little could be done to restore calm. Dr. Koeniger said that "panic spread among the native and European population because
cholera had not occurred since 1865, and especially since in the beginning
mortality exceeded 75 percent of the infected." Many people, as we have seen,
stayed indoors and did not dare eat anything but white rice, which seemed to
be the safest food. Since relatives were often unable to bury their dead, a burial
corps collected the corpses from hospitals and houses, using quicklime for general disinfection and for treating the bodies at interment. Typhoons, flooding,

and beriberi compounded the misery, and the contagion began to reach beyond the capital. As cholera spread throughout Luzon, it subsided in Manila by early December, having killed about 10 percent of the city's population.[23]

Breaking the pattern of twenty-year intervals between epidemics, cholera reappeared just six years later, in 1888. No new countermeasures were available, but enough acquired resistance may have remained in the population to afford a small measure of protection. As in the 1860s, the disease almost certainly arrived from the north. Alarm was raised in mid-June by the Manila press with reports of cholera in Hong Kong, but the Spanish consul in the Crown colony could not confirm them because of official stonewalling. Apprehension increased, however, when some Hong Kong newspapers affirmed that a number of sudden deaths had indeed occurred and also when the weekly health statistics there revealed a considerable increase in diarrheal and stomach illnesses. That was enough for the Central Board of Health in Manila to declare "suspicious" all ships arriving from Hong Kong, especially those carrying cargoes from Saigon, where cholera had appeared as well. Some of the vessels also brought "hundreds of crowded and filthy immigrants," who were promptly quarantined for ten days in a dirty isolation building across the bay in Mariveles before receiving permission to proceed into Manila.[24]

The epidemiology of the outbreak perplexed the health authorities. Dr. Francia finally concluded that its origin could not be explained with certainty "despite all the pompous academic theories" on the subject. No cases had developed among the detainees, and yet a suspicious case had appeared in the general population during the first half of July. Even more mystifying was the fact that the epidemic eventually erupted in a place nowhere near Mariveles: "In August, without communications, without traces of importation, cholera broke out in Taytay—a place well removed from the flow of commerce, situated almost in the interior, whose inhabitants are farmers—leaping those industrial river communities most in contact with persons from diverse places." The explanation may lie in an unconfirmed report that some infected sailors on a Hong Kong cargo ship had somehow made their way overland to Taytay after disembarking in Lucena, Tayabas. However cholera arrived, the first case was an elderly woman who had not left her house, and the second was a friend who came to visit her. Despite the usual frantic but tardy health measures, the disease then did follow the usual commercial routes, spreading within days to all of the towns along the Pasig River and inevitably to Manila. By the end of August the entire central plain was affected. In late February 1889, the disease was taken to Zamboanga—supposedly by an immigrant family from Manila or, alternatively, by a brigantine from Hong Kong that lacked the proper health clearances and docked under the pretext of an emergency. The epidemic spread to the Visayas thereafter, and death rates skyrocketed throughout the archipelago in 1889.[25]

Cholera returned for the third time in two decades early in 1902. Tragically, Filipinos had been better off under an inept colonial administration that was helpless to protect them from cholera and in effect, left them to the mercies of natural transmission factors. The Americans had both the will and the capability to act, along with boundless self-righteousness, but the power to intervene in the epidemic turned out to be only a power to make it worse. The 1902–1903 contagion was the 1888–1889 epidemic compounded. As before, rinderpest had already killed most of the bovine population, and malaria was epidemic in many regions. What separated this calamity from the earlier ones was not only the new administration's greater assertiveness but also the fact that the contagion erupted in the wake of war. Serious fighting had ended, to be sure, but the U.S. Army did not consider itself or the colonial enterprise completely out of danger. The American president's unilateral declaration that the war had ended was still several months away. The war and the cholera thus became entangled, and the situation was complicated further by the people's continuing dependence on the occupying force for some of their food. Ileto has identified the essence of the problem, pointing out that the second quarter of 1902 was a time "when the war against the cholera and the 'pacification' of Filipinos were barely differentiated, when medico-sanitary measures and popular resistance to such, were continuing acts of war."[26]

Cholera had been the U.S. Army medical department's worst nightmare from the beginning. Not only was the havoc of the 1882 and 1888–1889 Philippine outbreaks known, but most of the senior military officers remembered epidemic cholera among the soldiers in the United States three decades earlier. Henry Lippincott, the army's chief surgeon, was particularly apprehensive: "I had considerable experience of it on the plains in 1867 and knew what to expect." The anxiety was constant. Two suspicious cases developed as the fighting intensified in mid-1899, and the department advised Washington in a masterpiece of understatement that cholera "once introduced, would find favorable conditions for epidemic spread." After the war, Lippincott reflected that luck alone had saved everyone in the Philippines from cholera before 1902. It was less a matter of blind luck than the fact the disease had not become pandemic again until that year, but he was correct in suggesting that the consequences of an outbreak during the fighting a couple of years earlier are almost unthinkable. Good fortune did finally run out in 1902, when cholera's appearance in south China presaged its imminent entry into the islands.[27]

The first Philippine cases appeared on March 20 in a poor barrio situated on a slim tongue of land where the Pasig River flows into Manila Bay. The infection was immediately attributed to a cargo of supposedly contaminated cabbage from Canton, via Hong Kong, on a ship that had been denied entry into the port less than a week earlier because its bill of health had shown cholera. The crew had thereupon jettisoned the cabbage, "with the result that the whole bay was literally covered with this vegetable." Much of it was allegedly consumed within a couple of days of washing ashore. The hypothesis was thought to be buttressed by the fact that some steerage passengers on an army transport leaving Manila at about the same time had presumably eaten the vegetable and then introduced the infection at Nueva Caceres. Cabbage was probably not the culprit, however. The conclusion had been drawn simply on the basis that the vegetables had originated in an epidemic area of China, but it is not certain that cholera vibrios would have survived the voyage and the bath in the bay. Food-borne disease usually results from contamination with polluted water. It is more likely that the mode of introduction was by human carrier. The possibilities are endless. Many of the barrio residents were fishermen, stevedores, and small-time smugglers who had ample opportunity for contacts with people coming from the southeastern China coast. The volume of traffic, legitimate and not, between Hong Kong and Manila in 1902 was so high that it is pointless to try to pinpoint the exact source.[28]

The American colonial authorities in Manila were eager to apply the most up-to-date epidemiological theories so as to react more decisively and effectively than the Spanish officials ever had. Philippine Commissioner and Interior Secretary Dean C. Worcester immediately ordered the infected barrio burned to the ground and the inmates taken to detention camps. His order, well-intentioned as it may have been, stands in stark contrast to Dr. Alba's decision *not* to burn Julio Bautista's house in Zamboanga two decades earlier because of the risk to neighboring dwellings. The Guardia civil had occasionally executed government directives by forcibly taking cholera patients from their houses in prior epidemics, but the wholesale removals of victims and their contacts to hospitals and detention camps was an example of American efficiency run amok. Dr. Heiser later recalled the scene: "Uniformed men clattered up with ambulances and without ceremony lifted the sick from their mats and carted them away from their wailing families. Four times out of five this was the last they ever saw of their loved ones until shortly they received a curt notice to come to the hospital and claim their dead." Abuses such as the forcible administration of medicine occurred in the detention camps, giving rise to rumors throughout the islands of even worse outrages. American officials were not unaware of the hostility the measures engendered but wrote it off as the natural reaction of an unenlightened people. Luke Wright, the acting governor while William H. Taft was temporarily abroad, wrote that the "ignorant natives resent our modern methods of dealing with cholera," and they see compulsory quarantine and sanitation as a form of "arbitrary oppression." Such arrogance was absolutely counterproductive. The terror and resentment initiated by the implementation of Worcester's ill-conceived directive consigned the campaign to failure.[29]

The board of health attempted frantically to confine the outbreak to Manila, but cases quickly developed at a number of points on the Pasig River and around Manila Bay. Nevertheless, Worcester was optimistic in early April. He wrote the absent Governor Taft, who was involved in another kind of containment effort in Washington (a Senate committee was investigating alleged war crimes by American soldiers). The last thing the governor needed was more bad Philippine news, and he was undoubtedly relieved by Worcester's report: "By dint of the hardest work we have held the disease nearly stationary from the start." Unfortunately, cholera was even then filtering through the highly permeable cordon the medical authorities had placed around Manila. Worcester reversed his position when he submitted his annual report some months later, comparing the task with an earlier military attempt to seal off the capital from General Aguinaldo's soldiers: "What General Otis could not accomplish with thousands of soldiers was an impossibility for the board of health, aided by the city police and a few hundred men from the insular constabulary."[30]

The role of American soldiers as carriers is uncertain. Cholera first appeared outside of Manila in early April, and in an unconscious replay of the events of 1882 in Zamboanga, it was asserted by some that the disease had been introduced into that region by soldiers of the Eighth and Ninth U.S. Infantries. The army's medical department eventually concluded that cases had existed south of Manila before the first infected troops had arrived there. The evidence does not seem conclusive. In any case, ninety soldiers had contracted the disease by April 19, and medical officers reported angrily that every one of the cases had been preventable but had resulted from indiscriminate mixing with the people. Orders were issued again and again forbidding the soldiers throughout Luzon from entering houses and stores and were disobeyed just as regularly. When a cook for the Ninth U.S. Cavalry at San Pablo, Laguna, was found living with Filipinos in a house where cholera had developed, regulations were enforced with a vengeance, and the American army thereafter escaped serious mortality during the epidemic.[31]

American responsibility for the epidemic lay more generally in the creation of conditions that made epidemic diffusion a certainty. Its heavy-handed and insensitive response to the outbreak then aggravated the crisis. Hunger and fear are the keys to understanding the epidemiology of cholera in 1902. Several years of war-created agricultural dislocation and food shortages had left most people only months or even days away from serious nutritive deficiency. Under such circumstances the age-old pattern of small-scale movements of food from place to place took on renewed importance and proved too persistent for the quarantine to stop. Foodborne cholera transmission is relatively uncommon, so the significance of food in the epidemic lay less in its role as a medium of diffusion than as the principal reason that people were in motion. The health officials at that time had no way of knowing what is known today about transmission factors, so they were determined that no food should move. Under the hastily reinstituted pass system, no one and no foodstuffs could leave Manila without permission issued by the civil authorities.

Military officers alleged that those officials gave approval indiscriminately, even after the board of health was flooded with telegrams protesting the abuse of the privilege, but the passes were irrelevant. People had no difficulty moving in and out of the city whether they had them or not, so foodstuffs were transported illicitly right from the start. One of many methods of getting food inland was to take it in carriages to a point east of the road between Pasay and Parañaque, where it was off-loaded into small boats on the stream. The cargo was then floated up the Pasig River outside the quarantine and from there taken to the various lake ports around Laguna de Bay. As it happened, the first major explosion of cholera outside the city was caused by a cook who had obtained a pass allowing him to take coal oil to Binan, Laguna. Under that cover he smuggled food out to a fiesta there and died within a few hours. Eighty cases soon developed, all of which were traced to the fiesta. Other carriers regularly left Manila, with or without a pass but usually with food, for destinations that then served as new foci from which the disease radiated in all directions.[32]

The timing of the cholera outbreak could hardly have been worse for the residents of Laguna and Batangas, which were still under military administration. Following a series of directives issued in December 1901, the population had been reconcentrated. Commanding officers had specified "plainly marked limits surrounding each town bounding a zone within which it may be practicable, with an average sized garrison, to exercise efficient supervision over and furnish protection to inhabitants (who desire to be peaceful) against the depredations of armed insurgents." People who lived in barrios and outlying districts beyond those limits were encouraged to take themselves, along "with all their movable food supplies, including rice, palay, chickens, live stock, etc. to within the limits of the zone established at their own or nearest town." The property of anyone found outside of the zones after December 25 was "liable to confiscation or destruction." The ports in both provinces were closed on the first day of 1902 to make it difficult for the guerrillas to receive food and other provisions by sea. Overland shipments were prohibited as well, as was any movement by individuals outside zone limits without a pass, which was only to be issued in cases of extreme necessity. Colonel Arthur L. Wagner was sent to inspect "the concentration camps of the natives" and explained in his subsequent report that the residents were liable to be shot if found outside the "dead line," which was established 300 to 800 yards from the outer boundaries, but that "such a measure is never resorted to if it is possible to arrest them and turn them back to the camp." Residents were allowed to gather standing crops outside of the zone if accompanied by a military patrol, but in practice most troops were busy destroying whatever food supplies they could find in the countryside.[33]

Wagner reported, predictably, that he was unable to find any evidence of misery or neglect. Food was sufficient, houses were comfortable, health was "very good," and the "children look as happy and contented as any school children in the United States." The credibility of the Wagner Report can be judged from its author's conclusion that "the hombres, or common people, are perfectly content and have no desire to leave; they have scarcely more power of intelligent initiative than the same number of cattle." In fact, as May has demonstrated, life in the cramped, unsanitary, and food-scarce reconcentration zones increased susceptibility to disease, and in March and April dysentery and malaria became epidemic. The doctors could do little. In San Pablo, Laguna, the medical officer reported that the crowding and inadequate facilities made it impossible to enforce sanitary regulations or to institute curative measures that might lesson the mortality. Guerrilla resistance had been broken in the meantime, so in the midst of the dysentery and malaria outbreaks most of the ports were reopened, the zones were abolished, and the residents from outlying areas were allowed to return to their homes—just as the cholera was rushing southwards. An American military officer stationed in Batangas wrote home in mid-April that the "cholera scare" had become quite serious and was interfering with military operations, since ships and supplies were quarantined in Manila and other ports. He hoped that it would not develop into a grave epidemic: "It is the real Asiatic cholera and a very good thing to steer clear of." However, Majayjay, Laguna, was infected a week later. The cordon then seemed to hold, but cases appeared in Calamba, Laguna, on May 27 and in Lipa, Batangas, at the end of the month. The disease was unstoppable thereafter. The situation could hardly have been more chaotic. With a large proportion of the region's population unsettled, debilitated, hungry, and infected with one disease or another, cholera was readily propagated.[34]

Agriculture had come to a virtual standstill throughout much of southwest Luzon in late 1901 when the inhabitants were reconcentrated and the American army began its rampage. The winter rice harvest would have been inadequate to feed everyone during 1902 in any case, but the growing food crisis was compounded when the people were released from the zones too late for an adequate spring planting. Conditions varied throughout the region, of course. Binan, for instance, had a modest rice surplus that was available for purchase by barrios in the vicinity of Calamba, where military operations had prevented any planting at all. When cholera broke out, however, the quarantine proscribed movement and trade between the towns, and those in deficit areas like Calamba found themselves immediately dependent on rice that the U.S. Army provided. Smuggling became widespread, and its coincidence with the season for fiestas honoring various patron saints increased the illicit traffic. The quarantine stood no chance of success. Lieutenant B.J. Edger, the medical officer in charge of Binan and its military substations, explained why as he described the extensive rice fields that surrounded those towns and made it clear that "it would certainly take five, or ten regiments of soldiers, to put a cordon around them, and to keep up a perfect quarantine."[35]

To that situation were added the elements of fear and panic. As in Manila, the nipa houses of the poor were burned, the sick forcibly isolated, and household contacts rounded up and sent to detention camps either in the immediate area or in the capital. It also became known that the American authorities in Manila, fearing contamination of water sources, had started to cremate all corpses not buried in hermetically sealed metal coffins, which the poor could not afford. Ileto points out that "no Filipino in his right mind approves of cremation," and says, moreover, that Spaniards resident in the islands were well aware of Filipino horror at the idea. Presumably that was not a secret from the American officials, but reckless self-assurance and disdain for native "superstition" overrode good sense. Such methods invited resistance. Cholera deaths were everywhere concealed to avoid attracting official attention. Bodies were surreptitiously buried in shallow trenches, dumped in streams, or simply abandoned as family members took what possessions they could and fled in terror. With the main roads guarded, they followed side trails into remoter areas, often carrying infection with them. The population withdrawal typical of the war's earlier stages was re-created, and quite aside from the cholera, the cycle of malaria, untilled fields, malnutrition, disease, and impoverishment was set in motion again. Under the circumstances, it is not surprising that well over 10 percent of the combined population of Laguna and Batangas provinces died in 1902.[36]

That the official policy was backfiring was plain, especially after an incident in Batangas in which the burning of one house got out of control and set fire to eighty-one others. Appalled at the stupidity of the incident, General Bell remarked with calculated sarcasm that such runaway fires are "very likely to be the result in a town constructed almost entirely of bamboo." Bit by bit, first in Manila and then elsewhere, policy was reversed, at least on paper. Burning the houses of infectives was to be stopped, and the removal and isolation of contacts abandoned. The brigade commander in Batangas City sent orders to that effect to all stations on May 23, 1902. He explained that the burning and detention "leads people to conceal cases of cholera and even to throw their dead in rivers rather than take chances of having property burned and themselves sent to detention camp." Under the new procedure, the contacts were to be allowed to remain in their houses, while the sick were taken to hospitals. Unfortunately, the measures came too late to stem the course of the epidemic. They were also undercut by a new policy that represented an even greater abuse of power.[37]

The decision to stop burning applied only to the houses of cholera victims. There remained the problem of what to do about uninfected people who did not comply with the various sanitary regulations. Taking their cue from the army, which had almost literally burned its way through the Philippines during the war, civil officials suddenly appreciated that setting fire to houses was a particularly useful pressure tactic and measure of retribution. It is ironic that the most effective opposition to the new policy came from army officers like General Bell who, after the colony was pacified, fought the civil government's scheme to inflict further suffering on the people. Punitive houseburnings became policy only in areas under civil control, while the provinces still under military administration south of Manila were at least spared that outrage. North of Manila they continued, culminating in an incident in Dagupan, Pangasinan, in which the burning of a few houses under the direction of sanitary officers got out of hand and nearly destroyed the whole town.[38]

Two contrasting examples demonstrate how official overreaction increased cholera mortality. As early as March 26, 1902, a local board of health was created in Binan, rules and regulations were promulgated, and the town of about 9,500 residents was divided into districts with Filipino physicians acting as sanitary inspectors. Binan, like other towns, received a constant influx of nighttime visitors bringing in foodstuffs and other merchandise around the quarantine. The first case developed on April 22 when a woman coming from Muntinlupa, Rizal, slipped past all the guards and entered a house where she died the same night. No more cases were discovered for a month, but then they came in a torrent as a result of the fiesta mentioned earlier. A couple of American soldiers who had cohabited with local residents died the same week. Current procedure in the region mandated disinfection and cleansing of infected houses and a five-day quarantine for all inmates. The patient was isolated in a separate room in the care of a family member, who was given instructions regarding disposal of feces. All such houses were marked with a red flag, and three volunteer guards were put in charge of the house and inmates. That mild and sensible regime was abrogated almost immediately, however, after the Manila Central Board of Health sent a contract surgeon, Dr. R.A. Wilson, to Binan with instructions to establish a detention camp for contacts and a cholera hospital. He also brought what General Bell later described disapprovingly as a plan to "burn the houses of people who knowingly and intentionally disregarded sanitary regulations for the purpose of impressing upon the community the necessity for compliance with such regulations."[39]

From that day, it was impossible to find any contacts. The official report later stated that "the natives, notwithstanding the kindest, and best meaning words, were terrified at the idea of going into a detention camp, and fled to all parts of the pueblo, and its barrios, taking the disease with them wherever they went." The panic was heightened by newspaper accounts of the punitive house-burnings that were being carried out elsewhere. Lieutenant Edger suddenly started sending telegrams to his military superiors about a week after Wilson's arrival, registering frustration about quarantine violations and "the deceitfulness of the Filipino race." Then he formally requested permission to burn the houses of such offenders, pointing out that "the burning of refractory houses of persons was part of the successful tactics of the Civil Board of Health in the Northern Provinces." General Bell denied authorization. The detention camp was abolished, and it was announced that the old system of confining contacts in their houses was being resumed. Within two days, the number of cases began to decrease and continued to do so despite the indifferent enforcement of the quarantine and an influx of migrants who had hiked across the hills from municipalities in Cavite where no treatment was available. Bell's refusal to bow to administration pressure or to countenance Edger's houseburning request at least allowed the epidemic to fade out naturally thereafter, but the damage had been done. Zeal, arrogance, and cultural insensitivity had combined to intensify the epidemic, notwithstanding the incredible judgment of two army investigators who subsequently stated that "every evidence goes to show that cholera was very ably managed at this post." Edger reported 1,451 cases and 1,281 deaths among Filipinos in Binan and its substations, for an astounding case-fatality rate of 88.2 percent, which if anywhere near accurate is evidence of the debilitation the war and reconcentration had caused. According to census figures, almost one-fifth of Binan's population died in 1902. Although only about one-half of those fatalities were listed as cholera deaths, it was the panicked population dispersal that exposed the victims to the malaria and diarrheal diseases that accounted for most of the remaining mortality.[40]

Balayan, Batangas, was more fortunate. There the quarantine system and sanitary measures had little beneficial effect, but the Americans in charge at least refrained from peremptory methods that would have created a worse dis-

aster. Located farther than Binan from the focus in Manila, the military authorities in Batangas had more time to prepare and to learn from mistakes elsewhere. News of the original outbreak in late March arrived quickly, prompting
medical officers to recommend the use of dry-earth closets with chloride of
lime disinfectant, even though they thought an outbreak unlikely. The principle of sanitation was perfectly sound, but the report was academic given the
unreality of imagining that such an excreta disposal system could be quickly
instituted among those most at risk in a town of about 8,500 residents. More
recommendations regarding sanitation followed as the epidemic spread from
Manila, and the initial confidence in Balayan's immunity wavered. When the
disease reached Taal, Batangas, around the first of June, little hope remained.
The first cases developed on the outskirts of town on June 16 and were attributed to betel palm leaves brought in clandestinely from Taal. They had been
sprinkled with water, and indeed the evidence shows the importance of contaminated common water sources as the medium of transmission. Balayan residents got their water either from the river, into which the stools of those living
on its banks were washed, or from a spring. The victims, without exception,
lived near the river and took their water from it, while residents who instead
used the spring remained untouched by the epidemic. In a nearby barrio, a
quarter of the residents were wiped out by the disease, which did not subside
until heavy and prolonged rains flushed the contaminated stream that served as
the only water supply.

As the number of victims began to mount, the commanding officer of the
shorthanded army detachment in Balayan hired local guards to disinfect the
latrines and to patrol the town to prevent people from coming into contact with
the diseased. According to the medical officer, however, it was difficult to get
the guards to enforce the rules, thus rendering the whole system ineffective.
Residents of the river district, he said, could be seen going in and out of their
"infected houses" as they pleased. An overworked Filipino doctor treated the
cases, while an equally harried American physician devoted himself to prophylactic measures. No punitive measures were taken, no detention camps were
erected, and there was no talk of burning houses. The epidemic ran its course
in a month. In that time 300 cases and 173 deaths were reported for that period,
for a case-fatality rate of 57.7 percent. Mortality in Balayan for all of 1902, both
from all causes and from cholera alone, was somewhat less than half of Binan's
rate, and though various factors can account for the difference, foremost among
them was the decision to manage the epidemic with a lighter hand in Balayan.[41]

The epidemic stalked the entire Philippine archipelago. It attacked Capiz
City in early September 1902, and according to an American schoolteacher, "by
its ravages Capiz was reduced from a first-class city of twenty-five thousand
inhabitants to a second-class city of less than twenty thousand." When her
classes resumed in mid-November she wrote: "Began work again to-day. The
school is much fallen off. Many pupils are dead, and the rest have lost relatives.
It is a gloomy school, but the worst is over." The epidemic did not reach some
areas of the archipelago until 1903 and was not officially declared over until

early the next year. What happened in Binan and Balayan was representative of the experience in all regions. The same sequence of events occurred everywhere, just as it had in 1882 and 1888. First came the terrifying vigil and the frantic preparations. Then as the first cases began to appear, rumors started to circulate, increasing the hysteria. In Pontevedra, Negros Occidental, the people believed that someone was poisoning the wells. Poison or magic was suspected also in Sibalom, Antique, where it was noticed that cholera had exploded in a barrio immediately after a visit from the padre and his servant. Others insisted that a man was on the loose in the community whose touch produced vomiting, diarrhea, and almost immediate death. Still others had seen a powder scattered in the streets that caused anyone who stepped in it to die on the spot. Houses were burned and people fled to the hills, extending the range of infection. Survivors in Lipata, Antique, recalled half a century later that cholera had driven the people from the barrio and that only a few survived. Old-timers in one barrio of Tobaco, Albay, said that the people had died too fast to be taken to the cemetery, so the area in front of the chapel was converted into one. When it was filled, a new burial place was designated on a hill a short distance away. Finally, "the dead and the dying were buried together." According to official statistics, cholera accounted for 31.0 percent of the runaway Filipino mortality in 1902 and 19.1 percent in 1903.[42]

The epidemics abated in any particular area within a few months, but the effects of the dislocation persisted. Hunger was the most immediate, since food production and distribution were invariably in disarray, especially as a result of the concurrent malaria epidemic. Some found themselves situated like the people of Salcedo, Samar, who were reduced to "subsisting on the natural products of the forest and the stream." That sad predicament had occasionally been the lot of Filipinos since time immemorial when localized disasters temporarily incapacitated a community or region. What was new was that residents of a town on the remote southeastern coast of Samar were now highly vulnerable to an infection imported into the islands at places that only recently had been worlds away. The transformations that had knit the archipelago together by the 1860s had also upset its ecological equilibrium, leaving epidemic disease free to terrorize the islands for several decades impeded only by natural checks and facilitated by human actions.[43]

CONCLUSION

Intervention and Disease

There were no paths on the mountains, and no bridges over waters nor boats
upon them, nor were the rivers made navigable. Thus invasions and annexations
were not possible. The myriad beings participated in a mysterious equality and
forgot themselves in the Tao. Contagious diseases did not spread,
and long life was followed by natural death.

—*Pao Ching-yen*[1]

MASBATE was the most primitive island in the archipelago, according to
Guevedo in 1890, "desperately poor, with no instruction, no capital, no cultivation, no means of transportation, and no subsistence." Communications were in
a "truly lamentable state." Neither roads nor navigable rivers existed, so the
pueblos were linked only by narrow forest paths, which were frequently cut by
arroyos and rivers no vehicle could cross. All overland transport was accomplished by means of carabao, which was "irreplaceable as a mount on most of
the slopes." Movement between the pueblos was minimal in any case because
"when a stranger arrives who truly needs to eat, we can say that the others do
not eat." Guevedo was not a doctor, so he had nothing to say about the public
health, but one might expect high levels of disease and death in such an impoverished and "enfeebled" population group. But in fact, Masbate had the lowest
death rate, most favorable birth-death ratio, and highest population growth rate
in the Philippines. During the ten years (1876, 1885–1893) for which parish
statistics were subsequently available to the census enumerators, the island's
death rate averaged 15.3 per 1,000 inhabitants and its birth rate was 56.4. In the
very year Guevedo wrote, the death rate fell about as low as it was possible to
go, to 11.0 per 1,000. Without immigration of any consequence, the population
was growing by natural increase alone at an average annual rate of 4.1 percent.[2]

Here myth meets reality. Together they highlight the fact that humans participate in the creation of their own diseases. The epidemiological principles at
work in a dimly remembered but mostly imagined golden age in China were
the same as those that determined health in the late-nineteenth-century Philippines. Living conditions differed, to be sure. Food had been plentiful in the
never-never land of the Middle Kingdom, so "the people patted themselves on
the belly, and wandered about for pleasure." By contrast, Guevedo had stayed
with people in Masbate who "in effect don't eat, because in their houses they
have no fireplace and no food, except a little rice that they eat with some shell-

fish they get at the beach, which is sufficient to sustain the life of a man who is rooted in one place." The point is the same in each instance, however. If people could remain static in an unchanging total environment, lasting health would be possible, but in the real world "all living things and their environments change endlessly and no permanent equilibrium between them can ever be reached," as Dubos explained. Relatively isolated and immobile population groups might achieve a fragile ecological balance for a time, but Dubos also pointed out that "symbiosis is usually on the threshold of disease." That is especially so when low levels of disease have prevented the accumulation of acquired resistance, and in the case of Masbate, when undernutrition had pushed symbiosis right to the brink. After human intervention in the form of "invasions and annexations" upset equilibrium on the island at the turn of the century, both malaria and cholera became epidemic before the people's adaptive mechanisms could respond to the challenge. Death rates leaped to 43.1 and 58.4 per 1,000 in 1902 and 1903, respectively.[3]

Morse believes that historians bring a valuable perspective to the understanding of disease emergence because they focus on "the consequences of human actions, and the conditions that cause or permit certain developments." By contrast, biologists too often see causation as driven by natural processes alone, he says. The situation on Masbate demonstrates his point, since war was necessary to clear the way for epidemic disease in the debilitated and susceptible population group Guevedo had described a decade earlier. We historians have much to learn from the best thinkers in the health sciences, however, since we tend to focus too narrowly on the purely human round of existence—who decided what for whom, how, why, and what then. When the relationship of human decision and action to its surrounding environment is blurred or omitted altogether, the human role in causal processes tends to get inflated. Even when the relationship is addressed as one of agency and structure, conceptualization may still be limited by an anthropocentric bias if humans are thought to *act within* various frameworks. The boundaries are not so neatly delineated. Where human health is concerned, it is unclear, for instance, if the mosquito is simply part of the environment—a structural component of human existence—or if it has the ability to act and to produce effect that we associate with agency. Indeed, it becomes difficult to know who or what were the "agents of disease" in the Philippine story. The *Treponema pallidum* spirochete certainly was a causative factor of increased syphilis, but so too were soldiers, poverty, and cultural attitudes that opened the road to sexual, and thus infectious, traffic. We need to think about historical processes ecologically, and in Susser's sense of using the broadest possible formulation of causation, to understand how humans *interact with* an ever-changing environment—part living, part inanimate—that is fully capable of responding to insult in like measure. McNeill has put the matter bluntly: "We will never escape the ecosystem and the limits of the ecosystem. Whether we like it or not, we are caught in the food chain, eating and being eaten. It is one of the conditions of life."[4]

All human action is in some sense an intervention into ongoing processes. The complexity of multiple and reciprocal interaction is such that while the results are not random, neither are they easily predictable or controllable. Consequences are often unexpected, and as this history has shown, they are usually unintended as well. If a practical lesson emerges from the Philippine experience for policy makers today, it is that disease will result from initiatives that disturb equilibrium in the total environment, whether they be developmental, like road building in the Amazon basin, or destructive, like bombing Baghdad's electrical system. The more forceful the intrusion, the more likely it is that the ensuing diseases will become epidemic. Those who wanted to clear nineteenth-century Philippine forests so the riches of the land could be exploited can be excused for their unawareness of ecological principles and probable results. We have no such excuse today. Heightened awareness and understanding of the processes by which interventions yield epidemiological consequences should allow our modern proyectistas to proceed with increased caution, foresight, and wisdom.

Since the Spaniards and Americans were the most powerful intervenors in the Philippines, it is important to assess the role of colonialism as a determinant of the health crisis. The easy answer is that colonialism was the cause not only of epidemic disease in the late-nineteenth-century Philippines but of much else that occurred in Southeast Asia. Barbara Watson Andaya has rightly pointed out that "by their intrusion into the region, Europeans had fundamentally altered the manner in which its history was to develop." It can be argued further that the inherent nature of colonial rule tainted everything that followed. In Joseph Buttinger's eloquent statement of the principle, colonial regimes are "subject to a pernicious law, according to which ill effects are the fruit not only of malevolent but also of well-intentioned actions, just as though colonialism represents a given amount of evil that could be shifted about but not reduced."[5]

One can agree with Buttinger, as I do, and yet recognize that the processes of historical causation are more complex. To begin to untangle the Philippine network, it is helpful to keep two points in mind. First, moral valuations and principles of infectious disease should be kept separate. Evil is neither a useful interpretive tool nor a factor of disease transmission. When zoophilic anophelines are deprived of their usual bovine blood meals, for instance, malarial infection will spread regardless of whether the animals died in a flood, from rinderpest, or at the hands of an invading army. Second, colonialism—a general kind of power relationship—in and of itself does not cause anything. It is instead one of the interlocking systems in which epidemiological events were forced to work themselves out. Specific actions taken in consequence or in furtherance of that relationship help drive the disease process. That was the case in the Philippines, where the interventions that tipped the ecological balance most drastically were those set in motion by the Spanish-initiated campaign to develop the wealth of the land and the American military action to overcome resistance to colonial rule. The causal relationship between the colonial and disease processes was not always so clear or direct, however. Although the steamship was employed in the interests of Western imperialism and figures importantly in this story by increasing the mobility and velocity of infection, it is hard to see the kind of direct causal linkage that existed in the cases of cash cropping and war. The steamer's appearance on the seas was a development largely independent of the colonial system. The importation of rinderpest or cholera seems even less attributable to colonial action. Once pandemic, those diseases would have reached the archipelago regardless of whether Europeans controlled various Southeast Asian countries or not. What we can say finally is that the colonial process was neither necessary nor sufficient by itself to cause the abnormal level of illness and death in the late-nineteenth-century Philippines. It was instead a *contributory* determinant, but surely the major one.

The complexity of cause and consequence dominates this history. The Spanish conquest and pacification, accomplished after much Filipino suffering, brought about a long period of relative peace that reduced the instability of daily life and favored rapid population growth. Yet that very demographic factor eventually helped initiate the process that made it possible for epidemic disease to emerge 250 years later. The generally well-intentioned American attempt to control cholera, executed with dispatch and energy the Spanish administration had lacked, had the unforeseen effect of exacerbating the epidemic and increasing mortality. Just two years earlier, however, the U.S. Army—for motives that were more mixed—initiated a peremptory program to vaccinate every Filipino against smallpox, forcibly if necessary. It was implemented with no more regard for cultural sensitivities or human rights than the later campaign, yet its most striking result was that the Philippines later became the first Asian country in which smallpox was eradicated. Even then, the program may have left a residue of resentment that had its own consequences. Paul Greenough has come to just that conclusion in his study of the far less coercive Smallpox Eradication Programme in India and Bangladesh between 1973 and 1975, criticizing the program managers for failing to see the eradication of a disease as "only one part of a complex developmental puzzle whose overall historical and cultural design exhibited dozens of interpenetrating causes and effects." Such historical examples demonstrate Susser's point that causes have multiple effects and that to understand "the whole system of relationships" we must have a causal model that allows us not only to infer causes from a known manifestation, but also to "begin with an independent variable, or potential cause, and search out its effects."[6]

That kind of multicausal thinking is particularly useful for historians. Unfortunately, perhaps, it throws light on historical meanings more readily than it helps to prevent disease. For epidemiologists, explanatory models carry a predictive as well as an analytical function. Following Sir Ronald Ross's insistence on "exact enumerative methods" as a means of understanding the extent to which various factors determine an outcome, those models have always been mathematical. Two decades ago, however, Hans Enzenberger pointed out in another context that interlocking ecological systems are mediated by social factors, and so frustrate attempts at explanation by ecologists. His point raises the fundamental question of whether current epidemiological models are capable of translation into truly effective preventive action. Epidemiology encounters serious theoretical problems somewhere between the web of causation and the mathematical model, not to mention the practical problems of implementation between the model and disease prevention. The models inspire confidence to the extent that all the relevant variables are equally quantifiable, but the web of causation necessarily includes important variables that by their nature cannot be expressed in numbers since they are relationships, not things. Sylvia Noble Tesh points out that since the explanatory models can handle only empirical data, "they necessarily leave out exactly those nonquantifiable phenomena that constitute the strength of the web idea." Since cash cropping or resistance to colonial authority, for instance, sit uneasily in a mathematical formula alongside anopheline biting rates and numbers of secondary cases, they are omitted.[7]

Historians need not be mathematically exact in order to draw important insights. We can weigh causal factors, without reducing each to numerical values, according to a close reading of the historical record. Ross's injunction that the relative influence of variables be known exactly is met by sacrificing a degree of precision (which is only apparent in the mathematical models in any case) to an understanding of the historical process. Health scientists normally have a narrower focus, which is why health usually functions as the dependent variable in their formulations. Historians can set the various causal webs, each resulting in a specific health outcome, in the context of larger webs of historical causation. From that perspective it may even be possible to imagine how the system of health contains and is contained by other systems—like the boxes in Susser's Chinese conjuring trick. In any case, variables begin to lose their independent or dependent aspects, and as the distinction between cause and effect blurs, the interactive nature of forces becomes clearer. Enzenberger's observations on ecology imply that the tools of the health sciences, unassisted by the historical imagination, are ultimately insufficient to explain the dynamics of health. At the same time, we historians need those tools to interpret the significance of health in the history of populations. The complementary nature of the enterprise is evident.[8]

The essential meaning of the Philippine experience is perhaps best imagined on a level that is well beyond the reach of quantification. Epidemic disease on the scale Filipinos experienced it late in the nineteenth century is a metaphor for a human society out of harmony with itself and its enveloping environment. A final vignette is emblematic of that imbalance and the irony of a historical process whereby the conquerers became the healers and the victims themselves became corrupters. The incident occurred in Zamboanga early in 1903. American medical officer George W. Adair received a late-night visit from a Filipino who asked if the doctor would come to his home the next day to have a look at his face, which seemed a bit puffy. Arriving at the house, Adair was greeted by the man, his wife, and numerous small children. He also met a pretty, nineteen-year-old woman whose mother had brought her across the channel from Basilan. She was living with the family, but Adair was vaguely aware that "she did not belong there." Talking alone together, the man told him that he earned a livelihood for himself and his family by renting ponies and vehicles, mostly to American soldiers and sailors in Zamboanga. He also bought ponies and when he had gathered enough to justify the five-hundred-mile voyage, he accompanied them north to Manila and sold them there. Suddenly Adair thought he understood the situation: "Here an idea came. I said, 'The women?' A flush passed over his bloated features. He laughed, nodded and said yes—at the same time making a very impressive gesture imploring caution. He pointed to the open door of the next room where his wife was and said in a low but impressive tone, 'She does not know that.'" The man now had nearly enough "ponies" for a cargo, and he wanted Adair to examine him and write out a certificate of good health that he could show to the authorites in Manila if they troubled him. The physician refused: "No, the authorities in Manila would give more weight to the appearance of your face than to any paper I could give you—they have eyes." Adair had been able in the daylight to make an instant diagnosis as soon as he had walked in the house. The man had leprosy.[9]

A	*Agronómicas*
APSR	*Archivo de la Provincia del Santísimo Rosario*
Ar	*Aranceles*
ARSW	Annual Report of the Secretary of War
BHL	Bentley Historical Library
BIA	Bureau of Insular Affairs
BR	Blair and Robertson
C	*Cólera*
Ca	*Colonias agrícolas*
CHS	Cincinnati Historical Society
Cp	*Calamidades públicas*
CPI	Census of the Philippine Islands
CtM	Court-Martial Transcript
CZ	Central Zone
ECMC	East Carolina Manuscript Collection
EP	*Erección de pueblos*
GL	Genealogical Library of the Church of Jesus Christ of Latter-day Saints
HDP	Historical Data Papers
HHGL	Harlan Hatcher Graduate Library
HSP	Historical Society of Pennsylvania
ISHS	Iowa State Historical Society
L	*Langostas*
LC	Library of Congress
LL	Lilly Library
M	*Memorias*
MHC	Michigan Historical Collections
MHP	Medical History of Posts
MHS	Massachusetts Historical Society
Mm	*Memorias médicas*
NLM	National Library of Medicine
P	*Prostitución*
PNA	Philippine National Archives
PNL	Philippine National Library
RBHL	Rutherford B. Hayes Library
RG	Record Group
RHR	Regimental Health Records
RPC	Report of the Philippine Commission
S	*Sanidad*
SATS	St. Andrews Theological Seminary

SAWS   Spanish-American War Survey
SD   Southern District
SHC   Southern History Collection
SHM   Siouxland Heritage Museums
UCL   University of Colorado Library
USAL   United States Army Library
USAMHI   United States Army Military History Institute
USNA   United States National Archives
UVL   University of Virginia Library
WNRC   Washington National Records Center
WRPL   William R. Perkins Library

N O T E S

AUTHOR'S NOTE: All quotations and citations are documented at the end of the paragraph in which they occur. All translations are mine unless otherwise indicated specifically or unless it is evident from the bibliographic references.

PREFACE

1. On April 24, 1901, the chief of the U.S. War Department's Record and Pension Office was preparing index-record cards on each of the soldiers in the Philippines but was unsure of how to file them. He wrote a note to Secretary of War Elihu Root explaining that he needed an official name for the ongoing hostilities so these records could be distinguished from those of other wars. He suggested "Philippine Insurrection." A flurry of clerical activity turned up a legal memo in a recent deportation matter that had found the existence of an "insurrection" in the islands. On that basis Root agreed that the suggested title was appropriate, noting also that the description of the events there as an insurrection was already in common parlance. Thus the war was named. (F.C. Ainsworth to secretary of war, April 24, 1901, with endorsements, RG 112/26, 81721, USNA.) Most historians today refer to the conflict as the Philippine-American War. Because this book views it from the Filipino perspective, I call it simply the American war.

2. Dubos, *Mirage*.

3. The seminal works are Zinsser, *Rats*; Rosenberg, *Cholera Years*; Crosby, *Columbian Exchange*; McNeill, *Plagues*. For the health science concepts and quoted statements, see Burnet, *Biological Aspects*, 1–24 and Dubos, *Mirage*, 1–2, 29, 61, 64–65, 89, 102, 110–11, 137; Macdonald, *Epidemiology*, 121–28; Macdonald, "Dynamics," 489–506.

4. Susser, *Causal Thinking*, 30, 47–49. I use "health scientists" to include all those in the natural and social sciences who are concerned with issues of human health. For a strong criticism of multicausal models and their "generous egalitarianism," see Tesh, *Hidden Arguments*, 58–82. See also Turshen, *Political Ecology*, 11–19. For an admission of the problem by one who still believes that disease causation is best modeled multifactorily, see Oppenheimer, "In the Eye," 268.

5. Susan Sontag's famous argument in favor of "demetaphorizing" disease is buttressed by her belief in monocausality. She asserts that "it is diseases thought to be multi-determined (that is, mysterious) that have the widest possibilities as metaphors for what is felt to be socially or morally wrong" (Sontag, *Illness*, 60). Some metaphors plainly carry negative connotations that unfairly stigmatize victims of certain diseases, but it is more realistic to ask that we choose our analogies more carefully than to imagine that we will, or can, stop thinking metaphorically about what we do not understand, especially when it is something as frightening as disease. In my opinion, she is simply wrong on monocausality. For a discussion of those points, see Brandt, "AIDS," 93–96. The quoted phrases are in Morse, "AIDS," 28, 37. For his original statement of the "viral traffic" concept, see Morse, "Emerging Viruses," 389–409. Also see Morse, "Examining the Origins," 10–28. For more information on the development of Morse's idea, see Henig, *Dancing Matrix*, 12–20. William Muraskin has used the same metaphor in his work on hepatitis B, writing that the recent pandemic "demonstrated the existence of a series of infectious super 'highways'; transmission routes paved by major social, technological

and cultural changes." He says that we should erect "a series of roadblocks" to prevent emergence of such diseases (Muraskin,"Hepatitis B," 127–28).

6. For the evolution of epidemiological concepts and models, see Susser, *Causal Thinking*, 11–43, and Duncan, *Epidemiology*, 11–43.

7. For the most famous application of the thick description approach, see Geertz, "Thick Description," 3–30.

INTRODUCTION

1. Iloilo, 1891, *Mm*, 1, 9–10, PNA; Iloilo, 1892, *Mm*, 19–21, PNA; Iloilo, 1893, *Mm*, 11–12, PNA.

2. For the statements of the Spanish doctors, see Pangasinan, 1888, *Mm*, 16–18, PNA and Ilocos Sur, 1887, *Mm*, 1, PNA. For the use of the phrase "true mourning," see for instance, Iloilo, 1892, *Mm*, 16, PNA. The phrase "conflagration of disease" is from Heiser, *American Doctor's Odyssey*, 38, and Heiser, "Unsolved Health Problems," 178. Dr. Heiser was the first commissioner of health in the American colonial administration of the Philippines.

3. For approaches to contemporary Filipino understandings of the late-nineteenth-century epidemics, see Jocano, *Folk Medicine*, 71, and Ileto, *Pasyon*, 77, 84–85, 94, 168–70, 261, 276. Regarding population increase in South Vietnam, see FitzGerald, *Fire*, 534.

4. Dr. Gregorio Martín Blanco put the best possible light on the situation: "We doctors do not see enough sick persons to make an exact study of the pathology of the region, but others give us enough information to allow us to describe it sufficiently" (Ilocos Norte, 1879, *Mm*, 2, PNA). Also see Nueva Viscaya, 1884, *Mm*, 14, PNA; Laguna, 1886, *Mm*, 3, PNA; Cavite, 1886, *Mm*, 6–8, PNA; Cebu, 1886, *Mm*, 1–6, PNA; Ilocos Norte, 1886, *Mm*, 14, PNA; Albay, 1887, *Mm*, 2, 12, PNA; Pangasinan, 1888, *Mm*, 10, 25, PNA; Nueva Ecija, 1887, *M*, 16, PNA. Dr. M. Koeniger, a German physician resident in Manila during the early 1880s, explained the lack of autopsies: "The public opposes it on the grounds of mores, climate, and religious beliefs. The real reason, though, lies in the fact that the Spanish doctors have not yet tried to accustom the public to the practice of autopsy" (Koeniger, "Ueber epidemisches," 426). One médico titular said that the corpses were buried too promptly to permit autopsies to be performed. See Zambales, 1895, *Mm*, 4–5, PNA. For Dr. Gomez's remarks, see Iloilo, 1893, *Mm*, 14–17, PNA. The 1894 regulations are in Iloilo (CZ), 1894, *Mm*, 3, 10, PNA. For the 1909 study, see McLaughlin and Andrews, "Studies," 9–11.

5. The conclusions on disease prevalence are based on my reading of the entire archival record, but particularly the *Mm*. The estimate for 1902 is calculated from raw data in *CPI, 1903*, 3:276.

6. The quotes are from Martínez Cuesta, *History*, 196 and 188.

7. For an explanation of how population statistics were produced by church and civil officials and of the problems inherent in the records, see Cullinane, "Accounting," passim. See also May, "150,000 Missing Filipinos," 215–43, and Owen, "Measuring Mortality," 91–114. On the undercount, see Navarro, *Filipinas*, 28–34, and Sanciano, *El progreso*, 175–86. I have calculated the estimate of non-Christians from raw data in *CPI, 1903*, 2:14, 48–49.

8. *CPI, 1903*, 2:17–19, 48. The 1655 figure is derived by multiplying Owen's estimate, derived from Church sources, of the number of tribute-paying Filipinos in that year

(108,277) by four, the multiplier customarily used to convert to total population in the Philippines for that era. For Owen's figures, see Reid, "Seventeenth-Century Crisis," 649. It is impossible to know precisely how much of the long-term population gain is a reflection of increasing administrative and ecclesiastical control over non-Christians, but it can hardly amount to more than 10 percent. For the peak around 1840, see the tabulation of death rates by decade in Smith, "Crisis Mortality," 66.

9. Owen points out that although growth rates of 1.0 to 2.0 percent do not amaze us today, they were extraordinarily high for the nineteenth century, approached only in northern Europe and in some European settler colonies and exceeded only in the United States, where immigration was a major factor. See Owen, Paradox," 45–46. For Java, see Boomgaard, *Children*, 169–98. Boomgaard suggests a rate of 1.4 percent for the entire nineteenth century. For some contemporary rates worldwide, see *CPI, 1903*, 2:23–24.

10. *CPI, 1903*, 2:17–24.

11. The converging patterns are evident from the death rates by region and decade, in Smith, "Crisis Mortality," 66.

12. Gregorio Tenorio to Gobernador Superior Civil, Nov. 8, 1863, Zamboanga, 1863, C, PNA; Gabriel Albarez Quiñones to Gobernador Superior Civil, Mindanao, 1864, C, PNA; Smith, "Crisis Mortality," 67; Martínez Cuesta, *History*, 262.

13. For emerging evidence about the earlier crisis, see Reid, "Seventeenth-Century Crisis", 649–51.

14. I have calculated the demographic statistics from raw data in *CPI, 1903*, 3:12–17 and *CPI, 1918*, 2:971–72. The accuracy of the birth- and death rates and ratios depends, among other things, on the assumption that the same proportion of baptisms and burials were recorded relative to births and deaths that actually occurred. Cullinane has told me that he thinks burials were probably somewhat more underrecorded than baptisms because of the greater difficulty in bringing a corpse to the church (as opposed to bringing an infant) and because of the greater importance Filipinos attached to the baptismal sacraments (Cullinane, conversation with author, Aug. 14, 1993). His argument seems plausible, but I wonder at never having encountered it in any of the *Mm*, in which the chief physicians forwarded provincial demographic information to Manila each year. Many of them did not hesitate to point out why various official statistics were unreliable.

15. My speculation on the earlier trends for births and deaths is based on the raw data and graphs in Smith and Ng, "Components," 254, and Smith, "Crisis Mortality," 64–66.

16. My calculations of excess mortality assume a "normal" birth rate of 26.5 per 1,000, which is about the average rate for the relatively untroubled years 1876, 1886–1887, and 1904–1908 and an average death rate of about 36 per 1,000 for the period 1863–1903. For 1902 mortality, see *CPI, 1903*, 3:22–86. For the wartime death-rate estimate, see Macaraig, *Social Problems*, 177–79. On postwar infant mortality in Manila, see *CPI, 1918*, 2:1106. A standard population pyramid can be drawn from the census data. See especially *CPI, 1918*, 2:16.

CHAPTER 1

1. For the formulation, see Lilienfeld and Lilienfeld, *Foundations*, 46–48. The expanded definition of an agent is taken from Duncan, *Epidemiology*, 28. For the argument that any formulation based on the biomedical model of health is inadequate, see Morgan et al., *Sociological Approaches*, 11–44.

2. The quote is from Fenner, "Infectious Disease," 1043.

3. Despite the low probability of widespread epidemics, mortality from disease was undoubtedly substantial and helped to account for the presumably sluggish preconquest population growth rate. It is important to note that infectious agents vary widely in their ability to survive, and the archipelago's population profile was not protection against most of them. The critical population size necessary to sustain endemicity varies with each infection. Some can remain latent in inapparent hosts almost indefinitely and thus do not need to rely on chance introduction from outside reservoirs for continued existence in a population group. Others utilize nonhuman hosts either partially or wholly and are less dependent on large human populations. For the various epidemiological principles, see Bartlett, "Measles Periodicity," 48–70; Black, "Measles Endemicity," 207–11; Cliff et al., *Spacial Diffusion*, passim; Cliff and Haggett, "Island Epidemics," 138–47. For the basic infection transmission principles, see Brachman, "Principles," and "Transmission."

4. For the physical description and the argument that environmental diversity is the key to Philippine regionalism, see Wernstedt and Spencer, *Philippine Island World*, 3, 9–12, 39–62, 109–12, 142–43, 301–5. For further statistical information, see *CPI, 1903*, 2:29–30. Only 154 of the islands have an area of more than five square miles. Just 29 cover more than 100 square miles and together account for 99 percent of Philippine land area and (as of 1903) 95 percent of the population. Eleven islands exceed 1,000 square miles. The two largest, Luzon and Mindanao, are each more than seven times the size of the next biggest island and are 40,420 and 36,537 square miles, respectively. Luzon is almost precisely the same size as Iceland.

5. Scott reminded me that when we use phrases like "the history of the archipelago" or "Filipino history," we really mean the three and a half centuries of Spanish record keeping with all its built-in biases. The point about "asceptic isolation" (and the phrase) is his as well (Scott, personal communication, Jan. 11, 1991). For an estimate of 500,000 to 750,000 inhabitants in 1565, see *CPI, 1903*, 2:17–19, 48. A more recent estimate of 1,000,000 to 1,250,000 is in Corpuz, *Roots*, 2:529. The extended quotation is from Scott, *Looking*, forthcoming.

6. On settlement patterns, see Wernstedt and Spencer, *Philippine Island World*, 143, 158, 163–64, and Phelan, *Hispanization*, 15–17. For the quote about relations varying according to circumstances, see Scott, "Creation," 40. Loarca's statement is translated in Scott, *Looking*, forthcoming.

7. For the information on interisland trade, see Scott, "Boat-Building," 60–95. On slavery, see Scott, "Filipino Class Structure," 96–126, and Scott, "Oripun and Alipin," 138–55. The two quotations come from Scott, "Lost Visayan Literature," 26.

8. For trade routes and relations throughout the region, see Scott, *Filipinos in China*, passim. For the booster process, see Cliff and Haggett, *Spread*, 59. For early trade, both interisland and international, see also de la Costa, *Readings*, 9–15. As will be seen later in the text, infections survived the much longer five-week trip from San Francisco during the American war. The crucial difference in that case was that a regiment of more than a thousand soldiers served as a kind of floating booster population.

9. Martínez Cuesta, *History*, 31–32. The quoted passages describing how pacification was carried out are excerpted and translated in de la Costa, *Readings*, 22. The phrase "pain, tears and blood" is de la Costa's characterization of the conquest based on his reading of the Augustinian documents. For avoidance of tribute payment and flight, see "Paracer de P. Martín de Rada sobre tributos," June 21, 1574, in Lopez and Felix,

Christianization, 138. The distinction between friendly and unfriendly towns is from "Parecer de Guido de Lavezares sobre tributos," undated but probably 1574, ibid., 140–47. Lavezares's memorial to the Crown was in response to Rada's harsh criticism of the pacification campaign. While conceding that excesses had occurred, he blamed the initial violence on Filipino ambushes and strategies and its continuance on the need to protect friendly towns from the unfriendly ones. Historians reading the documentation generated by the Americans during their pacification more than three centuries later will have a strong sense of déjà vu.

10. For a description of the settlement patterns that evolved under Spanish rule, see Cullinane, "Accounting," 4–11. The quote about the unfamiliar way of life is from Martínez Cuesta, *History*, 181. On resettlement, see "Instructions to Juan de Bustamante, alcalde mayor of Camarines," Manila, Sept. 8, 1585, in San Antonio, *Crónicas*, 2:148–49, excerpted and translated in de la Costa, *Readings*, 27–28. For an overview of the policy and reasons why it was only partially successful, see Phelan, *Hispanization*, 44–49. Centripetal movement from small outlying islands to core islands seems to have occurred initially as well. See Wernstedt and Spencer, *Philippine Island World*, 143, 146, 164–67. For illness after resettlement, see de Jesus, *Tobacco Monopoly*, 113; Anton Malinski, carta al Rector de Brno., Apr. 21, 1733, translated and quoted in Martínez Cuesta, *History*, 112; Antolín, "Discurso," c. 1789, APSR.

11. For the burdens the impecunious government placed on Filipinos during the troubles of the first half of the seventeenth century, see the documents collected in de la Costa, *Readings*, 44–64. The quoted statement is from *ibid.*, 54.

12. For the quote about the reversal in raiding patterns, see Aganduru, "Historia general," 453. See also Scott, *Slavery*, passim. Fariz's statement is translated and quoted in Martínez Cuesta, *History*, 124. For Samar, including the translation and quotation of the priest's statement, see Cruikshank, *Samar*, 89–90.

13. For the first years of the galleon trade, see Schurz, *Manila Galleon*, 154–92 and passim. For the quote about calamities and apparently erroneous demographic conclusions drawn therefrom, see Phelan, *Hispanization*, 100–2. For the revised estimates, see Reid, "Seventeenth-Century Crisis," 639–59. Owen provided his statistics to Reid directly. The tree-ring series is highly persuasive evidence of an abnormally dry century in east-central Java, but it does not necessarily support Reid's conclusion that "the dry season must have been lengthened dangerously in those areas of eastern Indonesia and the Philippines where survival depended on a delicate balance between wet and dry monsoons." His only direct evidence for the Philippines during the entire century is one reported drought in East Borneo and Mindanao in 1660–1661. Ibid., 654–55.

14. The timing of the population rebound seems to have differed from region to region. That it began two or three decades later in the Visayas is suggested by the population data for Negros in Martínez Cuesta, *History*, 74, 108–9. For the freedom of the cabezas to squeeze the people, see Phelan, *Hispanization*, 115. Regarding earlier marriage, see Fr. Francisco de Paula Esteban's remark translated and quoted in Madrigal Llorente, *Blending*, 117. On the lack of references to epidemic disease in the early sources, it is worth noting that Father Martínez de Zúñiga pointed out two centuries ago that "the history of this country does not refer to any pestilence or any starvation due to famine that they [Filipinos] might have suffered in the past" (Martínez de Zúñiga, *Status*, 98). He overlooked the demographic consequences of the Dutch wars and much else, but it is true that the massive fifty-two-volume Blair and Robertson collection of documents contains only a handful of references to epidemics between the conquest and

1735. Smallpox and influenza were identified, but the other pestilences were unnamed. The references are as follows: (1) a "general malady" in Manila and surrounding towns in 1599 in Pedro Chirino, *Relación de las Islas Filipinas* (Roma, 1604), in BR, 12:297; (2) smallpox in Nueva Segovia (Cagayan) in 1600, in BR, 13:67–72; (3) a "plague" in Tinagoan, Buad, in 1601 in Diego Aduarte, *Historia de la provincia del Santo Rosario de la Orden de Predicadores* (Manila, 1640), in BR 30:309; (4) a pestilence in Silan, Cavite, in 1604 in Chirino, *Relación*, in BR, 13:194; (5) a pestilence "attended by pains in the stomach and head" in Bohol in 1604, in BR, 13:311; (6) a "grievous epidemic" in Manila and adjoining villages in 1628, perhaps imported from India, in Pedro Murillo Velarde, *Jesuit Missions in the Seventeeth Century* (Manila, 1749), in BR, 44:47–48; (7) "many illnesses" following typhoons on Luzon in 1639 in *Events in the Philippines for the year 1638 to that of 1639* (Cavite, 1639), in BR, 29:167–68; (8) smallpox in and around Luzon's central plain in 1658 in Casamiro Diaz, *Conquistas* (Manila, 1718), in BR, 41:310; (9) smallpox in and around Luzon's central plain mainly among uplanders in 1685, in BR, 42:234; (10) influenza in Pampanga in 1687 following a locust infestation the previous year in Diaz, *Conquistas*, in BR, 42:268–70; (11) a pestilence among Tagalogs in 1691, in *Document of Manila: Events at Manila* (Manila, 1691), in BR, 40:31; (12) disease in Tayabas in 1704 in Pedro de San Francisco de Assis, *Recollect Missions in the Philippines, 1661–1712* (Zaragoza, 1756), in BR, 41:98.

15. The quote is from Martínez de Zúñiga, *Status*, 98. The causes of the rapid population growth have been the subject of speculation for at least two centuries. See, for example, ibid., 119, 143 (end of Moro raiding, early marriage); Manuel Bernaldez Pizarro, *Reforms needed in Filipinas* (Madrid, 1827), in BR, 51:243 (the land's abundance); Echaúz, *Sketches*, 12 (end of *balos*, the custom of violent revenge); Martínez Cuesta, *History*, 155 (end of Moro raiding, smallpox vaccination); Owen, "Paradox," 52–53 (tranquility, smallpox vaccination). The introduction of smallpox vaccine at the beginning of the nineteenth century may well have given the already favorable growth rate a further boost, but grounds for skepticism exist, as will be shown in chapter 4.

16. Cullinane, "Accounting," 10.

17. Martínez de Zúñiga, *Status*, 79, 84, 97–98, 241, 259, 261–62, 391–92; Mendoza Cortes, *Pangasinan*, 6.

18. Cullinane, "Accounting," 10; Mendoza Cortes, *Pangasinan*, 6–11.

19. Martínez Cuesta, *History*, 169–91.

20. Cruikshank, *Samar*, 132–38.

21. Mendoza Cortes, *Pangasinan*, 1–4; Echaúz, *Sketches*, 27; Cruikshank, *Samar*, 138, 223.

22. Jagor was a German ethnographer who traveled in the islands from 1859–1861. For his observations on the role of priests and prisons, see Jagor, *Travels*, 99–100. On the forming of ritual links, see Cullinane, "Accounting," 11. For power distribution in the towns, see Bankoff, "Big Fish," 679–700.

23. Mendoza Cortes, *Pangasinan*, 56.

24. Measles is used as an example only because its diffusion mechanics are relatively well understood. By the nineteenth century, Filipinos no longer presented a virgin population for measles, and though the resulting mortality and blindness were not negligible, the disease did not produce demographic disaster as it did in the South Pacific region. For the growing Pacific Basin measles reservoirs, see Cliff and Haggett, *Measles*, 21–29. The surgeon-general of the U.S. Army stated officially that during the Philippine-American War measles "was imported into the Philippines [from San Francisco] on almost every transport" (Sternberg, "Report," 338). Although Manila did not officially

cross the population threshold for measles until 1907, the urban cluster in and around the city exceeded 250,000 by 1875 or so. See *CPI, 1903*, 3:12.

25. For commerce and the galleon, see Rodríguez, *El gobierno*, 145–52. Basco's statement of May 8, 1781, was made in an address to the first session of Manila's Sociedad económica de amigos del país. The speech appears in Montero, *Historia*, 2:291–93, and is translated and quoted in de la Costa, *Readings*, 114. Pedro Murillo Velarde made the statement about "more advanced nations" in 1749 (ibid., 97).

26. For the quote about sources of wealth, see Ortíz, *El Marqués*, 63, 105. For the quote about the archipelago's resources, and the proposals during the 1830s, see García, *El gobierno*, 132–38. For Calderón's statements, see ibid., 182. Murillo's observations are translated and quoted in de la Costa, *Readings*, 96–97. Proyectistas were persons advancing development or reform projects, plans, or schemes.

27. For additional information on the proposed reforms, see de la Costa, *Readings*, 106–120, 138–42; de Jesus, *Tobacco Monopoly*, 23–25, 32, 43–44; Diaz-Trechuelo, "Economic Development," passim. For Basco's statement, also from his 1781 address, see Montero, *Historia*, 2:291–93, translated and quoted in de la Costa, *Readings*, 113. For an overview of "commercial adventurism" throughout the region, see Kathirithamby-Wells, "Age of Transition," 599–612. For a detailed list of royal decrees and other important laws pertaining to agriculture, see Keyser, "Indice," 33–55. About the galleon's demise, see "Representation of Filipinas in Cortes," in BR, 51:284–85. Regarding the role of foreign merchant houses and the dynamics of the shift from a subsistence to cash-cropping economy, see Legarda, "American Entrepreneurs," 142–51, and "Foreign Trade," passim.

28. For a first-hand account of the cholera riots, see de la Gironiere, *Twenty Years*, 20–29. The Russian consul's remarks were made in a letter that is excerpted in a footnote to Montero, "Events of 1801–1840," in BR, 51:40–43. About the cholera and the riots, see also Bantug, *Medicine*, 29–30.

29. Regarding the implications of the riots for continued Spanish control and need for development, see "An Englishman," *Remarks on the Phillippine Islands, 1819–1822* (Calcutta, 1828), in BR, 51:179–80. Also see M. Gabriel's "testimony" in the appendix to de la Gironiere, *Twenty Years*, v, in which he says: "In 1828, the Spanish government, which had lost its American possessions, felt the necessity of taking vigorous measures for the development of its remaining colonies." Enrile's statement is translated and quoted in de la Costa, *Readings*, 176. That the Spaniards were fearful of rebellion is implicit in the remarks of Lt. Charles Wilkes, commander of an American naval scientific expedition that stopped at Manila for eight days in 1842. He wrote that rebellions were not infrequent in the provinces but that it was impossible to learn anything reliable about them "for all conversation respecting such occurrences is interdicted by the government" (Wilkes, *Narrative*, excerpted in *Travel Accounts*, 34–35). For the royal order of April 10, 1822, and succeeding legislation, see Keyser, "Indice," 45–46. Agricultural property and income were eventually exempted from taxation. See Robles, *Philippines*, 268.

30. For an example of the protectionist view, see Manuel Bernaldez Pizarro, *Reforms Needed in Filipinas* (Madrid, 1827), in BR, 51:182–273. For a more liberal approach, see the anonymous statement printed in an appendix to Bernaldez's memorial. For an outsider's appraisal of Spain's commercial system in the Philippines, see "An Englishman," *Remarks*, in BR, 51:144–60.

31. José Gabriel Gonzales y Esquivel, "Memoria sobre la Junta de Aranceles de las Islas Filipinas," July 6, 1876, *Ar*, PNA. For a more accessible, and less favorable, de-

scription and appraisal of the junta's work, see *CPI, 1903*, 1:356–61; 4:13, 559–60. For a mass of statistical and descriptive data on the commercialization of the economy in the nineteenth century, see ibid., 4, passim. For the enthusiastic observations of a contemporary outsider made during the early stages of the rapid economic growth (1846), see Mallat, *Philippines*," 83–84, 92, 129–30, 133–34, 151. For a similarly positive appraisal a little more than a decade later, see Bowring, *Visit*, passim. For a discussion of Spain's uncompetitive position in relation to Britain and the U.S., see Jagor, *Travels*, 264–67. For the secretary-general's comments, see Elías de Molíns, *Importación temporal*, 37, 42.

32. For a discussion of the royal decree of 1854, see Martínez Cuesta, *History*, 284. For the proposed reforms, see Keyser, *Medios*, 13–30; Jimeno, *Memoria*, 35–36; Ruíz, *El desestanco*, 4, 20–21, 28–29; Perez, *Situación*, 21–24; Azcarraga, *La libertad*, 7–11, 25–30. The phrase "emporium of production" is Perez's (*Situación*, 5). The following official reports contain representative examples of reform proposals: Ilocos Norte, 1876, *Mm*, 5–6, PNA; Nueva Viscaya, 1884, *Mm*, 4–8, PNA; Nueva Ecija, 1887, *Mm*, 10–15, PNA (also published in slightly different form—see Rajal, "Memoria," 290–359); Pampanga, 1889, *M*, 52b-60b, PNA; Pangasinan, 1891, *M*, 23–59, PNA; Cavite, 1892, *M*, 27b–31, PNA; Directores de Estaciones agronómicas, "Memoria agricola del distrito de Albay y Camarines," *A*, 1890, 1–2, PNA. For Graciano Lopez Jaena's assertion in 1887 that the Philippines was "flat broke," see de la Costa, *Readings*, 225–26.

33. For the point that wet-rice cultivators are more easily controlled, see Andaya, "Political Development," 426. For the development plan, see Martinez de Zúñiga, *Status*, 129, 218–19, 279, 342–45, 361–62. One lead worth following is the possibility that Java's nineteenth-century population was less mobile (thus retarding the spread of disease), which might help explain why it continued to grow rapidly after rates in the Philippines leveled off. Java did not have a comparable frontier or urbanization process. See Geertz, *Agricultural Involution*, 80; Boomgaard, *Children*, 110–16; Reid, "Economic and Social Change," 474–75.

34. Martínez de Zúñiga, *Status*, 108–12. For agreement that Moro raids peaked in the northern areas of the archipelago in the 1850s, see Bernad, "Father Ducos," 694.

35. For the government's decision in the 1790s to arm coastal villages and for inventories of coastal defenses of the bishoprics of Cebu in 1779 and Albay in 1799, see Warren, *Sulu Zone*, 171–76, 290–94. Regarding the curtailment of the Moros' raids in southeastern Luzon and the Visayas, see Mallari, "Camarines Towns," 453–73, and Owen, "Abaca," 192. For Samar, see Cruikshank, *Samar*, 84–100. For Negros, see Martínez Cuesta, *History*, 155–60. For the link between the end of the Moro raids and town formation in Sorgoson, see Dery, *Ibalon*, 116–17. For some details of preparations against raiders during 1827 in Camarines, see Mallari, "Alcalde," 464–71.

36. For the persistence of Moro raiding and Spanish countermeasures, including the attack on Balangingi, see Warren, *Sulu Zone*, 14–197. On steampower as the turning point, see Santayana, *La isla*, 66–67. On the effort to conquer the Muslim South, see the documents collected in de la Costa, *Readings*, 197–212; Bowring, *Visit*, 350; Foreman, *Philippine Islands*, 140–159; Ileto, *Magindanao*, passim. For the international and regional context, see Tarling, "Establishment," 5–28.

37. The phrase "magic of colonial alchemy" and the quote about acculturation are from Scott, "Cultural Minority," 40–41. On military expeditions and smallpox, see Guillermo Galvey Diaries, diary 8, on microfilm at SATS. See also Semper, "Trip," 25–26, and Scott, "Spanish Occupation," 47. The quotations about the ambushes are Governor Rajal's (Nueva Ecija, 1887, *Mm*, 10–10b, PNA). The remarks do not appear in the pub-

lished version of his report. On the success of military efforts against non-Christian hill peoples to secure land for pioneering, see Pampanga, 1890, *M*, 127b-129b, PNA.

38. On the Quadrilleros and Guardia civil, see Robles, *Philippines*, 69, 193–95, and Bankoff, "Big Fish," 697–700. For the creation of the Guardia civil, see *Reglamento para la organización*. About the bands of bandits, see Jagor, *Travels*, 165. Also, compare Martínez de Zúñiga, *Status*, 127, 142, 263, with Foreman, *Philippine Islands*, 263–65, 450–58, 488. The two men traveled through the same areas almost a century apart. Travelers in the priest's day were on their own outside of the towns. Foreman, by contrast, passed Guardia posts regularly, occasionally asked for and received an armed escort through the mountains, and even went on a manhunt as the invited guest of a captain of the guard. For the Negros expedition, see Weyler's Jan. 3, 1889 communication to the Overseas Ministry, translated and quoted in Martínez Cuesta, *History*, 236–37. On the subject of lawlessness and the government response, including the quoted circular, see Bankoff, "Deportation," 443–48. He says in another place that the link between agricultural development and the need for protection from lawless elements was direct: "Colonial officials were also concerned that the peasants' perception of personal insecurity was hampering agricultural production and effectively closing off some areas to cultivation" (Bankoff, *Big Fish*, 697).

39. For the government's awareness of the need for roads, as expressed in legislation, and the comment on the disparity, see Keyser, *Medios*, 23–24, 44–55. On Enrile, see Martínez Cuesta, *History*, 162–63. On the forced labor, see Robles, *Philippines*, 256–67. Regarding conditions of roads and bridges, see Panay, 1870, *M*, 1, PNA; Iloilo, 1886, *Mm*, 5, PNA; Pampanga, 1887, *M*, 25–25b, PNA; Nueva Ecija, 1887, *M*, 10–12, PNA; Pampanga, 1889, *M*, 65b-66, PNA. For the royal decree of July 12, 1883, and its consequences, see Sigson, "La Prestación Personal," 189–92. Weyler's comment is translated and quoted in Martínez, *Negros*, 306. For a road survey made shortly after the Americans assumed control, see Clark, "Labor Conditions," 793–94. On the effect of roads linking towns and facilitating exports, see Cavite, 1892, *M*, 28–29, PNA. On anticipated benefits of the railroad, see Nueva Ecija, 1887, *M*, 10, PNA, and Pampanga, 1890, *M*, 126b, PNA. For a passenger train timetable, see *Manila Times*, Jan. 19, 1899, and for 1902 statistics on passengers and tonnage hauled, see *CPI, 1903*, 4:595–98. For a summary of the demographic and transportation linkage of central Luzon after the late eighteenth century, see Doeppers, "Hispanic Influences," 88–92.

40. Larkin, "Place," 316–17. McCoy took that theme and elaborated the idea that the Philippines should be conceptualized as "an intensely dynamic society, or series of societies, that has changed constantly throughout its four centuries of recorded history in response to economic, demographic and technological stimuli" (McCoy, "Introduction," 4). Cruikshank's point is in "Continuity," 219–20, and he discusses Larkin's and McCoy's ideas about Philippine regional diversity in Cruikshank, *Samar*, 24–26.

41. Fegan, "Social History," 91–94. The Chinese-Filipino mestizos, who were far more numerous in the Philippines than the Spanish-Filipino mestizos, were the descendents of unions between Chinese fathers and Filipina mothers. As a group, they were a dynamic force in the commercialization of the Philippine economy, principally as landowners. By the end of the nineteenth century they were the principal constituent of the Filipino elite. Willem G. Wolters makes the same point about mutual interest binding landowners and their tenants in the land-opening process. In explaining how large landownership promoted such pioneering, he says that "landlords are in a position to send their tenants to do the clearing and the cultivating, while the landowner is able to pro-

vide them with a living in the meantime" (Wolters, "Sugar Production," 431). About the development of the export crop economy on the central plain, see also McLennan, *Central Luzon Plain*, 46–64. On sugar in the Philippines, see Larkin, *Sugar*.

42. McLennan, "Changing Human Ecology, 63–69. For a more detailed treatment of Ilocano migrations to the central plain, see McLennan, *Central Luzon Plain*, 103–45. See also Pangasinan, 1891, *M*, 12, PNA, and *CPI, 1903*, 1:516.

43. McCoy, " Queen," 311–26. Foreman asserted at the end of the century that "Negros Island was entirely opened up by foreign capital" (Foreman, *Philippine Islands*, 289).

44. Bankoff argues that deportation became the centerpiece of colonial strategy, explaining that "the state was able to pursue the aims of territorial expansion among the Muslim and tribal populations in the south through a policy of enforced migration under the guise of penal deportation" (Bankoff, "Deportation," 443). On penal colonies, see Montero, *Historia*, in BR, 51:70 and Foreman, *Philippine Islands*, 172–76, 266. For the recruitment of families, see especially the papers relating to penal colonies (1890), to Cotabato (1883–1885), and to Paragua (1884–1885) in *Ca*, PNA. The phrase "vicious habits" is from the latter. Regarding government encouragement of migration from Ilocos to Cagayan, see de Jesus, *Tobacco Monopoly*, 169–71. Immigration from Europe, and especially the Peninsula, was always greatly desired but probably not really expected. The Junta central de agricultura industria y comercio also encouraged Asian labor, going so far as to decide that Tonkinese would be the most suitable (del Busto, *Informe*, 5–22). On prospective lumber exports, see Jordana, *Memoria*, 14–15. Efforts were also made to disseminate basic information about agriculture. Typical was a handbook in a question-and-answer format aimed at both proprietors and colonists (Espejo, *Cartilla*, passim).

45. For an example of the age-old daily routine, see Taruc, *Born*, 16. The Daraga market is described in Jagor, *Travels*, 81. For the two statistical examples, see Foreman, *Philippine Islands*, 402, and "Number of men, women, and children and estimated quantity of food products going in and out from November 14, 1899 to February 5, 1900," RG 395/808, USNA.

46. Foreman, *Philippine Islands*, 420; Martínez de Zúñiga, *Status*, 126; Camarines Sur, 1886, *Mm*, 13–14, PNA. For another example of a burgeoning magnet city and the health problems that arose as it outgrew its municipal services, see Iloilo, 1888, *Mm*, 7–11, 13–14, PNA. For the increase in school matriculations in Manila, see Fernandez Frías, *Memoria*, appendix.

47. On the process of land acquisition by the urban elite and the expansion of tenancy with the rise of sugar on Cebu, see Fenner, *Cebu*, 91–95. On migration to Manila, see Doeppers, "Migration," 41 and passim. See also Ilocos Norte, 1876, *Mm*, 39, and the records collected in *P*, PNA. Also compare the wide variety of job categories in Manila with the relative few that existed in provincial towns. For that and population growth in Manila, see *CPI, 1903*, 2:20, 92–120, 865–1035. The average annual growth rate there was apparently 3.16 percent between 1876 (93,595) and 1903 (219,928). Because early population estimates vary as to what constituted Manila for census purposes, it is difficult to measure growth prior to 1876. On provincial magnet cities and reverse migration from Manila, see Owen, "Abaca," 199, 205–6.

48. Fegan, "Central Luzon Barrio," 95–98. For evidence of high death rates among pioneers, see papers relating to Paragua, 1884, *Ca*, PNA. On misfortune or oppression leading some to banditry or vagabondage, see Sancianco, *El progreso*, 230–31, and de Jesus, *Tobacco Monopoly*, 62–65, 95–96, 156, 202–3. On the fact that a floating popula-

tion had always existed, see Fenner, *Cebu*, 46, 52; Cushner, "Landed Estates," 116, 118 (vagabonds in the seventeenth century); Warren, *Sulu Zone*, 181 (villagers displaced by Moro raids, 1790–1848). On apparent increase in vagabondage, see Misamis, 1887, *M*, 10b, PNA, and Cruikshank, "Continuity," 233–34. Regarding the phenomenon of taking to the hills in Philippine history, see Ileto, *Pasyon*, 228–29 and Maceda, "Remontados," 313–21. The Spanish term for such a person was *remontado*. Ileto explains that it originally denoted one who refused to accept Christianity or to live "under the bells" but that by the nineteenth century the term referred to "one who had fled to the hills to avoid the payment of tribute and forced labor, to escape from the clutches of the law, or to live as a hermit and ascetic" (Ileto, *Pasyon*, 228). On the perceived connection between the floating population and a high death rate, see Cavite, 1887, *Mm*, 9, PNA. On passports, see de Jesus, *Tobacco Monopoly*, 95; de la Costa, *Readings*, 190–92; del Pan, *La Población*, 4–5; Foreman, *Philippine Islands*, 459, 518, 540–41.

49. On quarantine procedures, see the correspondence between Spanish consuls in the Southeast Asian region and Manila collected in *C*, PNA, and see also Heiser, *American Doctor's Odyssey*, 59. The comparison of entrants by destination is based on the 1,650 official arrivals in 1841, the only year for which I have such a figure. For that number and for the quarantine, see Mallat, *Les Philippines*, 2:356 and 299–305, respectively. For Chinese migration, see Wickberg, *Chinese*, 146–47,169–71; Warren, "Slavery," 434; Bowring, *Visit*, 181; Clark, "Labor Conditions," 859.

50. For the spread of infectious disease (in this case, influenza) among the peoples on the rim of the Southeast China Sea before the steamship, see Bennett, "Epidemic Catarrh," 522–26; Ward, "Account," 124–36; Kollman, "Grippe," 389–98. Regarding faster travel times, bigger ships, and the epidemiological consequences of the steamship, see Cliff and Haggett, *Measles*, 62. On the trip from Europe, see Foreman, *Philippine Islands*, 285. On the sugar trade with Australia and the opening of ports on Java, see Bowring, *Visit*, 412–13, 416. On the opening of Saigon, see Palanca, *Reseña*, passim. On the Southeast Asian rice trade, see Owen, "Rice Industry," 78–143. For touring entertainers, see *Manila Times*, Jan. 19 and June 8, 1899. On steamship service between Hong Kong and Manila, see Foreman, *Philippine Islands*, 298–99. For Dr. Gomez's comment, see Iloilo, 1892, *Mm*, 12, PNA.

51. Regarding communication between Manila and Cebu and within the Diocese of Cebu, along with the statistic about contact between Manila and Negros, see Martínez Cuesta, *History*, 161. The quoted opinion about interisland contacts is in Bowring, *Visit*, 98. For statistics on the merchant marine, see Azcarraga, *La libertad*, 20–21. For numbers of entries into and exits from Manila, see the 1862–1865 editions of the *Guía de forasteros*, 340, 331, 317, and 320, respectively. On Iloilo City, see McCoy, "Queen," 309–13. Arrivals from Manila increased from 254 in 1862 to 1,122 in 1871. Sailcraft arrivals from Negros rose from 75 to 405 in those same years. Additional shipping statistics for Panay in the single year of 1870 can be found in Panay, 1870, *M*, 24, 34, 44, 47, 75, 83, PNA.

52. Cruikshank, "Continuity," 222–35.

53. On both speed and rhythm, see Bowring, *Visit*, 22, 299, 407–8 (quoting from Nicolas Loney's 1857 report), and Foreman, *Philippine Islands*, 459–66, 507. For the effect on timing of epidemic waves, see Cliff and Haggett, *Measles*, 53–94.

54. For an appreciation of the complexity of the Philippine "revolutions," see Guerrero, "Luzon at War;" May, *Battle*; Ileto, *Pasyon*. For evidence that U.S. Army garrisons were sometimes used unwittingly to support one side or the other in local power struggles that were unrelated to the war, see "Statement of the Presidente of San Carlos and

forty-five others as to the Life of Faustino Gonzales and Antonio Morales," Mar. 11, 1900, RG 395/827, USNA. For a local factional struggle for power and money, see "Testimony of Teodoro Agarao and Frances Mariano Agarao in Court-Martial Transcript" contained in Report of Capt. Eli A. Helmick, Sept. 11, 1901, RG 395/2123, USNA. For banditry, see "Testimony of Mil. Gov. Eustacio Mololos" in Col. Cornelius Gardener, CtM, RG 94/421607, USNA, and Jack F.B. Mitchell to Violet Dandridge, Aug. 12, 1900, Bedinger-Dandridge Family Papers, box 14, file: "Correspondence 1900," WRPL. For the religious and class dimensions, see Gen. J.F. Bell to adjutant general, 2 Div., "Report on Situation at Cabaruan," Mar. 19, 1900, RG 395/851, USNA.

55. For flight as part of a historical pattern of "population withdrawal during crises in Philippine history," see Ileto, "Food Crisis," 101–17. On Batangas, see May, "150,000 Missing Filipinos," 215–43. For similar evidence on Samar, see Catbalogan, Samar, *MHP* 629, RG 94/547, USNA. For the account from Tanauan, see Lt. Alexander B. Coxe, Sr. to his aunt, Mar. 1, 1900, Alexander B. Coxe, Sr. Papers, 193, ECMC.

56. For dispersal and return home sick, see report of Maj. W.A. Holbrook, Feb. 8, 1900, RG 395/777, USNA; Indan, Camarines Norte, *MHP* 547, Oct. 1, 1900, RG 94/547, USNA; Talogtog, Abra, HDP, 1:175, PNL; Fee, *Woman's Impressions*, 131–33. Regarding patterns of flight in Sorgoson and the point that members of the principalía in the various towns perceived it in their interest to remain (or to return as soon as possible) in order to collaborate in the restoration of civil order, see Totanes, "Sorgoson's Principalia," 477–99. For contraction in Manila and garrison towns, see Maj. Frank S. Bourns, "Report of Board of Health," June 30, 1899, in *ARSW, 1899*, 260; report of Lt. E.S. Walton, Feb. 1, 1900, RG 395/2470, USNA; May, *Battle*, 192–94. Fleeing toward population centers rather than away from them finds its historical echo on Samar's west coast in the eighteenth century when people sought the security of fortified poblaciones during Moro raids. See Cruikshank, *Samar*, 93–94. For reconcentration in Albay, see Balading, Albay, HDP, 3:16, PNL; Taloto, Albay, HDP, 4:1–2, PNA; Allang, Albay, HDP, 5:80, PNL. For Marinduque, see RG 395/2458, USNA; Travelogue manuscript, James Alfred Leroy Papers, box 205–A, BHL; Brig. Gen. Luther R. Hale to Col. Harback and Col. Anderson, Oct. 22, 1900, RG 395/5175, USNA; Capt. W.M. Wright to Maj. Gen. J.C. Bates, Dec. 10, 1900, RG 395/2548, USNA; General Orders No. 11 and No. 13, Feb. 15 and Mar. 5, 1901, RG 395/318, USNA. For Batangas, see May, "Zones," 89–103, and M.L. Leepere, "Report from San Pablo," Apr. 14, 1902, RG 112/26, 90497/14, USNA. On the panic flight during the cholera epidemic, see Lt. B.J. Edger, Jr. "Special Report of Cholera Epidemic," May 23–July 18, 1902, RG112/26, 90497/19/B, USNA. For movement of Filipino soldiers and civilians, see Malolos testimony, 109, 111, 150–51, RG 94/421607, USNA; "Testimony of Natives Suspected of Aiding Insurgents," RG 395/5495, USNA; May, *Battle*, 186.

57. Spanish troop numbers are given in Foreman, *Philippine Islands*, 511–29. The quotation about the influx of prostitutes is from an unsigned and unidentified newspaper article, "The Crowning Infamy of Imperialism," in the Richard F. Pettigrew Papers, box: "R.F. Pettigrew Miscellaneous Papers Si–T," file: "Spanish-American War–2," SHM. For the quoted statements about emigrants, see *Manila Times*, June 7, June 13, Aug. 3, and Sept. 28, 1899. Announcement of the arrival of fortune seekers can be found in virtually every issue of that daily newspaper. They included dentists, doctors, lawyers, excursion directors, barkeepers, commercial agents, comic-opera troupes, self-described hustlers, prospectors, and missionaries—all said to be after a "Philippine Klondike." For the Spanish sick list, see Foreman, *Philippine Islands*, 540, 621; "Report of Henry Lippincott concerning Operations of the Medical Department in the Philip-

pine Islands, August 31, 1898," RG 112/26, 39109/63, USNA; Lippincott to surgeon general, Apr. 9, 1906, RG 112/26, 3866/v/3, USNA. For Filipino participation in the invasion of Annam and Cochin China three decades earlier and disease among the soldiers, see Taboulet, *La Geste*, 2:429–84, and Palanca, *Reseña*, passim. For numbers of Filipino troops entering and exiting the port of Manila, see the 1862–1865 editions of the *Guía de forasteros*, 315–20. Physicians had long considered military posts in the Philippines as foci for disease. See Iloilo, 1888, *Mm*, 11–12, PNA.

58. For the typhoid debate, see Heiser, "Unsolved Health Problems," 176; Sternberg, "Annual Report of the Surgeon General for the Year Ending June 1900," in *ARSW, 1900*, 651, 670; J.N. Glennan, "Report on Base Hospital at Batangas," 1900, RG 112/26, 2310/311/I, USNA; report of Joseph Curry, RG 112/26, 68075/G, USNA; J.B. Girard, "Report on Health of Troops in Division and Sanitation of Posts for Calendar Year 1904," Apr. 11, 1905, RG 112/26, 41842/C; Strong et al., "Medical Survey," 281–82, 292; Chamberlain, "Typhoid Fever," 311; Gutierrez, "Typhoid Fever," 367–78; Brillantes, "Disease-Carrier Problem," 110. For evidence of the preexistence of typhoid that the debaters were unaware of, see Cebu, 1884, *Mm*, 5–10, PNA; Abra, 1886, *Mm*, 5, PNA; Laguna, 1886, *Mm*, 4–5, PNA; Masbate y Ticao, 1886, *Mm*, 1, PNA; Albay, 1887, *Mm*, 8–9, PNA; Capiz, 1888, *Mm*, 11, PNA; Ilocos Norte, 1889, *Mm*, 16, PNA. Regarding variola minor, see McVail, *Smallpox*, 158. On hookworm, see Chamberlain, "Statistical Study," 249–66, and the discussion of his paper, which begins at 341. Chamberlain was probably wrong. For a more recent opinion that *Necator americanus* long predated the Americans in the Philippines, see Faust and Russell, *Craig*, 25. Still, American importations into regions other than the eastern Visayas, the traditional focus of hookworm infection, surely aggravated the problem.

59. See 26th U.S. Vol. Inf., RHR 346, RG 94, USNA. For Dr. Solivellas's reports, see Iloilo (CZ), 1894, 1895, *Mm*, PNA. The basic source for following the history of every American soldier admitted to sick list is the RHR, RG 94, USNA. Separate volumes exist for each regiment as well as for military hospitals, both ashore and afloat, in the Philippines. The MHP also contains a running general report about the health of the men at each of the posts throughout the island. Numerous official reports by and within the Army's medical department, RG 112/26, are also helpful. Official statements were made from time to time acknowledging the importation of substantial amounts of disease. See, for example, Sternberg, "Report," 338 (measles), and Henry C. Corbin, "Memorandum to the Secretary of War from Adjutant-General," Jan. 8, 1901, RG 94/356345, USNA (venereal disease). It is impossible, however, to know the significance of imported disease with any precision because the records do not trace the entire chain of transmission across the Pacific from specific Americans to specific Filipinos. Individuals who were infected sometime prior to embarkation and who later sailed can be identified, as can those who contracted disease and manifested symptoms en route; their subsequent contacts, whether American or Filipino, cannot, nor can asymptomatic or convalescent carriers. For a discussion and documentation of U.S. soldiers as carriers of disease to and in the Philippines, see De Bevoise, "Compromised Host," 188–210.

60. For evidence that soldiers and civilians shared the same diseases, see Maasin, Leyte, May 1901, *MHP* 560, RG 94/547, USNA; Nagcarlang, Laguna, Feb. 1902, *MHP* 578, RG 94/547, USNA; Santa Cruz, Ilocos Sur, July 1901, *MHP* 457, RG 94/547, USNA; Mangarin, Mindoro, Nov. 1, 1902, *MHP* 649, RG 94/547, USNA; 31st U.S. Vol. Inf., RHR 3475, RG 94, USNA. Some officers believed that the problem showed the need to move the garrisons away from the towns. See Maj. Henry D. Thompson and Lt. James M. Phelan to the chief surgeon, 3d Sep. Brig., July 28, 1902, RG 112/26, 90497/19,

exh. A, USNA. For the regimental sick lists, see the RHR. For sick-report admissions, see "Statistics from the Office of the Surgeon-General," RG 112/26, 10086/M, USNA. On sick reports as understatement of infectivity, especially of venereal disease, see Brig. Gen. George W. Sternberg to secretary of war, Feb. 4, 1899, in Sternberg, "Report of the Surgeon-General, Oct. 12, 1899," in *ARSW, 1899*, 453 and report of Maj. Samuel O.L. Potter, Oct. 16, 1898, in *ARSW, 1899*, 455.

61. On relations between soldiers and civilians, see May, *Battle*, 185–205. For the quoted statement and the establishment of garrisons from the medical department's point of view, see "Annual Report, 1900," in *ARSW, 1900*, 604. For a military point of view, see Gen. J.F. Bell to adjutant general, 2d Div., March 26, 1900, RG 395/851, box 8, USNA. For daily life, see "The Soldiers' Monotonous Life," *Manila Times*, Oct. 26, 1899. For the quote about hikes, see Maj. Frederick H. Sparrenberger, "Autobiographical Sketches," MS/C/44, box 2, NLM. For various quartering arrangements, see Alexander B. Coxe to his aunt, Mar. 1, 1900, and to Aunt Hall, Jan. 11, 1901, with hand-drawn map of Taal, Batangas, Alexander B. Coxe, Sr. Papers, ECMC; "Examination of Capt. William Wallace," RG 94/455906/C, USNA; E.S. Eby to Rev. I.L. Kephart, *Religious Telescope*, Mar. 12, 1902, 339; Balinag, Bulacan, Mar. 31, 1902, *MHP* 680, RG 94/547, USNA; 30th U.S. Vol. Inf., Tayabas, June 1900, RHR 2474, RG 94, PNA; Burgess, *Who Walk Alone*, 14–15. For intimate relations with women, queridas, and "marriages," see J. Edward Beattie to Reading K. Beattie, May 7, 1900, file: "Reading K. Beattie Papers, 1898–1906," WRPL; Arthur Valentiner to Clark Valentiner, Sept. 12, 1900, Arthur Valentiner Papers, CHS; Richard Johnson, "My Life in the U.S. Army," 22–23, 30–31, SAWS, U.S. Inf. 48th Reg., USAMHI. The quotation is from Blunt, *American Officer's Studies*, 19. On frequenting prostitutes, see Pvt. John Tucker, Hosp. Corps, CtM, RG 153, box 3163/20611, WNRC. The Wood-Forbes Report's figure on children of mixed parentage is cited in Macaraig, *Social Problems*, 281. I have checked the manuscript version of that report in RG 350, USNA, but was unable to find the reference. On mixed offspring, see also Arthur C. Johnson Diary, Jan. 9, 1900, box 2, diary 9, Arthur C. Johnson Papers, UCL; Heiser, *American Doctor's Odyssey*, 429–30; MacClintock, "Around the Island," 438–39. For the quote about chaffing the soldiers, see *Manila Times*, 4, Oct. 31, 1899. For the quote about soldiers going into nipa shacks, see Russell R. McPeak to his family, Dec. 29, 1900, Russell R. McPeak Papers, MHC. Regarding evidence of desire to keep U.S. garrisons, either for money or security, see report of Capt. J.F. Morrison, Nov. 25, 1901, RG 395/2354 and *Affairs in the Philippine Islands* 3:2461–543. For documentation of courts-martial involving drinking, gambling, and crimes against Filipinos as well as discussion of the U.S. Army in garrison towns, see De Bevoise, "Compromised Host," 179–88.

62. For the quoted statement, see Bautista, Pangasinan, Jan. 1900, *MHP* 378, RG 94/547, USNA. For American claims of cleaning the filth, see "Report of Henry Lippincott," Oct. 23, 1898, RG 112/26, 39109/79, USNA; Heiser, *American Doctor's Odyssey*, 60; Chamberlin, *Philippine Problem*, 113–22. For what was actually done, see reports of Lt. George R.D. MacGregor, Dec. 10 and 18, 1899, taking station in Pavia, Iloilo, RG 395/2470, USNA; reports of Lt. Homer B. Grant, Dec. 17 and 20, 1899, taking station in Santa Barbara, Iloilo, ibid.; report of Lt. George D. Rice, Feb. 20, 1900, from Molo, Iloilo, ibid; Surigao, Mindanao, *MHP* 516, RG 94/547, USNA; Letterbook, Oct. 14, 1901, Jay Johnson Morrow Papers, RBHL. On its merely cosmetic effect, see Jackson, "Sanitary Conditions," 432–33. On the wide spectrum of pathogenic microorganisms contained in feces and raw wastewater, see Shuval, "Public Health Considerations," 368–69, 379. On directions for proper feces disposal, see Gen. Robert Hughes, "Circular

Letter to all Commanding Officers," Dec. 29, 1899, RG 395/2464, USNA. The hundreds of volumes in the *MHP* series document the actual disposal practices at the various posts. For the problems of the men regulating their bowel movements, see Robert Dexter Carter to his father, Sept. 2, 1899, Robert Dexter Carter Papers, RBHL, and Seaman, "Native Troops," 247. For discussion and documentation of the problem of U.S. Army hygiene and sanitation in the Philippines, see De Bevoise, "Compromised Host," 210–19. On the Filipinos' use of the rivers, see George T. Newgarden, "Random Recollections of an Army Surgeon," 135, "Autobiographical Sketches," MS/B/141, NLM. Regarding the general problem in the U.S. Army in the second half of the nineteenth century, see Reed et al., *Report*, passim, and Cosmas, *Army*, 245–94.

CHAPTER 2

1. Susceptibility is defined broadly herein to include exposure and response to disease. On susceptibility, see Lilienfeld and Lilienfeld, *Foundations*, 46–48; Susser, *Causal Thinking*, 27–47; Patterson, "Infection," 741.

2. For the interrelationship between poverty and disease, see Walsh, "Estimating," 1073, and Dunn, "Social Determinants," 1086–96. For the cause- and-effect relationship and the quoted statement, see Payne, "Nature," 14. For the situation in the Philippines today, see Dougherty, "Medical Industry," 16, and the reports cited therein.

3. For wage scales and lists of occupations, see *CPI, 1903*, 2:92–120, 4:434–46. For typical observations by foreigners, see Clark, "Labor Conditions," 722, and Foreman, *Philippine Islands*, 320.

4. Ileto's remark was made in a personal communication during 1990. For the quotation about comparative poverty, see *CPI, 1903*, 1:513–14. For discussion and a proportional estimate of the wealthy elite in Batangas pueblos as 1.5 percent–2.0 percent of the population in the 1890s, see May, *Battle*, 8–25, 293–96. For the truly indigent as representing 3.1 percent of the population in another province, see Ilocos Norte, 1879, *Mm*, 6, PNA.

5. For Romblon, see Col. George W. Adair, "Autobiographical Sketches," MS/C/44, box 1, NLM; Clark, "Labor Conditions," 762; *CPI, 1903* 3:79, 139.

6. Zambales (SD), 1895, *Mm*, 7, PNA; Camarines Sur, 1884, *Mm*, 5; Camarines Sur, 1887, *Mm*, 13–14, PNA; Capiz, 1882, *Mm*, 28–28b, PNA; Pangasinan, 1883, *Mm*, 5, PNA; Ilocos Norte, 1886, *Mm*, 2, PNA; Abra, 1886, *Mm*, 4–5 PNA; Francia, *Unas palabras*, 9–10. On differential mortality by class, see also Owen, "Measuring Mortality," 106–7.

7. Fast and Richardson, *Roots*, 23–24, 38; McCoy, "Introduction," 7–8; Owen, "Abaca," 191; Pangasinan, 1891, *M*, 21b, PNA. The new Philippine crop patterns did not amount to monocropping in the strict sense because subsistence rice culture existed alongside cash crops in most regions, though in diminishing proportion to the population increase. In Bikol, as Owen has pointed out, "rice and abaca do not compete for land, so paddy-fields remain even as abaca expands" (personal communication, May 17, 1992).

8. Fast and Richardson, *Roots*, 21–23; Cullinane, "Changing Nature," 32; de Jesus, "Control," 32; Cagayan de Misamis, 1887, *M*, 12, PNA.

9. Pangasinan, 1891, *M*, 21b-22, PNA; Cavite, 1887, *Mm*, 26a-27, PNA.

10. For Nueva Ecija, see Rajal, "Memoria," 318–28, and the original version of the report in Nueva Ecija, 1887, *M*, 12b-18, PNA. On changing labor systems, see McCoy, "Introduction," 8; Fast and Richardson, *Roots*, 23–25, 28, 37–38, 42, 49, 96; McLennan, *Central Luzon Plain*, 111–21; Fegan, "Social History," 97; Roth, "Church Lands," 142–48. Owen reminds us, withal, that in 1898 "the agrarian landscape remained predomi-

nantly smallholder" (Owen, "Philippine Economic Development," 104). Prior to 1904 the unit of currency in the Philippines was the Mexican peso (Pfs), sometimes called the Mexican silver dollar ($Mex.). The rate relative to the U.S. dollar fluctuated from year to year. In 1904, the Philippine peso (P) was created, and its rate was set at P1.00 = $US 0.50.

11. For Negros, see McCoy, "Queen," 323, and Echaúz, *Sketches*, 60–63. See Iloilo, 1892, *Mm*, 13, PNA, for discussion of the "floating population," and Goa, Camarines Sur, HDP, 26:5, PNL for brigandage.

12. For crop export trends, see Fast and Richardson, *Roots*, 13, 38, 45, 49; Owen, "Abaca," 195, 210; Roth, "Church Lands," 148. See Kilbourne, "Food Salts," 127, for rice import statistics. For the Negros hunger crises, see Martínez Cuesta, *History*, 260–61.

13. As we shall see, the cost of light wood products every household needed had quintupled in some areas as early as 1868, a result of the drive to develop the land. See J. F., "Memoria," 460–61. For Philippine currency exchange rates against the U.S. dollar for the period 1870–1904, see *CPI, 1903*, 4:563; "RPC, 1907," in *ARSW, 1907*, 1018; Lt. Col. J.F. Kerr, "Memorandum regarding proposed amendment of paragraph 722, Army Regulations," Oct. 10, 1903, RG 112/26, 67680/Q/1, USNA. For reliance on imports, see McCoy, "Queen," 297; Fast and Richardson, *Roots*, 94; Cagayan de Misamis, 1887, *Mm*, 12–12b, PNA. See Pangasinan, 1891, *Mm*, 23, PNA, for Peñaranda's statement. I have calculated rice price fluctuations from raw figures in "RPC, 1907," in *ARSW, 1907*, 950. It is not clear if the prices therein are in Mexican or U.S. dollars. For Saigon rice prices in graphic form between 1878–1912 and the conclusion that no correlation existed between price (either in Saigon or on the world market) and Philippine purchases, see Miller, *Economic Conditions*, 34–35.

14. For 1903 wage rates, which had doubled since the war began, see "RPC, 1907," in *ARSW, 1907*, 1002.

15. On the immune system and host defense mechanisms, see Mandell et al., *Principles*, 33–146. For the quoted statement, see Patterson, "Infection," 741.

16. Schad and Banwell, "Hookworms," 362; Dammin, "Introduction," 1213–14.

17. Chandler and Reed, *Introduction*, 18–19. For the quoted statement, see Masur and Jones, "Protozoal Infections," 406.

18. For references to microparasites or "afecciones verminosas," see Ilocos Norte, 1876, *Mm*, 18, PNA. For discussion of the early "hit and miss" surveys, see Leech et al., "Hookworm Disease," 105. For the roundworm statistic, see Manalang, "Hookworm Campaign," 483–94. On worm infections as an indicator of living standards and for both Ascaris and Trichuris, see Hinz, *Human Helminthiases*, 190–202.

19. On iron deficiency, see Schad and Banwell, "Hookworms," 362. For the relative prevalence and geographical distribution today, see Hinz, *Human Helminthiases*, 202–7. For the 1922 findings, see Macaraig, *Social Problems*, 322. For prevalence in rural areas, see Leech, "Hookworm Disease," 105.

20. For the early surveys, see Garrison, "Prevalence," 191–210; Garrison and Llamas, "Intestinal Worms," 185–86; Strong et al., "Medical Survey," 257–69; Rissler and Gomez, "Prevalence," 267–76; Chamberlain, et al., "Examinations," 505–14; Willets, "Statistical Study," 211–14; Crowell and Hammack, "Intestinal Parasites," 157–74; Willets, "Intestinal Parasitism," 81–92; Willets, "Intestinal Helminthiasis," 233–40. For the prevalence of the four worms today, see Hinz, *Human Helminthiases*, 166–70, 207–11. For the 1903 survey, see Calvert, "Record," 484–85.

21. For the prison survey, see Garrison, "Animal Parasites," 206. The quoted phrase is from Mahmoud, "Schistosomiasis," 447. For the findings of the 1950s, see "Panel

Discussion on Schistosomiasis," in *Proceedings Eighth Pacific Scientific Congress*, 6A:334. See also Coller, *Barrio Gacao*, passim. For the situation in 1975, see Hinz, *Human Helminthiases*, 104.

22. For the 1908 finding, see Garrison, "Animal Parasites," 206. On the amoebiasis controversy, see Musgrave and Clegg, *Amebas*, passim; Musgrave, "Intestinal Amoebiasis," 229; Rogers, "Prevention," 219; Walker, "Comparative Study," 159; Walker and Sellards, "Amoebic Dysentery," 253. On *Giardia*, see Manson-Bahr and Bell, *Manson's Tropical Diseases*, 324–27, and Biggar, "Analysis," 13, 18.

23. For the Pasay survey, see Long, *Sanitation*, 7. For the Bilibid results, see Garrison, "Animal Parasites," 195. For the quoted statement about sapping the vitality, see Macaraig, *Social Problems*, 322. For the quoted remark about pathologic effect and for the threat to the community, see Faust and Russell, *Craig*, 53, 315.

24. Hinz, *Human Helminthiases*, 216–18; Garrison, "Animal Parasites," 208.

25. Strong et al., "Medical Survey," 207–10, 247.

26. Ibid., 211–18.

27. Ibid., 248–49.

28. Ibid., 232, 252.

29. Guthrie et al., "Water," 225–26. On the practical obstacles to implementing sanitary disposal systems, see Strong et al., "Medical Survey," 288.

30. For the quote about poor nutrition and poverty, see Norse, "Nutritional Implications," 25. The following quote is from McKeown, *Origins*, 55. For the basic connection with impoverishment, see Kosa et al., *Poverty*, passim. On antagonism and synergism, see Scrimshaw, "Interactions," 1679.

31. On measles and malnourishment, see Behar, "Deadly Combination," 29. On malnutrition and infection, see Newberne and Williams, "Nutritional Influences," 93.

32. For Dr. Cervantes's statement, see Samar, 1886, *Mm*, 7–8, PNA. For other observations on bad diets, see Panay, 1870, *Mm*, 42, PNA; Ilocos Norte, 1876, *Mm*, 33–35, PNA; Leyte, 1877, *Mm*, 20, PNA; Tarlac, 1884, *Mm*, 2, PNA; Ilocos Sur, 1886, *Mm*, 5–8, PNA; Cagayan de Misamis, 1886, *Mm*, 3–4, PNA; Albay, 1886, *Mm*, 6, PNA; Camarines Sur, 1887, *Mm*, 11–12, PNA; Antique, 1888, *Mm*, 5–6, PNA; Masbate y Ticao, 1889, *Mm*, 10, PNA; Abra, 1889, *Mm*, 5, PNA; Iloilo (CZ), 1894, *Mm*, 20, PNA; Zambales (SD), 1895, *Mm*, 4, PNA. For the current scientific understanding of the interrelationship between diet, anemia, and disease, see Girdwood, "Nutritional Anaemias," 441–64. For earlier and more positive views about diets, see San Antonio, *Chronicles*, 24–33, 36–37; Martínez de Zúñiga, *Status*, 58, 78, 343, 407, 417, 441, 453; Mallat, *Philippines*, 286–87; Jagor, *Travels*, 210. For the European case, see McKeown, *Origins*, 84–85. For the physical examination data, see "RPC, 1907," in *ARSW, 1907*, 1011–12.

33. For some of the contemporary descriptions of Filipino diets, see Leyte, 1877, *Mm*, 20, PNA; Masbate y Ticao, 1886, *Mm*, 2, PNA; Camarines Sur, 1887, *Mm*, 11–12, PNA; Antique, 1887, *Mm*, 1–2, PNA; Pangasinan, 1888, *Mm*, 8, PNA; Iloilo (CZ), 1894, *Mm*, 11, PNA; Arthur Valentiner to Clark Valentiner, Jan. 21, 1900, Arthur Valentiner Letters, CHS; "RPC, 1907," in *ARSW, 1907*, 1009; Heiser, *American Doctor's Odyssey*, 169. An observer noted in 1859 that except for the immediate vicinity of Manila, where some Chinese grew vegetables for that market, no such crops were grown in the rest of northern Luzon, "at least as a means of subsistence for the country, or as an article of commerce." He said that some few persons grew tomatoes and melons on their plots of ground after the rice was harvested but that the amount was negligible. Since he was concerned with commercial development, his description leaves open the possibility that most families grew fruits and vegetables for their own consumption. Still, he did not

say that, and no one else did either. See Fernandez Checa, "Memoria presentada," 122. It is important to keep in mind that diets, like everything else, differed from region to region. In some areas corn or root crops such as camotes or uvas replaced or supplemented rice, and the supply and varieties of fish also varied from place to place. See Leyte, 1881, *Mm*, 45, PNA, and "Memorandum from U.S. Army Board for the Study of Tropical Diseases as They Exist in the Philippine Islands," Sept. 30, 1909, RG 112/26, 68075/73, USNA. For the quoted phrases about supplements to rice and fish, see Capiz, 1887, *Mm*, 14, PNA, and Mallat, *Philippines*, 286, respectively. For the quotation about fruits, see San Antonio, *Chronicles*, 31. As to meat, poultry, and eggs being too expensive for all but the well-off, see Strong et al., "Medical Survey," 220, 226; "RPC, 1907," in *ARSW, 1907*, 753; Heiser, *American Doctor's Odyssey*, 169. For sugar in the Philippine diet, see Strong et al., "Medical Survey," 225, 230, and Wernstedt and Spencer, *Philippine Island World*, 216.

34. On the rice, see Kilbourne, "Food Salts," 127–29, and Strong et al., "Medical Survey," 231. On beriberi, see Andrews, "Infantile Beriberi," 68, and Darby, "Thiamine Deficiency," 545. For fish in Taytay, see Strong et al., "Medical Survey," 230. For food values, see Intengan et al., "Composition," 82:227–52, 83:187–216, 84:263–73, 84:343–63, 85:209, respectively; "Food Composition Table for the Western Pacific Region," in *Health Aspects*, 323–38; Lontoc et al., "Folic Acid Content," 311–20; Eusebio and Palad, "Vitamin A Content," 199–207. The suggested diet has been composed from data in Intengan, "Composition," 83:205; Food Composition Table in *Health Aspects*, 209; Strong, "Medical Survey," 230.

35. Strong et al., "Medical Survey," 221–30.

36. Ibid., 230–31. Another survey the same year showed that prisoners in Bilibid Prison consumed 2,646 kilocalories per day, which was thought to be representative of the average diet in the Philippines. See Aron, "Diet," 198–202. For the 1957 and 1974 survey results, see von Oppenfeld et al., "Labor Force," quoted in de Guzman et al., "Study," 63. On the problem of caloric deficit, see Fox, "Study," 63.

37. Jagor, *Travels*, 29; Iloilo (CZ), 1894, *Mm*, 9–11, PNA. For effects of modernization on nutrition in developing countries, see Pinstrup-Andersen, "Impact," 43–44.

38. For diets on Samar, see Cruikshank, *Samar*, 38, 117. A reading of the firsthand accounts by survivors of the Democratic Kampuchea years (1975–1979) in Cambodia indicates the importance of foraging skills under crisis conditions. It also seems clear that the "new" people (that is, the former urban residents) were at a severe disadvantage because they usually lacked those abilities. See, for instance, Pin, *Stay Alive*, passim.

39. For examples of accounts that describe an abundance of fruits and vegetables but are ambiguous as to whether the poorer segment of people grew them too, see Martínez de Zúñiga, *Status*, 58, and Goncharov, *Voyage*, 173–76. On kitchen gardening, see Pelzer, *Pioneer Settlement*, 43–47, and Wernstedt and Spencer, *Philippine Island World*, 183, 203. For the effect of declining land tenure on kitchen gardening, see Fegan, "Central Luzon Barrio," 121–23. The quoted statement is in San Antonio, *Chronicles*, 36. On the pervasiveness of chewing betel nut and tobacco (by cutting cigars into pieces), often together, see Jagor, *Travels*, 115. For the quote about tobacco, see Mallat, *Philippines*, 247.

40. The official complaint is translated and cited in Cruikshank, *Samar*, 115. For the rest, see Leyte, 1881, *Mm*, 5, PNA; Masbate y Ticao, 1889, *Mm*, 4, PNA; Zambales (SD), 1895, *Mm*, 3–4, 9, PNA.

41. On the U.S. Army as food purchaser, see Brig. Gen Marshall I. Ludington, "Report of the Quartermaster-General of the Army," Oct. 16, 1899, in *ARSW, 1899*, 181;

Luddington, "Report of the Quartermaster-General of the Army," Oct. 16, 1900, in *ARSW, 1900*, 445; report of Maj. Edw. E. Dravo, July 1, 1900, in *ARSW, 1900*, 104, 106; Maj. W.P. Kendall, "Report on the Bacoor Hospital," May 5, 1900, RG 112/26, 2310/311/8, USNA; Maj. Henry C. Fisher, "Report on the Post Hospital, Cebu, Cebu," May 1, 1900, RG 112/26, 2310/311/4, USNA; Maj. George Penrose, "Report on the Base Hospital at Calamba," May 8, 1900, RG 112/26, 2310/311/6, USNA; Aliaga, Nueva Ecija, *MHP* 385, June 1901–Jan. 1902, RG 94/547, USNA; Trinidad, Benguet, *MHP* 468, Feb. 1901, RG 94/547, USNA; Capt. William Alden, "Monthly Sanitary Report for Masinloc, Zambales," Apr. 4, 1902, "Hospital Papers, 1886–1912," box 1, folder 4, "Angeles and San Fernando," RG 94/548, USNA. On Warner Barnes, see Gen. Henry W. Lawton to Brig.-Gen. Theodore Schwan, Oct. 28, 1899, in Maj. Gen. Elwell S. Otis, "Report of Major-General E.S. Otis, U.S. Army, Commanding the Division of the Philippines and Military Governor of the Philippine Islands, September 1, 1899 to May 5, 1900," May 14, 1900, in *ARSW, 1900*, 223. Young Eulogio Rodriguez handled provisions for the 27th U.S. Vol. Inf. in Montalban (today Rodriguez), Rizal. Typical of those who used wartime opportunities to get ahead in life, Rodriguez went on to become president of the Philippine Senate and an invitee to the Eisenhower White House a half-century later. See Quirino, *Amang*, 7, 10–13, and De Bevoise, Review of *Amang*, 119–21. Daily pilferage of food by U.S. soldiers also drained nutritional resources from the poor. See De Bevoise, "Compromised Host," 161–63. For food contributions, both voluntary and not, to the Philippine Army, see May, *Battle*, 168–263.

42. McLennan, "Changing Human Ecology," 79–82. For the quoted passages, see J.B., "Estudio," 578, and Pampanga, 1887, *Mm*, 25b–26, PNA. For more detailed treatment of the ecology of pioneering on the central plain and especially the aridification process, see McLennan, *Central Luzon Plain*, 147–74.

43. For the early observation, see "Englishman," *Remarks*, in BR, 51:127. For action against the insects, see Gobernador de Pangasinan to Director Gral de Admin. Civil, June 20, 1887, *L*, PNA. For the cited infestations, which are just a few of many, see Gobernador P.M. de Visayas to Sr. Superintendente de Propios y Arbitrios de estas Islas, Nov. 17, 1866, file 29, *L*, PNA; Gobernador de Tarlac to Director Gral de Admin. Civil, July 16, 1886, file 54, *L*, PNA; Gobernador de Pampanga to Director Gral de Admin. Civil, Aug. 13, 1886, file 44, *L*, PNA.

44. Taft, "Report of the Civil Governor for the Period Ending December 23, 1903," Nov. 15, 1903, in *ARSW, 1903*, 18–20.

45. On the pass system and the resulting disruption of daily life, see Maj. J.J. Weisenburger, "Request for Instructions," July 9, 1899, RG 395/777, box 1, USNA; "Report of Larson Commanding U.S.S. *Napindan* regarding Action of Gunboat Cruising around Lake Examining Sailing Cascos, etc.," Aug. 6, 1899, RG 395/777, box 1, USNA; Capt. J.H.H. Peshine, "Request for Clarification on Conflicting Orders regarding Pass System," Aug. 6, 1899, RG 395/777, box 1, USNA. Actual restriction on civilian movement varied by place and time. Enforcement was generally relaxed after the Americans began garrisoning towns in 1900 and considered the surrounding areas pacified. May points out, for instance, that after occupation in January 1900, "residents of Batangas City were free, most of the time, to travel about the countryside" (May, *Battle*, 186). For a list of the open ports as of 1898, see *CPI, 1903* 4:579–80. For the letter from Cebu, see George S. Goodale to Miss Brown, May 27, 1899, Abbie Farwell Brown Papers, box 61, file: "May 1899–June 1900," UVL. For the cited petition and reports of others, see Calixto de Lara (Presidente of Las Pinas) and others to H.E. Captain General of Operations of Americans, July 13, 1899, RG 395/777, box 1, USNA, and Col. William H. Beck, "Report and

Recommendations Regarding Natives and Conditions at Paranaque, Bacoor, and Las Pinas," Jan. 19, 1900, RG 395/777, box 3, USNA. On "free" rice in exchange for roadwork, see Brig. Gen. F.D. Grant to adjutant general, 1st Div., July 24, 1899, RG 395/777, box 1, USNA, and Lt. J.C. Oakes, "Report on Roadwork in Silang, Indan Area," Feb. 2, 1900, RG 395/777, box 2, USNA. For the letter from Leyte, see Gordon Johnston to his parents, June 15, 1900, 12, B.S. Johnston Papers, SHC.

46. On rice destruction, see Lt. Henry Ripley, "Report Relating to Burning of Palay by U.S. Troops, Feb. 1900," and 12 endorsements, Apr. 11, 1900, RG 395/851, box 8, USNA. On the increasing unmanageability of the original policy, see Clarence R. Edwards to Capt. H.J. McGrath, July 11, 1899, and endorsements, especially the 5th, written at the instruction of Maj. Gen. Otis, RG 395/777, box 3, USNA. For the deliberate and purposeful shooting of animals, pursuant to orders, see Mauo, Samar, *MHP* 533, 1, 5–6, RG 94/547, USNA.

47. Regarding the destruction on Marinduque, see the archival record contained in entries 318, 517, 5175, and box 69 of RG 395, USNA. The enumeration is calculated from the raw data contained in the typewritten monthly summaries of reports of operations filed by detachment commanders. Burial data is derived from data contained in "Entierros, 1891–1909," Mogpog, Marinduque parish records, GL. May's work in the Batangas parish records has revealed a dramatic rise in mortality from disease in the eastern part of the province as soon as the Americans arrived to occupy it in 1900 (May, *Battle*, 205–7). The terror tactics used by the soldiers undoubtedly caused severe psychological stress in the populace. For evidence that stress increases susceptibility to infectious disease, see Totman et al., "Cognitive Dissonance Stress," 55–63; McKeown, *Origins*, 56; Petrich and Holmes, "Life Change," 825–38; Rabkin and Struening, "Life Events," 1013, 1018; Antonovsky, *Unraveling*, 27–32.

48. Ileto, "Food Crisis," 101–9.

49. For the quoted descriptions, see letter dated Jan. 4, 1901, *Grand Rapids (Michigan) Evening Press*, Feb. 28, 1900; Capt. E.F. Glenn to adjutant general, Dept. Visayas, Nov. 3, 1900, RG 395/2477, USNA; Col. J.T. Dickman to Manning, June 11, 1900, J.T. Dickman Papers, RBHL. For the secretary of war's comment, see Root to Weeks, Nov. 7, 1899, RG 94, 1856/277626. The campaign on Panay is documented in a number of different files and record groups in a number of different archives. However, for general information, see official reports in entries 2466, 2467, 2477, in RG 395, USNA. For more specific information, see report of Brig. Gen. Robert P. Hughes, Oct. 17, 1900, RG 395/2466, box 69, USNA; Capt. Alvin A. Barker to Hughes, Dec. 14, 1900., RG 395/2466, box 69, USNA; Col. J.T. Dickman, "Report of Operations in the Vicinity of Iloilo, Island of Panay, P.I., June 6 to July 16, 1900," RG 94/341412, USNA; Capt. C.M. Brownell, "Report of Operations in the Vicinity of Dumangas, Island of Panay, P.I., August 3 to 10, 1900, RG94/347792, USNA; Lt. G.R.D. MacGregor to adjutant general, 4th Dist., Jaro, Feb. 27, 1901, box 1, Moorfield Storey Papers, LC; Maj. Edwin F. Glenn, CtM, May 23–29, 1902, RG 153, box 3329, WNRC; Glenn, CtM, RG 153, box 3439, WNRC; Glenn to adjutant general, Dept Visayas, Nov. 3, 1900, RG 395/2477, USNA; Hughes to Col. Edward D. Anderson, Dec. 10, 1900, RG 395/2466, USNA; Hughes to Anderson, Dec. 29, 1900, RG 395/2466, USNA; Noble to commanding officer, Barotac Nuevo, Jan. 23, 1900, RG 395/2466, USNA; Simons to Maj. Guy V. Henry, Jr., Jan. 23, 1900, RG 395/2466, USNA; Noble to Henry, Jan. 24, 1900, RG 395/2466, USNA. The evidence in the previous sources should be contrasted with Gen. Hughes's testimony, which was clearly perjured, before a Senate committee in 1902 where he stated, for instance, that no burnings of towns occurred on Panay. At the most, he conceded that a barrio of a

half-dozen houses had been burned here and there (*Affairs in the Philippine Islands*, 1:558).

50. Dickman to Manning, Feb. 28, 1900, J.T. Dickman Papers, RBHL; Lt. Col. W.H. Van Horne to adjutant general, Dept. Visayas, Oct. 7, 1900, RG 395/2477, USNA.

51. For the cavalry experience, see the report of Lt. H.R. Richmond, 1st U.S. Cav., Jan. 12, 1902, RG 395/2354, box 2, USNA. For more information about that campaign in Batangas, see May, *Battle*, 225–64. For the medical officer's observation, see Alfred A. Woodhull, "Annual Report for the Year Ending June 30, 1899," RG 112/57592/76, USNA. For the observations at San Francisco del Monte, see report of Lt. James A. Moss, 24th U.S. Inf., Aug. 21, 1899, RG 395/777, box 1, USNA.

Chapter 3

1. Pedro de los Santos y Martina Rafael, Feb. 7, 1898, *P*, PNA. The facts were never established in court since the proceedings were aborted, so I have presented them as they appear to me, as I have done in most of the cases that follow. What happened was of course disputed. Rafael and de los Santos claimed that no "walk" ever took place. Instead, they said, Trias had stayed with them for just two or three days before disappearing, and when Ramos came looking for her, they had no idea of her whereabouts. All of that is highly doubtful, given what we learn from the *Prostitución* records about the way the system worked at that time. Rafael and de los Santos appear to have been two of a growing number of persons who were aware that money could be made by supplying young women to brothel proprietors. Much is unclear about this particular case, including the extent to which the two Spaniards (who probably knew each other) were conspirators. Perhaps they were not, and it was merely a matter of Trias and Ramos thinking that they could better their situation by changing jobs. But it is not impossible that Ramos was in league with the other couple. We know nothing about his marriage to Trias or even if it was legitimate. One contemporary said that prostitutes often told officials that their problems were the fault of their husbands. That reason could not have been too common, however, if the records are correct in showing that few prostitutes were married. On that point, though, see Rodríguez-Solís, *Historia*, 1893 ed., 246. For judicial procedure in the nineteenth-century Philippines, see Bankoff, "Inside the Courtroom," 287–304.

2. It is likely that venereal diseases existed in the Philippines before the Spanish conquest. Magellan's expedition is said to have encountered syphilis in all the islands of the Indonesian archipelago but especially in Timor. See Antonio Pigafetta, *First Voyage around the World* (1525), in BR, 34:125. For the contention that prostitution was not a part of traditional Philippine culture, see Infante, *Woman*, 61; Sturtevant, *Popular Uprisings*, 23; Sawyer, *Inhabitants*, 66. For the quote on the history of prostitution, see Rodríguez-Solís, *Historia*, 1921 ed., 111. Rodríguez-Solís concluded also that prostitution had not been an indigenous institution, saying that "it is more difficult to find information about prostitution in the Philippines than in Cuba, perhaps because it originally did not have as much importance in that archipelago as it later acquired." On the Los Banos hospital, see Fray Juan Manuel Maldonado de Puga, *The Order of St. John of God* (1742), in BR, 47:227. About the women the British left behind, see Ayerbe, *Sitio*, 130. We can infer from Le Gentil's observations that Spanish men in Manila were sexually active with prostitutes. See Le Gentil, *Voyage*, 94. For the quote about wayward women, see Martínez de Zúñiga, *Status*, 192, 223. For the ease of treating syphilis, see Mallat, *Philippines*, 74. Doeppers has made a couple of valuable observations. First, to

the extent that preconquest venereal diseases existed in the Philippines, they "presumably flourished in a different milieu," that is, without prostitution. Second, he cautions that the use of the term prostitution can be misleading in the Philippine cultural context, where the dividing line between it and *querida*-ship was often blurred. The term "querida" comprised relationships ranging from temporary but generally monogamous liaisons with soldiers to enduring ones, usually between Filipinos, involving companionship and sometimes household work. Doeppers has encountered in his research such relationships "of 20 or 30 years standing—virtual permanent additional marriages" (personal communication, Jan. 10, 1994).

3. Antolín, "Discurso," APS.

4. Regarding the distinction made in 1879 between the two diseases and for information about penicillin, see Spink, *Infectious Diseases*, 310–12. For the less serious diseases, see Heyman, "Chancroid," 958–59, and Manson-Bahr and Bell, *Manson's Tropical Diseases*, 1101–21. On the confusion with yaws, see ibid., 407–15, and Scott's forthcoming study of sixteenth-century society and culture. The latter reference appears in the section on Visayan health and hygiene, on 124 in the typescript Scott provided me. On the postwar concern about yaws in the Philippines, see Capt. Horace D. Bloomberg, "The Wasserman Reaction in Syphilis, Leprosy, and Yaws," Feb. 21, 1911, RG 112/26, 68075/89, USNA.

5. Heyman, "Syphilis," 1069–76; Spink, *Infectious Diseases*, 305–6; Piot and Holmes, "Sexually Transmitted Diseases," 850–54.

6. Bennett, "Pneumococcal Infections," 887–89; Spink, *Infectious Diseases*, 310; Piot and Holmes, "Sexually Transmitted Diseases," 846–47.

7. For the morbidity lists, see Cagayan de Misamis, 1886, *Mm*, appendix, PNA; Laguna, 1887, *Mm*, appendix, PNA; Ilocos Norte, 1891, *Mm*, 5–7, PNA. For the quotes, see Ilocos Norte, 1876, *Mm*, 26–27, PNA; Leyte, 1877, *Mm*, 35, PNA; Albay, 1887, *Mm*, 13, PNA.

8. For Dr. Farina's description of the diffusion process and his recommendations, see Leyte, 1877, *Mm*, 61, PNA. Dr. Solivellas's comments are in Iloilo (CZ), 1894, *Mm*, 14, PNA. About the military posts, see Meyer, "Igorots," 123. The correlation between STDs and the military increased. In the mid-1890s, the Spanish naval command was extremely concerned about an epidemic of syphilis among its sailors stationed in the pueblos of Cavite and San Roque, Cavite. See La Comandancia General del Apostadero y Escuadra de Estas Islas to Sr. Director Gral de Admin. Civil, Dec. 19, 1895, and Gobernador P.M. de Cavite to Inspector Gral de Beneficencia y Sanidad, Jan. 9, 1895, P, PNA.

9. Ilocos Norte, 1876, *Mm*, 26–27, PNA; Juzgado de Provincia, Bangued, Abra, to Regente de la Real Audiencia de Estas Islas, Apr. 22, 1885, P, PNA. About the house of detention, see Pvt. John B. Hallet, CtM, RG 153/30294, box 3366, WRNC. Doeppers called my attention to the existence of the *Gaceta* lists and also to the fact that the numbers are miniscule (Doeppers, conversation with author, Oct. 1, 1993). The quotation about clandestine prostitution in the larger provincial towns is from Gonzalez y Martín, *Filipinos*, 144.

10. Capiz, 1886, *Mm*, 8–9; Capiz, 1887, *Mm*, 24–26, PNA.

11. For an article based on research in the *Prostitución* records arguing that "onerous policies enforced by the Spaniards and the Americans in the Philippines brought stagnation and impoverishment to the inhabitants, and led indirectly to the continuance of prostitution," see Dery, "Prostitution," 475–89.

12. For the development of prostitution into a flourishing business in Singapore during the same period, see Warren, "Prostitution," 360–83.

13. The statistical profile that is presented here and in what follows is based on calculations from raw data contained in the case files, *P*, PNA. Doeppers has pointed to evidence suggesting a gender imbalance among migrants. He concludes that "women both outnumbered and came at higher rates than men relative to source populations in Rizal, Bulacan, Bataan, Cavite, and Pampanga—five of the six source provinces" (Doeppers, "Migration," 44). For the quoted statement, see Dery, "Prostitution," 477.

14. Morse, "AIDS," 28, 37. Often the decision to go into prostitution was not entirely free. Greg Bankoff tells of fourteen-year-old Felipa Almario, who came to Binondo in Manila to take work as a domestic when both of her parents died. She was seduced by one Mariano de Castro and when he promised to marry her, she left her job. After she realized that de Castro was not going to fulfill his promise, "she reluctantly agreed to become a prostitute." See Bankoff, "Servant-Master Conflict," 291. The subject of Filipino attitudes and behaviors regarding sex have not been studied extensively. One recent survey showed that compared to other nationalities, Filipinos are generally conservative on this subject. The author of an article discussing the findings hastens to add, however: "But these hold on the level of attitudes. Sexual *behavior* is another matter altogether." See Sandoval, "Filipino Attitudes," 318.

15. On paternal authority preventing women from becoming prostitutes in Manila, see *CPI, 1903*, 1:519.

16. About 90 percent (92 of 103) of those who can be identified by race were indio. Of the remainder, six were Chinese mestizo, two were Spanish mestizo, and the three others were listed as Spaniard, American, and English, respectively.

17. Some of the older women who were arrested may have had little or no connection with the trade at all. Denouncing someone as a prostitute was an effective means of harassment. Adriana Robles had come to Manila from San Rafael, Bulacan, probably as the result of her husband's death. Personal enemies denounced the thirty-five-year-old seamstress as a prostitute in 1884, and she was arrested, as she put it, "because of the unjust machinations of persons who took advantage of the good faith of the authorities." Her release was immediately ordered when the background investigation failed to reveal either a previous prison record or any known connection with prostitution. See Adriana Robles, Dec. 30, 1884, *P*, PNA. For another apparent frameup, this time of a man alleged to be involved in facilitating prostitution, see Ceferino Fernandes, July 1870, *P*, PNA. Fernandes seems to have been unfairly denounced by his rival in gambling and love, Espirion Atienza, to the warden of Mamante, Tondo, to whom Atienza was secretary. Fernandes was deported to Mindanao.

18. Maria Robles y Brigildo Ramirez, Mar. 24, 1877, *P*, PNA.

19. Maximiana de los Santos, May 6, 1877, *P*, PNA; Alejandra Rejes, Oct. 30, 1882, *P*, PNA; Benigna Raymundo, Feb. 17, 1887; Filomena de la Cruz, Feb. 19, 1887, *P*, PNA. Once out of Bilibid, however, some came back voluntarily. In 1886, the authorities were outraged to discover that some of the recently released prostitutes were returning on family visiting days—for business. The governor of Manila quickly agreed to a proposal to ban prison visits from former prostitute-inmates. See the correspondence between the warden of Bilibid and the governor of Manila, July 12–13, 1886, *P*, PNA.

20. Victoriana de la Rosa, Sept. 1871, *P*, PNA; Juana Rodriguez, Petrona Trinidad, Tomasa Dina, Francisca Garcia, Feb. 12, 1872, *P*, PNA.

21. Placida Javier, Oct. 21, 1874, *P*, PNA. Doeppers has rightly pointed out that this case "demonstrates the difficulty of separating serial prostitution from querida-ship" (personal communication, Jan. 10, 1994).

22. The earliest file that survives concerns a directive in 1858 to the mayors of all the

towns around Manila to apprehend four women who had been deported to Zamboanga for prostitution but had somehow escaped and were suspected to have come back to Luzon. See Cristina Miranda, Cirila Garcia, Sixta de la Cruz, Gervasia San Pablo, July 20, 1858, *P*, PNA. For the quoted legislation, see proclamation of Jan. 26, 1870, cited in Rafaela Mesa, Feb. 17, 1872, *P*, PNA, and art. 1 de la circular de 27 de Junio de 1872, quoted in Marguerita San Pedro, July 12, 1887, *P*, PNA. For the other twenty-five women, see the list of deportees on the boat *Marqués de la Victoria* to Puerta Princesa in Paragua, Feb. 21, 1872, and the various case files pertaining to them in *P*, PNA. The governor's comments appear in the Rafaela Mesa file. Dery doubts that many of the women ever returned. See Dery, "Prostitution," 485. He may be right, but there is no petition for permission to return in the files that was finally denied. The evidence is scant either way, however.

23. Matea San Juan, Josefa de la Cruz, Serapia Cuevas, Rafaela Quicias, Apr. 23, 1876, *P*, PNA.

24. Braulia Esquerra, Jan. 31, 1881, *P*, PNA. For other examples of women sent home who returned to prostitution in Manila, see Isidra Bitiera, Dec. 31, 1883, *P*, PNA, and Marguerita San Pedro, July 30, 1885, *P*, PNA. On arrests for suspected venereal disease, see, for example, Baldomera Miranda, Maria Garcia, Feliciana Pineda, Maria de la Cruz, Juana Valenzuela, Maria Romana, Lucia Arantio, Jan. 4, 1881, *P*, PNA.

25. Regarding the inchoate attempt at regulation in 1883, see "Antecedents sobre la organization de prostitución," and subsequent endorsement, May 16, 1883, *P*, PNA. For the governor-general's action, see "Secretaria del Gobierno General de Filipinas," July 13, 1887, *P*, PNA. About opposition to regulation and to Centeno, see St. Clair, *Katipunan*, 61, 65. For Dr. Mapa's argument, see Capiz, 1887, *Mm*, 26–28, PNA. One Spanish writer, who had never been to the Philippines but was relying on informants who had, said, "In Cavite, and in some other city, it seems also that prostitution is regulated in the same form as in Manila" (Rodríguez-Solís, *Historia*, 1893 ed., 245). I have seen nothing except for that uncertain reference to indicate that prostitution was regulated outside of Manila, but it would have made sense to extend it to Cavite, where there were so many sailors.

26. For the 1897 regulations, see "Reglamento especial de la Sección de Higiene de la Prostitución," July 31, 1897, *P*, PNA. For the preliminary consultation, see "Reglamento especial," Titulo 2, Articulos 3 y 7; Titulo 4, Articulo 9, *P*, PNA.

27. "Reglamento especial," Titulo 2, Articulos 12 y 15; Titulo 4, Articulos 26 y 27; Titulo 5, Articulos 32 y 35; Titulo 6, Articulos 41 y 42; Titulo 7, Articulos 45 y 47, *P*, PNA.

28. For the one roster that appears in the files, see the list of amas, amos, and prostitutes by house and address dated Sept. 7, 1893, *P*, PNA. For the quotes from the anonymous Spaniard (who is described as "a well-known writer") and for the statistic of 1,693 prostitutes, which also comes from him, see Rodríguez-Solís, *Historia*, 1893 ed., 246–47. In a later version of his book, he said that the governor and the publisher José del Perojo drew up a plan in 1889 to prohibit carnal traffic in the public roads, whether in coaches, behind houses, or against walls. It is not clear if such a regulation was ever issued, but there is no evidence to suggest that such practices were curtailed. See Rodríguez-Solís, *Historia*, 1921 ed., 259.

29. I have computed the various proportions from data in the files. Analyzing the test results by year shows a trend toward a larger proportion of negative results beginning in 1885, but the sample seems too small and the possible explanations too various to permit meaningful conclusions. For what it is worth, however, test results for venereal disease by year are as follows:

Year	Positive	Negative
1876	2	0
1877	25	2
1881	2	0
1882	1	3
1883	3	0
1885	6	13
1886	16	16
1887	2	8
1890	9	0

For the statistic from the anonymous Spaniard and for the military hospital figures, which he also provided, see Rodríguez-Solís, *Historia*, 1893 ed., 247.

30. For the Zabal-Simon investigation, see Don Mariano Zabala, July 31, 1890, *P*, PNA.

31. For the earlier matter, see Don Cipriano Subrido Fernandez, Don Angel Prensado Lojo, Don Estanislao Corral Perez, May 21, 1890, *P*, PNA.

32. For the follow-up on Encarnacion and Macalinao, see the 1893 registration list, September 7, 1893, *P*, PNA, and Maxima Macalinao, Sept. 22, 1893, *P*, PNA.

33. Florentina Caulas, Feb. 6, 1892, *P*, PNA.

34. For Irene Atienza's experience, see Maria Cruz Fernandez, Dec. 24, 1897, *P*, PNA.

35. For the quote about the criada system, see Clark, "Labor Conditions," 836–38. For Mojica's experience, see "Espediente gubernativo instruido en averignación de la conducta y antecedents de Victorina Garcia," Oct. 20, 1891, *P*, PNA.

36. For the statement about the "diseased woman," see Dickman to Manning, Dec. 6, 1899, J.T. Dickman Papers, RBHL.

37. On venereal infection in the U.S. population, see Holmes et al., *Sexually Transmitted Diseases*, 6. For the enlistment statistics, see Sternberg, "Annual Report for 1900," in *ARSW, 1900*, 916. It may be that the examining physicians at enlistment missed substantial numbers of infections. One World War I statistic suggests that 96 percent of the venereal diseases in the U.S. Army were contracted prior to enlistment (Bannister, "Military Surgeon," 14). For the problem of prostitution and venereal disease around military posts in the United States, see Maj. Gen. Henry C. Corbin, "Report of the Adjutant-General of the Army to the Secretary of War on the Canteen Section of the Post Exchange," Nov. 24, 1899, in *ARSW, 1899*, 81–277; Gen. S.B.M. Young to adjutant general, Oct. 22, 1901, RG 112/26, 43508/114, USNA; Sexton, *Soldiers*, 23. For venereal disease at Ft. McKenzie, see 3d U.S. Cav., RHR, RG 94, USNA. For examples of returning men with secondary syphilis to duty, see, for instance, 1st Tenn. Vol. Inf., RHR 2523, RG 94, USNA for the disposition of Pvt. Robert J. Bass in July 1898, Pvt. David Lomasney in Dec. 1898, and Pvt. Albert J. Fromme in Aug. 1899. See "Shall Men with Venereal Disease be Sent to the Philippine Islands?," Rg 112/26, 76655, USNA for that issue. For the anonymous statement, see William Lloyd Garrison, Jr. to the editor of the *Springfield Republican*, May 9, 1900, and enclosed in a letter from Erving Winslow to Sen. Richard F. Pettigrew, May 11, 1900, Richard F. Pettigrew Papers, box: "R.F. Pettigrew Miscellaneous Papers Pa–Pn," file: "Philippines," SHM.

38. On the British statistics, see Brig. Gen. T.J. Wint, "Report of Board of Officers regarding Military Administration in India, Burma, and Java," quoted in "Annual Report

of Chief Surgeon Smart for the Fiscal Year Ending June 30, 1903," RG 112/26, 24508/V, USNA. On the Asiatic Syphilis problem, see Lippincott to adjutant general, July 27, 1898, RG 395/777, USNA.

39. On increased incidence, see Maj. Gen. Henry C. Corbin, "Memorandum for the Secretary of War from the Adjutant-General," Jan. 8, 1901, RG 94/356345, USNA. For the brigade sick list, see report of Maj. Samuel O.L. Potter, Oct. 16, 1898, in *ARSW, 1899*, 455. For understatement of STD incidence, see Brig. Gen. George W. Sternberg to secretary of war in Sternberg, "Report of the Surgeon-General," Oct. 12, 1899, in *ARSW, 1899*, 453. On the separate wards, see Robert Dexter Carter to his father, Robert Dexter Carter Papers, RBHL. For the veteran's recollection, see John D. La Wall, "Memoirs," 103–4, SAWS, U.S. Vol. Inf., 27th Reg., USAMHI.

40. For the decree, see Taylor, *Philippine Insurrection*, 3:194–95. On Sampaloc, see "The Crowning Infamy of Imperialism," 2, in Richard F. Pettigrew Papers, box: "R.F. Pettigrew Miscellaneous Papers Si–T," file: "Spanish-American War," SHM. About the Calle Alix, see Garrison to editor of *Springfield Republican*, in Richard F. Pettigrew Papers, box: "R.F. Pettigrew Miscellaneous Papers Pa–Pn," file: "Philippines," SHM.

41. Regarding the influx from the treaty ports, the first two quoted phrases, and the bribes to the first mates, see, "Crowning Infamy," in Richard F. Pettigrew Papers, box: "R.F. Pettigrew Miscellaneous Papers Si–T," file: "Spanish-American War," SHM. On the nationality of the prostitutes and pimps, see A. Lester Hazlett, "A View of the Moral Conditions Existing in the Philippines," RG 94/368853/a/AGO, USNA, and Sexton, *Soldiers*, 57. For information about some of those individuals and their activities see *Manila Times*, Sept. 7, 1899, 2–3; Sept. 8, 1899, 1; Sept. 11, 1899, 7; Sept. 12, 1899, 1; Sept. 16, 1899, 1; Mar. 9, 1900, 1; Mar. 22, 1900, 1. The quoted phrase about "cosmopolitan harlotry" is from Sawyer, *Inhabitants*, 114. For the claim about 300 prostitutes, see Garrison to editor of *Springfield Republican*, Richard F. Pettigrew Papers, box: "R.F. Pettigrew Miscellaneous Papers Pa–Pn," Philippines, SHM. For those who slipped through, see *Manila Times*, Mar. 23, 1900, 1; Hazlett, "Moral Conditions," 33, RG 94/368853/2/AGO, USNA; report of Brig. Gen. Robert P. Hughes, Feb. 7, 1902, RG 94/343790, USNA. On the Filipina prostitutes, see Hughes, ibid., and report of Maj. Charles Lynch, May 18, 1901, RG 94/368853/a AGO, USNA. For Japanese prostitution in Manila, see Terami-Wada, "Early Years."

42. Terami-Wada, "Early Years," 3–4. The plague did not become epidemic and is generally thought to have been confined to Manila and to have disappeared quickly. Nevertheless, five cases (three fatal) were reported in Naic, Cavite, in Sept. 1901. See William Stephenson, "Reported Case of (Suspected) Plague at Naic, Cavite," Sept. 16, 1901, RG 112/52, 60276/59, MS 4968, USNA.

43. For statistics on the program, see reports of Brig.-Gen. George W. Davis, May 29, 1901; Capt. Albert Todd, May 16, 1901; Maj. Charles Lynch, May 18, 1901; Maj. F.A. Meacham, May 23, 1901; Maj. Ira C. Brown, May 16, 1901, all in RG 94/368853/a AGO, USNA. Also see Hughes, Report, Feb. 7, 1902, RG 94/343790, USNA, and Dr. Simon Flexner, Testimony, Aug. 17, 1900, in *Report of the Philippine Commission (Schurman), 1900*, 1:235. On gonorrhea, see Bennett, "Gonococcal Infections," 928. On the reinforcement system, see Cpl. C.W. Caville, CtM, RG 153/22636, box 3202, WNRC. On the runners, see report of Hughes, Feb. 7, 1902, RG 94/343790, USNA. For a view of the niches created by American money for saloon owners, musicians, flower and peanut girls, and assorted others, see "The Odd Side of Things—A Soldier's Resort in Manila," *Manila Times*, Nov. 11, 1899, 4.

44. About the European situation, see Pivar, *Purity Crusade*, 52–53. For the quote

about pious ignorance, see *Medical and Surgical History*, 1:894. For the quoted phrases from the moral reform standpoint, see Frances M. Robinson to Charles W. Fairbanks, Feb. 16, 1902, Charles W. Fairbanks Papers, LL. For the commanding general's semantic gymnastics, see Gen. Arthur MacArthur to adjutant general, Feb. 4, 1901, RG 94/ 343790, USNA.

45. "Crowning Infamy," Richard F. Pettgrew Papers, box: "R.F. Pettigrew Miscellaneous Papers Si-T," file: "Spanish-American War," SHM; Statement of Dr. Arthur L. Parker, Herbert Welsh Papers, HSP; Adrian Trench to Mr. Robbins, Oct. 30, 1901; memorandum from Col. Andrews, Feb. 18, 1902; Lt. Owen J. Sweet to adjutant general; and memorandum from Col. Andrews, Feb 24, 1902, all four from RG 94/343790, box 2307, USNA.

46. After initial reluctance or shyness on the part of the local women, some soldiers found that queridas were not difficult to get. See report of Lt. James A. Moss, Aug. 21, 1899, RG 395/777, USNA; J. Edward Beattie to Reading K. Beattie, May 7, 1900, Harry L. and Mary K. Dalton Collection, file: "Reading K. Beattie Papers, 1898–1906," WRPL; Maugat, Batangas, HDP, 12:118, PNL; Blunt, *American Officer's Studies*, 19; "Statement of Joseph A. Florence," Dean C. Worcester Philippine Collection, HHGL. For the economic basis of liasons and the quote about "priestly injunctions," see Richard Johnson, "My Life in the U.S. Army," 22–23, 30–31, SAWS, U.S. Inf. 48th Reg., USAMHI. For the statement about rising incidence of illicit relationships, see Blunt, *American Officer's Studies*, 19. On the church in the nineteenth century, see Schumacher, *Revolutionary Clergy*, and Anderson, *Studies*. On marriages, see Spencer A. Kuhn to Walter L. Mains, Apr. 1, 1901, SAWS, U.S. Inf., 17th Reg., USAMHI; E.S. Eby to Rev. I.L. Kephart, in *Religious Telescope*, Mar. 12, 1902, RG 94/425584, 339, USNA; Balinag, Bulacan, *MHP* 680, RG 94/547, USNA; William Jennings Bryan to Elihu Root, May 28, 1903, and Root to Bryan, June 5, 1903, RG 94/487381, box 3418, USNA; 25th U.S. Inf., RHR, RG 94, USNA; report of Maj. Charles E. Woodruff, June 20, 1902, RG 94/548, box 1, USNA. For the quote about leaving queridas, see Arthur Valentiner to Clark Valentiner, Sept. 12, 1900, CHS. Also see Immanuel H. Warrington Diary, vol. 2, Sept. 4, 1901, HSP. For estimates of prevalence, see Johnson, "My Life in the U.S. Army," 31, and MacClintock, "Around the Island," 439. For the quote about alliances, see John D. La Wall, "Memoirs," 104, SAWS, U.S. Vol. Inf., 27th Reg., USAMHI.

47. For an example of prostitutes in a garrison town, see William Harvey, CtM, RG 153/23788, box 3226, WNRC. On lack of cooperation, see Tuguegarao, Cagayan, Oct. 31 and Dec. 2, 1901, *MHP* 632, RG 94/547, USNA; Lt. M.A. De Laney to the municipal president, and other correspondence in "Prostitution and Venereal Disease in Dagupan," RG 112/26, 88939/B, USNA; Ch. Surg. Smart, "Annual Report for the Fiscal Year Ending June 30, 1903," RG 112/26, 24508/V, USNA; J.B. Girard, "Report of Health of Troops in Division and Sanitation of Posts for Calendar Year 1904," Apr. 11, 1905, RG 112/26, 41842/C, USNA. For the transient women, see Binalonan, Pangasinan, *MHP* 494, RG 94/547, USNA.

48. On the call for stringent measures, see Santa Cruz, Ilocos Sur, and other stations, Aug. 1, 1901, *MHP* 459, RG 94/547, USNA. For the observation about scattered quarters, see Baliuag, Bulacan, Mar. 31, 1902, *MHP* 680, RG 94/547, USNA. For the experience on the southern island, see Siasi, Sulu (Jolo) Group, *MHP* 664, RG 94/547, USNA.

49. Statement of Fred F. Newell, Dean C. Worcester Philippine Collection, Philippine Atrocities, Statements, etc., HHGL; Pvt. Phineas Foutz, 19th U.S. Inf., CtM, RG 153/23345, box 3217, WNRC.

50. Report of Maj. F.A. Meacham, May 22, 1901, RG 94/368853/a AGO, USNA. For the statement about the Hawaiian experience, see report of Maj. Charles Lynch, May 18, 1901, RG 94/368853/a, USNA. Charles R. Greenleaf, "Report of Medical Department of Period Ending May 31, 1901," May 31, 1901, RG 112/26, 57592/183/B, USNA. For admissions data, see "U.S. Army Venereal Disease Statistics," RG 112/26, 58512/H, USNA.

51. General Orders No. 101, Manila, May 21, 1901, in "General Orders and Circulars, Hqtrs. Division of the Philippines, 1901," vol. 60, RG 350, USNA. For the later study, see Maj. Gen. C.R. Reynolds, "Summary of the History of the Control of Venereal Disease in the United States Army," Dec. 7, 1937, USAL.

52. For the reported rates, see 24th U.S. Inf., Santa Rosa, June 1901, RHR, RG 94, USNA, and Bugason, Antique, June 17, 1901, RG 94/547, USNA. For initial improvement, see 24th U.S. Inf., Penaranda, Nueva Ecija, Nov. 1901, RHR, RG 94, USNA, and 25th U.S. Inf., Dasol, Zambales, Nov. 1901, RHR, RG 94, USNA. For the theory about the decline of "military necessity," see Elihu Root to Margaret Dye Ellis, Apr. 3, 1902, RG 94/430201, USNA.

53. About the Civil War experience, see *Medical and Surgical History*, 1:894. For claims of success (often nullified by developments months later), see Tagbilaran, Bohol, Feb. 1, 1902, *MHP* 496, RG 94/547, USNA; 4th Sep. Brigade, Jan. 1902, *MHP* 522, RG 94/547, USNA; Baliuag, Bulacan, Mar. 31, 1902, *MHP* 680, RG 94/547, USNA; Surigao, Mindanao, June 30 and Sept. 20, 1902, *MHP* 516, RG 94/547, USNA; 24th U.S. Inf., Penaranda, Nueva Ecija, Feb. 1902, RHR, RG 94, USNA. For the quote about the men not recognizing their contacts, see Tuguegarao, Cagayan, Oct. 31 and Dec. 2, 1901, *MHP* 632, RG 94/547, USNA. Regarding the system at Tayug, see 24th U.S. Inf., Tayug, Pangasinan, Jan.–Feb. 1902, RHR, RG 94, USNA. Recent experience has shown how difficult it is to control, let alone eradicate, venereal disease. Gonorrhea is particularly persistent. The reporting of infected women has been shown to be ineffective. Programs using modern "speed zone" epidemiology in which 85 percent of contacts have been located and treated within seventy-two hours have failed to control infection. Epidemiologists have almost none of their usual weapons: quarantine is politically and practically impossible, no vaccine exists, and no animal reservoirs or vectors await eradication. Specific treatment is the only recourse, but since infection confers no acquired resistance, the patient is returned to the population as a susceptible, and transmission of the disease continues. See Bennett, "Gonococcal Infections," 928.

54. For the quoted phrases about "temporary treatment" and "lack of funds," see 24th U.S. Inf., Tayug, Pangasinan, Jan.–Feb. 1902, RHR, RG 94, USNA. On "noncooperation," see Tuguegarao, Cagayan, Oct. 31 and Dec. 2, 1901, *MHP* 632, RG 94/547, USNA. For a more detailed treatment of Filipino "resistance-through-inaction" in other respects during the war, see Ileto, "Cholera," 141. For an account of everyday humiliations and indignities, see Ileto, "Towards a Local History," 11. For the complexities of power in the towns and the possibilities for corruption, see Bankoff, "Big Fish," 679–700.

CHAPTER 4

1. For Dr. Llanera's experience, see Abra, 1884, 1886, 1887, 1889, 1890, 1891, 1894, *Mm*, PNA. Also see Gobierno P.M. de Abra to Director Gral. de Administración Civil, Oct. 19, 1887, *Cp*, PNA, and Tayum, Abra, HDP, 1:604, PNL.

2. For the summary of indigenous beliefs and practices in the following paragraphs, I have relied principally on Jocano, *Folk Medicine*, passim; Pal, *Resources* 189–94; Pal,

"Philippine Barrio," 431–32; Lieban, "Qualification," 511; Bantug, *Medicine*, 1–35; Scott's forthcoming study of sixteenth-century Visayan society and culture (122–29 in the typescript he provided me); and my reading of the *Mm* and *M*. Folk beliefs are persistent, and thus modern studies like those of Jocano, Pal, and Lieban are valuable. For an example of the use of modern ethnographic sources as evidence of earlier beliefs and an argument for that methodology, see Martin, *Keepers*, 7 and passim. On attitudes toward insane persons and victims of leprosy, see Iloilo (CZ), 1894, *Mm*, 15, PNA, and Ilocos Norte, 1876, *Mm*, 50, PNA, respectively. On the subject of leprosy in the Philippines, which is unfortunately outside the scope of this study, see Rogel, *Lepra*, and Burgess, *Who Walk Alone*. On venereal disease and measles, respectively, see Ilocos Norte, 1876, *Mm*, 26–27, PNA, and "Medical Officers, Henry Lippincott," RG 112/26, 3866/V/3, USNA.

3. For the quoted statement, see Jocano, *Folk Medicine*, 40–41. For an example of contemporary perceptions of disease periodicity, see Iloilo (CZ), 1895, *Mm*, 3, PNA.

4. For contemporary evidence of the people's trust in the local healers, see Ilocos Norte, 1876, *Mm*, 30, PNA; Capiz, 1882, *Mm*, 29b–31, 54; Cebu, 1886, *Mm*, 1, PNA; Antique, 1887, *Mm*, 3, PNA; Camarines Sur, 1887, *Mm*, 8–9, PNA; Ilocos Norte, 1888, *M*, 81b, PNA; Pangasinan, 1891, *M*, 53b, PNA; Capiz, 1892, *M*, 62, PNA; Zambales, 1892, *M*, 120, PNA, quoting from Zambales, 1892, *Mm*. For modern evidence, see Pal, "Philippine Barrio," 431–32, and Lieban, "Qualification," 511–21. For the various kinds of healers, see Jocano, *Folk Medicine*, 126–54.

5. On the role of the priests, see Pangasinan, 1892, *M*, 120b, PNA, and Amigos del país, *La situación*, 20–21. For the quote on healers and religion, see Jocano, *Folk Medicine*, 128. For the quote about the devil, see Bantug, *Medicine*, 35. For the cited examples, see Pangasinan, 1892, *M*, 120b, PNA, and Albay, HDP, 2:26–27, PNL.

6. For Dr. Martín's comment and also an example of the ambivalent attitude of the physicians, see Ilocos Norte, 1876, *Mm*, 6–7, 22, PNA. Regarding limited contact between médicos titulares and the people, see Cebu, 1884, *Mm*, 11, PNA, and Martínez Cuesta, *History*, 267–68. On the Santo Tomas graduates, see Bantug, *Medicine*, 17, and Ileto, "Outlines," 136–44. Sometimes the best way to accomplish smallpox vaccination was to give the vaccine to the padre (Iloilo, 1893, *Mm*, 19–20, PNA). Regarding the popularity of Filipino médicos today who use both traditional and modern methods, see Jocano, *Folk Medicine*, 149–50. On various remedies that were used, see Bantug, *Medicine*, 26–27, 36–37; Capiz, 1882, *Mm*, 29b—31, 54, PNA; Buga, Albay, HDP, 3:413, PNL; del Rosario and Rizal, "Some Epidemiological Features," 1–5. Oil of manungal is coconut oil containing macerated pieces of the wood (or scrapings of it) and is a common traditional remedy of great usefulness. It is taken as a purgative and is also applied externally to the abdomen for stomach pain and indigestion. It cannot prevent death from cholera, however.

7. For the origins of smallpox in Asia and endemicity in the Philippines, see Fenner, et al., *Smallpox Eradication*, 210–16, 228. On preconquest contact with smallpox, see Phelan, *Hispanization*, 107. For the threshold population figure, see Fenner, "Smallpox in Southeast Asia," 34.

8. Martín de Rada, "Letter to the Viceroy of Nueva España, Martín Enriquez," (Manila, June 30, 1574), in BR, 34:292. Fenner and his colleagues say that a late-sixteenth-century outbreak in Manila was set off by a virus imported from Mexico. Perhaps that was the one de Rada lived through. On endemic patterns of smallpox and the importation from Mexico, see Fenner et al., *Smallpox Eradication*, 195–96, 228. It is possible that the 1574 contagion was worsened by the consternation in Manila that year when "a

large Chinese fleet under the filibuster Li Ma Hong, or Limahon, with over four thousand men on board, attacked the newly-founded town on Manila Bay" (Schurz, *Manila Galleon*, 26).

9. For Nueva Segovia, see Diego Aduarte, *Historia de la Provincia del Sancto Rosario de la Orden de Predicadores* (Manila, 1640), in BR, 30:309, 31:156, 32:93–94. For Bohol, see Manuel Antonio de Rojo y Vieyra, *Rojo's Narrative* (Manila, 1763), in BR, 49:179. For Sulu, see Wilkes, *Narrative*, 1844 ed., 5:349–50, 357. For Leyte-Samar, see Juan Antonio Tornos, *Retrato geográfico-histórico-apologético de las Islas Filipinas*, 1789, translated and cited in Martínez Cuesta, *History*, 109. For the Chinese importation, see letters from the Archbishop of Manila to the King, Jan. 12, 1790, the governor of Manila to Antonio Valdes, Jan. 18, 1790, and Gov.-Gen. Fernandez de Folgueras to the Secretary of State, Grace and Justice, Apr. 25, 1809, which are cited and translated in Martínez Cuesta, *History*, 109–10.

10. On wave patterns, see Fenner et al., *Smallpox Eradication*, 178–79. For the quoted statement, see Pedro de San Francisco de Assis, *Recollect Missions in the Philippines, 1661–1712* (Zaragoza, 1756), in BR, 41:156.

11. Marc H. Dawson has explained the changing patterns of smallpox infection in nineteenth-century Kenya as a response to the changing environment and especially famine, which "altered usual social and economic patterns, thus presenting the opportunity for endemic smallpox to become epidemic." Specifically, he points out that "increased trade, large and more frequent population movements, and greater population densities could have little other effect on the disease." He concludes that "in much of colonial Kenya, smallpox appears to have become a more frequent but less fatal disease, due to the rising level of immunity in the population" (Dawson, "Smallpox," 245–50).

12. For the types of smallpox and case-fatality rates, see Fenner et al., *Smallpox Eradication*, 4–40.

13. On the immunology of smallpox, see ibid., 32, 38, 146–66.

14. For the clinical features of smallpox, see ibid., 5–40; Manson-Bahr and Apted, *Manson's Tropical Diseases*, 276–77; Christie, *Infectious Diseases*, 205, 217–18, 221, 232, 234–35. For a contemporary description of symptoms, see Ilocos Norte, 1886, *Mm*, 2–9, PNA.

15. For Dr. Ares's statement, see Cebu, 1884, *Mm*, 7–9, PNA. On direct transmission, see Fenner et al., *Smallpox Eradication*, 191; Manson-Bahr and Apted, *Manson's Tropical Diseases*, 275, 278; Christie, *Infectious Diseases*, 213, 248–49. The observations about the culture are in Ileto, "Cholera," 135, 139. For Western observations, see Iloilo, 1891, *Mm*, 12, PNA; Strong et al., Medical Survey, 254; Charles W. Hack, "Report of Special Sanitary Inspection of the Islands of Cebu, Bohol, Samar, and Leyte," May 15, 1903, in *ARSW, 1903*, 231. About the nine days of mourning (*novenarios*), see Iloilo (CZ), 1894, *Mm*, 12, PNA. For effective control measures, see Manson-Bahr and Apted, *Manson's Tropical Diseases*, 275, 278.

16. I use the term "resistance" throughout the book instead of the more common but imprecise word "immunity." The distinction is less important, however, with a disease like smallpox, in which survivors of attacks acquire lifelong protection amounting to immunity. On immunity (resistance) and immunologic responses, see Duncan, *Epidemiology*, 33, and Barrett, *Textbook of Immunology*, 287–89. For the distinction between control and eradication, see Andrews and Langmuir, "Philosophy," 1.

17. For the lifelong protection, see Manson-Bahr and Apted, *Manson's Tropical Diseases*, 276.

18. On herd immunity, see Susser, *Causal Thinking*, 61–62, and Lilienfeld and Lilienfeld, *Foundations*, 61–62.

19. On Jenner, see Hopkins, *Princes*, 77–81. About the Balmis expedition, see Smith, *Real Expedición*, passim. For vaccinations in the Visayas in 1808, see letter from Gov.-Gen. Mariano F. de Folgueras to the president of the Supreme Junta of Spain, Apr. 25, 1809, and for Dr. Casas's statement, see *Informe sobre el estado de la vacuna*, 1823, both of which are cited and translated in Martínez Cuesta, *History*, 160–61. The quote comparing the Balmis mission to an epic poem is in Bantug, *Medicine*, 38. The 1838 quotation is in D.J.M.B., *Principios*, 3–4. For Dr. Martín's opinion, see Ilocos Norte, 1876, *Mm*, 44–45, PNA. The final quote is from Gonzalez, *Anuario*, 142, 145.

20. Records and reports referring to smallpox and the vaccination program, mostly after 1870, are filed under "*Sanidad*," "*Calamidades públicas (Viruelas)*," "*Memorias médicas*," "*Memorias*," and other titles in the PNA. The quote is from Gonzalez, *Anuario*, 143. For the colonial administration's administrative structure, see Robles, *Philippines*, 60–166.

21. For the quotes regarding Negros, see Martínez Cuesta, *History*, 266–67. For Dr. Martín's statement, see Antique, 1886, *Mm*, 9, PNA. For the journalist's comment, see Feced, "Beneficencia," 90. For the physician's remarks, see Un médico aplatanado, "Ligeras Consideraciones," 259. Another observer said in 1896 that "smallpox is so obstinate and general in the Philippines that it can be properly said to be *endemic* in these islands." See Gonzales y Martín, *Filipinas*, 132.

22. For the Binondo epidemic, see M.R. Cura Parroco de Binondo to Gobernador Superior Civil de Manila, Feb. 17, 1872, Rafaela Mesa, *P*, PNA. For Cotabato, see Cotabato Distrito P.M. de Mindanao to Luis Fernandez, Dec. 23, 1871–Feb. 27, 1872, *Cp*, PNA. For Lepanto, see Basilio Avelino to Director Gral. de Administración Civil (Manila), Apr. 6, 1875, *Cp*, PNA. Owen alerted me to the epidemic in Camarines Sur (personal communication, June 16, 1990). The Davao outbreak is reported in Davao, 1890, *M*, 85, PNA. Dr. Gomez's statement is in Iloilo, 1892, *Mm*, 14, PNA. For Bulacan, see Fegan, "Central Luzon Barrio," 100, and *CPI, 1903*, 3:15. For Pampanga, see Gobierno Civil de la Provincia de la Pampanga to Director Gral. de Administración (Manila), March 28, 1894, *Cp*, PNA. For Zamboanga, see Médico titular, Zamboanga to Inspector de Beneficencia y Sanidad, May 15, 1895–Aug. 16, 1895, *Cp*, PNA. Regarding the remaining epidemics, see Leyte, 1881, *Mm*, 15–17, PNA; Pangasinan, 1883, *Mm*, 9–9b, PNA; Nueva Viscaya, 1884, *Mm*, 21, PNA; Cagayan de Misamis, 1886, *Mm*, 1, PNA; Antique, 1886, *Mm*, 7, PNA; Antique, 1887, *Mm* 2, PNA; Abra, 1887, *Mm*, 1–8, PNA; Abra 1894, *Mm* 2–3, PNA. For U.S. Army figures, see report of Charles R. Greenleaf, July 13, 1900 in Sternberg, "Annual Report for 1900," in *ARSW, 1900*, 635; Maj. L.M. Maus, "Report of Department of Northern Luzon Made to the Chief Surgeon, Division of the Philippines," June 15, 1900, ibid., 636; Aparri, Cagayan, April 30, 1900, *MHP* 669, RG 94/547, USNA; Pandan, Antique, Feb. 1901, *MHP* 405, RG 94/547, USNA.

23. The quote is from Corpuz, *Bureaucracy*, 146. For progress elsewhere, see Hopkins, *Princes*, 81–96, 267–90, and Boomgaard, *Children*, 190. Martínez Cuesta holds official "inertia and negligence" accountable for the lack of health care. In another place he says that government projects were customarily "plagued by defects of implementation." See Martínez Cuesta, *History*, 266–67 and 181, respectively.

24. For folk ideas about smallpox, see Iloilo (CZ), 1895, *Mm*, 3, PNA. Monthly breakdowns of disease in the *Mm* show the highest incidence of smallpox in the cool, dry months reflecting both the superior viability of the virus in lower temperatures and humidity as well as social factors such as ease of travel and increased interpersonal

contact in that season. (The next highest incidence was in the hot, dry months, indicating that mobility was a more important factor than temperature.) A German physician resident in Manila remarked in the early 1880s that "the healthiest time is the cool dry, the so-called winter, with the exception that then usually the smallpox rage" (Koeniger, "Ueber epidemisches," 421). For a more complete discussion of seasonality, see Fenner et al., *Smallpox Eradication*, 179–82. For appeals to the spirits, see Albay, HDP, 2:26–27, PNL. On vaccination and predisposition to skin disease, see *CPI, 1918*, 2:985. On vaccination and transmission of smallpox, see Nueva Viscaya, 1884, *Mm*, 6, PNA. The quoted phrase is from Masbate y Ticao, 1886, *Mm*, 6, PNA. For Dr. Amide's experience, see Pangasinan, 1883, *Mm*, 16, PNA.

25. On the board's difficulties with the civil administration, see the correspondence of Médico titular, Zamboanga to Inspector Gral. de Beneficencia y Sanidad, May 15–Aug. 16, 1895, *Cp*, PNA. On financial constraints, see Davao, 1890, *M*, 85, PNA, and Corpuz, *Bureaucracy*, 137–42. For underpaid vaccinators, see Abra, 1887, *Mm*, 7, PNA, and Cavite, 1886, *Mm*, 4–5, PNA. The conclusion about padded totals arises from analysis of the figures, which sometimes exceed the number of children in the particular province. Other inferences are possible, but given the universal complaints about mothers hiding children, the difficulty of reaching people outside the urban centers, and the testimony that vaccinators commonly abandoned their jobs, the reported numbers of vaccinations sometimes is suspicious. Moreover, under the American administration, it was well established that vaccinators often filed false reports. It seems reasonable to assume that they did so in earlier years as well. See Heiser, *American Doctor's Odyssey*, 188–89. For Dr. Janay's comments, see Nueva Viscaya, 1884, *Mm*, 16, PNA. For the decree against abuses, see "Decreto del Gobr. Gral contra algunos abusos cometidos en la administración de la vacuna," Mar. 7, 1894, in *Gaceta de Manila*, Apr. 29, 1894.

26. For vaccination procedure, see Bantug, *Medicine*, 66. On avoidance, see Leyte, 1877, *Mm*, 15, PNA; Masbate y Ticao, 1884, *Mm*, 6–7, PNA; Zambales (SD), 1895, *Mm*, 8, PNA. For neglect of revaccinations, see Laguna, 1886, *Mm*, 10–11, PNA, and Pangasinan, 1888, *Mm*, 52, PNA. The *Mm* for Ilocos Norte (1876, 1879, 1886, 1891) give statistics for six years showing revaccinations of 24,798 females and 20,726 males (54.5 percent–45.5 percent). For the estimate of number of children vaccinated, see Martínez Cuesta, *History*, 161.

27. On the legislation, see Bantug, *Medicine*, 39. For the provision about fines, see Articles 56 and 59 of the 1893 regulations as reprinted in Un médico aplatanado, "Ligeras consideraciones," 260. Abra, 1887, *Mm*, 6, PNA, contains a typical proposal for mandatory vaccination and punishment for avoidance. For the Batangas governor's view, see Sastrón, *Batangas*, 71, and Sastrón, *La insurrección*, 27. For Dr. Peres's statement, see Cavite, 1887, *Mm*, 5–6, PNA. As to the military presence, only 1,500 Spanish soldiers were in the Philippines as late as 1896, when the revolution against Spain began. There were an additional 14,000 Filipino soldiers commanded by Spaniards and 4,000 Filipino civil guards, it is true, but that force did not begin to match the coercive potential of the U.S. Army during the war. In addition, the Spanish civil administration never considered army and police enforcement of smallpox immunization since it did not see the disease as a threat to its vital interests as the U.S. Army later would. See Robles, *Philippines*, 181.

28. For vaccination, its successes and failures worldwide in the nineteenth century and arm-to-arm propagation, see Fenner et al., *Smallpox Eradication*, 261–73. For the latter, also see Cavite, 1886, *Mm*, 4–5, PNA, and Ilocos Norte, 1890, *Mm*, 10, PNA. For transfer of infection, see Antique, 1888, *Mm*, 6, PNA.

29. On the various methods in the Philippines, see Bantug, *Medicine*, 66. On those methods in general and the various problems involved, see Fenner et al., *Smallpox Eradication*, 283–86, and Hopkins, *Princes*, 84, 95. On reconstitution, see Abra, 1890, *Mm*, 6–7, PNA. On refrigeration, see "Annual Report of the Quartermaster-General, 1900," in *ARSW, 1900*, 286, and "Annual Report of the Acting Commissary-General of Subsistence, 1900," ibid., 470. For viability without refrigeration in the Philippines, see Heiser, *American Doctor's Odyssey*, 182. The scope of the treatment herein makes vaccination seem a good deal less complex than it was. For the difficulty nineteenth-century doctors had in interpreting the results of vaccination and revaccination, see Fenner et al., *Smallpox Eradication*, 277–314.

30. Basilio Avelino to Director Gral. de Administración Civil (Manila), Apr. 6, 1875, *Cp*, PNA; Médico titular, Romblon to Inspector Gral. de Sanidad y Beneficencia, July 29, 1891, *Cp*, PNA; Davao, 1890, *M*, 85, PNA; Nueva Viscaya, 1884, *Mm*, 16, PNA; Antique, 1886, *Mm*, 8–12, PNA; Antique, and 1888, *Mm*, 6–7, PNA; Capiz, 1888, *Mm*, 42–44, PNA; Iloilo, 1891, *Mm*, 24, PNA; Iloilo, 1893, *Mm*, 9, PNA; Camarines Sur, 1888, *Mm*, 17, PNA; Cavite, 1886, *Mm*, 4–5, PNA; Pangasinan, 1883, *Mm*, 9b, PNA; Pangasinan, 1888, *Mm*, 32–35, PNA. For the episode in Cotabato, see Cotabato Distrito P.M. de Mindanao to Luis Fernandez Golfín, Dec. 23, 1871–Feb. 27, 1872, *Cp*, PNA. For the official admission, see Gov.-Gen. Rafael de Izquierdo to Ministry of Overseas Territories, May 3, 1872, translated and cited in Martínez Cuesta, *History*, 281–82.

31. See the references to Antique, Iloilo, and Pangasinan in the preceding endnote.

32. See Masbate y Ticao, 1884, 1886, 1888, 1889, 1890, 1891, 1892, 1894, *Mm*, PNA.

33. Médico titular, Zamboanga, to Inspector Gral. de Beneficencia y Sanidad, May 15–Aug. 16, 1895, *Cp*, PNA. On discontinuance, see Maus, "Report," in *ARSW, 1900*, 633–34.

34. Owen's research in the parish burial records of three Kabikolan towns suggests that eighteenth-century epidemics may have been worse than any that occurred in the nineteenth century (Owen, "Paradox," 38). I generally agree, but we should be careful about equating explosiveness with long-term mortality totals. As already discussed, occasional importations of the virus into nonendemic areas will set off more dramatic outbreaks all along the age spectrum than those that occur where it arrives more frequently or is constantly present. As the Bikol and other regions established more regular interisland contacts, the pattern of smallpox mortality changed. Whether the evolving pattern, which was more regular but less explosive, actually resulted in lower smallpox mortality has yet to be established. Fenner's observation applied to Southeast Asia generally, but the Philippines is one of the areas that he specifically discussed. See Fenner, "Smallpox in Southeast Asia," 195. For the conclusion that vaccination was the cause of dramatically reduced smallpox mortality during the nineteenth century on Java, see Boomgaard, *Children*, 190. On cause-of-death inaccuracies, see Cavite, 1886, *Mm*, 6, PNA; Cebu, 1886, *Mm*, 7, PNA; Albay, 1887, *Mm*, 11, PNA; Antique, 1887, *Mm*, 3, PNA; Zambales (SD), 1895, *Mm*, 5, PNA. For the opinions of Dr. Llanera and Dr. Ares, see Abra, 1887, *Mm*, 6, PNA, and Cebu, 1884, *Mm*, 7–10, PNA.

35. For the studies in Asia and also for the problem of assessing case-fatality rates among various populations, see Fenner et al., *Smallpox Eradication*, 50–54, 101. For yearly population, birth, and death totals, see *CPI, 1903*, 2:18, and 3:12–17. I have calculated average annual death rates by decade from the regional data in Smith, "Crisis Mortality," 66.

36. Ilocos Norte, 1876, *Mm*, 45–46, PNA; Ilocos Norte, 1879, *Mm*, 10–11, PNA; Ilocos Norte, 1888, *M*, 82, PNA; Cavite, 1887, *Mm*, appendix, PNA; Nueva Viscaya, 1884,

Mm, 11, PNA; Antique, 1886, *Mm*, 8, PNA; Masbate y Ticao, 1891, *Mm*, appendix, PNA; Iloilo (CZ), 1895, *Mm*, 6, PNA; Abra, 1894, *Mm*, 2, PNA; Cagayan de Misamis, 1886, *Mm*, appendix, PNA.

37. I am indebted to Owen for the parish statistics, which he compiled and sent me on his own motion (personal communication, June 16, 1990). For Dr. Delgado's comments, see Camarines Sur, 1888, *Mm*, 8–9, 12, PNA.

38. Montero, *Historia*, in BR, 51:25; Fenner et al., *Smallpox Eradication*, 263–71.

39. See Ilocos Norte for the following years: 1876, *Mm*, 41–46, PNA; 1879, *Mm*, 12, PNA; 1886, *Mm*, 1–11 (which contains the one minor outbreak), PNA; 1888, *M*, 81–82, PNA; 1888–1889, *Mm*, 1, PNA; 1890, *Mm*, 2, 5–6, PNA; 1891, *Mm*, 4, PNA.

40. Hospitals Afloat, RHR 3462, RG 94, USNA; Maj.-Gen. W.R. Shafter to adjutant general, Sept. 19 and Nov. 18, 1899, RG 112/26, 57783/A, USNA; report of Charles F. Keiffer, Sept. 1899, RG 112/26, 57783/B, USNA; report of William Grey Miller, Sept. 18, 1899, RG 112/26, 57783/G, USNA.

41. About the Intensified Programme, see Fenner et al., *Smallpox Eradication*, 185–203. For susceptibility to imported strains, see Manson-Bahr and Apted, *Manson's Tropical Diseases*, 276. On the 1891 importation, see Iloilo, 1891, *Mm*, 1–2, PNA.

42. Brig. Gen. George W. Sternberg, "Report of the Surgeon-General," Oct. 12, 1899, in *ARSW, 1899*, 601; Hopkins, *Princes*, 287–88; John P. Kelly, "Report and History of Epidemic Diseases on Board the USA Transport *Kilpatrick*," May 13, 1901, Ms. #4948, RG 112/52, 65241, USNA; Stephen Wythe, "Report of Smallpox Case," April 8, 1902, Ms. #5019, RG 112/52, USNA. On presence of variola minor after U.S. occupation, see McVail, "Smallpox," 158. On variola minor case-fatality rate, see Fenner et al., *Smallpox Eradication*, 4.

43. Joseph A. Curry, "Report on Diseases," June 20, 1901, RG 112/26, 68075/G, USNA; report of Lt. Col. Henry Lippincott, Oct. 2, 1898, RG 112/26, 39109/79; Maj. Frank S. Bourns, "Report on Board of Health," June 30, 1899, in *ARSW, 1899*, 260. The vaccine sent out from San Francisco was said to have been inert from the long sea voyage. See Sternberg, "Annual Report for 1900," in *ARSW, 1900*, 717. For the quote about the medical corps' concern and the figure of 80,000 vaccinated persons, see Sexton, *Soldiers*, 56–57.

44. Gen. Harrison G. Otis to adjutant general, 2d Div., Jan. 5, 1899, RG 395/851, box 2, USNA; Gen. MacArthur to provost marshall, Jan. 6, 1899, ibid.; Otis to adjutant general, 2d Div., Jan. 15, 1899, ibid.; Maj. John A. Rafter, "Weekly Inspection Report," Jan. 24, 1899, ibid.; Otis to adjutant general, 2d Div., Feb. 3, 1899, ibid.; Lt.-Col. Henry Lippincott, "Report of the Medical Department, Oct. 23–Dec. 31, 1898," RG 112/26, 39109/99, USNA; Brig. Gen. Frank Royce Keefer, "Autobiographical Sketches," box 2, MS/C/44, NLM; Bourns, "Report of Board of Health," in *ARSW, 1899*, 260; Col. Charles R. Greenleaf, "Report on Medical Department for the Period Ending May 31, 1901," RG 112/26, 57592/183/B, USNA; Joseph A. Curry, "Report on Diseases," RG 112/26, 68075/G, USNA.

45. For the western Visayas, see report of C.W. Chiene, vice consul, U.S. consulate, Iloilo, Jan. 28, 1899, RG 395/2470, box 2, USNA; La Carlotta and Valladolid, Negros, *MHP* 508, RG 94, USNA; Maj. H.W. Cardwell to assistant adjutant general, Nov. 1, 1899, RG 395/2470, box 2, USNA; report of Capt. Marion C. Rayson, Feb. 22, 1900, RG 395/2470, box 2, USNA; 26th U.S. Vol. Inf., RHR 3468, RG 94, USNA; Banate, *MHP* 508, Jan. 6, 1900, RG 94/547, USNA. For northern Luzon, see Maj. C.M. Drake, "Report on Existence of Smallpox Epidemic at Pandan, Ilocos Sur," Jan. 27, 1900, and other reports therein, RG 395/2157, USNA.; Lt. J.M. Flemister, "Report of Lapog and Magsin-

gal for July 1900," Aug. 1, 1900, and other reports therein, RG 395/2170, USNA; "1st Dist., N. Luz., Inspection Reports, May 1900–Nov. 1900," Namacpagan, Union, Sept. 1900, RG 395/2180, USNA; 24th U.S. Inf., RHR, RG 94, USNA; report of Maj. L.M. Maus, in *ARSW, 1900*, 635.

46. Report of Maj. L.M. Maus, in *ARSW, 1900*, 635. Maus later recalled that more than 800,000 persons were finally vaccinated during the campaign and that as a result, smallpox was "practically eradicated" in the region. See Col. L.M. Maus, "Autobiographical Sketches," 4, MS/C/44, box 2, NLM, and Maj. L.W. Crampton, "Report on Operations of Medical Department in the Department of the Visayas, Jan.–May 1900," RG 112/26, 2310/311/V, USNA. Actually, many more years of vaccination, control, and surveillance were necessary before endemic smallpox was practically eradicated around 1930. See De Bevoise, "Until God Knows When," 181–85.

47. Dickman to Manning, May 16, 1900, J.T. Dickman Papers, RBHL; Pandan, Antique, *MHP* 405, Feb. 1901, RG 94/547, USNA; Ligao, Albay, *MHP* 463, RG 94, USNA. For mortality statistics by disease, see *CPI, 1903*, 3:141, 163, 495, 500. I have adapted Geertz's seminal idea that "radical discontinuities" between culture and social structure are some of the driving forces in change. See Geertz, "Ritual," 144.

48. San Pablo, Laguna, Jan. 16, 1902, *MHP* 528, RG 94/547, USNA; Maj. William Stephenson, "Annual Report," RG 395/2345, box 5, USNA. For Bell's campaign, see May, *Battle*, 242–69.

49. For death statistics, see *CPI, 1903*, 3:276, and *CPI, 1918*, 2:1042. For the quoted estimate of yearly deaths, see Heiser and Lynch, "Vaccination," 40. In another place, he stated: "Forty thousand unvaccinated were uselessly slaughtered each year by smallpox." See Heiser, *American Doctor's Odyssey*, 38. Historians of smallpox routinely use Heiser's statistics and sometimes leave the erroneous impression that 40,000 Filipinos died annually of smallpox throughout the nineteenth century. That could not possibly have been the case, as has been shown. Heiser's numbers are often suspect. Of the archipelago's last major smallpox epidemic, between 1918 and 1920, he stated that 50,000 died of smallpox in 1918 and that "almost 100,000" eventually died. The official figures, however, were about 17,000 and 75,000, respectively. It could well be that the official numbers were inaccurate, but Heiser's bias in favor of everything American should be recognized. Thus, if the Spanish program looked ineffective and the Filipino officials who administered vaccination just prior to 1918 appeared incompetent, American achievements were enhanced by contrast.

CHAPTER 5

1. Koeniger, "Ueber epidemisches," 419–21. I am indebted to Petra Goedde for her translation of this article. On the process that created the scarcity in light building materials, which had already quintupled in price by the late 1860s, see chapter 6 of this book.

2. For Dr. Gomez's observations, see Iloilo, 1892, *Mm*, 12, PNA. For the German doctor's speculations about causation, see Koeniger, "Ueber epidemisches," 428–30.

3. Koeniger, "Ueber epidemisches," 419, 428–30. For the developments in Japan and for the theoretical dispute, see Inouye and Katsura, "Etiology," 6–15.

4. 25th U.S. Inf., RHR, Oct. 1901, USNA; Strong et al., "Medical Survey," 293.

5. For the 1960s statistic, see Caasi et al., "Studies," 24.

6. For a recent summary of the longstanding debate as to whether Southeast Asian history has been driven by internal or external influences, see Legge, "Writing," 1–50.

For a more promising conceptual model to understand how cultures and societies continually "reinvent" themselves, see Clifford, *Predicament*, 1–17, 277–346. On the importance of the Industrial Revolution on trade relations between the colonial powers and Southeast Asian peoples, see Tate, *Modern Southeast Asia*, 2:1–24. For the remark about the new trading system, see Coclanis, "Distant Thunder," 1055. See also Coclanis, "Southeast Asia's Incorporation," 251–67. For the quote about government interference and also an overview of the rice trade before 1860, see Owen, "Rice Industry," 83–86. For more detailed information on each of the three exporting regions, see Cheng, *Rice Industry*; Adas, *Burma Delta*; Ingram, "Thailand's Rice Trade"; Ingram, *Economic Change*; Coquerel, *Paddys*; Robequain, *Economic Development*. The quoted phrase about the port of Saigon is from the field marshal who led the Spanish forces (including Filipino troops) in the invasion and seems to have considered the port opening the principal mission of the campaign (Palanca, *Reseña Histórica*, 43).

7. For supply factors at Rangoon, Bangkok, and Saigon/Cholon, see Owen, "Rice Industry," 78–82, 112–20. For the complexity of interregional and intraregional commercial contacts, see Huff, "Bookkeeping Barter," 161–89; Baker, "Economic Reorganization," 325–49; Bray, *Rice Economies*, 128–29.

8. Owen, "Rice Industry," 93–103; Huff, "Bookkeeping Barter," 93–103.

9. For the development of agricultural infrastructure in Pangasinan, see Gonzalez, *Labor Evangélica*, 18–22. Doeppers called my attention to a report documenting the introduction of the bamboo *noria* waterwheel into the municipality of Manaoag sometime after the mid-nineteenth century. The article contains a photo of the water-hoist. See *Quarterly Bulletin of the Bureau of Public Works* 3 (April 1914), 41. Doeppers says that "the impact of the *noria* on rice culture would have been to get an early and secure start on the seed beds" (personal communication, Feb. 21, 1994). For the move toward free trade in rice, see Keyser, *Medios*, 48–50.

10. For the quote and a discussion of the success of free trade legislation, see Sancianco, *El progreso*, 233. On Pangasinan, see Mendoza Cortes, *Pangasinan*, 53–55; Craig and Benitez, *Philippine Progress*, 71; Regino Garcia, "Cultivation of Rice," in *CPI, 1903*, 4:92.

11. For legislation permitting imports, see Keyser, *Medios*, 50. Calculation of the export-import ratio has been made from statistics in Kilbourne, "Food Salts," 127. For the statistics on paddy acreage, see Fast and Richardson, *Roots*, 40. Their page citation to vol. 4 of the 1903 Census is erroneous, however.

12. Pangasinan, 1891, *Mm*, 13–21, PNA; Owen, "Abaca," 200; Directores de Estación Agronómica, "Memoria agrícola del distrito de Albay y Camarines," 1890, A, 39, PNA.

13. Sawyer, *Inhabitants*, 130.

14. Import-export ratios for the entire period as well as Philippine purchases for 1899–1903 by source have been calculated from data in Kilbourne, "Food Salts," 127. Coclanis also says that the rice trade was not "heavily sinicized" in Southeast Asia west of the Malacca Straits (Coclanis, "Southeast Asia's Incorporation," 264). That judgment is erroneous if he intends it to include Saigon/Cholon and Manila. Owen supposes, in fact, that one determining factor of the Philippine pattern of rice purchases was the special tie that existed between the Hokkien Chinese importers in Manila and exporters in Saigon/Cholon (personal communication, May 17, 1992). For statistics on Philippine purchases at Rangoon, Bangkok, and Saigon, see Owen, "Rice Industry," 97–101. On extraordinary imports and crisis years see Miller, *Economic Conditions*, 33–38. On shortages of food during the revolution, see Ileto, "Food Crisis," 101–117. For the statement about crop replacement occasioning no loss to the people, see *CPI, 1903*, 4:87.

15. For the quoted statements, see Miller, *Economic Conditions*, 36–37 and *CPI, 1903*, 4:87, respectively.

16. On subsistence during severe crises, see Goa, Camarines Sur, HDP, 26:4, PNL, and Ileto, "Food Crisis," 101–17. Doeppers points out that "crisis years" have resulted from a number of circumstances, including economic depression, but that significant mortality increases seem to be tied to an interruption of the food supply (personal communication, Feb. 21, 1994). On the point, see Owens, "Subsistence," and Doeppers, "Metropolitan Manila," 530–33.

17. Owen, "Subsistence Crisis," 35–46.

18. William H. Taft, "Report of the Civil Governor for the Period Ending December 23, 1903," in *ARSW, 1903*, 23–24; Stewart, "Report," 39.

19. After processing, the grain is classified as either partially milled, milled (clean), or highly milled (white) rice. The amount of retained thiamine varies accordingly. For the milling process, see Cheng, *Rice Industry*, 9–10, 77–111; Grist, *Rice*, 420–48; Manson-Bahr and Apted, *Manson's Tropical Diseases*, 529. The effect of storage is noted by Fehily, "Human-Milk Intoxication," 591.

20. Mallat, *Philippines*, 83; *RPC (Schurman), 1900*, 3:245; Garcia, "Cultivation of Rice," in *CPI, 1903*, 90–91; Miller, *Economic Conditions*, 32; Foreman, *Philippine Islands*, 318–19.

21. Owen, "Rice Industry," 111. The statement about Spanish protectionist legislation is in Elías de Molíns, "Importación temporal," 39. The secretary-general of Barcelona's society of credit and docks was arguing for legislation allowing the import of Southeast Asian (and particularly Philippine) rice for processing and reexport only.

22. Robequain, *Economic Development*, 309–10.

23. For the quote about Western entreprenurial disinterest, see Owen, "Rice Industry," 91. Also see Foreman, *Philippine Islands*, 319. Foreman states that steam power was used first in Camarines province by Spaniards in 1888. He also says that steam mills were built along the Manila-Dagupan railroad in places other than the four he named, but he is not specific as to numbers or locations. For Peñaranda's comments, see Pangasinan, 1891, *Mm*, 18, PNA. Increasingly, Tutuban barrio in Manila, where the railroad station and yards were located, became the center of the domestic rice trade. Doeppers has called my attention to a Tutuban rice mill whose proprietors as of Aug. 17, 1898 were one Chas. H. Cundall and one W.A. Fitton (personal communication, Feb. 21, 1994). For subsequent development of the Tutuban-centered domestic rice trade, see "Rice Distribution," 13, 36.

24. The import-export statistics were calculated from data in Kilbourne, "Food Salts," 127.

25. Kilbourne, "Food Salts," 129; "Report of W.B. Wilcox and L.R. Sargent," 3–4.

26. Foreman says that Pardo's mill opened in 1896. See Foreman, *Philippine Islands*, 319. Owens's source is an 1894 newspaper article, however. Owens also points out that although Spaniards pioneered rice milling in the Philippines, the Chinese soon controlled it. See Owen, *Prosperity*, 70, 173–74.

27. For a discussion of minimum requirements, see Inouye and Katsura, "Diagnosis," 71–72; Neal and Sauberlich, "Thiamin," 195; Manson-Bahr and Bell, *Manson's Tropical Diseases*, 836; Caasi et al., "Studies," 29–30; Luna et al., "Thiaminase," 145–51. For dietary sources of thiamine, see Neal and Sauberlich, "Thiamin," 195, 217–18. On depletion of thiamine, see Manson-Bahr and Bell, *Manson's Tropical Diseases*, 837, and Sandstead, "Clinical Manifestations," 687. More recently, widespread beriberi developed in Democratic Kampuchea (Cambodia) during the Khmer Rouge years. For in-

stances of what was evidently the dry (atrophic) form of beriberi, which the author confuses with one of its symptoms—"oedema," see Pin, *Stay Alive*, 121–38.

28. Koeniger, "Ueber epidemisches," 419–23.

29. For all aspects of beriberi, see Manson-Bahr and Bell, *Manson's Tropical Diseases*, 835–40; Sandstead, "Clinical Manifestations," 685–88; Inoye and Katsura, "Clinical Signs," 29–47; Valyasevi and Munro, "Beriberi," 1006–7; Woodruff, *Medicine*, 426–29; Maegraith, *Adams*, 331–35; Katsura and Oiso, "Beriberi," 136–45. The most acute thiamine deficiency disease is Wernicke's encephalopathy, but it is rare in Asia and appears to have played no role in nineteenth-century Philippine public health. It occurs primarily in alcoholics.

30. Koeniger, "*Ueber epidemische*, 423, 427.

31. Ibid., 425.

32. For Koeniger's remarks, see ibid., 419–27. The case-fatality rate on the *Riujo* in 1882 was apparently 9.1 percent (25 deaths out of 276) (Inouye and Katsura, "Etiology," 9–10). Such rates have less meaning than with other diseases, since they are apparently dependent on the extent of the thiamine deficiency. We can safely assume, for instance, that the Japanese sailors were taking in slightly more vitamin B_1 than those Manila residents who stayed in their houses that year and ate nothing whatever except for highly milled rice. On Malabon, see del Pan, *Las Islas Filipinas*, 357, 362; Wickburg, *Chinese*, 34, 68, 101–02, 107, 136, 149; Magno, "Politics," 204–09. Dr. Gomez's statement is in Iloilo, 1892, *Mm*, 14, PNA.

33. For beriberi in Japan, see Inouye and Katsura, "Etiology," 1. For Southeast Asia, see Schneider, "Beriberi," 170–204, and Fiebig, "Beriberi," 437–39 and citations therein.

34. Colín, *Labor Evangélica*, 1:106; Bantug, *Medicine*, 39; Antonio de Morga, *Sucessos de las Islas Filipinas* (Mexico, 1609), in BR, 15:57; *Relation of Events in the Filipinas Islands, 1618–1619* (Manila, 1619), ibid., 17:22; [Francisco de Figeroa?], *Events in Filipinas, 1668* (Manila, 1669), ibid., 37:28. For the Zamboanga reference, see Schneider, "Beri-Beri," 194.

35. Gonzalez, *Anuario*, 141.

36. Foreman, *Philippine Islands*, 207.

37. Capiz, 1887, *Mm*, 33–37, PNA. Dr. Mapa provided no references to particular newspapers or writers.

38. For Dr. Martín's comments, see Ilocos Norte, 1876, *Mm*, 20, 24, PNA. Dr. Peres's lists are in Cavite, 1886, *Mm*, 3, PNA. For the catch-all category, see the appendices to the *Mm* for Ilocos Norte in 1888–1889 and 1891, PNA. For the 20,000 deaths, see those appendices plus the ones for Cavite in 1886 and 1887, PNA.

39. Maus, "Report," in *ARSW, 1900*, 636; Maj. L.W. Crampton, "Report on Operations," RG 112/26, 2310/311v, USNA; Dickman to Manning, June 11, 1900, 6, J.T. Dickman Papers, RBHL.

40. *CPI, 1903*, 3:139, 494; Herzog, "Studies," 755.

41. For the experiments of Japanese researchers, see Inouye and Katsura, "Clinical Signs," 47. Researchers believe it likely that thiamine deficiency is not the sole cause of infantile beriberi and that some of its features may be attributable to various toxic properties in breast milk. Lydia Fehily pointed out in 1944 that in the process of B_1 avitaminosis, intermediary products of incomplete carbohydrate oxidation, like pyruvic acid and sodium pyruvate, accumulate in human milk in amounts that may be beyond infantile tolerance. Indeed, she argued that "breast-milk intoxication" would be a more suit-

able term than "infantile beriberi." See Fehily, "Human-Milk Intoxication," 590–91. For a typical description of a foreign physician's view of the generally anemic physical state of Filipinos, see Iloilo (CZ), 1894, *Mm*, 16–17, PNA.

42. On the clinical course of infantile beriberi, see Inouye and Katsura, "Clinical Signs," 47–49; Sandstead, "Clinical Manifestations," 688; Manson-Bahr and Bell, *Manson's Tropical Diseases*, 838–39. For the experience in Hong Kong, see Fehily, "Human-Milk Intoxication," 590–91.

43. Statistics exist in the *Memorias médicas* for Ilocos Norte (1879, 1889, 1891) and Cavite (1886, 1887) from which an infant mortality rate can be calculated. The Ilocos Norte composite rate for those years was 255.2 infant deaths per 1,000 live births. The figure for Cavite was 180.7. The years in question for Ilocos Norte included one normal year and two disastrous ones, while those for Cavite were two of the healthiest, so the average annual mortality rate from 1870 to 1902 was probably somewhere in between. That would indicate that Philippine infant mortality was among the highest of the recorded rates in the world—far worse than those in any of the Western industrialized countries, about equal with that of India, and slightly better than those of only Chile and Russia. For a list of those countries for which rates can be calculated, see Cipolla, *Economic History*, 100.

44. Ilocos Norte, 1876, *Mm*, 24, PNA; Ilocos Norte, 1886, *Mm*, 12–15, PNA.

45. Iloilo, 1891, *Mm*, 3–7, PNA.

46. Iloilo, 1892, *Mm*, 1–15, PNA.

47. Iloilo, 1893, *Mm*, 24–28, PNA.

48. Iloilo (CZ), 1894, Mm, 22, PNA; Iloilo (CZ), 1895, Mm, 9–23, PNA.

49. McLaughlin and Andrews, "Studies," 149–59.

50. *CPI, 1918*, 2:1106; "Conditions in the Philippine Islands, Report of the Special Mission to the Philippine Islands to the Secretary of War" (Wood-Forbes Report), 1922, 5, RG 350, USNA; Heiser, *Odyssey*, 38, 101.

51. The quoted phrase about civilization is U.S. President William McKinley's. See Karnow, *In Our Image*, 134, 160. For annexation and the war, see Miller, *"Benevolent Assimilation."*

CHAPTER 6

1. The *Memoria* presented at Philadelphia is excerpted in Jimeno, *Población*, 116. For the rest, see Jordana, "Memoria," 3, 15.

2. For the quoted passage about those who fled to the hills, see Ileto, *Pasyon*, 228. For forced timber cutting, see Roth, "Church Lands," 140. Roth says that timber cutting as a labor obligation was abolished sometime in the eighteenth or nineteenth centuries.

3. For the history of medical understanding of malaria, see Harrison, *Mosquitos*. Dr. Amide's remarks are in Pangasinan, 1883, *Mm*, 11–11b, PNA.

4. Siasi, Sulu (Jolo) Group, *MHP* 664, Sept. 30, 1899, RG 94/547, USNA; Maj. George H. Penrose, "Report into Cause of Sickness at San Pablo," June 9, 1900, RG 112/26, 2310/311w, USNA; Ilagan, Isabela, *MHP* 610, May 1901, RG 94/547, USNA; Maasin, Leyte, *MHP* 560, Oct.-Nov. 1901, RG 94/547, USNA.

5. For the governor's insights, see Rajal, "Memoria," 292. For an account of Philippine observers being "fooled" for seventeen years after the role of mosquito as vector was understood because of the assumption that malaria was always a marsh disease, see Russell, *Malaria*, 10. For all aspects of Philippine anopheline vectors, see Russell et al.,

Practical Malariology, 296; Bispham, *Malaria*, 50; Craig, "Observations," 524; Manalang, "Malaria Transmission," 241–50; Delfinado et al., "Checklist," 433; Urbino, "Control," 23–25; Mieldazis, "Preferential Breeding Conditions," 59–60; King, "Three Philippine Anopheles," 488–91; Mendoza and Abinoja, "Observations," 57; Urbino, "Development," 6A:425–27. A. *minimus flavirostris* is the most important vector everywhere in the archipelago except on Mindoro, where A. *mangyanus* is the principal one.

6. For Urbino's remarks on lowland settlement patterns minimizing the extent of malarial infection, see Urbino, "Development," 6A:407. The quoted phrase is taken from a royal order of Jan. 21, 1864, recommending the development of the germs of wealth buried in the country and ordering the colonial goverment to propose methods of attaining that objective. See Keyser, *Medios*, 53.

7. For the quoted statement, see Taylor, *Cinchona*, 24. For the plasmodium lifecycle, see Manson-Bahr and Bell, *Manson's Tropical Diseases*, 3–6; Miller, "Malaria," 223–39; Woodruff, *Medicine*, 30–33. The invading parasites are sporozoa of the genus *Plasmodium*. Three of them—*P. vivax, P. malariae*, and *P. ovale*—are species of subgenus *Plasmodium*, while the more dangerous *P. falciparum* is a species of subgenus *Laverania*. Each species comprises numerous different strains. Vivax malaria is synonomous with tertian, benign tertian, and simple intermittent fever, all of which describe an infection characterized by a high fever that recurs every forty-eight hours, or a little less, and which rarely terminates in death. Falciparum malaria has been variously known as malignant tertian, subtertian, aestivo-autumnal, and pernicious. The fever cycle is less regular, as the name subtertian suggests. If untreated, primary attacks are often fatal. No nineteenth-century Philippine data on the relative proportions of the two species exists. The two earliest reliable studies produced conflicting data. The first was an examination in 1906 of 84 positive blood smears taken from 180 children that found *P. falciparum* in 52.4 percent of the cases and *P. vivax* in 40.5 percent. A more comprehensive survey in 1928 of 1,849 positive smears from 13,972 persons in sixteen provinces revealed *P. vivax* in 70.5 percent of the patients and *P. falciparum* in 24.1 percent. See Bowman, "Incidence," 291, and Russell, *Malaria*, 19.

8. For lists of deaths by cause, see the statistical appendices to the following reports: Albay, 1887, *Mm*, PNA; Laguna, 1886, 1887, 1888, *Mm*, PNA; Pangasinan, 1888, *Mm*, PNA; Ilocos Norte, 1889, 1891, *Mm*, PNA. Malaria may or may not have been overreported. On the one hand, it must have been tempting to assume that most mortal fevers in the countryside were malarial. (The *Memorias médicas* usually attributed a large proportion of deaths to fever, however, so it looks as if the physicians tended to report the data as they received it from the parishes instead of diagnosing cases they had not seen.) The Americans, less experienced with tropical disease, were more likely to see malaria behind every fever. As U.S. Army physician Joseph J. Curry put it in 1901, "[Fever] is for [the Filipino physician] as malaria is to us, a cloak for ignorance" (Curry, "Report to the Surgeon General," June 20, 1901, RG 112/26, 68075/G, USNA). Dr. Chamberlain agreed, asserting that "Malaria has been the scapegoat for the diagnostic shortcomings of the tropical practitioner" (Chamberlain, "Typhoid Fever," 300). On the other hand, some of the undifferentiated fevers must have been malaria. Additionally, the real difficulty in diagnosis was that malaria mimicked other diseases rather than vice versa. See Manson-Bahr and Apted, *Manson's Tropical Diseases*, 50. It seems enough to conclude that malaria accounted for substantially more deaths during the last part of the nineteenth century than any other disease in the Philippines. For the tendency of Spanish and Filipino doctors to use fever as a catch-all category as well as for a guide to the huge amount of early literature on Philippine malaria, see Russell, *Malaria*, 9, and pas-

sim. For the quote about latent and relapsing malaria, see Bowman, "Incidence," 292. On malaria's consequences and the following quotation, see Black, "Epidemiology," 136. Vivax patients experience *relapses* caused by late-maturing parasites (merozoites) that remain behind in the liver and eventually invade the blood stream at regular intervals. Falciparum survivors suffer *recrudescences* due to the persistence of parasites in the body after they have already invaded the red blood cells.

9. For measurements of endemicity and all aspects of immunity (resistance), see Manson-Bahr and Bell, *Manson's Tropical Diseases*, 12–15, 44; Miller, "Malaria," 226–27, 233; Woodruff, *Medicine*, 27–28, 37–39. Natural genetic resistance and passive transmission of maternal resistance to infants both exist to some degree. No genetic shield has ever been noted in Filipinos as a racial subgroup, but variation among individuals may occur. The natural passive protection in infants lasts four to six months but is lost thereafter. With regard to acquired resistance, it should be noted that the immune system, *when not otherwise compromised*, responds with reasonable effectiveness to any malarial invasion. In a primary attack, lymphoid macrophages and humoral antibodies can destroy most of the invaders, but their counterattack is only mounted against the parasites during their development in the red cells. Ironically, incomplete victory is the best result, the more so for those who will continue to live in regions of high endemicity. So long as some red cells remain parasitized, the immune reaction is stimulated, and resistance is maintained—and even builds—against succeeding attacks. If all parasites are destroyed, however, acquired resistance is rapidly and easily lost. Modern antimalarial drugs also produce that result, as does prolonged absence from an endemic area. For the quoted statement about the benefits to the community of acquired resistance and the dangers to migrants of meeting new strains, see Black, "Epidemiology," 136, 138.

10. Quinine is not active against falciparum malaria. It does have great usefulness against *P. vivax*, however, attacking the parasite in the red cell (erythocytic) phase, but even successful treatment leaves the patient open to relapses, since the drug does not touch parasites in the liver (which they invade prior to eruption into the blood stream). And though the drug blocks the cycle at the erythrocytic phase, it does nothing to halt continuing vectoral transmission of new parasites through subsequent bites. For the history of quinine, see Taylor, *Cinchona*. On eventual production in the Philippines, which began after 1930, see Maranon and Bartlett, "Cinchona Cultivation," 111–87. For disproportionate mortality among pobres for lack of quinine, see Abra, 1890, *Mm*, 5., PNA. Gov. Millan's story is in Ilocos Norte, 1888, *M*, 81b, PNA. The description of malaria victims waiting resignedly without medicine is from Albay, 1886, *Mm*, 10–11, PNA. Some physicians urged the government to provide free medicines for the needy, but that was clearly beyond the administration's resources. For a typical plea, see Dr. Ares's repeated arguments in Cebu, 1884, *Mm*, 14–17, PNA; Cebu, 1886, *Mm*, 7–8, PNA.

11. The list of transmission factors is taken from Manson-Bahr and Bell, *Manson's Tropical Diseases*, 43.

12. Macdonald, *Epidemiology*, 17–43. The quoted phrase is on 17. Also see the selection of Macdonald's essays arranged under the subheading "Quantitative Epidemiology of Malaria" in Bruce-Chwatt and Glanville, *Dynamics*, 68–169. The introductory essay is also helpful. See Bruce-Chwatt, "Quantitative Epidemiology," 8–17. As an example of malaria's potential explosiveness, Macdonald posits a patient infected with *P. falciparum* who is infective to all the anophelines that take blood meals from him for eighty days. If ten bite each day, he infects 800 mosquitos, each of which might have a 90 percent

probability of survival thereafter through one day (and each succeeding day). If the temperature were such that the extrinsic incubation cycle took twelve days, about 28 percent of the 800 anophelenes would live long enough to produce infective sporozoites ready for transmission. Each would still have a subsequent ten-day life expectancy. If the vectors were entirely anthropophilic (taking their blood meals from humans exclusively), feeding once every other day, each would infect five persons, on the average. As a result, the primary infection would have generated some 1,200 new cases of falciparum malaria. Even though the reproduction rate would not be as high in nature as the mathematical model suggests (because the 1,200 bites would probably have been distributed among fewer than 1,200 separate persons), such a reproduction rate obviously could not long sustain itself because everyone in the community would soon be infected. Three natural restraints on the reproduction rate exist: (1) the development of resistance in the population group, which restricts the length of time that its individual members will remain infective, (2) the rapidly increasing incidence of individuals who are already infected when they receive subsequent infective bites, so that the creation of new cases apparently declines, and (3) the increasing occurrence of such superinfection (the imposition of a second infection on the first) in mosquitos, so that subsequent infections do not substantially increase their infectivity.

13. Macdonald, *Epidemiology*, 40–43. Pampana's statement is quoted in Harrison, *Mosquitos*, 201.

14. The first two quoted passages are from Macdonald, *Epidemiology*, 45. The third is in Macdonald, "Analysis," 258. For speculation about the development of the main vector's zoophilism, see Baisis, "Notes," 500–1. On the relationship between population movements and malarial transmission in Africa, see Prothero, *Migrants*.

15. Keyser, *Medios*, 14–16; Pelzer, *Pioneer Settlement*, 88–90.

16. Sanciano, *El progreso*, 48–49; Keyser, *Medios*, 16. For temporary huts as foci, see Prothero, *Migrants*, 36.

17. For malaria and hill-country agriculture this century, see Pelzer, *Pioneer Settlement*, 33. Dr. Nolasco's comments are in Masbate y Ticao, 1886, *Mm*, 2, PNA.

18. For the creation of the *Inspección*, see Robles, *Philippines*, 140, 211–12. For the decrees of 1863 and 1866, see del Busto, *Medios*, 53, 55. The bad effects of allowing provincial governors to engage in trade and commerce and the decision to abolish that privilege are treated in Robles, *Philippines*, 111–17, 123–24.

19. For the creation of the junta, see Robles *Philippines*, 55. For the argument in support of the new regulations, see J.F., "Memoria," 460–61.

20. Unsigned letter from Inspector de Montes to Gobernador Gral, Aug. 1869, abstracted in Leitz, *Calendar*, 131/31, and Jordana, *Memoria*, 3–13. Total income from the sale of forest products and from fines amounted to Pfs 60,206—not negligible but hardly significant in comparison with other kinds of income the state received. During the fiscal year 1878–1879, for instance, receipts from municipal rentals and fees alone amounted to Pfs 2,026,653. See Robles, *Philippines*, 252.

21. By 1903, lumber ranked as the fourth leading industry (behind tobacco, liquor and beverages, and food and its products) and its output represented 9.1 percent of total value of products by industry groups. That was somewhat deceiving, however, since the Philippines was almost entirely nonindustrialized and though the industry was of moderate importance domestically, it was not big enough or mechanized enough yet to be a major exporter. Only 2,039 wage earners worked in lumber and its remanufacture. Sawing was carried on at seventy-eight establishments in eleven provinces, but the census report stated that "Lumber for building and other purposes is, for the most part, sawed

by hand, slowly and laboriously. In Manila, however, and at a few other points, steam sawmills are in operation." See *CPI, 1903*, 4:470, 482–86. For the junta secretary's remarks, see del Busto, *Informe*, 15–16.

22. For the creation of the commission, see Robles, *Philippines*, 268–69. For the station director's remarks, see José Guevedo, "Memoria agrícola del distrito de Albay y Camarines," Feb. 1, 1890, 118–160, A, PNA.

23. For the quoted phrase and the lack of money the research stations received, see José Guevedo, "Memoria agrícola," 45. For the dynamic between the various groups of people engaged in the lumbering industry, see J.F., "Memoria sobre el comercio de maderas," 154–55. For the comments of Jordana and the journalist, see "Estudio forestal," 238.

24. For Dr. Gomez's remark, see Iloilo, 1892, *Mm*, 22–23, PNA.

25. Urbino, *Proceedings*, 429.

26. The quoted phrase is from Heiser, *American Doctor's Odyssey*, 449. The longer statement about working on shares is from Miller, *Economic Conditions*, 28. For the study on insecticide spraying, see Urbino, "Control," 67.

27. For the research on the seasonal peaks of sporozoite rates, see Urbino, *Proceedings*, 430. On Ilocos Norte's geography, population movements, harvesting, and malaria, see Ilocos Norte, 1879, *Mm*, 13–19, PNA.

28. For malaria in the nineteenth-century United States, see Faust, "Malaria Incidence," 749–63, and Boyd, "Historical Sketch," 226–38.

29. 1st Tenn. Vol. Inf., RHR 2523, RG 94, USNA. Fortunately for the Filipinos, most of the recruits from western Tennessee went to Cuba in the 2d Tenn. Vols. The Philippine-bound regiment comprised men predominantly from the eastern part of the state. 29th U.S. Vol. Inf., RHR 2473, RG 94, USNA; 32nd U.S. Vol. Inf., RHR 3476, RG 94, USNA; 6th U.S. Cav., RHR, RG 94, USNA. For transmission principles explaining the continuing infectivity of the soldiers after the trip across the Pacific, see Manson-Bahr and Apted, *Manson's Tropical Diseases*, 42, 50–55.

30. 27th U.S. Vol. Inf., RHR 3469, RG 94, USNA; 32nd U.S. Vol. Inf., RHR 3476, RG 94, USNA; 11th U.S. Vol. Cav., RHR 3467, RG 94, USNA.

31. 28th U.S. Vol. Inf., RHR 3470, RG 94, USNA.

32. Ligao, Albay, *MHP* 463, RG 94/547, USNA; report of Capt. Claude E. Sawyer, Mar. 14, 1900, RG 395/777, box 2, USNA; Col. L.M. Maus, "Report," June 15, 1900, in *ARSW, 1900*, 636.

33. Indan, Camarines Norte, *MHP* 746, RG 94/547, USNA; report of Col. Jas. T. Pettit, with endorsements, Jan. 19, 1900, RG 395/777, box 3, USNA; Banate, Panay, *MHP* 449, Jan. 1900, RG 94/547, USNA.

34. The disease presents three distinct forms, and in ascending order of gravity, they are: inapparent, abortive, and frank clinical reactions. In the last, which characterized the Philippine epizootics, a sudden, sharp fever marks the onset of the infection. Febrile illness and restlessness are manifest within twenty-four hours. A rough and lusterless coat, shallow and rapid breathing, a dry muzzle, congested mucous membranes, loss of appetite, and constipation are typical. The fever peaks in two or three days and subsides with the onset of diarrhea. Depression is evident, and lesions appear in the mucosa of the mouth, nose, and genital tract. The diarrhea persists for about a week, containing specks of blood in fatal cases. Extremely rapid dehydration ensues, leading to severe emaciation, prostration, and death. For all aspects of the disease, see Hall, *Diseases*, 30–32, 54; Scott, *Diagnosis*, 2–17; Chalmers, "Nutrition," 189; Cockrill, "Aspects," 203–06, 212. For the early research in the Philippines, see Ruediger, "Observations,"

381–83; Ruediger, "Difference," 431; Boynton, "Rinderpest," 10. Other studies imply that Philippine carabaos and cattle were generally in as poor physical condition as their human counterparts. As in man, poor nutrition and multiple infection compromise bovine host defenses, and weakened immune systems may have contributed to the almost total mortality during the epizootics of 1888 and 1900. The most common intercurrent infection in the Philippines was foot-and-mouth disease, which by itself was not particularly troublesome but in combination with rinderpest was almost always fatal. Texas fever and surra were somewhat less prevalent, but when encountered in connection with cattle plague, both were "very destructive to life." Anthrax was enzootic in the islands, but its relationship and interaction with rinderpest is unclear. Writing in 1922, the Philippine Bureau of Agriculture's chief veterinarian said that several people staunchly maintained that rinderpest was first introduced no later than 1882. (Youngberg, "Brief History," 205). If that were the case, it is difficult to see how an epizootic was avoided, especially during the chaos of that epidemic cholera year.

35. May is one historian who has understood the link between rinderpest and malaria (and consequent food shortages) in the Philippines. He provides an extensive application of the epidemiological principles governing that process to the situation in Batangas during the war. See May, *Battle*, 26, 60–61, 264–66, 271, 291. For return to equilibrium, see Macdonald, "Community Aspects," 83. The insecticide study in the mid-1950s showed the importance of the availability of bovine blood meals as a transmission factor. Even though the anopheline population increased in Santa Maria, Laguna, the mosquitos could not be induced to increase their human-biting rate because of the large number of carabaos in that rice-growing municipality. In fact, it declined. See Urbino, "Control," 65. For the minimum estimate of five years for replenishment under the circumstances, see Shealy, "Some Facts," 399.

36. For the beginning of the epizootic, see Pangasinan, 1888, *Mm*, 27–30, PNA. For the belief that the virus was imported from French Indochina, see Youngberg, "Brief History," 205. The Cambodian epizootic is described in Moura, *Royaume*, 172. For the clogged rivers, see Francia, *Unas palabras*, 21. Francia's source for the priest's report is Dr. R. Berriz Roberto's *Mm* for Bulacan in 1888. That document is not included in the medical reports held in the PNA.

37. Ilocos Norte, 1888–1889, *Mm*, 2–3, PNA; Pangasinan, 1888, *Mm*, 28–29, 46, PNA.

38. For bovine statistics and agricultural consequences of the epizootic, see Pangasinan, 1891, *Mm*, 59, PNA; Morong, 1892, *M*, 9, PNA; Ilocos Sur, 1888, *Mm*, 6–11, PNA. For prices of carabaos, see Pampanga, 1889, *M*, 58a–59, PNA. The best contemporary data about the 1887–1889 epizootic/epidemics are contained in the *Mm* for Ilocos Norte, 1888–1891. The slow recovery is documented in the various *Mm* from Luzon in the following years. The inability to till the land and consequent famine was still remembered more than sixty years later. See Agupit, Camarines Sur, HDP, 26:31, PNL. The epizootic at the end of the century disrupted transportation from the abaca fields to market in the Bikol region as it must have after 1887. See Owen, "Abaca," 198. For the effect of the 1896–1897 revolt on the bovine population, see Ileto, "Food Crisis," 111–13.

39. Shealy, "Some Facts," 397, 399, 403. Shealy was writing about his experiences between 1905 and 1908, but it seems likely that the conditions were similar at the end of the previous decade.

40. For the association of war and rinderpest, see Scott, *Diagnosis*, 10. For the speculation that the disease appeared in 1898, see Ileto, "Food Crisis," 111. For the Balayan and Tuy reports, see Ileto, "Food Crisis," 111. For the Camp Stotsenburg survey, see

Craig, "Observations," 523. For the bionomics of *A. balabacensis*, see Russell et al., *Practical Malariology*, 296.

41. For the U.S. Army's use of carabaos for haulage, see Brig. Gen. Theodore Schwan to Lawton, Oct. 24, 1899, in "Report of Major-General E.S. Otis, U.S. Army, Commanding the Division of the Philippines, and Military Governor of the Philippine Islands, September 1, 1899 to May 5, 1900," in *ARSW, 1900*, 221, and Pvt. Albert Gay, 17th U.S. Inf., CtM, RG 153/16174, box 3080, WNRC. For the almost total depopulation and slow replacement, see William H. Taft to Henry Cabot Lodge, Nov. 27, 1902, "Lodge Papers, 1902, H–Z (incoming)," Henry Cabot Lodge Papers, MHS, and Nelson A. Miles to War Department (telegram), RG 94/489592, box 3370, USNA. On the consequences of the animal shortage on plowing, see Lt. F.J. Morrow, "Report on Status of Affairs in Pueblo of Rosales," Jan. 12, 1900, RG 395/851, box 6, USNA. On the resulting inflated carabao prices, black market, and rustling, see Quirino, *Amang*, 7. For the effect on the American army, see Brig. Gen. Marshall I. Ludington, "Report of the Quartermaster-General of the Army," Oct. 16, 1900, in *ARSW, 1900*, 297, and report of Maj. C.P. Miller, July 11, 1900, in *ARSW, 1900*, 101.

42. On transmission during the dry months, see Ruediger, "Observations," 381. For the situation in Aparri, see Sternberg, "Report of the Surgeon-General for 1900," in *ARSW, 1900*, 644, and Aparri, Cagayan, Apr. 20 and June 3, 1901, *MHP* 669, RG 94/547, USNA. For the remaining places, see Pili, Camarines Sur, Nov. 1900–Jan. 1902, *MHP* 485, RG 94/547, USNA; Buhi, Camarines Sur, Mar.–Sept 1900, *MHP* 413, RG 94/547, USNA; Cagayan de Misamis, Jan. 31, 1901, *MHP* 502, RG 94/547, USNA; Palompan, Leyte, July 31, 1901, *MHP* 377, RG 94/547, USNA.

43. Typical of the casual killings was an incident involving a mounted soldier outside of San Jose de Buenavista, Antique, who rode by and shot Francisco Joyel's carabao as the animal and its owner were plowing a rice field. For that offense, which was not the one at issue in the soldier's subsequent court-martial, see Pvt. Henry Harding, 38th U.S. Vol. Inf., CtM, RG 153/24397, box 3239, WRNC. Although such "joy-killings" accounted by themselves for only a tiny fraction of the animal depopulation, they increased the probability that individuals like Joyel would be bitten, which then increased other transmission factors in their immediate vicinity. For the ecological connection in the other areas, see Daet, Camarines Norte, *MHP* 746, RG 94/547, USNA; Boac, Marinduque, *MHP* 545, Jan. 31, 1902, RG 94/547, USNA; Gazan, Marinduque, *MHP* 548, Apr. 1902, RG 94/547, USNA; Boac, Marinduque, *MHP* 553, RG 94/547, USNA; W.H. Cook, "Report of Tayabas Province," May 15, 1903, in *ARSW, 1903*, 194–206; Santa Rosa and Cabuyao, *MHP* 628, May 31, 1903, RG 94/547, USNA. For the mortality data on Cabuyao, see *CPI, 1903*, and 3:82, 146–47, 501.

44. *CPI, 1903*, 4:228–29 (carabao mortality), and 3:138, 494 (human mortality). For the Batangas estimates, see May, *Battle*, 265. For the two surveys on levels of infection, see Bowman, "Incidence," 291, and Russell, *Malaria*, 19.

CHAPTER 7

1. For the nineteenth-century pandemics, see Cliff and Haggett, *Atlas*, 5–6. Major outbreaks occurred in the Philippines in 1820, 1843, and 1865. We know little about their scope. Gironiere, an eyewitness to the first, said only "I had only resided a short time at Cavite when that terrible scourge, the cholera, broke out at Manilla, in September, 1820, and quickly ravaged the whole island." Nothing in the account of his subsequent activities on Luzon suggests that the island was paralyzed, however. See Giro-

niere, *Twenty Years*, 20, and passim. The Smith-Cullinane data are too scanty to throw much light on the issue, but the only parishes in their sample of eleven in 1820 that seem to have experienced crisis mortality at that time were in the Ilocos region (six out of seven). The other four in Laguna, Batangas, Albay, and Cebu did not. In 1843, only four of nineteen sampled parishes show crisis mortality, all in the Ilocos provinces again. The epidemic around 1865 seems to be the first with real interisland diffusion, since it spread from Manila to Zamboanga and from there north, and sixteen parishes on both Luzon and Cebu in the sample of twenty-six registered abnormal death totals. See Smith, "Crisis Mortality," 67. For its origin in Shanghai, see Francia, *Unas palabras*, 7. Some turn-of-the-century observers alleged that cholera had been present in the Philippines in between the major epidemics. Philippine Commissioner Worcester asserted that cholera cases had existed between the 1882 and 1888 outbreaks but that the governor-general had covered them up ("Editorial," 65–66). Heiser believed that cholera vibrios were constantly present in the Manila water supply and awaiting optimum conditions to set off an epidemic (Heiser, "Some Considerations," 95). Dr. Francia claimed that sporadic cases of cholera had existed in the Philippines in most years ever since 1820, but he distinguished the local strain from Indian cholera (Francia, *Unas palabras*, 8). The implication from the foregoing views is that cholera had become endemic in the Philippines sometime during the century. Indeed, archival sources reveal that sporadic cases of *cólera endémico* were being officially reported to Manila in nonepidemic years. See, for instance, correspondence from the governors of Zambales, Mindanao, and Cagayan to the governor-general of the Philippines in July 1861, Nov. 1863, and April 1864, respectively, *Cp*, PNA. Also see Cebu, 1884, *Mm*, 4, PNA. Those authorities were probably mistaken, however. Bantug argues persuasively that cholera was not endemic in the Philippines during the nineteenth century. He contends that each epidemic resulted from imported infection and that the sporadic cases in intervening years were simply misdiagnosed. See Bantug, *Medicine*, 28–37. For the correspondence regarding the Bangkok outbreak, see *Cp*, 1873, PNA.

2. Among the specimens seized from visiting French zoologists in Manila as evidence of the plot to exterminate the population and take over the islands was "a quantity of Peruvian bark" (Dobell letter, in BR, 51:44). The government set up stalls in the streets to dispense free medicines as well. The source for that information is Dr. Carlos Luis Benoit, who many years later was a physician in the Philippines and who died in the 1888–1889 cholera epidemic. He said that the medicines given out free in 1820 had been quinine and alcohol, usually brandy. The passage, which I have translated, is in Bantug, *Medicine*, 30. I am assuming that the ingredient was the bark (cinchona), not quinine. If the Frenchmen were thinking of beginning the cultivation of that plant in the islands, as is probable, the irony becomes overwhelming given the fact that malaria was the greatest threat to life in the Philippines. It will be recalled that quinine was first isolated from cinchona in that very year, 1820, but that the Philippines had to import that antimalarial drug until well into the twentieth century. Regarding the 1820 epidemic, see de la Gironiere, *Twenty Years*, 20–29. For examples of recommended precautions against cholera in the nineteenth-century Philippines, see Bantug, *Medicine*, 36–37, and del Rosario and Rizal, "Some Epidemiological Features," 1–5.

3. Asiatic cholera is to be distinguished from El Tor cholera, which seems not to have been implicated in the nineteenth-century epidemics but which has plagued the Philippines in more recent times. The use of the term "cholera" herinafter should be understood to refer to Asiatic cholera. For the history of the use of fluid and salt replacement, the only effective treatment, as well as its first use in the Philippines in 1909, see "Doc-

uments communicated," 274; Lectures on Communicable Diseases, 1904, "Cholera," lecture 7, United States Army Medical School, Washington, D.C., MS/C/15, 5, NLM; Nichols and Andrews, "Treatment," 81; Rogers, "Treatment," 99; Sellards, "Tolerance," 363.

4. For all aspects of cholera, see Manson-Bahr and Bell, *Manson's Tropical Diseases*, 259–72; Barua and Burrows, *Cholera*, passim; Feachem, "Environmental Aspects," 1–47. Malnourishment is thought to compromise natural resistance by neutralizing the host's protective gastric juices. Cholera is transmitted orally between people via three routes: water, food, or other people (fecal-oral). It has always been assumed that water is the most important. Vibrios can survive in water for up to a year, and thus wells, rivers, and reservoirs are natural sources. Primary transmission occurs with drinking water. The parasite is also spread secondarily in water used to irrigate or freshen foods. The simultaneous development of a large number of cases in a community is normally attributed to a common water source that has been contaminated by fecal discharge containing cholera vibrios. Surveys that consistently show lower-than-infective vibrio levels in wells and standing surface water in villages with cases of the disease have cast some doubt on the primacy of transmission via water, but no one doubts its importance. Polluted water is almost always the original culprit, for instance, in foodborne transmission, especially in the case of inadequately cooked fish. The vibrio also survives well in boiled rice, and the addition of salt to rice or fruit enhances propagation. The epidemiological significance of the fecal-oral route has sometimes been discounted, but it would be unwise to overlook it given the low level of hygiene and sanitation in most nineteenth-century Filipino households. The custom of eating with the fingers from common receptacles without prior washing of the hands obviously brought the person-to-person route into play. Cholera spreads among household contacts within two days of the index case, and it is well documented that such transmission is much more common in low-income families with inadequate cleanliness. The ease with which infection could be spread by each of the three routes among the Filipino poor accounts for the explosiveness of the outbreaks.

5. For Koch's statement, see Feachem, "Environmental Aspects," 11. Infectives who excrete vibrios for more than three weeks are classified as chronic carriers. Because the chronic state is rare, though, such persons are much less important to the epidemiology of cholera than are the acute carriers.

6. Prevention and control of cholera were virtually impossible under nineteenth-century conditions in the Philippines. Even today, when few mysteries remain about the disease or its epidemiology, strategies aimed at forestalling or containing transmission in developing countries are easily frustrated. At a minimum, governments must have the capacity to maintain comprehensive surveillance and reporting of all enteric and diarrheal diseases. In addition, the means must be found to finance, construct, and maintain sanitation facilities and improved water supplies. That is difficult enough to accomplish in a network of remote villages, but the task becomes truly formidable in burgeoning urban areas undergoing tremendous socioeconomic changes. Immunization does not give protection beyond three or four months, and quarantines have limited effect. International contacts through trade and tourism vastly complicate the problem. When prevention and long-term control fail, successful management of cholera epidemics in developing countries depends on the construction of temporary hospitals and provision of intravenous and oral fluids *in advance of* the epidemic. After the outbreak, immediate treatment of cholera cases, carriers, and contacts is basic. Proper advance organization that allows for prompt fluid and salt replacement among cases can reduce

mortality to less than 1 percent. Mass or individual antibiotic treatment of those who develop diarrhea and of direct contacts of cases is useful in reducing infectivity and severity of clinical manifestations. It is rare that cholera epidemics are managed with optimum efficiency, however. Prior to 1903 in the Philippines, neither colonial administration had the knowledge, resources, or organizational capabilities to deal successfully with a cholera epidemic.

7. For Dr. Gomez's comments, see Iloilo, 1886, *Mm*, 16–17, PNA, and 1891, *Mm*, 22–23, PNA. Another observer said that local boards of health did not exist in pueblos other than provincial capitals and that the "immense majority" of Philippine towns had no licensed physician. See Gonzalez y Martín, *Filipinas*, 137.

8. For the correspondence regarding the Nagasaki outbreak, see *Cp*, 1878, PNA.

9. For the correspondence about the various outbreaks in 1881, see *Cp*, 1881, PNA.

10. For the following account of the 1882 epidemic in Zamboanga, see Alba, *Memoria*. The phrase "guest from the Ganges" appears in Dr. Francisco Javier de Castro's introduction (ibid., 13). That name for cholera, which was commonly used, referred to the disease's presumed origins in India.

11. For the quote about frequent communications, see ibid., 27.

12. In the original document, the arrival of the *España* is dated July 14. Because of the apparent inconsistency with the rest of the narrative, I am assuming that the date is a simple misprint and that the ship in fact arrived on June 14. In any case, the matter is not essential to epidemiology of the cholera in 1882. For the doctor's quoted remarks, see Alba, *Memoria*, 91.

13. For the quote about preparing for cholera, see Alba, *Memoria*, 88. The other quotations are from ibid., 40.

14. For the two quoted statements, see ibid., 34 and 32, respectively.

15. For the sultan's quoted phrase, see ibid., 32. Writing at the end of the decade, Dr. Francia said that the disease had been imported into Jolo on steamship *Johk-ang*, which sailed periodically between Singapore, Hong Kong, Sumatra, Java, Sandakan, Borneo, and Jolo. He said that two hundred persons died in Maibung in forty days. See Francia, *Unas palabras*, 7.

16. For the doctor's quoted comments about isolation, attenuating measures, ridiculous methods, and the importance of time, see Alba, *Memoria*, 92, 93, 95, and 19, respectively.

17. The apparent case-fatality rates for Zamboanga (45.1 percent for the cabecera and 43.5 percent for the district) seem low and should be accepted with skepticism. For the information about Basilan, see Father Pablo Cavalleria to Father Francisco Sanchez, Isabela de Basilan, Dec. 31, 1886, in BR, 43:261.

18. About cholera in Capiz City, which is described in the following paragraphs, see Capiz, 1882, *Mm*, PNA. For some reason, perhaps because this was a special report, this document is filed under *M* rather than with the other *Mm*. The quotations are from pages 21, and 21b, respectively.

19. For the four quotations, see ibid., 22b, 23, 23b.

20. For the three quoted passages, see ibid., 29, 25, and 54, respectively.

21. The quoted remarks are in ibid., 52, 51b, 36, and 24, respectively. At the end of the account of his "observations during that very sad time," he cited a statistic of 9,256 cholera deaths for the province, presumably out of 230,000 residents, which would mean that about 4 percent of the population died. The vagaries of demographic reporting were such, however, that the provincial population was reported in the 90,000 range in some years and around 230,000 in others. If the official death toll represents the

mortality in the area comprising the lower population base, then around 10 percent of the people in that part of Capiz province died. About 8.6 percent of the population on the neighboring island of Negros died. See Martínez Cuesta, *History*, 263–65.

22. For the importation into Manila, see Alba, *Memoria*, 34, and Francia, *Unas palabras*, 7. The quoted phrase is in Koeniger, "Ueber epidemisches," 419.

23. For the preparations in Manila, see del Rosario and Rizal, "Some Epidemiological Features," 1–5; Bantug, *Medicine*, 30–31. For the quoted statement about the spreading panic, see Koeniger, "Ueber epidemisches," 419. For the spread of cholera from Manila through the Lingayen Bay ports on October 20, see Pangasinan, 1883, *Mm*, 3b–4, PNA. Owen has called my attention to the existence of documents in *Ep*, Camarines Sur, 1881–1883, PNA, in which Manila reprimanded the provincial governor and others for letting cholera arrive in Nueva Caceres in 1882 (on a ship that evaded the quarantine) and for their subsequent failure to take action once it broke out (personal communication, May 17, 1992). Estimates of the final death total in Manila vary widely. The official count of the Sub-Delegation de Medicina was based on woefully incomplete hospital records and listed only 5,413 deaths. By contrast, one priest claimed that 1,300 persons died in a single day when the epidemic was at its peak. Koeniger estimated a more realistic total of between 15,000 and 20,000 deaths in the city, while Sawyer claimed that 30,000 perished. Manila's population was around 200,000 at the time (although Koeniger thought it was double that), so perhaps as many as one out of every ten residents died. See Koeniger, "Ueber epidemisches," 419, and Sawyer, *Inhabitants*, 400–1.

24. For a firsthand account of the epidemic, see Francia, *Unas palabras*, passim. At that time he was the inspector general of beneficence and health. The quoted phrase is at page 17.

25. For Dr. Francia's quoted remarks, see ibid., 12–13. Fragmentary data precludes any reliable comparison of overall mortality on Luzon or in the Philippines for the two epidemics, but it is clear that fewer people died from cholera in the later one. That was especially so in Manila, where just 1,603 persons died, according to Francia. Official death counts for those years, which show no increase in overall mortality during 1888 and 1889 in the capital, make that statistic plausible. The numbers of deaths in Manila for the relevant years are as follows: 1885—12,052; 1886—7,403; 1887—9,889; 1888—9,061; 1889—10,383; 1890—6,817; 1891—6,871; 1892—10,939. How complete they were for any year is unknown. See *CPI, 1903*, 2:12–14. If acquired resistance played a part in holding down cholera mortality in 1888–1889, we could expect that a greater proportion of victims survived their attacks during the latter contagion. Unfortunately, data that would allow a comparison of case-fatality rates during the two epidemics are not available. One random statistic does exist, however. In 1889 on Negros, 14,819 persons were said to have contracted the disease, and of them, 7,798 died, for a case-fatality rate of 52.6 percent, a statistic which does not indicate that acquired resistance had a dramatic effect. See Martínez Cuesta, *History*, 263–65. In any event, the 1882 epidemic is the one that standard histories of the Philippines emphasize in any catalogue of late-nineteenth-century catastrophes. As detailed in the preceding chapter, however, the conjunction of cholera with rinderpest and malaria ensured that the 1888–1889 disaster would have longer-lasting consequences. Overall mortality was undoubtedly higher as well, though it was spread out over several years.

26. For the quoted statement, see Ileto, "Cholera," 127. Also see Sullivan, "Cholera," 284–300.

27. For cholera among the soldiers in the United States during the late 1860s, see War Department, *Report*, v–xvii, 17–80. For the two quoted statements from the medi-

cal department, see Lt. Col. Henry Lippincott, "Brief Outline of Events and Matters Related to Medical Department in Expedition to the Philippines, July 25, 1898–April 18, 1899," Apr. 9, 1906, RG 112/26, 3866/V/3, USNA, and Alfred A. Woodhull, "Annual Report for the Year Ending June 30, 1899," RG 112/26, 57592/76, USNA.

28. For the initial outbreak in Manila, see Heiser, "Some Considerations," 91, and Ileto, "Cholera," 127. The quoted description is Heiser's.

29. For Worcester's order and the quoted description, see Heiser, *American Doctor's Odyssey*, 105–6. The practice that was followed subsequently during the epidemic—that of simply disinfecting wood houses while continuing to burn nipa huts—gives substance to Ileto's charge that the poor and "ignorant classes" were unjustly oppressed. See Ileto, "Cholera," 136, citing General Order No. 66, Headquarters, Division of the Philippines, Mar. 25, 1902, RG 395/3287, USNA. For Guardia civil actions, see Abra, HDP, 2:26–27, PNA. For the acting governor's remark, see Luke Wright to Root, July 20, 1902, Elihu Root Papers, box 164, LC. The American actions can also be understood as a manifestation of a collective image of themselves sent to cleanse the islands. The Philippines was seen as a veritable Augean stables waiting to be exhumed from centuries of accumulated filth. Americans used that metaphor (or variations of it) constantly, and a book could be written on the cultural assumptions it contained. See Heiser, *American Doctor's Odyssey*, 59–78, and Chamberlin, *Philippine Problem*, 113–22. Indeed, the relevant chapter in the former book is entitled "Washing Up the Orient." For recent comment on the American attitude, see Ileto, "Cholera," 132, and Sullivan, "Cholera," 287–89.

30. For a brief overview of the Senate investigation, see Karnow, *In Our Image*, 192–93. The testimony before the committee is contained in the three-volume *Affairs in the Philippine Islands*. For Worcester's two statements, see Worcester to Taft, Apr. 5, 1902, Elihu Root Papers, box 164, LC, and "Annual Report of the Secretary of the Interior to 31 August 1902," RPC, 1902, in *ARSW, 1902*, 273, quoted in Ileto, "Cholera," 127.

31. For all of the issues surrounding the cholera cases among the soldiers, see Maj. Charles A. Woodruff, "Sanitary Report on Cholera Conditions," Aug. 12, 1902, RG 112/26, 90497/19, USNA; Lt. B.J. Edger, Jr., "Special Report of Cholera Epidemic, May 23–July 18, 1902," RG 112/26, 90497/19/B; Maj. Henry D. Thompson and Lt. James M. Phelan, "Report of Investigations," July 28, 1902, RG 112/26, 90497/14, USNA; C.A. Cattermole, "Report from Pila," Aug. 13, 1902, RG 112/26, 90497/19/V, USNA.

32. For military complaints, see Thompson and Phelan, "Report of Investigations," July 28, 1902, RG 112/26, 90497/19/A, USNA. For illicit movement to Laguna de Bay, see Rhodes to Manila Board of Health, Apr. 27, 1902, RG 112/26, 90497/14, USNA. So too with longer-range movements of people. The maritime quarantine against ships leaving Manila proved almost useless because travelers simply went overland to ports that as yet had no restrictions and embarked from there. See Heiser, "Some Considerations," 91. About the cook, see Woodruff, "Sanitary Report," Aug. 12, 1902, RG 112/26, 90497/19, USNA.

33. For the zones, see May, *Battle*, 243–50, 263–69. For a pamphlet compilation of the various military directives, see M.F. Davis, *Telegraphic Circulars and General Orders Issued by Brigadier-General J. Franklin Bell*, RG 94/AGO/415839, USNA. For the quoted portions of the inspection report, see report of Col. Arthur L. Wagner, Mar. 22, 1902, Joseph B. Foraker Papers, CHS.

34. For Wagner's conclusions and the quoted passage, see report of Wagner, Mar. 22, 1902, Joseph B. Foraker Papers, CHS, 1–7. For the actual situation, see May, *Battle*,

262–69. On conditions in San Pablo, see Maj. M.L. Leepere, "Report from San Pablo," Apr. 14, 1902, RG 112/26, 90497/14, USNA. For the officer's letter home, see William E. Horton to Grenville Dodge, Apr. 17, 1902, Grenville Dodge Papers, vol. 35, "General Correspondence," ISHS. For the epidemic's progress south, see C.F. Kuhn, "Report from Majayjay," June 20, 1902, RG 112/26, 90497/19/K, USNA; Franklin McEvoy, "Report from Lipa," June 24, 1902, RG 112/26, 90497/19/D. For the situation after the zones were abolished, see Maj. Gresham's order, May 5, 1902, ibid., and "Hospital Papers, 1886–1912," box 1, file 4, "Correspondence from Tarlac and Caloocan, Apr. 27–18, 1902," in "Passes File, Surgeons in 2d Sep. Brigade," RG 94/548, USNA.

35. For the rice situation and the attempts to evade the quarantine, see Ileto, "Cholera," 130–31. For the concluding quote, see Edger, "Special Report," RG 112/26, 90497/19/B, PNA.

36. On cremation, see Ileto, "Cholera," 137–38. On the flight, see Edger, "Special Report," RG 112/26, 90497/19/B, PNA. For the mortality figure, see *CPI, 1903*, 3:79, 82.

37. For the change in policy, see Davis, "AG to all station commands," May 23, 1902, RG 112/26, 90497/19, USNA. Bell's comment is contained in his Dec. 9, 1902 endorsement to Woodruff, "Sanitary Report," Aug. 12, 1902, RG 112/26, 90497/19, USNA. Although the remark was retrospective, it reflects his consistent attitude toward burning as a weapon against cholera.

38. Most historians today criticize American commanders such as Gens. J. Franklin Bell, Jacob "Howling Jake" Smith, and Adna R. Chaffee for the severity of their military campaigns. The censure seems to me to be richly deserved, and Gen. Hughes can be added to the list. But if America's military adventure was unjust and if war crimes were committed, its representatives were not uniformly or consistently villainous. Gen. Bell, in particular, was not a one-dimensional figure. He was a prototype of those military men who are relentless in war but compassionate once the fight has ended. After directing a harsh pacification campaign in Abra less than a year earlier, he personally solicited donations of money from officers and enlisted men throughout northern Luzon to relieve the suffering of "these helpless people [who] are now suffering the pangs of hunger and are on the verge of starvation as a consequence of circumstances over which they had no control" (July 29, 1901 telegram from Bell in Immanuel Warrington Diary, vol. 1, Aug. 1, 1901, HSP). He began his personal relief effort when the civil government deemed it "impracticable," as he put it bitterly, to furnish aid to the people. Bell's military tactics have not been universally condemned. For strong support, see Gates, *Schoolbooks*, 260–63, and for qualified support, see Linn, *U.S. Army*, 159–60. About the fire in Dagupan, see *Manila Times*, July 9, 1902, cited in Ileto, "Cholera," 147.

39. Bell's description appears in his endorsement to Woodruff, "Sanitary Report," July 18, 1902, RG 112/26, 90497/19, USNA.

40. For the course of events in Binan, see Edger, "Special Report," RG 112/26, 90497/19/B, USNA.

41. Balayan, Batangas, *MHP* 624, 1–22, RG 94/547, USNA, and Woodruff, "Sanitary Report," 3–4, Aug. 12, 1902, RG 112/26, 90497/19, USNA. On overall mortality statistics for Binan and Balayan, see *CPI, 1903*, 3:141, 146.

42. For one person's experience of the epidemic in Capiz City, see Fee, *Woman's Impressions*, 221–31. Regarding the vigil and preparations in a Cebu municipality, see diary of Capt. George H. Caulkins, Argao, Cebu, *MHP* 600, RG 94/547, USNA. For the rumors, see Pontevedra, Negros Occidental, Bacolod, HDP, 8:140, PNA, and Sibalom, Antique, HDP, 7:1, PNL. About burning and flight, see Maj. Jos. M. Heller, "Report from San Felipe Neri, Rizal," May 3, 1902, "Hospital Papers, 1886–1912," box 1, file 4,

RG 94/548, USNA. The remembrances are in Lipata, Antique, HDP, 7:1, PNA, and Banquerohan, Albay, HDP, 3:4, PNL. The proportion of cholera mortality has been calculated from death totals in *CPI, 1903*, 3:139, 494. Parish records were either non-existent or fragmentary in 1902, so the census enumerators in 1903 had no means of accurately counting the number of cholera deaths. We can be sure that the mortality was worse than the official figures suggest. American medical officers reported case-fatality rates as high as 80 percent in northern Luzon. I have derived that figure from data contained in the daily statistics in "Cholera Reports, 1902," Division of the Philippines, Dept N. Phil., Hqtrs 3d Brig., RG 395/2377, box 1, USNA.

43. For the experience in Salcedo, see Lt. Nolan V. Ellis to adjutant general, 6 Sep. Brig., July 30, 1902, RG 395/2571, box 3, USNA.

Conclusion

1. Quoted in Dubos, *Mirage*, 11.

2. Guevedo, "Memoria agrícola," 125–30, A, PNA. I have calculated the demographic statistics from data in *CPI, 1903*, 3:12–17.

3. Dubos, *Mirage*, 1, 2, 11, 27, 29, 49, 89, 93; Gueveda, *Memoria agrícola*, 128–29; *CPI, 1903*, 3:83, 148, 503.

4. Morse, "AIDS," 38; McNeill, "Patterns," 36.

5. Andaya, "Political Development," 453; Buttinger, *Vietnam*, 1:36.

6. For the remarks about the eradication campaign in South Asia, see Greenough, "Intimidation," 24–25. About the causal model, see Susser, *Causal Thinking*, 46–47. In arguing that the usual formulation of necessary and sufficient cause restricts conceptualization of causal models, Susser points out that most determinants likely to be discovered in epidemiology are in the category of causes that are neither necessary nor sufficent but that are able to contribute to a disease outcome. In those cases, independent variable (cause) X may or may not be present when dependent variable (manifestation) Y is present. If X is present with Y, some additional factor must also be present. Causality is ultimately too complex to describe adequately, but it should be kept in mind that the two colonial campaigns (and every other determinant that can be identified in this study) were themselves as much effect as cause and were embedded in their own causal processes—the system of imperial rivalries, for one. Susser's ideas also encourage the historian to think about whether Buttinger's dictum might be expanded to accommodate the possibility that good effects might sometimes have been the fruit of colonial action, whether malevolent or well-intentioned. Put another way, the issue is whether some colonial interventions were less bad than others. The American smallpox program was indeed less bad than its cholera campaign, and we can be confident that the hundreds of thousands of Filipinos whose lives were ultimately saved as a result of vaccination would agree. The wholesale quarantines, detentions, and houseburnings that were mandated to fight cholera outraged a deeply embedded cultural belief system regarding health and disease. They also terrorized the people, causing panic and flight, which spread the contagion. By contrast, the intervention against smallpox engendered no such terror and resistance, not only because its methods were less severe but because no serious cultural insult was involved. In addition, however unwelcome vaccination might have been, it had been a familiar and at least partially effective procedure for a century. Consequences are too indirect and various to allow an accurate accounting, and in addition to the points Greenough makes it can certainly be argued that one adverse outcome of the smallpox program was that its very success simply increased the power of the

colonial state to accomplish other more pernicious objectives. The fact remains, however, that intervention against cholera killed people while intervention against smallpox
saved lives. And for what it is worth, the Historical Data Papers do not indicate that any
trace of resentment against compulsory vaccination remained in the Filipino historical
memory a half-century later.

7. Ross, *Prevention*, xi, 209; Enzenberger, "Critique," 17; Tesh, *Hidden Arguments*,
66.

8. Susser, *Causal Thinking*, 49.

9. Col. George W. Adair, "Autobiographical Sketches," MS/C/44, 29, NLM.

BIBLIOGRAPHY

ARCHIVES AND MANUSCRIPT COLLECTIONS

Archivo de la Provincia del Santísimo Rosario, Quezon City

Francisco Antolín, "Discurso sobre el gentio y población de esta Misión de Ituy y Paniquí," *Tercera Duda: si los infieles reducidos a pueblos formados enferman mas presto y mueron muchos,* c. 1789, M.S., Sección, "Cagayán," (Relaciones).

Bentley Historical Library, University of Michigan, Ann Arbor, Michigan

James Alfred Leroy Papers

Cincinnati Historical Society, Cincinnati, Ohio

Joseph B. Foraker Papers
Arthur Valentiner Papers

East Carolina Manuscript Collection, J.Y. Joiner Library, East Carolina University, Greenville, North Carolina

Alexander B. Coxe, Sr. Papers

Genealogical Library of the Church of Jesus Christ of Latter-day Saints, Salt Lake City, Utah

"Entierros, 1881–1909," Mogpog, Marinduque

Harlan Hatcher Graduate Library, University of Michigan, Ann Arbor, Michigan

Dean C. Worcester Philippine Collection
Michigan Historical Collections
Russell B. McPeak Papers

Historical Society of Pennsylvania, Philadelphia, Pennsylvania

Immanuel H. Warrington Diary
Herbert Welsh Papers

Iowa State Historical Society

Grenville Dodge Papers

Library of Congress, Washington, D.C.

Elihu Root Papers
Moorfield Storey Papers

Lilly Library, University of Indiana, Bloomington, Indiana

Charles W. Fairbank Papers

Massachusetts Historical Society

Henry Cabot Lodge Papers

National Library of Medicine, Bethesda, Maryland

United States Surgeon General's Office: Autobiographical Sketches of Medical Officers

William R. Perkins Library, Duke University, Durham, North Carolina

Harry L. and Mary K. Dalton Collection
Bedinger-Dandridge Family Papers

Philippine National Archives, Manila

Agronómicas
Aranceles
Calamidades públicas
Cólera
Colonias agrícolas
Langostas
Memorias
Memorias médicas
Prostitución
Sanidad

Philippine National Library, Manila

Historical Data Papers

Rutherford B. Hayes Library, Fremont, Ohio

Robert Dexter Carter Papers
J.T. Dickman Papers
Jay Johnson Morrow Papers

St. Andrews Theological Seminary, Quezon City

Guillermo Galvey Diaries

Siouxland Heritage Museums, Sioux Falls, South Dakota

Richard F. Pettigrew Papers

Southern History Collection, University of North Carolina Library, Chapel Hill, North Carolina

B.S. Johnson Papers

United States Army Library, Washington, D.C.

United States Army Military History Institute, United States Army War College, Carlisle Barracks, Carlisle, Pennsylvania

Spanish-American War Survey

United States National Archives, Washington, D.C.

Record Group 94. Records of the Adjutant-General's Office
Record Group 112. Records of the Surgeon-General's Office
Record Group 350. Records of the Bureau of Insular Affairs
Record Group 395. Records of United States Army Overseas Operations and Commands

University of Colorado Library, Boulder, Colorado

Arthur C. Johnson Papers

University of Virginia Library, Charlottesville, Virginia

Abbie Farwell Brown Papers

Washington National Records Center, Suitland, Maryland

Record Group 153. Records of the Judge Advocate General's Office

NEWSPAPERS AND PERIODICALS

Gaceta de Manila, April 29, 1894
Grand Rapids (Michigan) Evening Press, February 28, 1900
La política de España en Filipinas, 1891–1894
Manila Times, 1899–1902
Religious Telescope, March 12, 1902
Revista de Filipinas, 1876

ARTICLES, BOOKS, DISSERTATIONS, GOVERNMENT DOCUMENTS,
UNPUBLISHED PAPERS

Adas, Michael. *The Burma Delta: Economic Development and Social Change on an Asian Rice Frontier*. Madison, Wis., 1974.
Affairs in the Philippine Islands: Hearings before the Committee on the Philippines of the United States Senate. 3 vols. 57th Cong., 1st sess., 1902, S. Doc. 331.
Aganduru Moriz, Rodrigo de. "Historia general de las Islas accidentales a la Asia adyacentes llamadas Philippinas." In *Colección de documentos ineditos para la historia de España*. Madrid, 1882.
Alba y Martín, D.R. *Memoria sobre el cólera morbo asiático con ligeras nociones sobre la etiología de esta enfermedad*. Madrid, 1884.
Amigos del país. *Guía de forasteros en las Islas Filipinas*. Manila, 1862–1865.
―――――. *La situación del país, colección de artículos publicados por "La Voz Española."* 2d ed. Manila, 1897.
Andaya, Barbara Watson. "Political Development between the Sixteenth and Eighteenth Centuries." In Vol. I of *Cambridge History of Southeast Asia*, edited by Nicolas Tarling. Cambridge, 1992.
Anderson, Gerald, ed., *Studies in Philippine Church History*. Ithaca, 1969.
Andrews, Justin M., and Alexander D. Langmuir. "The Philosophy of Disease Eradication." *American Journal of Public Health* 53 (1963): 1–6.
Andrews, Vernon L. "Infantile Beriberi." *Philippine Journal of Science* 7 (1912): 67–90.
Annual Report of the Secretary of War, 1899. 56th Cong., 1st sess., 1899. H. Doc. 2.
Annual Report of the Secretary of War, 1900. 56th Cong., 2d sess., 1900. H. Doc. 2.
Annual Report of the Secretary of War, 1902. 57th Cong., 2d sess., 1902. H. Doc. 2.
Annual Report of the Secretary of War, 1903. 58th Cong., 2d sess., 1903. H. Doc. 2.
Annual Report of the Secretary of War, 1907. 60th Cong., 1st sess., 1907. H. Doc. 2.
Antonovsky, Anton. *Unravelling the Mystery of Health: How People Manage Stress and Stay Well*. San Francisco, 1987.
Aron, Hans. "Diet and Nutrition of the Filipino People." *Philippine Journal of Science* 4 (1909): 198–202.

Ayerbe, Marqués de. *Sitio y conquista de Manila por los Ingleses en 1762*. Zaragosa, 1897.

Azcarraga y Palmero, Manuel. *La libertad de comercio en las islas Filipinas*. Madrid, 1871.

Baisis, F.E. "Notes on Philippine Mosquitos. XVII. The House-Frequenting Habit of Philippine *Flavirostris*." In *Proceedings of the Eighth Pacific Science Conference*. Vol. 6A. Quezon City, 1960.

Baker, C. "Economic Reorganization and the Slump in South and Southeast Asia." *Comparative Studies in Social and Economic History* 22 (1981): 325–49.

Banister, W.B. "The Military Surgeon and the Civilian Practitioner." *Philippine Journal of Science* 17 (1920): 11–18.

Bankoff, Greg. "Big Fish in Small Ponds: The Exercise of Power in a Nineteenth-Century Philippine Municipality." *Modern Asian Studies* 26 (1992): 679–700.

———. "Deportation and the Prison Colony of San Ramon, 1870–1898," *Philippine Studies* 39 (1991): 443–57.

———."Inside the Courtroom: Judicial Procedure in Nineteenth-Century Philippines." *Philippine Studies* 41 (1993): 287–304.

———."Refining Criminality: Gambling and Financial Expediency in the Colonial Philippines, 1764–1898." *Journal of Southeast Asian Studies* 22 (1991): 267–81.

———."Servant-Master Conflicts in Manila in the Late Nineteenth Century." *Philippine Studies* 40 (1992): 281–301.

Bantug, Jose P. *A Short History of Medicine in the Philippines during the Spanish Regime, 1565–1898*. Manila, 1953.

Barrett, James T. *Textbook of Immunology: An Introduction to Immunochemistry and Immunobiology*. 3d ed. St. Louis, 1978.

Bartlett, Maurice S. "Measles Periodicity and Community Size." *Journal of the Royal Statistical Society* 120 (1957): 48–70.

Behar, M. "A Deadly Combination." *World Health* (February–March 1974): 29.

Bennett, George. "On the Epidemic Catarrh, or Influenza, Which Prevailed at Manila (Island of Luconia) during the Month of September 1830." *The London Medical Gazette* 8 (1831): 522–26.

Bernad, Miguel A. "Father Ducos and the Muslim Wars: 1752–1759." *Philippine Studies* 16 (1968): 690–728.

Biggar, W.D. "Analysis and Treatment of Immunodeficiency Diseases." In *Infection in the Compromised Host*, edited by James C. Allen. Baltimore, 1976.

Bispham, William N. *Malaria: Its Diagnosis, Treatment and Prophylaxis*. Baltimore, 1944.

Black, Francis L. "Measles Endemicity in Insular Populations: Critical Community Size and Its Evolutionary Implication." *Journal of Theoretical Biology* 11 (1966): 207–11.

Black, Robert H. "The Epidemiology of Malaria in the Southwest Pacific: Changes Associated with Increasing European Contact." *Oceania* 27 (1956): 136.

Blair, Emma H., and James A. Robertson, eds. *The Philippine Islands, 1493–1893*. 55 vols. Cleveland, 1903–7.

Blunt, J.Y. Mason. *An American Officer's Philippine Studies*. Manila, 1912.

Boomgaard, Peter. *Children of the Colonial State*. Amsterdam, 1989.

Bowman, Fred D. "The Incidence and Complications of Malaria in the Philippines with Special Reference to Its Treatment with Arsenophenylglycin." *Philippine Journal of Science* 5 (1910): 291–302.

Bowring, John. *A Visit to the Philippine Islands*. London, 1859.

Boyd, Mark F. "An Historical Sketch of the Prevalence of Malaria in North America." *American Journal of Tropical Medicine* 21 (1941): 226–38.

Boynton, William Hutchins. "Rinderpest, with Special Reference to Its Control by a New Method of Prophylactic Treatment." *Philippine Journal of Science* 36 (1928): 1–35.

Brachman, Philip S. "Principles and Methods." In *Principles and Practices of Infectious Diseases*, 3d ed., edited by Gerald L. Mandell, R. Gordon Douglass, Jr., and John E. Bennett. New York, 1990.

———. "Transmission and Principles of Control." In *Principles and Practices of Infectious Disease*, 3d ed., edited by Gerald L. Mandell, R. Gordon Douglass, Jr., and John E. Bennett. New York, 1990.

Brandt, Allan M. "AIDS and Metaphor: Toward the Social Meaning of Epidemic Disease." In *In Time of Plague: The History and Social Consequences of Lethal Epidemic Disease*, edited by Adrian Mack. New York, 1991.

Bray, Francesca. *The Rice Economies: Technology and Development in Asian Societies*. Oxford, 1986.

Brillantes, Concha. "The Disease-Carrier Problem in the Philippine Islands." *Philippine Journal of Science* 17 (1920): 110.

Bruce-Chwatt, L.J. "Quantitative Epidemiology of Tropical Diseases." In *Dynamics of Tropical Disease: The Late George Macdonald*, edited by L.J. Bruce-Chwatt and V.J. Glanville. London, 1973.

Bruce-Chwatt, L.J., and V.J. Glanville, eds. *Dynamics of Tropical Disease: The Late George Macdonald*. London, 1973.

Burgess, Perry. *Who Walk Alone*. New York, 1940.

Burnet, F.M. *Biological Aspects of Infectious Diseases*. Cambridge, 1940.

Buttinger, Joseph. *Vietnam: A Dragon Embattled*. 2 vols. New York, 1967.

Caasi, Priscilla I., Zenaida G. Luna, and Gloria A. Camcam. "Studies on the Nutrient Requirement of Filipinos: I. Thiamine Requirements as Estimated from Urinary Thiamine Excretion of Ten Adult Filipinos on Controlled Intake." *Philippine Journal of Science* 94 (1965): 23–42.

Calvert, W.J. "Record of Parasitic Infections in the Philippines." *Boston Medical Survey Journal* 145 (1903): 484–85.

Census of the Philippine Islands, 1903. 4 vols. Washington, D.C., 1905.

Census of the Philippine Islands, 1918. 4 vols., Manila, 1921.

Chalmers, Margaret I. "Nutrition." In *The Husbandry and Health of the Domestic Buffalo*, edited by R. Ross Cockrill. Rome, 1974.

Chamberlain, Weston P. "A Statistical Study of Uncinariasis among White Men in the Philippines." *Philippine Journal of Science* 5 (1910): 249–66.

———. "Typhoid Fever in the Philippine Islands." *Philippine Journal of Science* 6 (1911): 299–334.

Chamberlain, Weston P., H.D. Bloomberg, and E.D. Kilbourne. "Examinations of Stools and Blood among the Igorots of Baguio, P.I." *Philippine Journal of Science* 5 (1910): 505–14.

Chamberlin, Frederick. *The Philippine Problem*. Boston, 1913.

Chandler, Asa C., and Clark P. Reed. *Introduction to Parasitology*. 10th ed. New York, 1962.

Cheng Siok-Hwa. *The Rice Industry of Burma: 1852–1940*. Kuala Lumpur, 1968.

Christie, A.B. *Infectious Diseases: Epidemiology and Clinical Practice*. Edinburgh, 1974.

Cipolla, Carlo M. *The Economic History of World Population*. Middlesex, England, 1979.

Clark, Victor S. *Labor Conditions in the Philippines*. Bulletin of the Bureau of Labor, no. 108. Washington, D.C., 1905.

Cliff, Andrew D., and Peter Haggett. *Atlas of Disease Distributions: Analytic Approaches to Epidemiological Data*. Oxford, 1988.

———. "Island Epidemics." *Scientific American*, June 1984, 138–47.

———. *The Spread of Measles in Fiji and the Pacific: Spatial Components in the Transmission of Epidemics through Island Communities*. Canberra, 1985.

Cliff, Andrew D., Peter Haggett, J.K. Ord, and G.R. Versey. *Spatial Diffusion: An Historical Geography of Epidemics in an Island Community*. Cambridge, 1981.

Clifford, James. *The Predicament of Culture: Twentieth-Century Ethnography, Literature, and Art*. Cambridge, 1988.

Cockrill, R. Ross. "Aspects of Disease." In *The Husbandry and Health of the Domestic Buffalo*, edited by R. Ross Cockrill. Rome, 1974.

Coclanis, Peter A. "Distant Thunder: The Creation of a World Market in Rice and the Transformations It Wrought." *American Historical Review* 98 (1993): 1050–78.

———."Southeast Asia's Incorporation into the World Rice Market: A Revisionist View." *Journal of Southeast Asian Studies* 24 (1993): 251–67.

Colección de documentos ineditos para la historia de España. Madrid, 1882.

Colín, P. Francisco. *Labor Evangélica de los Obreros de la Compañía de Jesús en las Islas de Filipinas*. 3 vols. Barcelona, 1900.

Coller, Richard W. *Barrio Gacao: A Study of Village Ecology and the Schistosomiasis Problem*. Quezon City, 1960.

Coquerel, Albert. *Paddys et riz de Cochinchine*. Lyon, 1911.

Corpuz, Onofre D. *Bureaucracy in the Philippines*. Quezon City, 1957.

———. *The Roots of the Filipino Nation*. 2 vols. Quezon City, 1989.

Cosmas, Graham A. *An Army for Empire*. Columbia, 1971.

Cowan, C.D., ed. *The Economic Development of South-East Asia: Studies in Economic History and Political Economy*. London, 1964.

Craig, Austin, and Conrado Benitez. *Philippine Progress Prior to 1898*. Manila, 1916.

Craig, Charles F. "Observations upon Malaria: Latent Infection in Natives of the Philippine Islands—Intracorpuscular Conjugation." *Philippine Journal of Science* 1 (1905): 523–31.

Crosby, Alfred W. *The Columbian Exchange: Biological and Cultural Consequences of 1492*. Westport, Conn. 1972.

Crowell, B.C., and R.W. Hammack. "Intestinal Parasites Encountered in Five Hundred Autopsies, with Report of Cases." *Philippine Journal of Science* 8 (1913): 157–74.

Cruikshank, Bruce. "Continuity and Change in the Economic and Administrative History of Nineteenth Century Samar." In *Philippine Social History: Global Trade and Local Transformations*, edited by Alfred W. McCoy and Ed. C. de Jesus. Quezon City, 1982.

———. *Samar: 1768–1898*. Manila, 1985.

Cullinane, Michael. "Accounting for Souls." In *Philippine Historical Demography: Sources and Applications*, edited by Michael Cullinane and Peter Xenos. Forthcoming.

———. "The Changing Nature of the Cebu Urban Elite in the Nineteenth Century." In *Philippine Social History: Global Trade and Local Transformations*, edited by Alfred W. McCoy and Ed. C. de Jesus. Quezon City, 1982.

Cushner, Nicholas P. "Landed Estates in the Colonial Philippines: Their Origins and Social Consequence." Paper delivered to the Association for Asian Studies, March 1973.

D.J.M.B. *Principios de vacunación para el uso de los vacunadores de las provincias de las Islas Filipinas*. Manila, 1838.

Dammin, Gustave J. Introduction to "Diseases Produced by Worms." In *Principles of Internal Medicine*, 4th ed., edited by T.R. Harrison et al. New York, 1962.

Darby, William J. "Thiamine Deficiency (Beriberi)." In *Principles of Internal Medicine*, 4th ed., edited by T.R. Harrison et al. New York, 1962.

Dawson, Marc H. "Smallpox in Kenya." *Social Science and Medicine* 13B (1979): 245–500.

De Bevoise, Ken. "The Compromised Host: The Epidemiological Context of the Philippine-American War." Ph.D. diss., University of Oregon, 1986.

———. Review of *Amang*, by Carlos Quirino. *Pilipinas* 7 (1986): 119–21.

———. "Until God Knows When: Smallpox in the Late-Colonial Philippines." *Pacific Historical Review* 59 (1990): 149–85.

De Guzman, Ma. Patrocinio E., et al. "A Study of the Energy Expenditure, Dietary Intake, and Pattern of Daily Activity among Various Occupational Groups: I. Laguna Rice Farmers." *Philippine Journal of Science* 103 (1974): 53–65.

De Jesus, Ed. C. *The Tobacco Monopoly in the Philippines: Bureaucratic Enterprise and Social Change, 1766–1880*. Quezon City, 1980.

De la Costa, H. *Readings in Philippine History*. Manila, 1965.

De la Gironiere, Paul P. *Twenty Years in the Philippines*. New York, 1854.

Del Busto, Manuel. *Informe sobre la inmigración de colonos europeos y braceros asiáticos en estas islas*. Manila, 1884.

Delfinado, M.D., G.B. Viado, and C.T. Coronel. "A Checklist of Philippine Mosquitos with a Larval Key to Genera (Diptera, Culicidae)." *Philippine Journal of Science* 91 (1962): 433–58.

Del Pan, José Felipe. *Las Islas Filipinas. Progresos en 70 años*. Manila, 1878.

———. *La Población de Filipinas*. Manila, 1883.

Del Rosario, S.V., and L. Lopez Rizal. *Some Epidemiological Features of Cholera in the Philippines*. Bulletin of the Philippine Health Service, no. 25. Manila, 1922.

Dery, Luis Camara. *From Ibalon to Sorgoson: A Historical Survey of Sorgoson Province to 1905*. Quezon City, 1991.

———. "Prostitution in Colonial Manila." *Philippine Studies* 39 (1991): 475–89.

Díaz-Trechuelo Spínola, Lourdes. "The Economic Development of the Philippines in the Second Half of the Eighteenth Century," *Philippine Studies* 11 (1963), 12 (1964), 13 (1965), and 14 (1966).

"Documents Communicated by the Central Board of Health, London, Relative to the Treatment of Cholera by the Copious Injection of Aqueous and Saline Fluid into the Veins." *Lancet* 2 (1832): 274.

Doeppers, Daniel Frederick. "Hispanic Influences on Demographic Patterns in the Central Plain of Luzon, 1565–1780." *University of Manila Journal of East Asiatic Studies* 12 (1968): 11–96.

———. "Metropolitan Manila in the Great Depression: Crisis for Whom?" *The Journal of Asian Studies* 50 (1991): 511–35.

———. "Migration, Urban Structure, and Labor Market 'Conspiracies': Metropolitan Manila, 1893–1903." In *Philippine Historical Demography: Sources and Applications* edited by Michael Cullinane and Peter Xenos. Forthcoming.

Dougherty, Charles. "Medical Industry Thrives, Health Care Fails." *Science for the People* (March/April 1981), 16–21.

Dubos, René. *Mirage of Health: Utopias, Progress, and Biological Change*. New Brunswick, New Jersey, 1959.

Duncan, David F. *Epidemiology: Basis for Disease Prevention and Health Promotion*. New York, 1988.

Dunn, Frederick L. "Social Determinants in Tropical Disease." In *Tropical and Geographical Medicine*, edited by Kenneth S. Warren and Adel A.F. Mahmoud. New York, 1984.

Echaúz, Robustiano. *Sketches of the Island of Negros*. Trans. Donn V. Hart. Athens, Ohio, 1978.

"Editorial: Discussion of Doctor McLaughlin's Paper on 'The Suppression of a Cholera Epidemic in Manila.'" *Philippine Journal of Science* 4 (1909): 59–68.

Elías de Molíns, D. José. *Importación temporal de los arroces de la India y Filipinas*. Barcelona, 1883.

Enzenberger, Hans Magnus. "A Critique of Political Ecology." *New Left Review* 84 (1974): 3–31.

Espejo, Zoilo. *Cartilla de agricultura Filipina*. Manila, 1870.

Eusebio, Emerina C., and Jose G. Palad. "Vitamin A Content of Philippine Foods." *Philippine Journal of Science* 94 (1966): 199–207.

Fast, Jonathan, and Jim Richardson. *Roots of Dependency: Political and Economic Revolution in the Nineteenth Century Philippines*. Quezon City, 1979.

Faust, Ernest Carroll. "Malaria Incidence in North America." In Vol. 1 of *Malariology*, edited by Mark F. Boyd. Philadelphia, 1949.

Faust, Ernest Carroll, and Paul Farr Russell. *Craig and Faust's Clinical Parasitology*. 6th ed. Philadelphia, 1957.

Feachem, Richard G. "Environmental Aspects of Cholera Epidemiology. III. Transmission and Control." *Tropical Disease Bulletin* 79 (1982): 1–47.

Feced, Pablo. "Beneficencia y Sanidad." In *La política de España en Filipinas* 8 (1891): 90–91.

Fee, Mary H. *A Woman's Impressions of the Philippines*. Chicago, 1910.

Fegan, Brian. "The Social History of a Central Luzon Barrio." In *Philippine Social History: Global Trade and Local Transformations*, edited by Alfred W. McCoy and Ed. C. de Jesus. Quezon City, 1982.

Fehily, Lydia. "Human-Milk Intoxication Due to B_1 Avitaminosis." *British Medical Journal* 2 (1944): 590–91.

Fenner, Bruce Leonard. *Cebu under the Spanish Flag, 1521–1896: An Economic-Social History*. Cebu City, 1985.

Fenner, Frank. "Infectious Disease and Social Change." *The Medical Journal of Australia* 1 (1971): 1043–47.

————. "Smallpox in Southeast Asia." *Crossroads: An Interdisciplinary Journal of Southeast Asian Studies* 3 (1987): 34.

Fenner, Frank, et al. *Smallpox and Its Eradication*. Geneva, 1988.

Fernandez Checa, José. "Memoria presentada al General Norzagaray en Setiembre de 1859." *Revista de Filipinas* 2 (1876): 121–24.

Fernandez Frías, Evaristo. *Memoria historico-estadística sobre la enseñanza secundaria y superior en Filipinas*. Manila, 1883.

Fiebig, M. "Beriberi Onder de Dessabevolking in Nederlandsch-Indie." *Geneeskundig tijdschrift voor Nederlandsch-Indie* 30 (1890): 437–39.

FitzGerald, Frances. *Fire in the Lake: The Vietnamese and the Americans in Vietnam*. New York, 1972.

Foreman, John. *The Philippine Islands*. New York, 1899.

Fox, R.H. "A Study of Energy Expenditure of Africans Engaged in Various Rural Activities." Ph.D. diss., University of London, 1953.

Francia y Ponce de Leon, Benito. *Unas palabras sobre el cólera en Filipinas. Epidemia de 1888–1889.* Manila, 1889.

García Gonzalez, Antonio F. *El gobierno en Filipinas del Ilmo. Sr. Don Fray de Arechederra y Tovar, Obisbo de la Nva. Segovia.* Granada, 1976.

Garrison, Philip E. "The Prevalence and Distribution of the Animal Parasites of Man in the Philippine Islands, with a Consideration of Their Possible Influence upon the Public Health." *Philippine Journal of Science* 3 (1908): 191–210.

Garrison, Philip E., and Rosendo Llamas. "The Intestinal Worms of 385 Filipino Women and Children in Manila." *Philippine Journal of Science* 4 (1909): 185–86.

Gates, John Morgan. *Schoolbooks and Krags: The United States Army and Counterinsurgency in the Philippines.* Chapel Hill, 1989.

Geertz, Clifford. *Agricultural Involution: The Processes of Ecological Change in Indonesia.* Berkeley, 1963.

——. "Thick Description: Toward an Interpretive Theory of Culture." In *Interpretation of Cultures,* Comp. Clifford Geertz. New York, 1973.

——. "Ritual and Social Change: A Javanese Example." In *Interpretation of Cultures,* Comp. Clifford Geertz.

Girdwood, R.H. "Nutritional Anaemias and Small Intestinal Diseases in the Tropics." In *Medicine in the Tropics,* edited by A.W. Woodruff. Edinburgh, 1974.

Goncharov, Ivan. *Voyage of the Frigate "Pallada."* In *Travel Accounts of the Islands.* Manila, 1974.

Gonzalez, Jose Ma. *Labor Evangélica.* Manila, 1946.

Gonzalez Fernandez, Ramon. *Anuario Filipino para 1877.* Manila, 1877.

Gonzalez y Martín, R. *Filipinas y sus inhabitantes. Lo que son y lo que deben ser.* Bejar, Spain, 1896.

Greenough, Paul. "Intimidation, Resistance and Coercion in the Final Stages of the South Asian Smallpox Eradication Campaign, 1973–75." *Social Science and Medicine.* Forthcoming.

Grist, D.H. *Rice.* 6th ed. London, 1986.

Guerrero, Milagros A. "Luzon at War: Contradictions in Philippine Society, 1898–1902." Ph.D. diss., University of Michigan, 1977.

Guthrie, George M., et al. "Water, Waste and Well-Being in the Rural Philippines." *Philippine Quarterly of Society and Culture* 2 (1983): 225–26.

Gutierrez, Perpetuo. "Typhoid Fever in the Philippines." *Philippine Journal of Science* 9 (1914): 367–78.

Hall, H.T.B. *Diseases and Parasites of Livestock in the Tropics.* London, 1977.

Harrison, Gordon. *Mosquitos, Malaria, and Man: A History of the Hostilities since 1880.* New York, 1978.

Health Aspects of Food and Nutrition. 3d ed. Manila, 1979.

Heiser, Victor. *An American Doctor's Odyssey.* New York, 1936.

——. "Some Considerations with Regard to the Cause of the Frequent Reappearance of Cholera in the Philippine Islands, with Statistics Beginning with the Outbreak in 1902 to January 1, 1908." *Philippine Journal of Science* 3 (1908): 95.

——. "Unsolved Health Problems Peculiar to the Philippines." *Philippine Journal of Science* 5 (1910): 171–78.

Heiser, Victor, and Charles N. Lynch. "Vaccination in the Philippines Still Effective. *Journal of the American Medical Association* 74 (1922): 40–41.

Henig, Robin Marantz. *A Dancing Matrix: Science Confronts Emerging Viruses.* New York, 1993.

Herzog, Maximilian. "Studies in Beriberi." *Philippine Journal of Science* 1 (1906): 711–55.

Heyman, Albert. "Chancroid." In *Principles of Internal Medicine*, 4th ed., edited by T.R. Harrison et al. New York, 1962.

Hinz, Erhard. *Human Helminthiases in the Philippines: The Epidemiological and Geo-medical Situation*. Berlin, 1985.

Holmes, King K., Per-Anders Mardh, P. Frederick Sparling, and Paul J. Wiesner. *Sexually Transmitted Diseases*. New York, 1984.

Hopkins, Donald R. *Princes and Peasants: Smallpox in History*. Chicago, 1986.

Huff, W.G. "Bookkeeping Barter, Money, Credit, and Singapore's Rice Trade, 1870–1939." *Explorations in Economic History* 26 (1981): 161–89.

Ileto, Reynaldo C. "Cholera and the Origins of the American Sanitary Order in the Philippines." In *Imperial Medicine and Indigenous Societies*, edited by David Arnold. Manchester, 1988.

————. "Food Crisis During the Revolution." *Kebar Sebaring Sulating Maphilindo* 15 (1985): 101–17.

————. *Magindanao, 1860–1888*. Ithaca, 1971.

————. "Outlines of a Non-linear Emplotment of Philippine History." In *Reflections on Development in Southeast Asia*, edited by Lim Teck Ghee. Singapore, 1988.

————. *Pasyon and Revolution: Popular Movements in the Philippines, 1840–1910*. Quezon City, 1979.

————. "Towards a Local History of the Philippine-American War: The Case of Tiaong, Tayabas (Quezon) Province, 1901–1902." Typescript, 1983.

Infante, Teresita R. *The Woman in Early Philippines and among the Cultural Minorities*. Manila, 1975.

Ingram, James C. *Economic Change in Thailand 1850–1970*. Stanford, 1971.

————. "Thailand's Rice Trade and the Allocation of Resources." In *The Economic Development of South-East Asia: Studies in Economic History and Political Economy*, edited by C.D. Cowan. London, 1964.

Inouye, Katashi, and Eisuke Katsura. "Clinical Signs and Metabolism of Beriberi Patients." In *Review of Japanese Literature on Beriberi and Thiamine*, edited by Norio Shimazono and Eisuke Katsura. Tokyo, 1965.

————. "Diagnosis, Prevention and Therapy of Beriberi." In *Review of Japanese Literature on Beriberi and Thiamine*, edited by Norio Shimazono and Eisuke Katsura. Tokyo, 1965.

————. "Etiology and Pathology of Beriberi." In *Review of Japanese Literature on Beriberi and Thiamine*, edited by Norio Shimazono and Eisuke Katsura. Tokyo, 1965.

Intengan, Carmen. LL., et al. "Composition of Philippine Foods." Parts 1–5. *Philippine Journal of Science* 82 (1953): 227–52; 83 (1954): 187–216; 84 (1955): 263–73; 84 (1955): 343–63; 85 (1956): 209.

J.B. "Estudio sobre las inundaciones de Pangasinan." *Revista de Filipinas* 1 (1876): 578–82.

J.F. "Estudio forestal acerca de la India Inglesa, Java, y Filipinas." *La política de España en Filipinas* 20 (1891): 238.

————. "Memoria para la Real Sociedad Económica sobre los medios por los cuales puede y debe promoverse el desarrollo de la agricultura del país." *Revista de Filipinas* 1 (1876): 429–61.

————. "Memoria sobre el comercio de maderas en Filipinas." *La política de España en Filipinas* 87 (1894): 154–55.

Jackson, Thomas W. "Sanitary Conditions and Needs in Provincial Towns." *Philippine Journal of Science* 3 (1908): 431–37.

Jagor, Fedor. *Travels in the Philippines*. Manila, 1965.

Jimeno Agius, José. *Memoria sobre el desestanco del tabaco en las Islas Filipinas*. Binondo, 1871.

———. *Población y comercio de Filipinas*. Madrid, 1884.

Jocano, F. Landa. *Folk Medicine in a Philippine Municipality*. Manila, 1973.

Jordana y Morera, Ramon. *Memoria sobre la producción de los montes públicos de Filipinas durante el ano económico de 1874–1875*. Madrid, 1876.

Karnow, Stanley. *In Our Image: America's Empire in the Philippines*. New York, 1989.

Kathirithamby-Wells, J. "The Age of Transition: The Mid-eighteenth to the Early Nineteenth Centuries." In Vol. 1 of *The Cambridge History of Southeast Asia*, edited by Nicolas Tarling. Cambridge, 1992.

Katsura, E., and T. Oiso. "Beriberi." In *Nutrition in Preventive Medicine: The Major Deficiency Syndromes, Epidemiology, and Approaches to Control*, edited by G.H. Beaton and J.M. Bengoa. Geneva, 1976.

Keyser y Muñoz, Antonio de. *Medios que el gobierno y la sociedad económica de amigos del país de Filipinas pueden emplear para obtener el desarrollo de la agricultura en el país*. Manila, 1869.

Kilbourne, E.D. "Food Salts in Relation to Beriberi." *Philippine Journal of Science* 5 (1910): 127–36.

King, W.V. "Three Philippine Anopheles of the *Funestus-Minimus* Subgroup." *Philippine Journal of Science* 48 (1932): 488–521.

Koeniger, M. "Ueber epidemisches Auftreten von Beriberi in Manila 1882/83." *Deutches Archiv für Klinische Medezin* 34 (1884): 419–32.

Kollman, [Dr.] "Die Grippe in Java in Jahre 1831." *Wissenschaftliche Annalen de gesamten Heilkunde* 26 (1833): 389–98.

Kosa, John, Aaron Antonovsky, and Irving Kenneth Zola. *Poverty and Health: A Sociological Analysis*. Cambridge, Mass., 1969.

Larkin, John. "The Place of Local History in Philippine Historiography." *Journal of Southeast Asian History* 8 (1967): 306–17.

———. *Sugar and the Origins of Modern Philippine Society*. Berkeley, 1993.

Leech, Charles N., Benjamin Schwartz, and Florence Dixon Leech. "Hookworm Disease: A Clinical Entity in the Philippine Islands." *Philippine Journal of Science* 23 (1923): 105–22.

Legarda, Benito, Jr. "American Entrepreneurs in the Nineteenth Century Philippines." *Explorations in Entrepreneurial History* 9 (1957): 142–59.

———. "Foreign Trade, Economic Change and Entrepreneurship in the Nineteenth Century Philippines." Ph.D. Diss., Harvard University, 1955.

Le Gentil, Guillaume. *A Voyage to the Indian Seas*. Manila, 1964.

Legge, J.D. "The Writing of Southeast Asian History." In Vol. 1 of *The Cambridge History of Southeast Asia*, edited by Nicolas Tarling. Cambridge, 1992.

Leitz, Paul S., ed. *Calendar of Philippine Documents in the Ayre Collection of the Newberry Library*. Chicago, 1956.

Lieban, Richard. "Qualification for Folk Medical Practice in Sibulan, Negros Oriental, Philippines." *Philippine Journal of Science* 91 (1962): 511–21.

Lilienfeld, Abraham M., and David E. Lilienfeld. *Foundations of Epidemiology*. 2d ed. New York, 1973.

Linn, Brian McAllister. *The U.S. Army and Counterinsurgency in the Philippines*. Chapel Hill, 1989.

Long, John. *Sanitation in the Philippine Islands*. Washington, D.C., 1916.

Lontoc, Aurea V., Olympia N. Gonzalez, and Leogarda B. Dimaunahan. "Folic Acid Content of Some Philippine Foods." *Philippine Journal of Science* 95 (1966): 311–20.

Lopez, Rafael, and Alfonso Felix, Jr., eds. *The Christianization of the Philippines*. Manila, 1965.

Luna, Zenaida G., et al. "Thiaminase in Some Species of Fish, Clams, and Crustaceans in the Philippines." *Philippine Journal of Science* 97 (1968): 145–51.

Macaraig, Seraphim E. *Social Problems*. Manila, 1929.

MacClintock, Samuel. "Around the Island of Cebu on Horseback." *American Journal of Sociology* 8 (1903): 433–41.

McCoy, Alfred W. "Introduction." In *Philippine Social History: Global Trade and Local Transformations*, edited by Alfred W. McCoy and Ed. C. de Jesus. Quezon City, 1982.

————. "A Queen Dies Slowly: The Rise and Decline of Iloilo City." In *Philippine Social History: Global Trade and Local Transformations*, edited by Alfred W. McCoy and Ed. C. de Jesus. Quezon City, 1982.

Macdonald, George. "The Analysis of Malaria Epidemics." In *Dynamics of Tropical Disease: The Late George Macdonald*, edited by L.J. Bruce-Chwatt and V.J. Glanville. London, 1973.

————. "Community Aspects of Immunity to Malaria." In *Dynamics of Tropical Disease: The Late George Macdonald*, edited by Bruce-Chwatt and V.J. Glanville. London, 1973.

————. "The Dynamics of Helminth Infections, with Special Reference to Schistosomes." *Transactions of the Royal Society of Tropical Medicine and Hygiene* 59 (1965): 489–506.

————. *The Epidemiology and Control of Malaria*. London, 1957.

Maceda, Generosa. "The Remontados of Rizal Province." *Philippine Journal of Science* 64 (1937): 313–21.

McKeown, Thomas. *The Origin of Human Disease*. Oxford, 1988.

McLaughlin, Allan J., and Vernon L. Andrews. "Studies on Infant Mortality." *Philippine Journal of Science* 5 (1910): 149–61.

McLennan, Marshall S. *The Central Luzon Plain: Land and Society on the Inland Frontier*. Quezon City, 1980.

————. "Changing Human Ecology on the Central Luzon Plain." In *Philippine Social History: Global Trade and Local Transformations*, edited by Alfred W. McCoy and Ed. C. de Jesus. Quezon City, 1982.

McNeill, William H. *Plagues and Peoples*. Garden City, 1976.

————. "Patterns of Disease Emergence in History." In *Emerging Viruses*, edited by Stephen S. Morse. New York, 1993.

McVail, J.C. "Smallpox and Vaccination in the Philippines." *British Medical Journal* 1 (1923): 158–62.

Madrigal Llorente, Ana Maria. *A Blending of Cultures: The Batanes 1686–1898*. Manila, 1983.

Maegraith, Brian. *Adams and Maegraith: Clinical Tropical Diseases*. 8th ed. Oxford, 1984.

Magno, Francisco A. "Politics, Elites and Transformation in Malabon." *Philippine Studies* 41 (1993): 204–16.

Mahmoud, Adel A.F. "Schistosomiasis." In *Tropical and Geographical Medicine*, edited by Kenneth S. Warren and Adel A.F. Mahmoud. New York, 1984.

Mallari, Francisco. "Alcalde Versus Friar in Camarines." *Philippine Studies* 40 (1992): 464–79.

_____. "Camarines Towns under Siege." *Philippine Studies* 38 (1990): 453–73.

Mallat de Bassilan, Jean. *Les Philippines: histoire, geographie, moeurs, agriculture, industrie et commerce des colonies espagnoles dans l'Oceanie.* 2 vols. Paris, 1861.

_____. *The Philippines: History, Geography, Customs, Agriculture, Industry and Commerce of the Spanish Colonies in Oceania.* Trans. P. Santillan-Castrence in collaboration with Lina Castrence. Manila, 1983.

Manalang, C. "A Hookworm Campaign in Cebu." *Philippine Journal of Science* 27 (1925): 483–94.

_____. "Malaria Transmission in the Philippines: I. The Natural Vector." *Philippine Journal of History* 45 (1931): 241–50.

Mandell, Gerald L., R. Gordon Douglass, Jr., and John E. Bennett, eds. *Principles and Practices of Infectious Diseases.* 3d ed. New York, 1990.

Manson-Bahr, P.E.C., and F.I.C. Apted. *Manson's Tropical Diseases.* 18th ed. London, 1982.

Manson-Bahr, P.E.C., and D.R. Bell. *Manson's Tropical Diseases.* 19th ed. London, 1987.

Maranon, Joaquin, and Harley Harris Bartlett. "Cinchona Cultivation and the Production of Totaquina in the Philippines." *University of the Philippines Natural and Applied Sciences Bulletin* 7 (1941): 111–87.

Martin, Calvin. *Keepers of the Game: Indian-Animal Relationships and the Fur Trade.* Berkeley, 1978.

Martínez Cuesta, Angel. *History of Negros.* Trans. Alfonso Felix, Jr. and Sor Caritas Sevilla. Manila, 1980.

Martínez de Zúñiga, Joaquín. *Status of the Philippines in 1800.* Trans. Vicente del Carmen. Manila, 1975.

Masur, Henry, and Thomas C. Jones. "Protozoal and Helminthic Infections." In *Infections in the Abnormal Host*, edited by Michael H. Grieco. New York, 1980.

May, Glenn A. *Battle for Batangas: A Philippine Province at War.* New Haven, 1991.

_____. "150,000 Missing Filipinos: A Demographic Crisis in Batangas, 1887–1903." *Annales de Démographie Historique* (1985): 215–43.

_____. "The Zones of Batangas." *Philippine Studies* 29 (1981): 89–103.

Medical and Surgical History of the War of the Rebellion. 2 vols. Washington, D.C., 1888.

Mendoza, Jose B., and Benito Abinoja. "Observations on Supposedly Unusual Breeding of the Philippine Malaria Vector." *Philippine Journal of Science* 81 (1951): 53–60.

Mendoza Cortes, Rosario. *Pangasinan, 1801–1900: The Beginnings of Modernization.* Quezon City, 1990.

Meyer, Hans. "The Igorots." In *German Travellers on the Cordillera (1860–1898)*, edited by William Henry Scott. Manila, 1975.

Mieldazis, J.J. "Preferential Breeding Conditions of Anopheles in the Philippine Islands." *Philippine Journal of Science* 41 (1930): 59–64.

Miller, Hugo. *Economic Conditions in the Philippines.* Boston, 1913.

Miller, Louis. "Malaria." In *Tropical and Geographical Medicine*, edited by Kenneth S. Warren and Adel A.F. Mahmoud. New York, 1984.

Miller, Stuart Creighton. *"Benevolent Assimilation": The American Conquest of the Philippines 1899–1903.* New Haven, 1982.

Montero y Vidal, José. *Historia general de Filipinas.* 3 vols. Madrid, 1887–95.

Morgan, Myfanwy, Michael Calnan, and Nick Manning. *Sociological Approaches to Health and Medicine.* London, 1985.

Morse, Stephen S. "AIDS and Beyond: Defining the Rules for Viral Traffic." In *AIDS:*

The Making of a Chronic Disease, edited by Elizabeth Fee and Daniel M. Fox. Berkeley, 1992.

Morse, Stephen S. "Emerging Viruses: Defining the Rules for Viral Traffic." *Perspectives in Biological Medicine* 34 (1991): 387–409.

———. "Examining the Origins of Emerging Viruses." in *Emerging Viruses*, edited by Stephen S. Morse. New York, 1993.

Moura, Jean. *Le Royaume du Cambodge*. Paris, 1883.

Muraskin, William. "Hepatitus B as a Model (and Anti-Model) for AIDS." In *History*, edited by V. Bernidge and P. Strong. Cambridge, 1993.

Murillo Velarde, Pedro. *Historia de la provincia de Philipinas de la Compañía de Jesús*. Manila, 1749.

Musgrave, W.E. "Intestinal Amoebiasis without Diarrhea." *Philippine Journal of Science* 5 (1910): 229–31.

Musgrave, W.E., and Moses T. Clegg. *Amebas: Their Cultivation and Etiological Significance*. Manila, 1904.

Navarro, Eduardo. *Filipinas. Estudio de algunos asuntos de actualidad*. Madrid, 1897.

Neal, Robert A., and Howerde E. Sauberlich. "Thiamin." In *Modern Nutrition in Health and Disease*, 6th ed., edited by Robert W. Goodhart and Maurice E. Shils. Philadelphia, 1980.

Newberne, P.M., and G. Williams. "Nutritional Influences on the Course of Infections." In *Resistance to Infectious Disease*, edited by R.H. Dunlop and H.W. Moon. Saskatoon, 1970.

Nichols, Henry J., and Vernon L. Andrews. "The Treatment of Asiatic Cholera during the Recent Epidemic." *Philippine Journal of Science* 4 (1909): 81–91.

Norse, David. "Nutritional Implications of Resource Policies and Technological Change." In *Nutrition and Development*, edited by Margaret Biswas and Per Pinstrup-Andersen. Oxford, 1985.

Oppenheimer, Gerald M. "In the Eye of the Storm: The Epidemiological Construction of AIDS." In *AIDS: The Making of a Chronic Disease*, edited by Elizabeth Fee and Daniel M. Fox. Berkeley, 1992.

Ortíz de la Tabla Ducasse, Javier. *El Marqués de Ovando Gobernador de Filipinas (1750–1754)*. Sevilla, 1974.

Owen, Norman G. "Abaca in Kabikolan: Prosperity without Progress." In *Philippine Social History: Global Trade and Local Transformations*, edited by Alfred W. McCoy and Ed. C. de Jesus. Quezon City, 1982.

———. "Measuring Mortality in the Nineteenth Century Philippines." In *Death and Disease in Southeast Asia*, edited by Norman G. Owen. Singapore, 1987.

———. "The Paradox of Nineteenth-Century Population Growth in Southeast Asia." *Journal of Southeast Asian Studies* 18 (1987): 45–57.

———. "Philippine Economic Development and American Policy: A Reappraisal." In *Compadre Colonialism: Studies on the Philippines under American Rule*, edited by Norman G. Owen. Ann Arbor, 1971.

———. *Prosperity without Progress: Manila Hemp and Material Life in the Colonial Philippines*. Berkeley, 1984.

———. "The Rice Industry of Mainland Southeast Asia 1850–1914." *Journal of the Siam Society* 109 (1972): 78–143.

———. "A Subsistence Crisis in the Provincial Philippines 1845–1846." *Kinaadman* 8 (1986): 35–46.

———. "Subsistence in the Slump: Agricultural Adjustment in the Provincial Philippines." In *The Economics of Africa and Asia in the Inter-War Depression*, edited by Ian Brown. London, 1989.

Pal, Agaton P. "A Philippine Barrio." *University of Manila Journal of East Asiatic Studies* 5 (1956): 431–32.

_____. *The Resources, Levels of Living, and Aspirations of Rural Households in Negros Oriental*. Quezon City, 1963.

Palanca Gutierrez, Carlos. *Reseña histórica de la expedición de Cochinchina*. Cartagena, 1869.

Patterson, Philip Y. "Infection in the Compromised Host." In *The Biologic and Clinical Basis of Infectious Diseases*, 2d ed., edited by Guy P. Youmans, Philip Y. Paterson, and Herbert M. Sommers. Philadelphia, 1980.

Payne, Philip R. "The Nature of Malnutrition." In *Nutrition and Development*, edited by Margaret Biswas and Per Pinstrup-Andersen. Oxford, 1985.

Pelzer, Karl. *Pioneer Settlement in the Asiatic Tropics: Studies in Land Utilization and Agricultural Colonization in Southeastern Asia*. New York, 1945.

Perez Valdes, Gabino. *Situación económica de Filipinas y medios de mejorarla*. Madrid, 1871.

Petrich, John, and Thomas H. Holmes. "Life Change and Onset of Illness." *Medical Clinics of North America* 61 (1977): 825–38.

Phelan, John Leddy. *The Hispanization of the Philippines: Spanish Aims and Filipino Responses 1565–1700*, Madison, Wis., 1959.

Pin Yathay. *Stay Alive, My Son*. New York, 1989.

Pinstrup-Andersen, Per. "The Impact of Export Crop Production on Human Nutrition." In *Nutrition and Development*, edited by Margaret Biswas and Per Pinstrup-Andersen. Oxford, 1985.

Piot, Peter, and King K. Holmes. "Sexually Transmitted Diseases." In *Tropical and Geographical Medicine*, edited by Kenneth S. Warren and Adel A.F. Mahmoud. New York, 1984.

Pivar, David J. *Purity Crusade: Sexual Morality and Social Control, 1868–1900*. Westport, Conn., 1973.

Proceedings of the Eighth Pacific Scientific Congress of the Pacific Scientific Association. 7 vols. Quezon City, 1960.

Prothero, R. Mansell. *Migrants and Malaria*. London, 1965.

Quarterly Bulletin of the Bureau of Public Works, 3. Manila, 1914.

Quirino, Carlos. *Amang: The Life and Times of Eulogio Rodriguez, Sr*. Quezon City, 1983.

Rabkin, Judith G., and Elmer L. Struening. "Life Events, Stress, and Illness." *Science* 3 (1976): 113–20.

Rajal y Larre, Joaquín. "Memoria de la provincia de Nueva Ecija, en Filipinas." *Boletín de la Sociedad Geográfica de Madrid* 27 (1889): 290–359.

Reed, Walter, V.C. Vaughan, and E.O. Shakespeare. *Report on the Origin and Spread of Typhoid Fever in U.S. Military Camps during the Spanish War of 1898*. Washington, D.C., 1904.

Reglamento para la organización, régimen y servicio de la Guardia civil de las Islas Filipinas. Manila, 1868.

Reid, Anthony. "Economic and Social Change, c. 1400–1800." In Vol. 1 of *The Cambridge History of Southeast Asia*, edited by Nicolas Tarling. Cambridge, 1992.

_____. "The Seventeenth-Century Crisis in Southeast Asia." *Modern Asian Studies* 24 (1990): 639–59.

Report of the Philippine Commission (Schurman) 1900. 4 vols. 56th Cong., 1st sess., 1900. S. Doc. 138.

Report of W.B. Wilcox and L.R. Sargent on Trip through the Island of Luzon, 56th Cong., 1st sess., 1900. S. Doc. 196.

"Rice Distribution in the Philippines and the Tutuban Rice Exchange." *The Philippine Journal of Commerce* 12 (April 1936): 13, 36.

Rissler, R.S., and Liborio Gomez. "The Prevalence of Intestinal Parasites in Rizal and Cavite Provinces and in Cagayan Valley." *Philippine Journal of Science* 5 (1910): 267–76.

Robequain, Charles. *The Economic Development of French Indo-China.* London, 1944.

Robles, Eliodoro. *The Philippines in the Nineteenth Century.* Quezon City, 1969.

Rodríguez Garcia, Vicente. *El gobierno de Don Gaspar Antonio de la Torre y Ayala en las islas Filipinas.* Granada, 1976.

Rodriguez-Solís, Enrique. *Historia de la prostitución en España y América.* 2d ed. Madrid, 1893.

———. *Historia de la prostitución en España y América.* Madrid, 1921.

Rogel Lebres, Manuel. *Lepra en Bisayas.* Manila, 1897.

Rogers, Leonard. "The Prevention and Treatment of Amoebic Abscess of the Liver." *Philippine Journal of Science* 5 (1910): 219–28.

———. "The Treatment of Cholera by Injections of Hypertonic Saline Solutions with a Simple and Rapid Method of Intraabdominal Administration." *Philippine Journal of Science* 4 (1909): 99–106.

Rosenberg, Charles E. *The Cholera Years: The United States in 1832, 1849, and 1866.* Chicago, 1962.

Ross, Sir Ronald. *The Prevention of Malaria.* 2d ed. New York, 1910.

Roth, Dennis M. "Church Lands in the Agrarian History of the Tagalog Region." In *Philippine Social History: Global Trade and Local Transformations,* edited by Alfred W. McCoy and Ed. C. de Jesus. Quezon City, 1982.

Ruediger, E.H. "The Difference in Susceptibility to Cattle Plague Encountered among Cattle and Carabaos." *Philippine Journal of Science* 4 (1909): 425–52.

———. "Observations on Cattle Plague in the Philippines and the Methods Employed in Combating It." *Philippine Journal of Science* 4 (1909): 381–90.

Ruíz de la Escalera y Oraá, Toribio. *El desestanco del tabaco en Filipinas.* Bilbao, 1871.

Russell, Paul F. *Malaria and Culicidae in the Philippine Islands: History and Critical Bibliography, 1898 to 1933.* Manila, 1933.

Russell, Paul F., Luther S. West, Reginald D. Manwell, and George Macdonald. *Practical Malariology.* 2d ed. London, 1963.

St. Clair, Francis. *The Katipunan, or the Rise and Fall of the Filipino Commune.* Manila, 1902.

San Antonio, Juan Francisco de. *The Philippine Chronicles of Fray San Antonio.* Trans. D. Pedro Picornell. Manila, 1977.

Sanciano y Goson, Gregorio. *El progreso de Filipinas. Estudios económicos, administrativos y políticos.* Madrid, 1881.

Sandoval, Gerardo A. "Filipino Attitudes Towards Sexual Relations." *Philippine Studies* 41 (1993): 305–18.

Sandstead, Harold H. "Clinical Manifestations of Certain Classical Deficiency Diseases." In *Modern Nutrition in Health and Disease,* 6th ed., edited by Robert W. Goodhart and Maurice E. Shils. Philadelphia, 1980.

Santayana, Agustín. *La isla de Mindanao, su historia y su estado presente, con algunas reflexiones acerca de su porvenir.* Madrid, 1862.

Sastrón, Manuel. *Batangas y su provincia*. Malabon, Philippines, 1895.

_____. *La insurreccción en Filipinas y guerra hispano-americana en el archipelago*. Madrid, 1901.

Sawyer, Frederic H. *The Inhabitants of the Philippines*. New York, 1900.

Schad, Gerhard A., and John B. Banwell. "Hookworms." In *Tropical and Geographical Medicine*, edited by Kenneth S. Warren and Adel A.F. Mahmoud. New York, 1984.

Schneider, F. "Beriberi." *Geneeskundig tijdschrift voor Nederlandsch-Indie* 23 (1883): 170–204.

Schumacher, John. *Revolutionary Clergy: The Filipino Clergy and the Nationalist Movement 1850–1903*. Quezon City, 1981.

Schurz, William L. *The Manila Galleon*. New York, 1939.

Scott, G.R. *Diagnosis of Rinderpest*. Rome, 1977.

Scott, William Henry. "Boat-Building and Seamanship in Classic Philippine Society." In *Cracks in the Parchment Curtain and Other Essays in Philippine History*, edited by William Henry Scott. Quezon City, 1985.

_____. "The Creation of a Cultural Minority." In *Cracks in the Parchment Curtain and Other Essays in Philippine History*, edited by William Henry Scott. Quezon City, 1985.

_____. "Filipino Class Structure in the Sixteenth Century." In *Cracks in the Parchment Curtain and Other Essays in Philippine History*, edited by William Henry Scott. Quezon City, 1985.

_____. *Filipinos in China before 1500*. Manila, 1989.

_____, *Looking for the Prehistoric Filipino and Other Essays in Philippine History*. Quezon City. Forthcoming.

_____. "Lost Visayan Literature." *Kinaadman* 14 (1992): 26.

_____. "*Oripun* and *Alipin* in the Sixteenth Century Philippines." In *Slavery, Bondage and Dependency in Southeast Asia*, edited by Anthony Reid. New York, 1983.

_____. *Slavery in the Spanish Philippines*. Manila, 1991.

_____. "The Spanish Occupation of the Cordillera in the Nineteenth Century." In *Philippine Social History: Global Trade and Local Transformations*, edited by Alfred W. McCoy and Ed. C. de Jesus. Quezon City, 1982.

Scrimshaw, Nevin S. "Synergistic and Antagonistic Interactions of Nutrition and Infection." *Federation Proceedings* 25 (1968): 1679–81.

Seaman, Louis Livingston. "Native Troops for Our Colonial Possessions." *Journal of the Association of Military Surgeons of the United States* 10 (1910): 237–52.

Sellards, A.W. "Tolerance for Alkalies in Asiatic Cholera." *Philippine Journal of Science* 5 (1910): 363–401.

Semper, Carl. "Trip through the Northern Provinces of the Island of Luzon." In *German Travellers on the Cordillera (1860–1898)*, edited by William Henry Scott. Manila, 1975.

Sexton, William T. *Soldiers in the Sun*. Harrisburg, 1939.

Shuval, H.I. "Public Health Considerations and Excreta Re-use for Agriculture." in *Water, Wastes and Health in Hot Climates*, edited by Richard G. Feachem, Michael McGarry, and Duncan Mara. London, 1977.

Sigson, Adolfo. "La Prestación Personal." *La política de España en Filipinas* 4 (1894): 189–92.

Smith, Michael M. *The "Real Expedición Maritime de la Vacuna" in New Spain and Guatemala*. Philadelphia, 1974.

Smith, Peter C. "Crisis Mortality in the Nineteenth Century Philippines: Data from the Parish Records." *Journal of Asian Studies* 38 (1978): 51–76.

Smith, Peter C., and Shui-Meng Ng. "The Components of Population Change in Nineteenth-Century South-East Asia: Village Data from the Philippines." *Population Studies* 36 (1982): 237–55.

Sontag, Susan. *Illness as Metaphor*. New York, 1979.

Spink, Wesley W. *Infectious Diseases: Prevention and Treatment in the Nineteenth and Twentieth Centuries*. Minneapolis, 1978.

Sternberg, George W. "Report for 1900–1901." *Journal of the Association of Military Surgeons of the United States* 10 (1901): 322–46.

Stewart, Alonzo, *Report to the Secretary of Agriculture regarding Conditions in the Philippine Islands*. 60th Cong., 1st Sess., 1908. S. Doc. 535.

Strong, Richard P., et al. "Medical Survey of the Town of Taytay." *Philippine Journal of Science* 4 (1909): 205–302.

Sturtevant, David R. *Popular Uprisings in the Philippines, 1840–1940*. Ithaca, 1976.

Sullivan, Rodney. "Cholera and Colonialism in the Philippines." In *Disease, Medicine and Empire: Perspectives on Western Medicine and the Experience of European Expansion*, edited by Roy MacLeod and Milton Lewis. London, 1988.

Susser, Mervyn. *Causal Thinking in the Health Sciences: Concepts and Strategies in Epidemiology*. New York, 1973.

Taboulet, Georges. *La Geste Francaise en Indochine*. 2 vols. Paris, 1956.

Tarling, Nicolas. "The Establishment of the Colonial Régimes." In Vol. 2 of *The Cambridge History of Southeast Asia*, edited by Nicolas Tarling. Cambridge, 1992.

Taruc, Luis. *Born of the People*. New York, 1953.

Tate, D.J.M. *The Making of Modern South-East Asia*. 2 vols. Kuala Lumpur, 1979.

Taylor, John R.M. *The Philippine Insurrection against the United States, 1899–1903: A Compilation of Documents with Notes and Introduction*. 5 vols. Pasay City, 1971–73.

Taylor, Norman. *Cinchona in Java: The Story of Quinine*. New York, 1945.

Terami-Wada, Motoe. "The Early Years of the Japanese Community in Manila, 1890–1910." Presented at the Sixth National Conference on Local-National History, Philippine Social Science Council, Diliman, Quezon City, Dec. 11–14, 1984.

Tesh, Sylvia Noble. *Hidden Arguments: Political Ideology and Disease Prevention Policy*. New Brunswick, 1988.

Totanes, Stephen Henry S. "Sorgoson's Principalia and the Policy of Pacification, 1900–1903." *Philippine Studies* 38 (1990): 477–99.

Totman, R., S.E. Reed, and J.W. Craig. "Cognitive Dissonance Stress and Virus-Induced Common Colds." *Journal of Psychosomatic Resistance* 21 (1977): 55–63.

Turshen, Meredeth. *The Political Ecology of Disease in Tanzania*. New Brunswick, 1984.

Un médico aplatanado. "Ligeras consideraciones sobre el reglamento provisional para la propagación y conservación de la vacuna en Filipinas." *La politica de España en Filipinas* 71 (1893): 258–61.

Urbino, Cornelio M. "Control of *Anopheles minimus flavirostris* Ludlow by Residual Spraying Along Stream Banks." *Philippine Journal of Science* 94 (1965): 23–42.

———. "Development of Malaria Control against *Anopheles minimus flavirostris* in the Philippines." In *Proceedings of the Eighth Pacific Science Conference*. Vol. 6A. Quezon City, 1960.

Valyasevi, Aree, and Hamish N. Munro. "Beriberi, Pellagra, and Scurvy." In *Tropical and Geographical Medicine*, edited by Kenneth S. Warren and Adel A.F. Mahmoud. New York, 1984.

Walker, E.L. "A Comparative Study of Healthy People, and in Amoebic Dysentery." *Philippine Journal of Science* 6 (1911): 259–79.

Walker, E.L., and A.W. Sellards. "Experimental Amoebic Dysentery." *Philippine Journal of Science* 8 (1913): 253–331.

Walsh, Julia A. "Estimating the Burden of Illness in the Tropics." In *Tropical and Geographical Medicine*, edited by Kenneth S. Warren and Adel A.F. Mahmoud. New York, 1984.

Ward, T.M. "An Account of Epidemic Catarrh, which Prevailed at Penang, in July and August 1831." *Transactions of the Medical and Physical Society of Calcutta* 6 (1833): 124–36.

War Department, Surgeon General's Office, Circular No. 1, *Report on Epidemic Cholera and Yellow Fever in the Army of the United States during the Year 1867*, Washington, D.C., 1868.

Warren, James Francis. "Prostitution and the Politics of Venereal Disease: Singapore, 1870–98." *Journal of Southeast Asian Studies* 21 (1990): 360–83.

_____. "Slavery and the Impact of External Trade." In *Philippine Social History: Global Trade and Local Transformations*, edited by Alfred W. McCoy and Ed. C. de Jesus. Quezon City, 1982.

_____. *The Sulu Zone 1768–1898*. Singapore, 1981.

Wernstedt, Frederick L., and J. E. Spencer. *The Philippine Island World: A Physical, Cultural, and Regional Geography*. Berkeley, 1967.

Wickberg, Edgar. *The Chinese in Philippine Life, 1850–1898*. New Haven, 1965.

Wilkes, Charles. *Narrative of the United States Exploring Expedition during the Years 1838, 1839, 1840, 1841, 1842*. 5 vols. Philadelphia, 1844.

_____. *Narrative of the U.S. Exploring Expedition*. In *Travel Accounts of the Islands (1832–1858)*. Manila, 1974.

Willets, David G. "Intestinal Helminthiasis in the Philippine Islands as Indicated by Examination of Prisoners upon Admission to Bilibid Prison, Manila, P.I." *Philippine Journal of Science* 9 (1914): 233–40.

_____. "Intestinal Parasitism, Particularly Entamoebiasis, in Patients in the Philippine General Hospital, Manila, P.I." *Philippine Journal of Science* 9 (1914): 81–92.

_____. "A Statistical Study of Intestinal Parasites Found in Cavite Province." *Philippine Journal of Science* 6 (1911): 211–14.

Wolters, Willem G. "Sugar Production in Java and in the Philippines during the Nineteenth Century." *Philippine Studies* 40 (1992): 411–34.

Woodruff, A.W., ed. *Medicine in the Tropics*. Edinburgh, 1974.

World Health Organization. *The Health Aspects of Food and Nutrition*. 3d ed. Manila, 1979.

Youngberg, Stanton. "A Brief History of Rinderpest in the Philippine Islands." *Philippine Agricultural Review* 15 (1922): 205–17.

Zinsser, Hans. *Rats, Lice and History*. Boston, 1935.

abaca, 39, 152. *See also* cash crops
Abra: poverty and disease in, 47; smallpox in, 94, 111; vaccinators in, 106
Adair, George W., 189
Adell, Patricio, 8
Aduarte, Diego, 98
Aganduru Moriz, Rodrigo de, 21
Agase, 170–71
agronomical commission, 152
Aguinaldo, Emilio, 86
Albay, malaria in, 157; rinderpest in, 162; syphilis in, 72
Alba y Martín, D. R., 168–72
Alcina, Francisco, 19
amas, 76
amebiasis, 53
American war, 13, 193n. 1; and migration, 40–41; and Philippine economy, 50
Amide Castro, José, 47, 105, 142–43
Amoeba, 53
Ancylostoma duodenale, 51, 52
Andaya, Barbara Watson, 187
Andrews, Vernon L., 139–40
Anglo-Burmese War of 1852, 120
Anopheles balabacensis, 161; *A. minimus flavirostris*, 143–44, 148, 153, 154, 159
Antique, smallpox in, 111
Antolín, Francisco, 20, 70
Arce, Julian de, 6
Ares, Gaudencio, 101, 110
Ascaris lumbricoides, 51, 52
Association for Philanthropic Labor, 88
Atienza, Irene, 83–84
Ayarra, Francisco, 8
Azcarraga y Palmero, Manuel, 31

Balantidium, 53
Balmis, Francisco Xavier de, 102, 103
banditry, 33–34
Bankoff, Greg, 34
Bantug, Jose P., 96, 103
barangay, 18, 24
barrios, 20
Basco y Vargas, José, 27, 28
Batangas: cholera in, 182–83; malaria in, 157; migration from, 40; reconcentration in, 179–80; smallpox vaccination in, 117
Bell, J. Franklin, 117, 181, 243n. 38
beriberi, 8, 58; case-fatality rates, 131, 132; and cash-crop agriculture, 120; cause, 118–19, 129; and cholera, 134, 138; dry, 130, 131; and economic changes, 119–20, 126; epidemiological theory, 17; fulminating, 130, 131; history of 133–34; and lactation, 131; mortality, 120, 135–36, 140–41; and rice imports, 126; and rice milling, 126; Shoshin, 130, 131, 132; symptoms of, 130–32; types of, 130–31; and U.S. Army, 135; and war, 135; wet, 130, 131. *See also* infantile beriberi
Bikol plain, 10, 123–24
Binan, cholera in, 181–82
birth statistics. *See* demographic statistics
Black, Robert H., 145
blood fluke, 52
Bohol, smallpox on, 98
bookkeeping barter, 121, 124
Borneo-Luzon-Fujian trade route, 19
Bowman, Fred B., 145
Bowring, John, 39
British army, and venereal disease, 85
bronchitis, 95
Bulacan, pioneering in, 35
Burnet, F. Macfarland, x
Buttinger, Joseph, 187

cabezas de barangay, 22
caciques, 148, 149
Cagayan: rinderpest in, 162; smallpox in, 98, 111
Calamidades públicas records, 104
Calderón Enríquez, Pedro, 28
Camarines Norte, rinderpest in, 162
Camarines Sur: poverty and disease in, 47; rinderpest in, 162; smallpox in, 111–12
Capiz: poverty and disease in, 47; prostitution in, 73
Capiz City, cholera in, 172–74, 183
carabao, 158, 160–63
Casas, Fernando, 103
cash crops, 47, 121–22, 123; and beriberi, 120; exports of, 49; and poverty, 47, 49
cattle, 160–63
Caulas, Florentina, 83
causality, xi, 244n. 6
Cavite: beriberi in, 135; infant mortality in, 231n. 43; smallpox in, 111; vaccinators in, 106

Cebu, roundworm incidence on, 51
Cebu City, 30
Centeno y García, José, 80, 88
Central Board of Health. *See* Manila Board of Health
Central Board of Vaccination, 94, 103, 105
Cercomonas, 53
Cervantes, Mariano, 57
Chamberlain, Weston P., 41–42
Chinese: as merchants, 121, 122, 125, 126, 127; migration of, 38; as mill owners, 129; in Philippines, 38
Chinese-Filipino mestizos, 201n. 41; as landlords, 35, 47; as merchants, 36, 60; and Philippine development, 30
cholera, 8, 28, 164–65, 239n. 6; 1820 epidemic, 164; 1863 epidemic, 10; 1882 epidemic, 10, 118, 168; 1888 epidemic, 10, 175; 1902 epidemic, 11, 175–84; American reaction to, 177; and beriberi, 130, 134, 138; case-fatality rates for, 182, 183; cause of, 165; and detention camps, 182; endemicity of, 237n. 1; and food crisis, 180; and migration, 178–79; mortality of, 165, 172, 174–75, 184, 237n. 1, 240n. 21, 241n. 23, 241n. 25; prevention of, 167, 168, 169, 171–73, 174, 239n. 6; resistance to, 165; in Southeast Asia, 164, 167; transmission of, 165–66, 239n. 4; and U.S. Army, 176, 177–78, 181–82
Cinchona ledgeriana, 146
Civil Guard, 34, 177
Clive, Robert, 120
Coclanis, Peter A., 120, 124
Colín, Francisco, 133
colonialism, and disease, 187–88
commercial adventurism, 28
compulsory labor. See *polo*
Corpuz, Onofre D., 104
Costa, Horacio de la, 21
Cotabato, smallpox epidemic, 108
Crampton, L. W., 135
cremation, American policy of, 180
criadas, 83, 84
crisis mortality episodes, 10, 11–12
crop specialization. *See* monoculture
Cruikshank, Bruce, 25, 26–27, 32, 35, 39
Cuerpo de Quadrilleros, 33
Cullinane, Michael, 10, 23, 24, 26

death statistics. *See* demographic statistics
del Busto, Manuel, 151–52
Delgado, Ezequiel, 37, 47, 111

demographics, and disease transmission, 17, 27
demographic statistics, 9–10; for Java, 9; limitations of, 7, 8; for Manila, 24; for Philippines, 8–13, 17–18, 21–22, 38, 140, 185–86; for Siam, 9
Department of Beneficence and Health, 62
deportation: for prostitution, 78–79; in settlement efforts, 36
de Rada, Martín, 98
Dery, Luis Camara, 32, 75
detention camps, 182
Dickman, J. T., 65, 135
diet: and caloric intake, 59; composition of, 57–59, 60, 125
diphtheria, 8
disease: agent of, 17; and causation, xii, 95–96, 186–88, 189; and colonialism, 187–88; endemic, 17; and environment, 186–87; epidemic, 17; latency of, 196n. 3; and malnutrition, 56–57; Philippine concept of, 94–97, 101, 105; and poverty, 45, 46–47, 50; types of, in Philippines, 8
disease transmission: and demographics, 17, 27; and migration, 37–38; by military, 41; and pueblo formation, 26–27; and sanitation practices, 43–44; and Spain, 20, 23; and steamship, 38–39, 40; by U.S. Army, 41–42; and trade, 19
Dobell, Peter, 29
Doeppers, Daniel F., 37
Dubos, René, ix, x, 186
Dutch wars, and Spanish colonial economy, 21
dwarf tapeworm, 52
dysentery, 8, 42, 43

Echaúz, Robustiano, 49
ecological equilibrium, xi, 7; changes in and food supply, 61–63; and malaria, 147, 148
economic development: agricultural, 27–28, 29–30; and beriberi, 119–20; commercial, 29–31; and migration, 31; and poverty, 47–50; and *proyectistas*, 28, 30–31; and steamship, 38–40
Edger, B. J., 180, 182
1896 revolution, 40, 41
Eighth U.S. Infantry, 178
Eijkman, Christian, 119
Eleventh U.S. Cavalry, 114, 156
encomendero, 20
encomienda system, 20
Enrile y Alcedo, Pascual, 29, 34
Enterobius vermicularis, 52
Enzenberger, Hans, 188, 189

epidemic disease, 7, 10; Philippine concept of, 96–97
epidemiology: models of, 188–89; modern theory of, 17

Fariña y Tabares, Regino, 61, 72
Fariz, Pedro, 21
Fast, Jonathan, 48
Fegan, Brian, 35, 38
Fehily, Lydia, 230n. 41
Fenner, Frank, 17, 97–98, 109, 112, 225n. 34
Fernandez de Folgueras, Mariano, 28
First Tennessee Volunteers, 155
fish, in diet 57–58; varieties, 58
flatworms, 52
food supply: and ecological changes, 61–63; economic effects on, 60–61; and exports to cities, 60–61; famine relief, 125–26; and rinderpest, 62; and town formation, 60; and U.S. Army, 61, 63–66
forced labor. See *polo*
Foreman, John, 37, 129, 134
Foutz, Phineas, 90
Francia y Ponce de Leon, Benito, 174, 175
Francisco de San Antonio, Juan, 58
free trade, 29–30, 122–23

galleon trade, 21, 27
García Gonzales, Antonio F., 28
Garrison, Philip E., 54
General Orders No. 101, 91
Giardia lamblia, 53
Glenn, Edwin F., 65
Gomez y Arce, José, 6, 39, 104, 108, 118, 132, 153; on infantile beriberi, 138–39; on prevention of cholera, 166–67
gonorrhea, 71–72, 91, 220n. 53; incidence of, 87; and U.S. Army, 85
Gonzalez Fernandez, Ramón, 133–34
Greenleaf, Charles R., 90–91
Greenough, Paul, 188
Guardia civil, 34, 177
Guevedo, José, 152, 185–86

Heiser, Victor, 117, 177
helminthic infections, 8, 51
hemp. See abaca
herbalist, 96
herd immunity, 102, 113
Herrera, Diego de, 20
Herzog, Maximilian, 136
Hinz, Erhard, 53
Historical Data Papers, ix
Hong Kong, 30, 124

hookworm, 41–42, 51, 52, 53
host resistance. See resistance
Huff, W. G., 121
Hughes, Robert P. , 64
Hymenolepis nana, 52

Ibanags, 33
Ibarra, Leandro, 86
Ileto, Reynaldo C., 46, 64, 92, 101, 142, 161, 176, 180
Ilocanos, 33
Ilocos Norte: beriberi mortality in, 135; cholera in, 160; infantile beriberi in, 137–38; infant mortality in, 231n. 43; malaria in, 159; migration and malaria in, 154; poverty and disease in, 47; rinderpest in, 159; smallpox in, 111; syphilis in, 72; vaccination in, 112–13
Ilocos region: pioneers from, 35; smallpox in, 99
Ilocos Sur, 6
Iloilo, 6; beriberi in, 132, 139; diet in, 59; infantile beriberi in, 138–39; malaria in, 158; smallpox case-fatality rate in, 111
Iloilo City, 30, 39
immune system: factors affecting, 45; and intestinal parasitism, 51; and poverty, 50
indios, 47–48
infantile beriberi: cause of, 230n. 41; and lactation, 136; symptoms of, 136–38
infant mortality, 139–40
infieles, 9, 33, 36
influenza, 8
insanity, 95
Inspección des Montes, 150, 151
Inspección general de Beneficencia y Sanidad, 62
Intensified Smallpox Eradication Programme, 113
intestinal parasitism, 51; and immune system, 51; incidence of, 53; and sanitation, 53
Isnegs, 33
Izquierdo, Rafael de, 108

Jagor, Fedor, 26, 30, 34, 36, 59
Janay, Octavio, 106
Java, demographic statistics, 9
Javier, Placida, 78
Jenner, Edward, 102
Jimeno, Romualdo, 25
Jimeno Agius, José, 31
Jocano, F. Landa, 95, 96
Jolo, 32, 88
Jones, Thomas C., 51

Jordana y Morera, Ramon, 142, 150, 151, 153
Junta de agricultura, industria y comercio, 150
Junta de Aranceles, 29–30
Junta Superior de Sanidad. *See* Manila Board of Health

kakke, 118, 119, 133
Kathirithamby-Wells, J., 28
Keyser y Muñoz, Antonio, 30, 34, 148, 149
Kilbourne, E. D., 128
Koch, Robert, 165–66
Koeniger, M., 118, 130, 131–32, 133, 134, 174

Laguna: malaria in, 163; reconcentration in, 179–80; rinderpest in, 163
Lamblia, 53
land development, 149–53
land title system, 148
Larkin, John, 34–35
Legazpi, Miguel López de, 20
Le Gentil, Guillaume, 70
leprosy, 8, 95
Leyte: rinderpest on, 162; smallpox on, 99; syphilis on, 72
Lippincott, Henry, 85–86, 114, 176
liver fluke, 52
Llanera, Agustín, 47, 94, 105–6, 109, 110
Llorente, Ana Maria Madrigal, 22
Loarca, Miguel de, 19
locusts, 62
Lopez de Séneca, Enrique, 72
Ludington, Marshall I., 162
lung fluke, 52
Luzon: beriberi on, 135; locusts on, 62; malaria on, 157; Moro raids on, 31, 32; pioneering on, 35; population growth on, 23; rice imports and exports, 128; rinderpest on, 160, 162; smallpox on, 115; vaccination on, 108. *See also specific provinces*; Manila

Macalinao, Maxima, 82–83
Macaraig, Seraphim E., 53
MacArthur, Arthur, 88, 91
Macdonald, George, xi, 147
Mahmoud, Adel A. F., 52
Malabon, beriberi in, 132
malaria, 8, 10, 11, 95, 143; cause of, 142–44; diagnosis of, 232n. 8; and ecological equilibrium, 147, 148; endemicity in uplands, 142; epidemiology of, 145–48; and forest clearing, 151–52, 153–54; life cycle of parasite, 144; and migration, 144, 148, 154–55, 157;

pathogenesis of, 144; and poverty, 145; propagation of, 233n. 12; recrudescence of, 232n. 8; relapse of, 232n. 8; resistance to, 145–46, 147, 233n. 9; and rinderpest, 158–60; transmission of, 146–48, 149, 155–57; treatment of, 146; in United States, 155–57; in U.S. Army, 42, 155, 156
Malinski, Anton, 20
Mallat de Bassilan, Jean, 60, 70, 71, 72, 127
malnutrition: and disease, 56–57; and poverty, 56; and smallpox, 100
Manila: beriberi in, 130; cholera in, 28–29, 174–75; and entry of disease, 23; food exports to, 60–61; hookworm, 52; migration to, 37, 75; population of, 24; port of, 28, 30; poverty and disease in, 47; prostitution in, 74–75, 79–84, 86–88; smallpox in, 98, 99, 114–15; trade with other Philippine areas, 39–40; venereal disease in, 70, 72
Manila Board of Health, 87, 90, 140, 164, 167, 174, 175
Manila-Dagupan railroad, 34, 128
Manila Galleon, 21
Mapa y Belmonte, Cornelio, 73–74, 134
Maria de Aguilar, Rafael, 31
Marinduque: destruction of food supply on, 64; rinderpest on, 162
Marqués de Villadarias, 28
Martín Blanco, Gregorio, 72, 73, 97, 103, 135, 137, 154
Martínez Cuesta, Angel, 20, 32, 103, 105, 106
Martínez de Zúñiga, Joaquín, 23, 24, 31, 32, 37, 70
Masbate, 152, 185–86
Masur, Henry, 51
Maus, L. M., 116, 135, 157
May, Glenn A., 40, 46
McCoy, Alfred W., 35–36, 39
McKeown, Thomas, 56, 57
McLaughlin, Allan J., 139–40
McLennan, Marshall S., 35, 62
McNeill, William H., 186
Meacham, F. A., 90
measles, 8, 27, 56–57, 95
médico titular, 6, 97
Memorias médicas, 7, 11, 104, 109, 112, 134
Mendoza Cortes, R., 26, 122
meningitis, 8
mestizo traders, 122
migration, 35–37; and American war, 40–41; between barrio and *población*, 36–37; of Chinese, 38; and cholera, 178–79; and economic development, 31; and 1896 revolution, 40; epidemiological significance of,

37–38; and malaria, 144, 148, 154–55, 157; and prostitution, 75; and U.S. Army, 41; and venereal disease, 69

Millan, Camilo, 146

Mindanao: malaria on, 158; Moros on, 21; wars against Moros on, 32

Mindoro, Moro bases on, 31

Mojica, Apolonia, 84

Mongkut, King (Rama IV), 120

monocausality, 194n. 6

monoculture, 47, 118, 123–24

Monserrat, Rafael, 6, 108, 160

Montero y Vidal, José, 112

Morong, rinderpest in, 160

Moros, 21, 31, 33; and cholera, 168, 169, 172; government action against, 31–32; quarantine of boats, 169; raids, 32

Morquecho, Manuel Valdivieso, 25

Morse, Stephen S., xii, 186

mosquitoes. See *Anopheles*

Moss, James A., 65

municipal elites, 24

Murillo Velarde, Pedro, 28

Muslim Filipinos. *See* Moros

Necator americanus, 41, 51, 52

Negros, locusts on, 62; and Moros, 32; pioneering on, 35–36; pueblo formation on, 25, 26; smallpox vaccination on, 103–4; workers on, 49

Negros Occidental, 8

Newberne, P. M., 57

Newell, Fred F., 90

1908 Bilibid Prison survey, 52, 53

Ninth U.S. Infantry, 178

Nolaso, Bibiano, 108–9, 149, 152

Nueva Ecija: 48, 128; pioneers from Ilocos, 35

Nueva Viscaya: smallpox case-fatality rate in, 111; vaccinators in, 106

Opisthorchis japonicum, 52

Orthopoxvirus variola, 99

Ortíz de la Table Ducassse, Javier, 27

Owen, Norman G., 21, 225n. 34; on rice trade, 120, 121, 123, 128, 129; on vaccination effectiveness, 109, 112

Oxyuris, 52

pacification, and disease, 20

padre, 97; as healer, 96

palay, 127

Pampana, Emiliano, 47

Pampanga, 62, rinderpest in, 160

Panay: beriberi on, 135; typhoid on, 42; U.S. Army destruction on, 64–65; vaccination on, 108. *See also* Capiz City

Pangasinan, 6; demography of, 24; flooding and food deficit in, 61–62; poverty and disease, 47; pueblo formation, 26; rice production, 122, 123; rinderpest in, 160; smallpox in, 116

Paragonimus westermani, 52

parasites, transmission of, 53

Pardo, Manuel, 129

pass system, 63, 178, 179

Patterson, Philip Y., 50

Payne, Philip R., 45

Peñaranda, Carlos, 47, 48, 50, 123, 128

Peres, Juan, 106, 107, 135

Perez Valdez, Gabino, 31

Phelan, John L., 21

Philippine-American War. *See* American war

Philippine Civil Service Board, 57

Philippine concept of health, 94–97, 101, 105

Philippine economy: and American war, 50; development of, 121–23; instability of, 49–50

Philippine Islands, geography of, 17, 196n. 4

pinworm, 52

pioneering, 34–36

Plasmodium spp., 232n. 7; *P. falciparum*, 144, 232n. 7; *P. vivax*, 144, 232n. 7

población, 20, 23

población-barrio-sitio system, 23–24

polo, 21, 22, 34, 142

poverty, 45–47; and cash cropping, 47, 49; and disease, 45, 46–47, 50; and economic development, 47–50; and immune system, 50; and malaria, 145; and malnutrition, 56; and sanitation practices, 55; and sharecropping, 48

principalía, 24

Prostitución records, 74, 80

prostitutes: age of, 76; socioeconomic status of, 75–76; suppliers of, 83–84; venereal disease in, 81, 87

prostitution, 70, 73–84, 86–89; and corruption, 74, 81–84; and migration, 75; punishment for, 77–79; regulation of, 79–81, 87–88; socioeconomic context of, 74–75; and transmission of venereal disease, 73; in United States, 88; and U.S. Army, 88, 89; and venereal disease, 79

protectionists, 29

protozoa, 53

protozoal infection, 51

proyectistas, 28, 30–31

pueblo formation, 23–24; and disease transmission, 26; factors influencing, 24–26; and food supply, 60
puerperal fever, 8

quarantines, 164, 166, 167–68
queridas, 43, 89, 213n. 2
quinine, 146, 233n. 10

Rafael, Martina, 69
Rajal y Larre, Joaquín, 48, 143
rancherias, 20
Rangoon, 120
Rao, A. R., 100
Raquel, Eulogio, 47, 137–38, 159
Real Compañía de Filipinas, 28
Rebelo, Guillermo, 47, 173–74
reconcentration, 41, 179, 180
Regimental Health Records, 43, 85
Reid, Anthony, 22
remontado, 202n. 48
resistance: acquired, 101–2, 186; to cholera, 165; group, 102; individual, 102; to malaria, 145–46; to smallpox, 100
rheumatic fever, 8
rice, 39, 47, 119; in diet, 58; exports of, 49, 128; and free trade, 122–23; grades of, 128–29; imports of, 123–25, 128; milling of, 126–27, 128–29; price fluctuations of, 50; production of, 120–21, 123–24; from Saigon, 126, 127, 129, 132, 134, 135; threshing of, 127; worldwide trade of, 127–28
rice-export industry: Philippine, 122–23; Southeast Asian, 120–21
Richardson, Jim, 48
rinderpest, 8, 10; cause of, 158; effect on agriculture, 160; and food supply, 62; and malaria, 158–60; mortality of, 160, 163; in Southeast Asia, 159, 161; symptoms of, 235n. 34; transmission of, 158, 161; and U.S. Army, 161–62
Robequain, Charles, 127
Robles, Maria, 77
Rodríguez-Solís, Enrique, 70
Romblon, poverty and disease on, 46
Root, Elihu, 88
Ross, Ronald, 143, 188, 189
roundworms, 51, 52
Ruíz de la Escalera y Oraá, Toribio, 31

Saigon, 120, 124
Samar: economic development on, 39; Moro raids on, 21, 32; pueblo formation on, 25, 26; smallpox on, 99

San Antonio, Juan Francisco de, 60
Sancianco y Goson, Gregorio, 149
San Francisco de Assis, Pedro de, 99
sanitation practices, 54–55; and disease transmission, 43–44; and intestinal parasitism, 53; and poverty, 55
San Juan, Matea, 79
Santos, Pedro de los, 69
Sarmiento, Gregorio, 83
Sawyer, Frederic H., 124
scabies, 8
Schistosoma japonicum, 52
schistosomiasis, 52–53
Scott, William Henry, 18, 19, 33
Scrimshaw, Nevin S., 56
settlement patterns, 18–19, 20; and disease transmission, 23
sharecropping, 35, 48
Shoshin. *See* beriberi
Siam: demographic statistics for 9; rice production in, 120
Siasi, venereal disease on, 89–90
Simon, Pedro, 81–83
Sims, George K., 143
Singapore, 30, 121, 124
sitios, 20
Sixth U.S. Cavalry, 115, 155
slave raiding, and disease transmission, 19
smallpox, 8, 95, 100–101; case-fatality rates of, 100, 110–11; cause of, 99; endemicity of, 97–98; epidemics of, 98–99, 104, 109; epidemiology of, 99, 102; flat, 100; haemorrhagic, 100; and malnutrition, 100; modified, 100; mortality of, 110–12, 116, 117, 225n. 34, 227n. 49; noneruptive, 100; ordinary, 100, 101; resistance to, 100, 102; in Sulu Archipelago, 98–99; transmission of, 100, 101, 113; in United States, 114; in U.S. Army, 42, 113, 114–15
Smallpox Eradication Programme, 188
smallpox vaccination, 102–113, 116, 117; effectiveness, 109–111, 112–13
smallpox vaccination programs: effectiveness, 117; Spanish, 102–4, 105–7, 109; of U.S. Army, 116–17
smallpox vaccine, 94, 102–3, 107–8
Smith, Peter C., 10
Sociedad económica de amigos del país, 150
Solivellas, Bernardino, 42, 59, 72, 139
Sontag, Susan, 193n. 6
Spain: colonization and pacification of Philippines, 18, 20–21; and disease transmission, 20, 23; and Philippine economic development, 27–31; war against Moros, 32–33

Spanish-Filipino mestizos, 201n. 41
Spanish military, 224n. 27; and venereal disease, 72–73
STDs (sexually transmitted diseases). *See* venereal disease
steamship: and disease transmission, 38–39,
  40; and economic development, 38–40; and
  trade, 38–40, 126; and wars against Moros,
  32–33
Strongyloides stercoralis, 52, 53
Sual, 30
Suez Canal, 38, 120
sugar, 28, 36, 39. *See also* cash crops
Sulu Archipelago: Moros in, 21, 32; smallpox
  in, 98–99
Sulu Sultanate, 32
Susser, Mervyn, xi, 186, 188, 244n. 6
Sweet, Owen J., 88
syphilis, 70, 71, 90; and U.S. Army, 85–86

Taenia solium, 52
Taft, William H., 177
Takaki, Kanehiro, 119
tapeworm, 52
tariff board. *See* Junta de Aranceles
tariffs, 29–30
Tarling, Nicholas, 32
Taylor, Norman, 144
Taytay: diet in, 58–59; rinderpest in, 159; sani-
  tation in, 54–55
Tercios de Guardia civil, 34, 177
Terramon Caballero, Ricardo, 47
Tesh, Sylvia Noble, 189
tetanus, 8
thiaminase, 129
thiamine, 58, 118, 126, 127, 130; dietary requirement, 129; sources, 129
Third U.S. Cavalry, 85
Thirteenth Minnesota Volunteers, 114
Thirty-first U.S. Volunteer Infantry, 113
Thirty-second U.S. Volunteer Infantry, 155,
  156
threadworm, 52
Ticao, smallpox on, 108–9
Tornos, Juan Antonio, 99
Torre, Luis de la, 62
total environment, x, 7, 23, 118, 146, 186
town formation. *See* pueblo formation
trade, 19; and disease transmission, 19, 72;
  and steamship, 38–40
traditional healers, 96
transportation infrastructure, 34
Treponema pallidum, 71, 186
Trias, Faustina, 69

Trichuris trichiura, 51, 52, 53
tuberculosis, 8
Twentieth Kansas Volunteers, 115
Twenty-eighth U.S. Volunteer Infantry, 156–
  57
Twenty-ninth U.S. Volunteer Infantry, 155
Twenty-seventh U.S. Volunteer Infantry, 156
Twenty-sixth U.S. Volunteer Infantry, 42,
  115
Twenty-third U.S. Infantry, 88, 89–90
typhoid, 8, 41, 42

United States: malaria in, 155–57; prostitution
  in, 88; smallpox in, 114; smallpox vaccination in, 113
U. S. Army, 10, 27, 50; and beriberi, 135; and
  cholera, 176, 177–78, 181–82; diseases of,
  42; and disease transmission, 41–42; and
  food supply, 61, 63–64; interaction with Filipinos, 43; and malaria, 155–57; pass system,
  63; policy of burning, 177, 181, 182; and
  prostitution, 87, 88, 89; and *queridas*, 43;
  raids on Panay, 64–65; and reconcentration, 41, 179–80; and rinderpest, 161–62;
  sanitation practices, 43; smallpox in, 113,
  114–15; smallpox vaccination program, 116–
  17; and venereal disease, 84–86, 89–90, 91,
  92
U.S. Public Health and Marine Hospital Service, 57
Urbino, Cornelio, 144, 153

vaccinators, 103, 105–6
vandala, 21, 22
Van Horne, W. H., 65
variola major, 99–100, 114. *See also* smallpox
variola minor, 41, 99, 114. *See also* smallpox
venereal disease, 8, 70, 71–72, 85, 95; control
  of, 91–92, 220n. 53; epidemiology of, 72;
  and migration, 69; and military, 70; in prostitutes, 81, 87; transmission of, 72–73, 89–90;
  and U.S. Army, 42, 84–86, 89–90, 91, 92
Vibrio cholerae, 165
Villamil, L., 108
Visayas, 10; beriberi in, 135; hookworm in, 41;
  Moros in, 21, 32; rinderpest in, 162; smallpox in, 115
visitas, 23, 24
vitamin B$_1$. *See* thiamine

Wagner, Arthur L., 179
Western medicine, in Philippines, 97
Weyler, Valeriano, 34
whipworm, 51, 53

whooping cough, 8
Wilkes, Charles, 98–99
Williams, G., 57
Wilson, R. A., 182
Women's Christian Temperance Union, 88
Wood-Forbes Mission, 43
Worcester, Dean C., 177–78

World Health Organization, 56
Wright, Luke, 177

Zabala, Mariano, 81–83
Zambales, poverty and disease in, 47
Zamboanga, 30, 32; cholera in, 170–72; quarantine of, 168–70; smallpox in, 109